SHIKI TSUKAI

3

Story by To-ru Zekuu

Art by Yuna Takanagi

Translated and adapted by Mayumi Kobayashi

Lettered by North Market Street Graphics

DEL REY

Ballantine Books · New York

Shiki Tsukai volume 3 is a work of fiction. Names, characters, places, and incidents are the products of the author's imagination or are used fictitiously. Any resemblance to actual events, locales, or persons, living or dead, is entirely coincidental.

A Del Rey Manga/Kodansha Trade Paperback Original

Published in the United States by Del Rey Books, an imprint of The Random House Publishing Group, a division of Random House, Inc., New York.

Del Rey is a registered trademark and the Del Rey colophon is a trademark of Random House, Inc.

Publication rights arranged through Kodansha Ltd.

First published in Japan in 2007 by Kodansha Ltd., Tokyo

ISBN 978-0-345-50415-9

Printed in the United States of America

www.delreymanga.com

9 8 7 6 5 4 3 2 1

Translator and adaptor: Mayumi Kobayashi
Lettering: NMSG

Contents

Since *Shiki Tsukai* is about the seasons, calendars are very important to the story. Two types of calendars are referenced throughout this series. One is the Gregorian calendar, the familiar 12-month January-through-December system that is commonly used throughout the West and in many other parts of the world. But the lunisolar calendar—the one that was used in Japan until 1873, when Japan adopted the Gregorian calendar—is also referred to often. A lunisolar calendar is one that indicates both the moon phase and the time of the solar year.

Under the Gregorian calendar, in Japanese the months are literally called "first month (January)," "second month (February)," "third month (March)," etc.

But under the lunisolar calendar, each month has a name specifically tied to the seasons. They are as follows, with the names literally translated, and where the name is derived from.

January = *Mutsuki*, affection month. Family and friends get together to celebrate the New Year.

February = *Kisaragi*, layering clothes month. This month, wear layers for protection from the cold.

March = *Yayoi*, new life month. Derived from Spring.

April = *Uzuki*, Deutzias flower month. This month is when the Deutzias flowers bloom.

May = *Satsuki*, crop month. This is the best month to plant crops.

June = *Minazuki*, water month. End of the rainy season.

July = *Fumizuki*, letter month. Derived from the *Tanabata* holiday where you write a wish or a song on a piece of paper and hang it on bamboo.

August = *Hazuki*, leaf month. Month when the leaves fall.

September = *Nagazuki*, long month. The time of year when nights grow longer.

October = *Kannazuki*, God month. Gods gather in October for an annual meeting at the Izumo shrine.

November = *Shimotsuki*, frost month. The first frost of the Winter.

December = *Shiwasu*, priest month. Priests are busy making end-of-year prayers and blessings.

The lunisolar calendar is also divided into 24 *sekki*. The 24 *sekki* are days that divide the lunisolar calendar into 24 equal sections and have special names to mark the change in seasons. The dates below are approximate and shift due to the differences in the lunisolar and Gregorian calendars.

Rishhun. February 4. First day of Spring.

Usui. February 19.

Keichitsu. March 5.

Shunbun. March 20. Vernal equinox. Middle of Spring.

Seimei. April 5.

Kokuu. April 20.

Rikka. May 5. First day of Summer.

Shouman. May 21.

Boushu. June 6.

Geshi. June 21. Summer solstice. Middle of Summer.

Shousho. July 7.

Taisho. July 23.

Rishuu. August 7. First day of Autumn.

Shouho. August 23.

Hakuro. September 7.

Shuubun. September 23. Autumnal equinox. Middle of Autumn.

Kanro. October 8.

Shoukou. October 23.

Rittou. November 7. First day of Winter.

Shousetsu. November 22.

Taisetsu. December 7.

Touji. December 22. Winter solstice. Middle of Winter.

Shoukan. January 5.

Daikan. January 20.

Honorifics Explained

Throughout the Del Rey Manga books, you will find Japanese honorifics left intact in the translations. For those not familiar with how the Japanese use honorifics and, more important, how they differ from American honorifics, we present this brief overview.

Politeness has always been a critical facet of Japanese culture. Ever since the feudal era, when Japan was a highly stratified society, use of honorifics—which can be defined as polite speech that indicates relationship or status—has played an essential role in the Japanese language. When addressing someone in Japanese, an honorific usually takes the form of a suffix attached to one's name (example: "Asuna-san"), is used as a title at the end of one's name, or appears in place of the name itself (example: "Negi-sensei," or simply "Sensei!").

Honorifics can be expressions of respect or endearment. In the context of manga and anime, honorifics give insight into the nature of the relationship between characters. Many English translations leave out these important honorifics, and therefore distort the feel of the original Japanese. Because Japanese honorifics contain nuances that English honorifics lack, it is our policy at Del Rey not to translate them. Here, instead, is a guide to some of the honorifics you may encounter in Del Rey Manga.

-*san*: This is the most common honorific, and is equivalent to Mr., Miss, Ms., or Mrs. It is the all-purpose honorific and can be used in any situation where politeness is required.

-*sama*: This is one level higher than "-san" and is used to confer great respect.

-*dono*: This comes from the word "tono," which means "lord." It is an even higher level than "-sama" and confers utmost respect.

-*kun*: This suffix is used at the end of boys' names to express familiarity or endearment. It is also sometimes used by men among friends, or when addressing someone younger or of a lower station.

-*chan*: This is used to express endearment, mostly toward girls. It is also used for little boys, pets, and even among lovers. It gives a sense of childish cuteness.

Bozu: This is an informal way to refer to a boy, similar to the English terms "kid" and "squirt."

Sempai/Senpai: This title suggests that the addressee is one's senior in a group or organization. It is most often used in a school setting, where underclassmen refer to their upperclassmen as "sempai." It can also be used in the workplace, such as when a newer employee addresses an employee who has seniority in the company.

Kohai: This is the opposite of "sempai" and is used toward underclassmen in school or newcomers in the workplace. It connotes that the addressee is of a lower station.

Sensei: Literally meaning "one who has come before," this title is used for teachers, doctors, or masters of any profession or art.

[blank]:   This is usually forgotten in these lists, but it is perhaps the most significant difference between Japanese and English. The lack of honorific means that the speaker has permission to address the person in a very intimate way. Usually, only family, spouses, or very close friends have this kind of permission. Known as *yobisute*, it can be gratifying when someone who has earned the intimacy starts to call one by one's name without an honorific. But when that intimacy hasn't been earned, it can be very insulting.

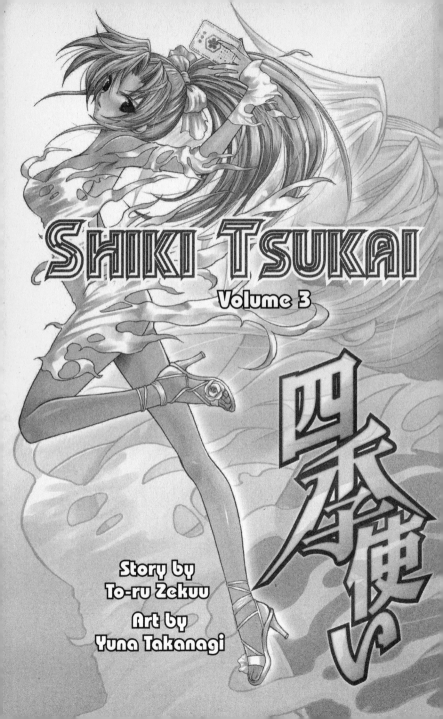

SHIKI TSUKAI

Volume 3

四季使い

Story by
To-ru Zekuu

Art by
Yuna Takanagi

Table of Contents

SHIKI TSUKAI

Akira Kizuki, a kindhearted boy, once lived a peaceful life as an ordinary middle school student. But his fate would forever change after meeting Koyomi Sakuragi, a *Shiki Tsukai*. A *Shiki Tsukai* controls the seasons using magical objects, known as *Shikifu*.

As the *Shiki Tsukai* of March, Koyomi has a mission to protect Akira, the boy who has the power to become the *Shinra*, a great warrior who can control all the seasons, from the *Shiki Tsukai* of Summer. The *Shiki Tsukai* of Summer believe humans are to blame for the destruction of Earth's natural order, and that they must destroy all mankind to save it…but in order to do so, they need Akira's power. Should Akira save humanity…or save the Earth from humanity? While Akira hesitated over his decision, Koyomi was shot. Now that Akira has seen how truly ruthless the *Shiki Tsukai* of Summer are, he is determined to fight to save all humanity.

Just like Akira, the *Shiki Tsukai* of Spring and Winter are on the side of mankind. The leaders of the *Shiki Tsukai* of Spring and Winter are Junichiro Kizuki, Akira's father, and Kenshin Sakuragi, Koyomi's father. Their base is the Sakuragi Corporation, which is run by Kenshin. Ryuka Kato, the *Shiki Tsukai* of July, and also the sniper who shot Koyomi, was captured by Moe Mutsuki, the *Shiki Tsukai* of January, and was taken to the Sakuragi Corporation.

After recovering, Koyomi invites Akira and his two childhood friends to her house but Rinsho, the *Shiki Tsukai* of June, appears, and Moe Mutsuki tries to stop him. Moe has the advantage against Rinsho, but then Nanayo Rangetsu, the most powerful *Shiki Tsukai* of July, appears. Moe is outnumbered, and therefore is wounded in the fighting. Akira and Koyomi come to help but they are helpless against Nanayo. After overpowering Akira, Nanayo sees how afraid Akira is. She tells Akira, "This is boring. Get stronger," and cuts short the battle.

Rei Seichouji, the *Shiki Tsukai* of February, heals Moe with a healing incantation. Rei and Moe manage to get information out of Ryuka that Fall has sided with Summer. At the same time, the American office of the Sakuragi Corporation is under attack…

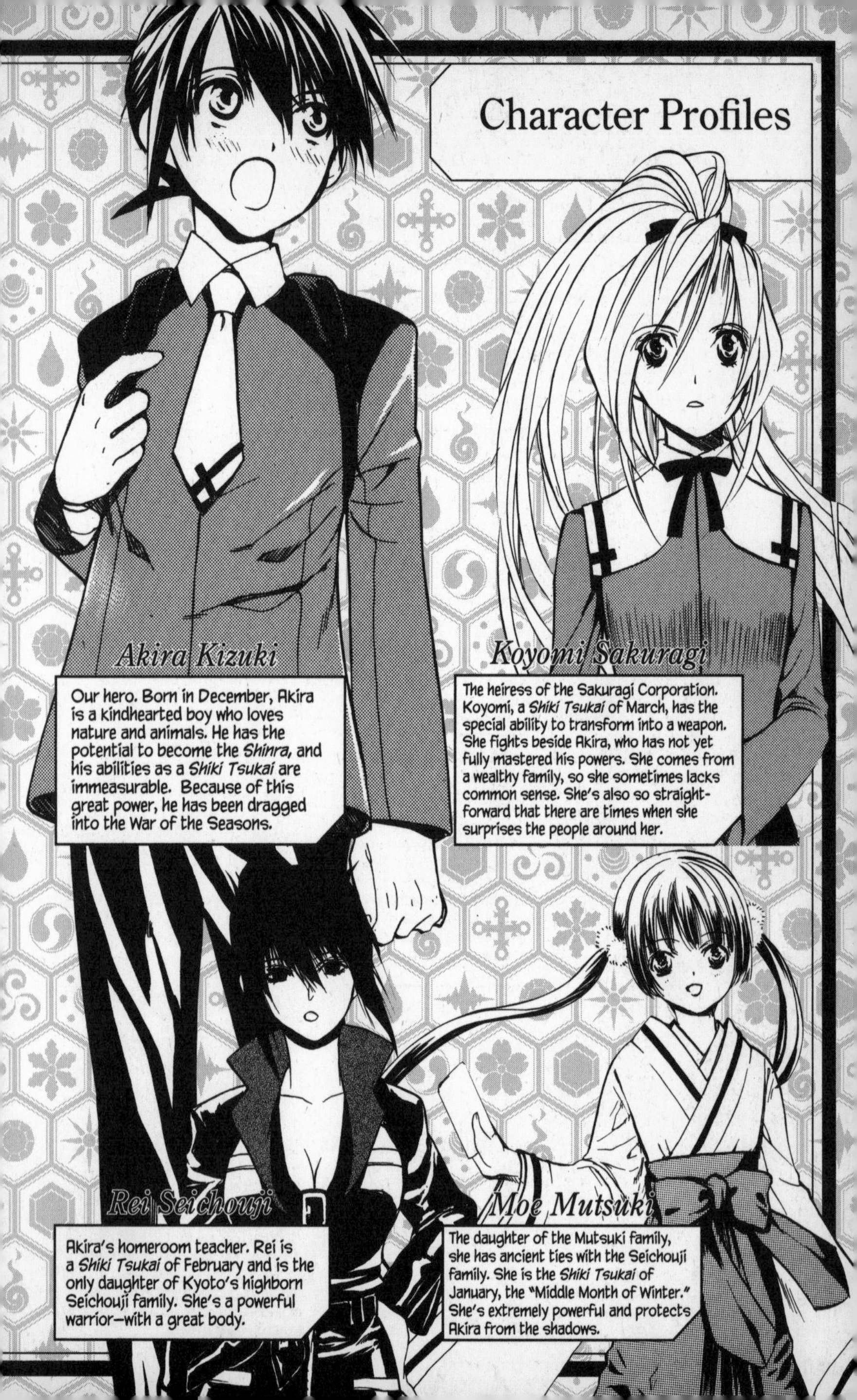
Character Profiles
Akira Kizuki
Our hero. Born in December, Akira is a kindhearted boy who loves nature and animals. He has the potential to become the *Shinra,* and his abilities as a *Shiki Tsukai* are immeasurable. Because of this great power, he has been dragged into the War of the Seasons.
Koyomi Sakuragi
The heiress of the Sakuragi Corporation. Koyomi, a *Shiki Tsukai* of March, has the special ability to transform into a weapon. She fights beside Akira, who has not yet fully mastered his powers. She comes from a wealthy family, so she sometimes lacks common sense. She's also so straight-forward that there are times when she surprises the people around her.
Rei Seichouji
Akira's homeroom teacher. Rei is a *Shiki Tsukai* of February and is the only daughter of Kyoto's highborn Seichouji family. She's a powerful warrior—with a great body.
Moe Mutsuki
The daughter of the Mutsuki family, she has ancient ties with the Seichouji family. She is the *Shiki Tsukai* of January, the "Middle Month of Winter." She's extremely powerful and protects Akira from the shadows.

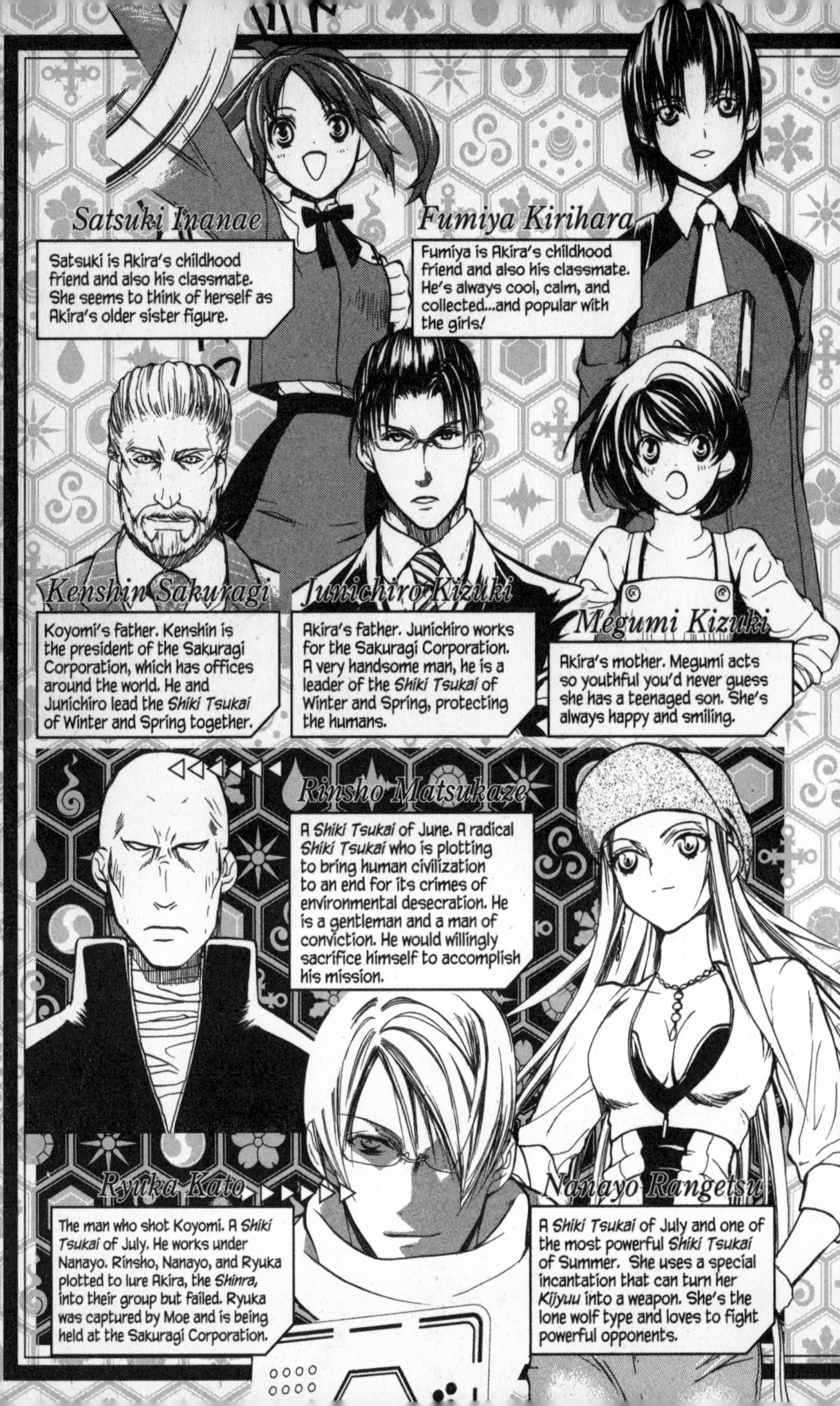
Fumiya Kirihara
Fumiya is Akira's childhood friend and also his classmate. He's always cool, calm, and collected...and popular with the girls!
Satsuki Inanae
Satsuki is Akira's childhood friend and also his classmate. She seems to think of herself as Akira's older sister figure.
Megumi Kizuki
Akira's mother. Megumi acts so youthful you'd never guess she has a teenaged son. She's always happy and smiling.
Junichiro Kizuki
Akira's father. Junichiro works for the Sakuragi Corporation. A very handsome man, he is a leader of the Shiki Tsukai of Winter and Spring, protecting the humans.
Kenshin Sakuragi
Koyomi's father. Kenshin is the president of the Sakuragi Corporation, which has offices around the world. He and Junichiro lead the Shiki Tsukai of Winter and Spring together.
Rinsho Matsukaze
A Shiki Tsukai of June. A radical Shiki Tsukai who is plotting to bring human civilization to an end for its crimes of environmental desecration. He is a gentleman and a man of conviction. He would willingly sacrifice himself to accomplish his mission.
Nanayo Rangetsu
A Shiki Tsukai of July and one of the most powerful Shiki Tsukai of Summer. She uses a special incantation that can turn her Kijyuu into a weapon. She's the lone wolf type and loves to fight powerful opponents.
Ryuka Kato
The man who shot Koyomi. A Shiki Tsukai of July. He works under Nanayo. Rinsho, Nanayo, and Ryuka plotted to lure Akira, the Shinra, into their group but failed. Ryuka was captured by Moe and is being held at the Sakuragi Corporation.

Eleventh Season

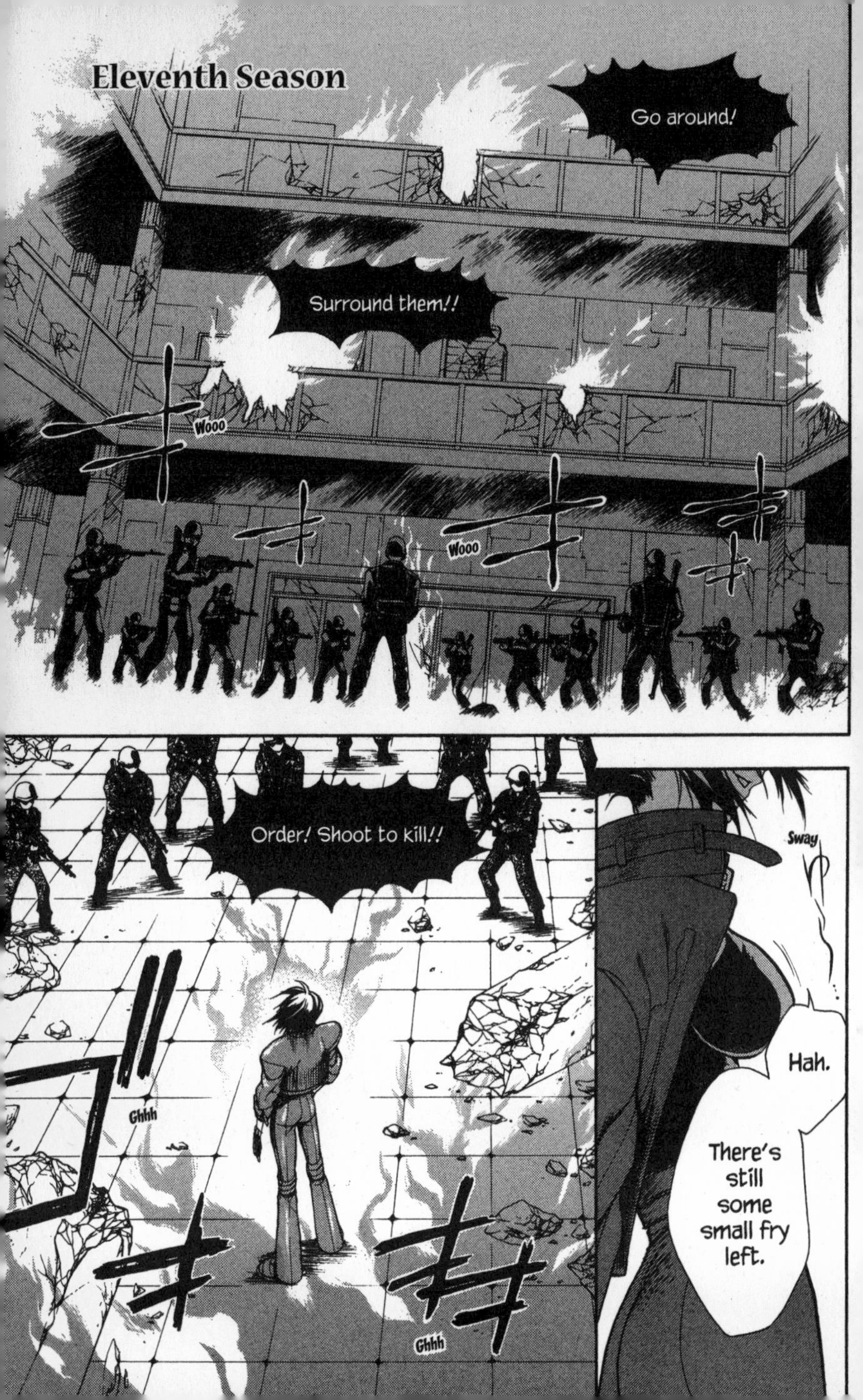
Go around!
Surround them!!
Wooo
Wooo
Sway
Hah.
There's still some small fry left.
Order! Shoot to kill!!
Ghhh
Ghhh

Eleventh Season
Activity of Discord

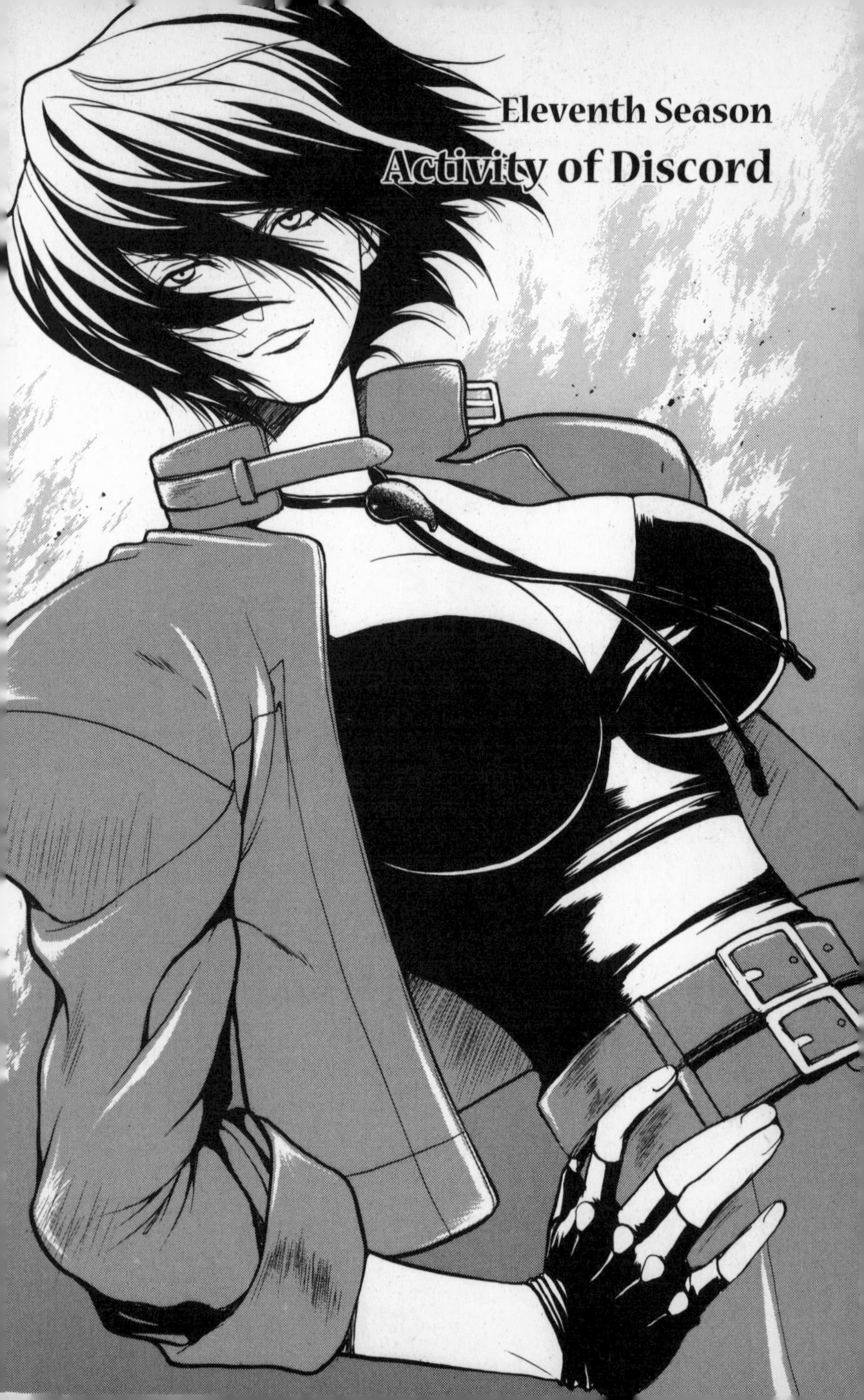

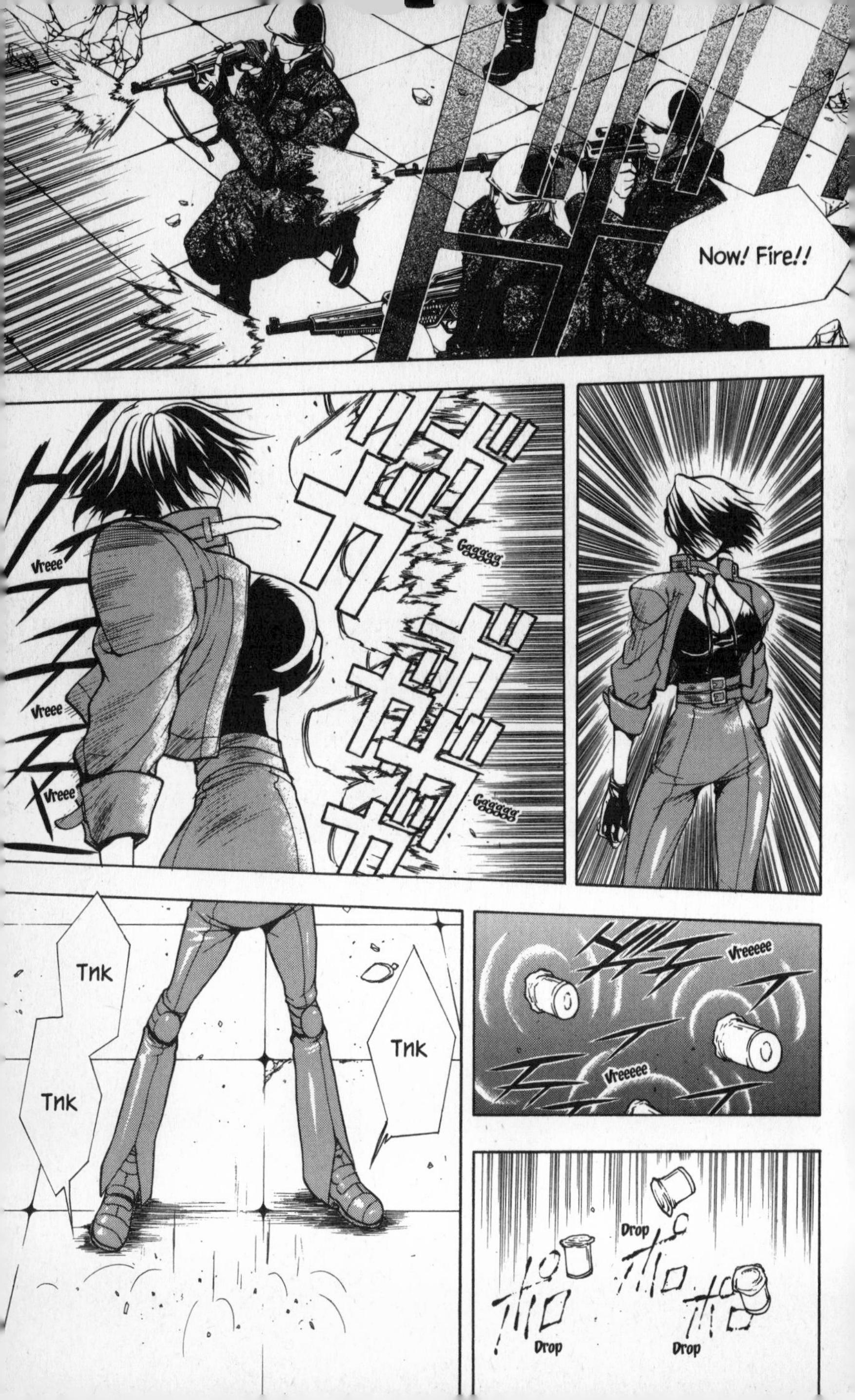

Now! Fire!!
Gagggg
Vreee
Vreee
Vreee
Gagggg
Vreeee
Vreeee
Drop
Drop
Drop
Tnk
Tnk
Tnk

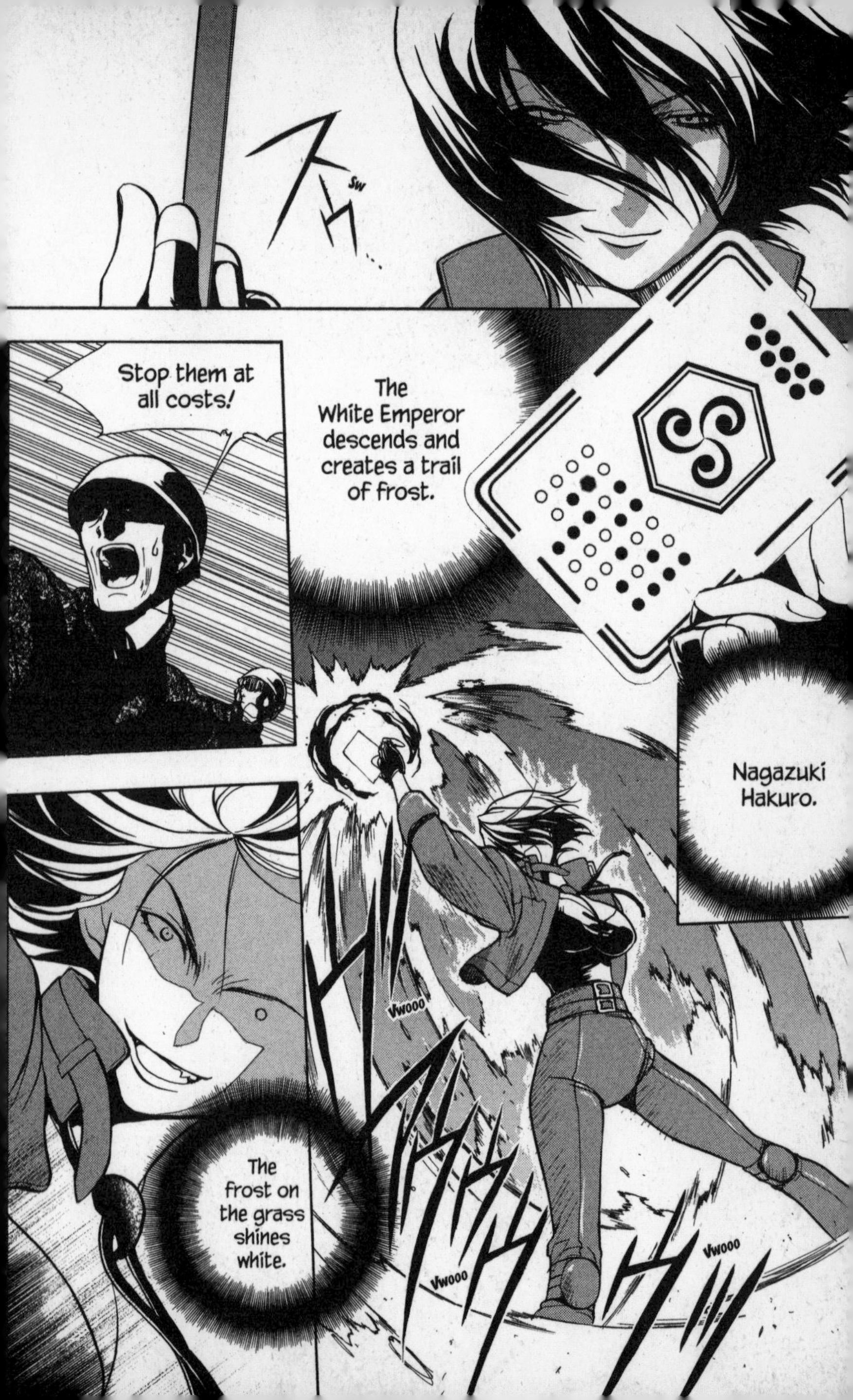
SW...
The White Emperor descends and creates a trail of frost.
Nagazuki Hakuro.
Vwooo
Vwooo
Vwooo
Stop them at all costs!
The frost on the grass shines white.

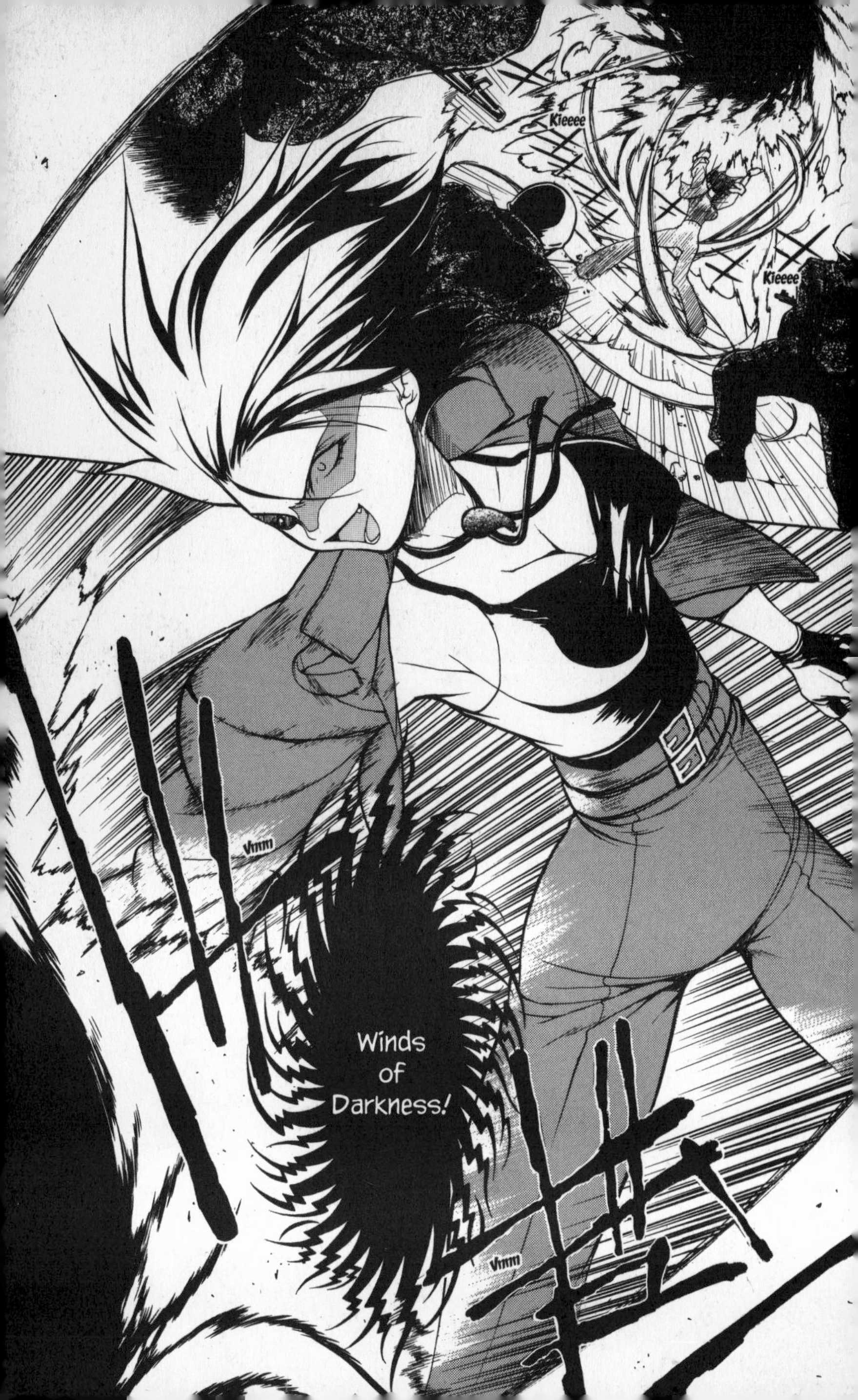
Kieeee
Kieeee
Vmm
Winds of Darkness!
Vmm

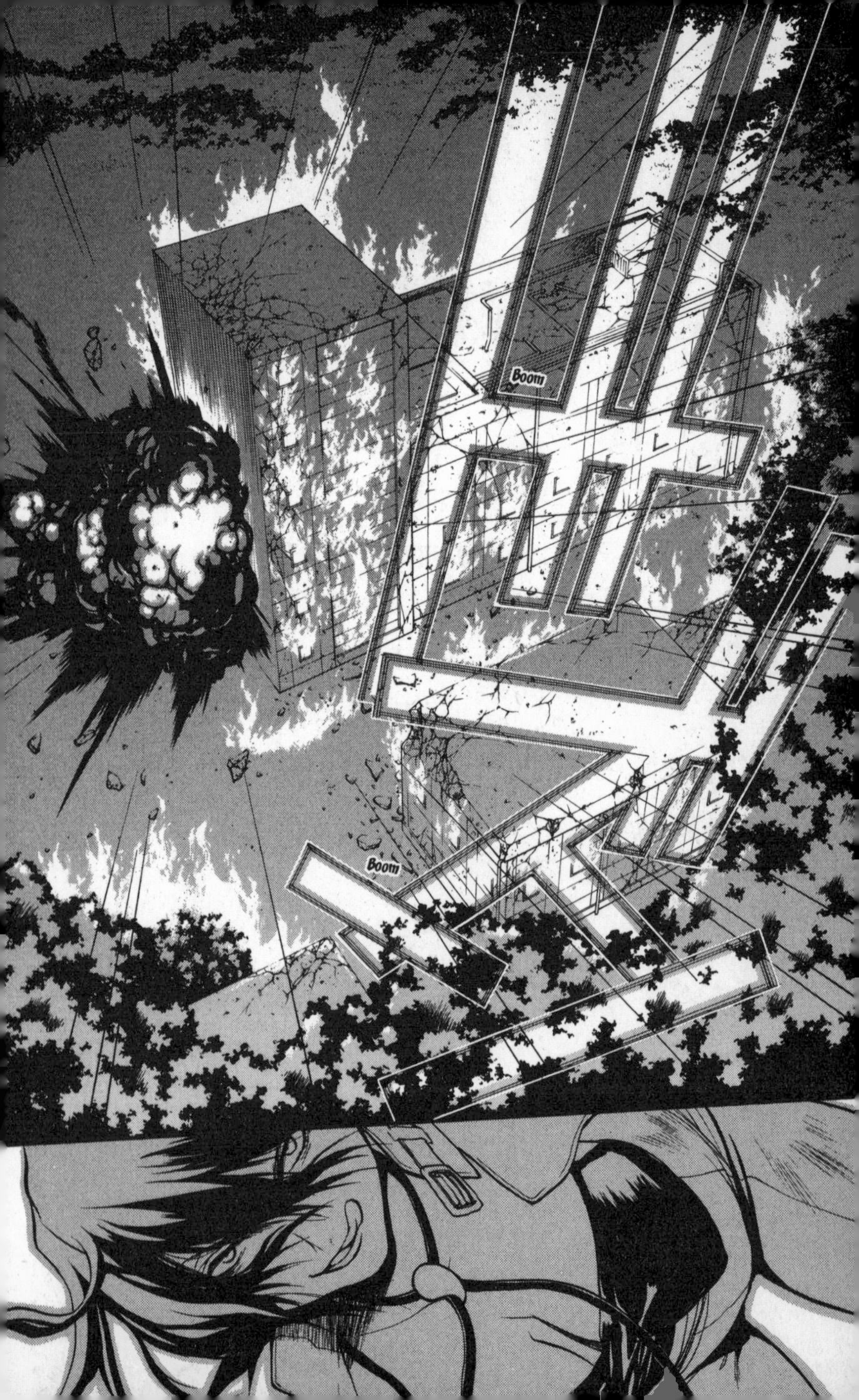
Boom
Boom

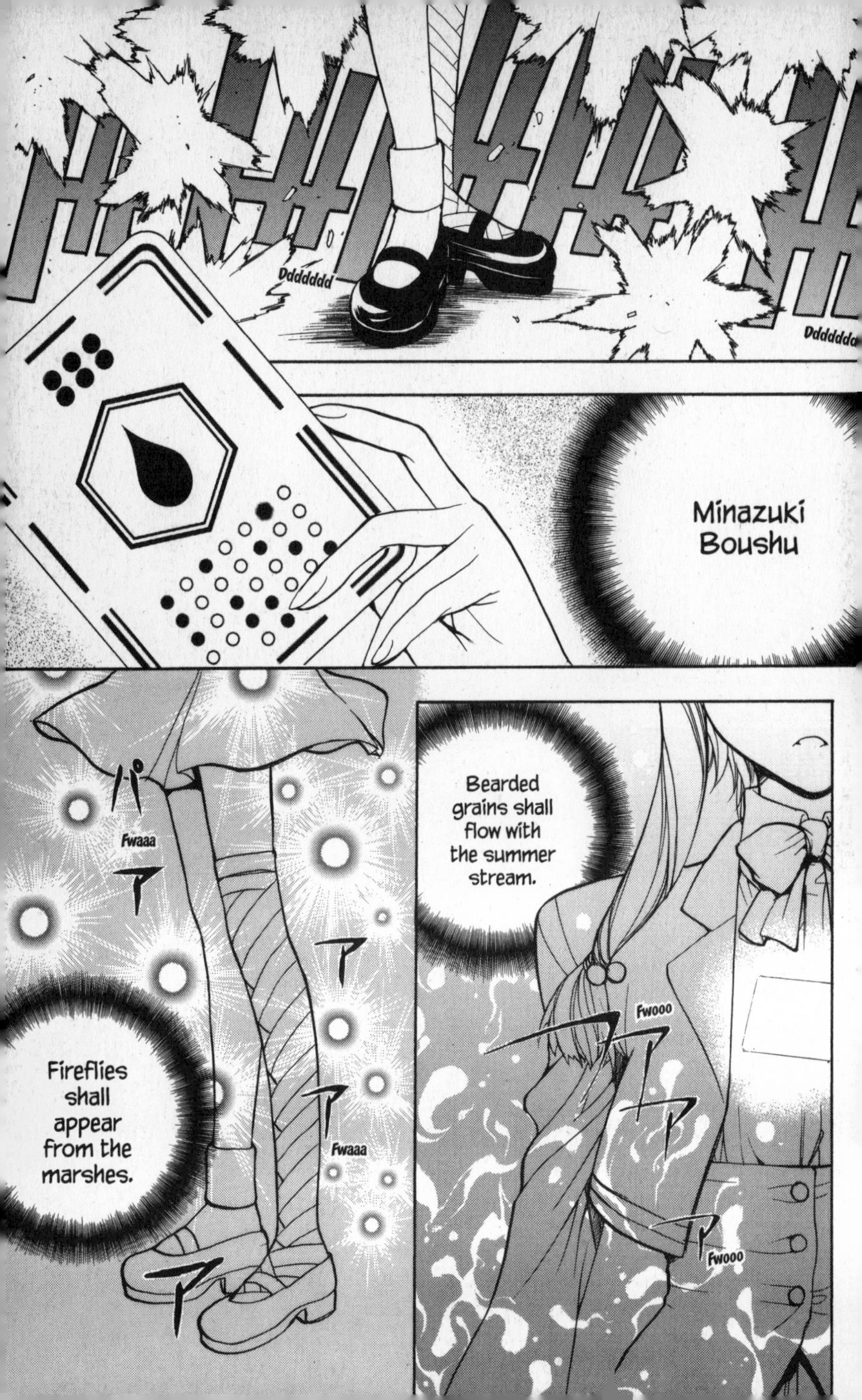

Dddddd
Ddddddd
Minazuki Boushu
Bearded grains shall flow with the summer stream.
Fwooo
Fwooo
Fwaaa
Fireflies shall appear from the marshes.
Fwaaa

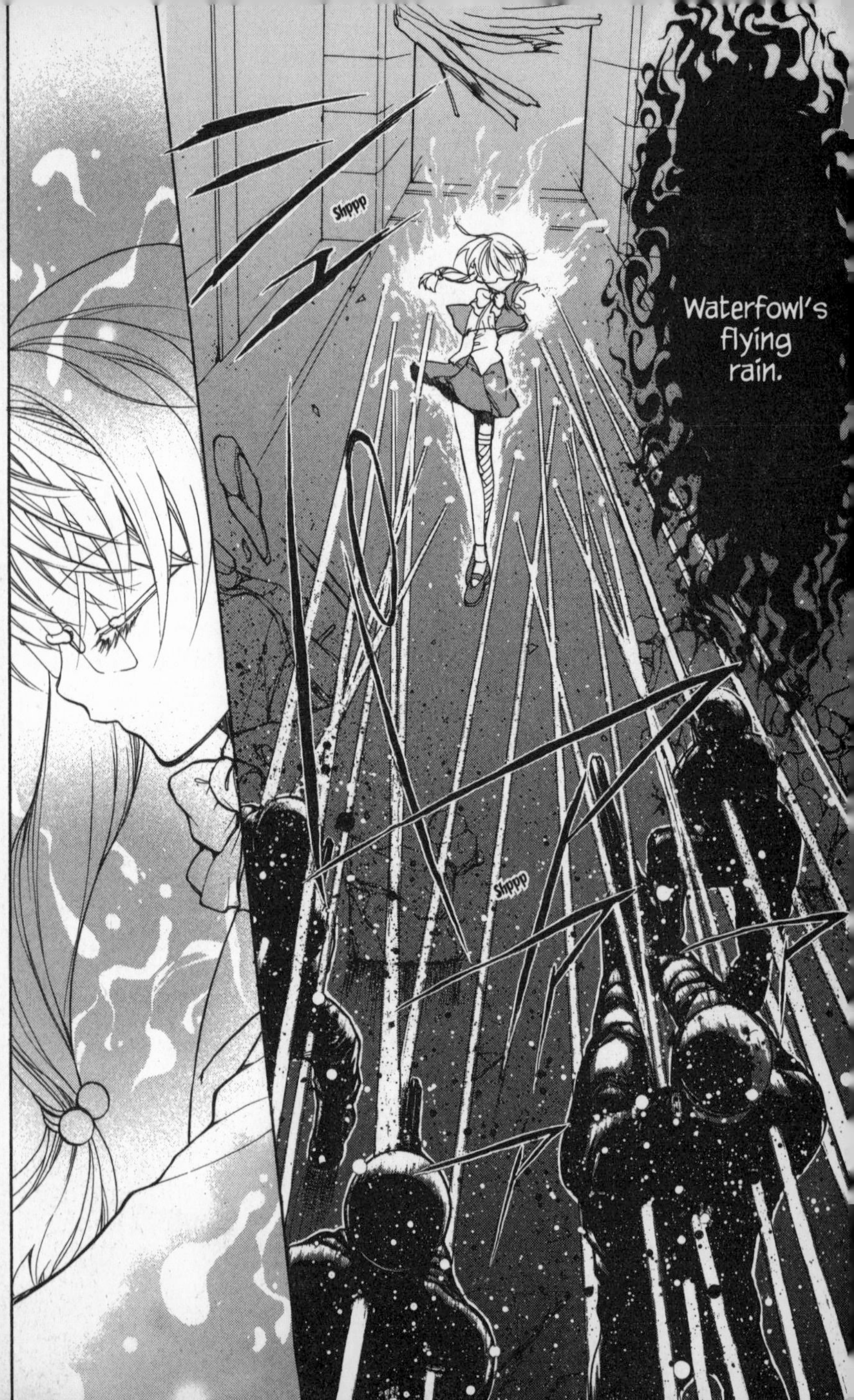
Waterfowl's flying rain.
Shppp
Shppp

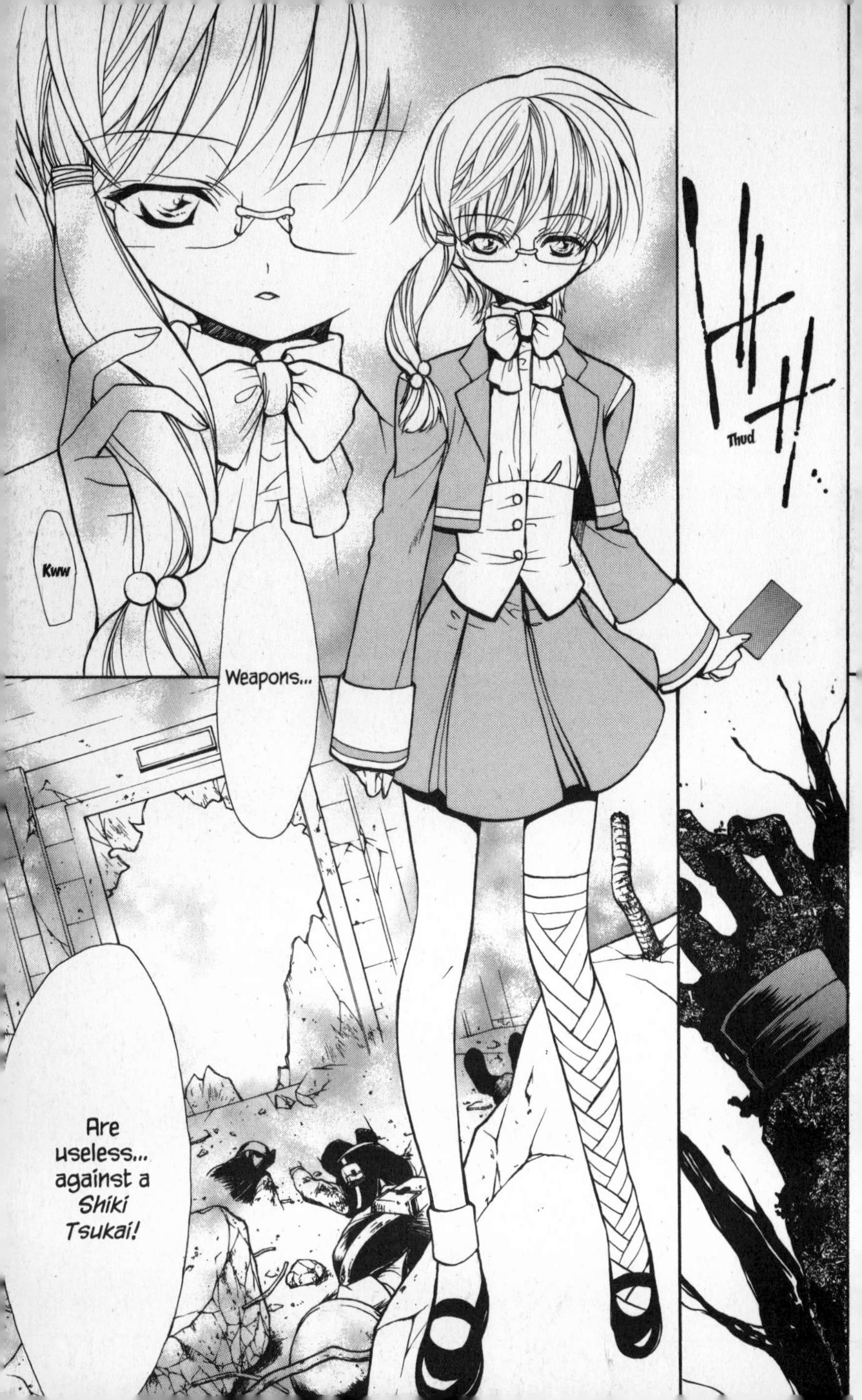
Thud
...
Kww
Weapons...
Are useless... against a Shiki Tsukai!

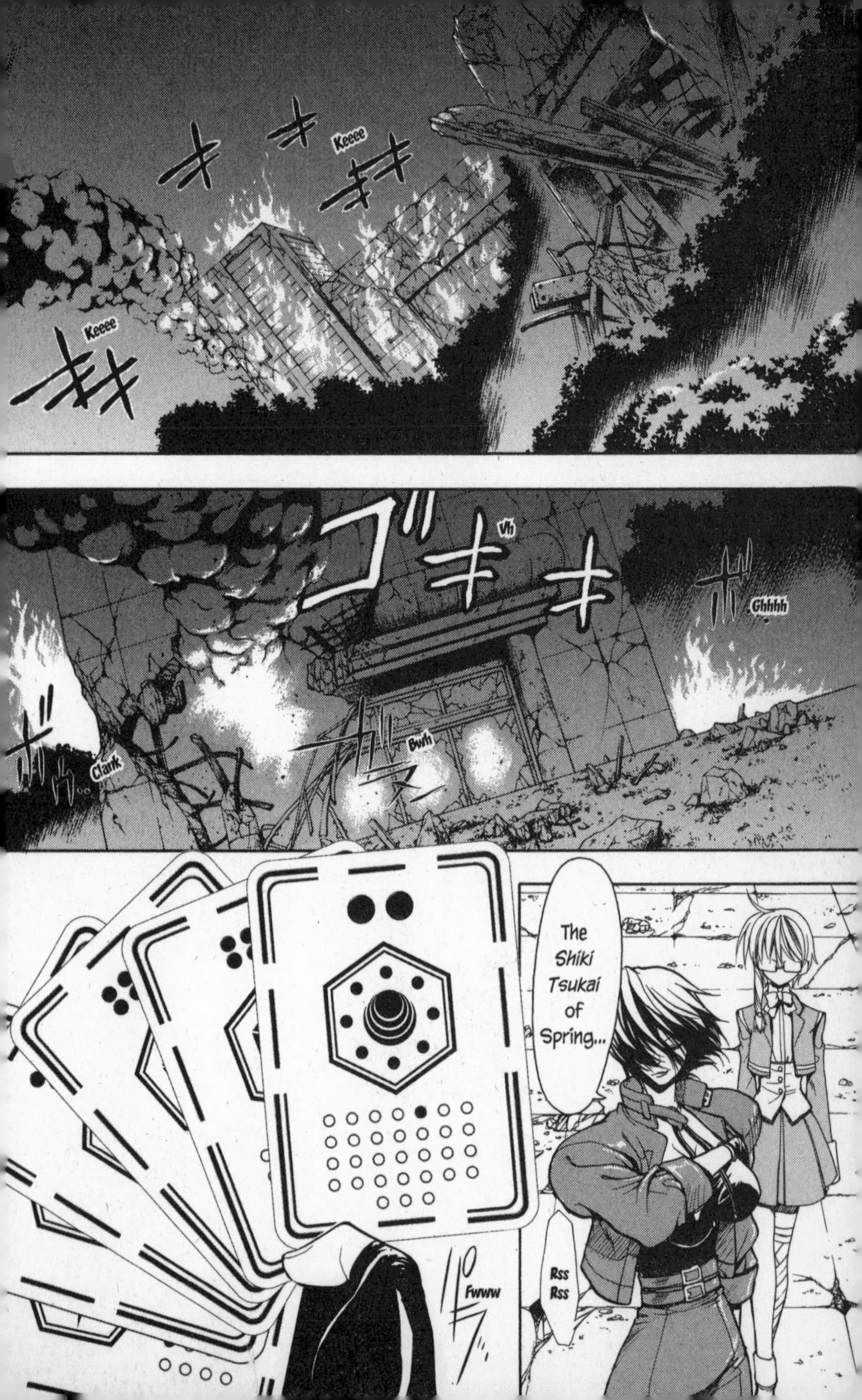

Keeee
Keeee
Ghhhh
Vi
Bwh
Clank
The Shiki Tsukai of Spring...
Rss Rss
Fwww

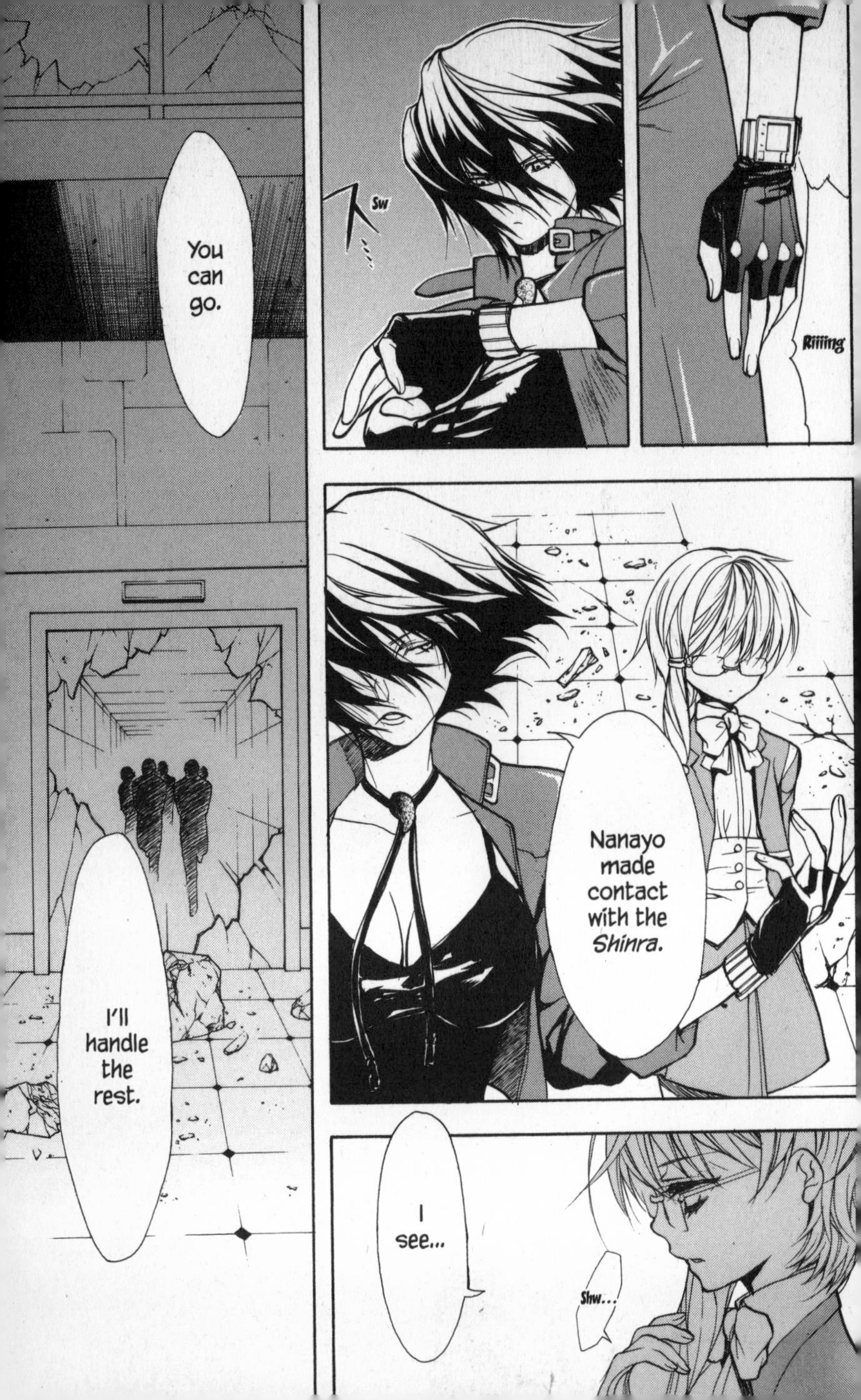
Riiing
Sw
Nanayo made contact with the *Shinra*.
I see...
Shw...
You can go.
I'll handle the rest.

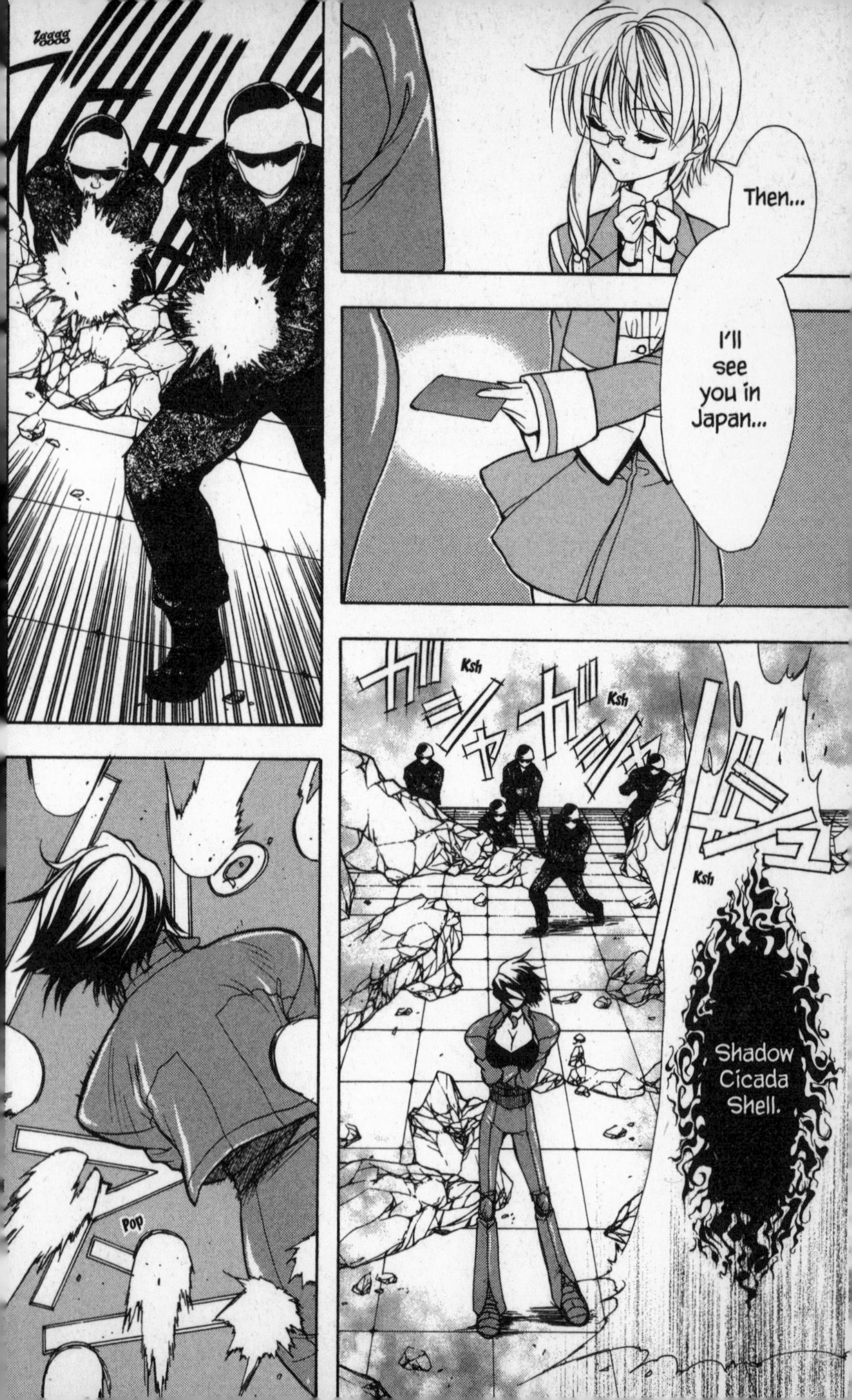
Then...
I'll see you in Japan...
Zgggg
Ksh
Ksh
Ksh
Shadow Cicada Shell.
Pop

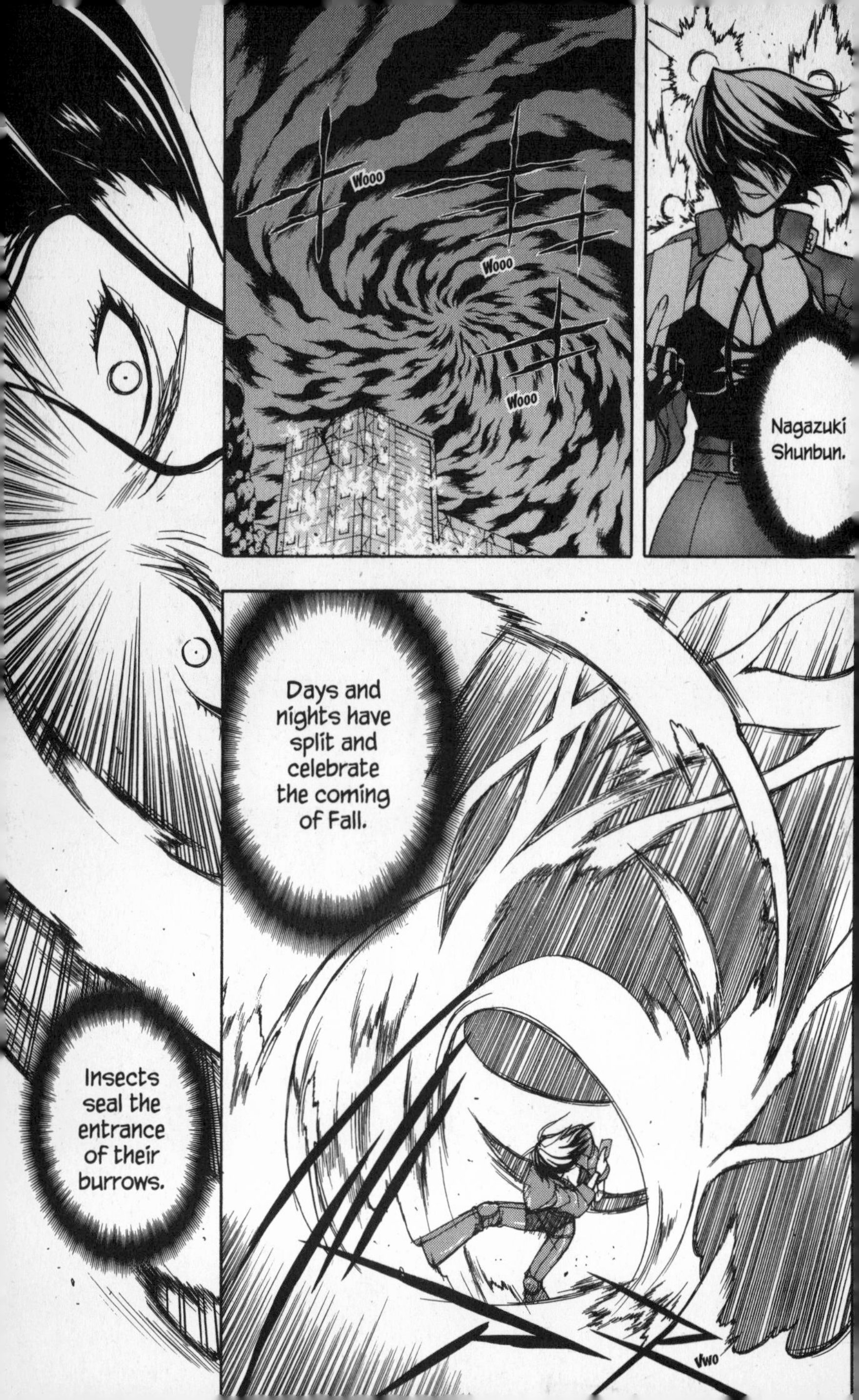
Nagazuki Shunbun.
Wooo
Wooo
Wooo
Days and nights have split and celebrate the coming of Fall.
Vwo
Insects seal the entrance of their burrows.

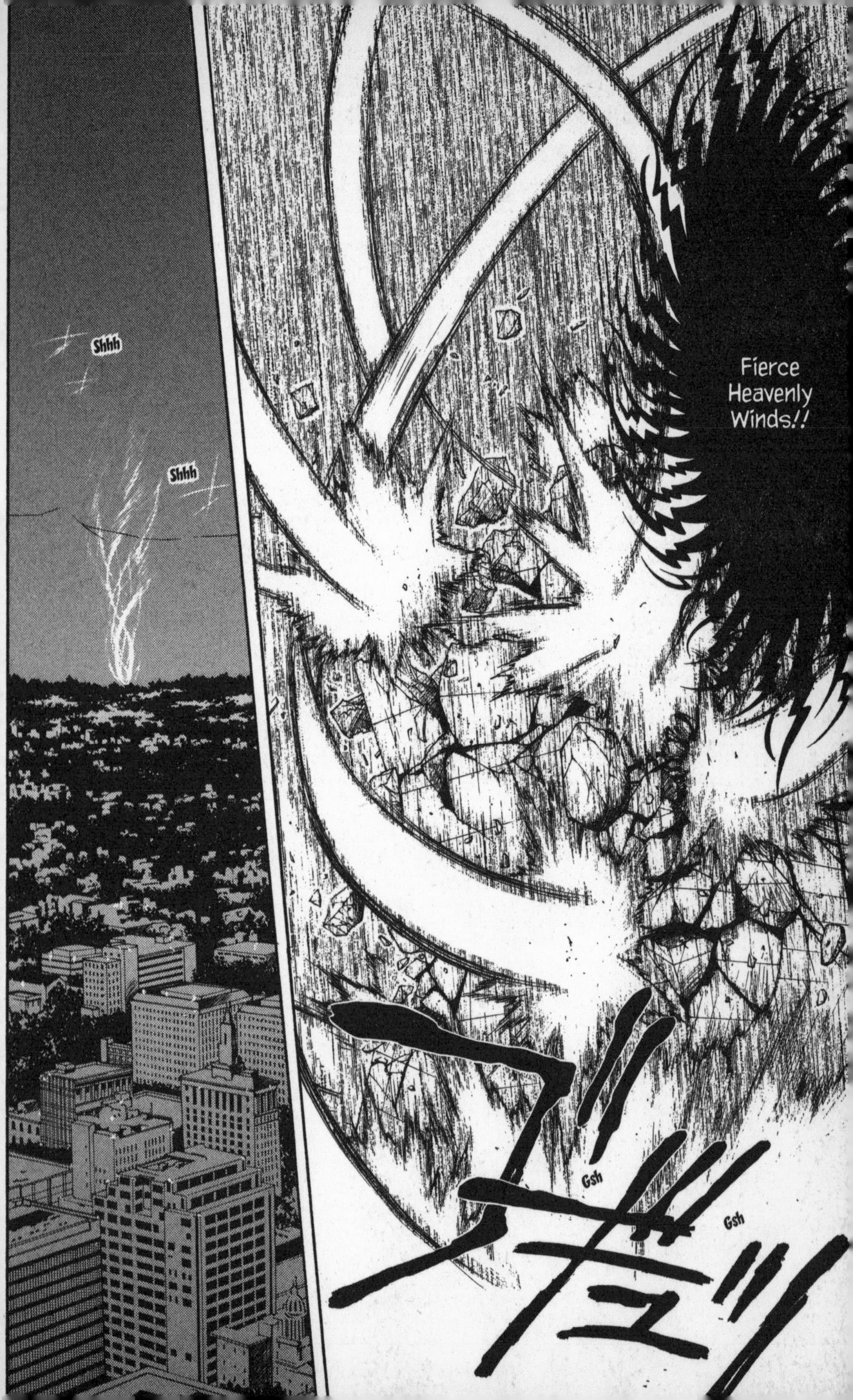
Fierce Heavenly Winds!!
Gsh
Gsh
Shhh
Shhh

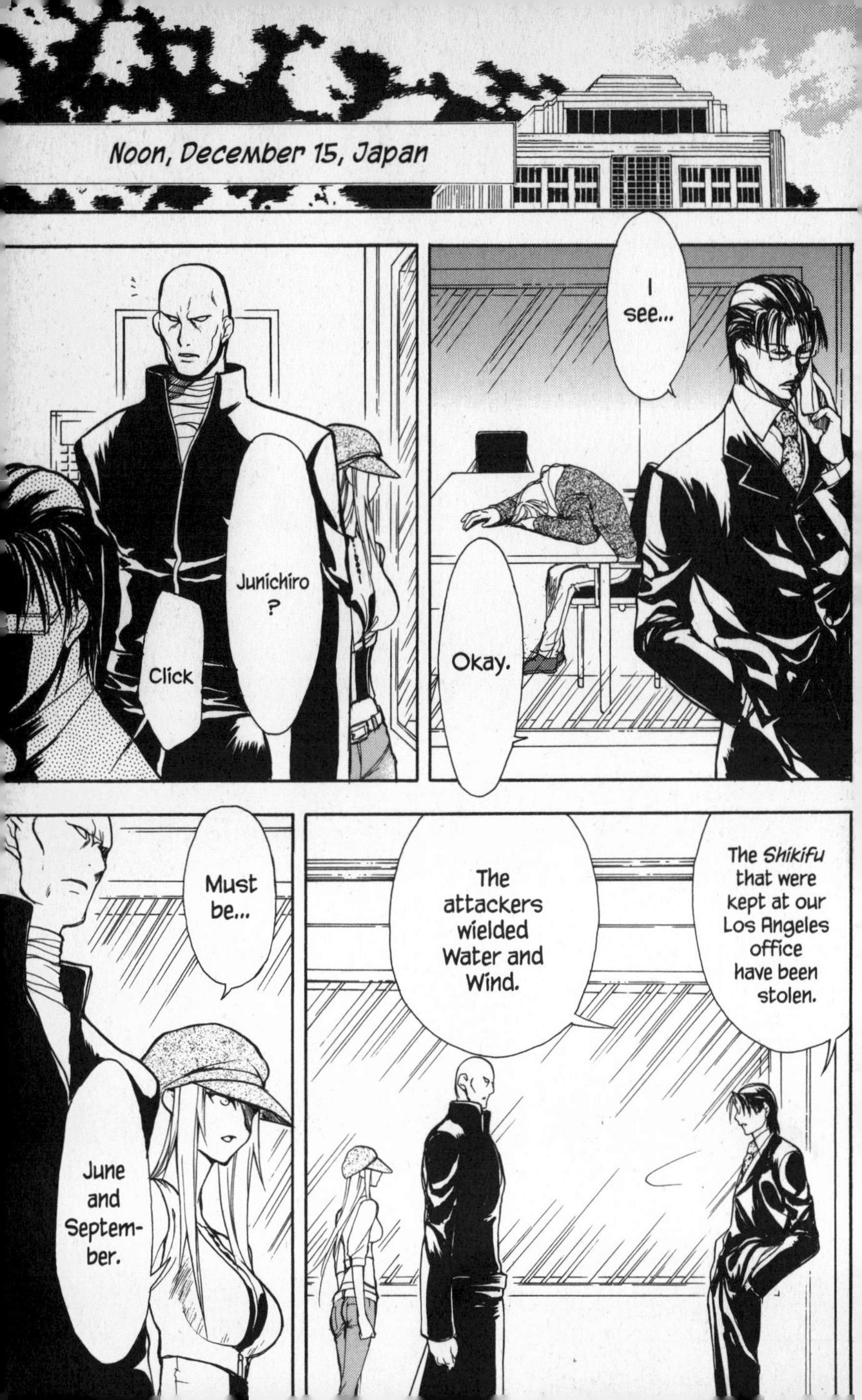
Noon, December 15, Japan
I see...
Okay.
Junichiro ?
Click
The *Shikifu* that were kept at our Los Angeles office have been stolen.
The attackers wielded Water and Wind.
Must be...
June and September.

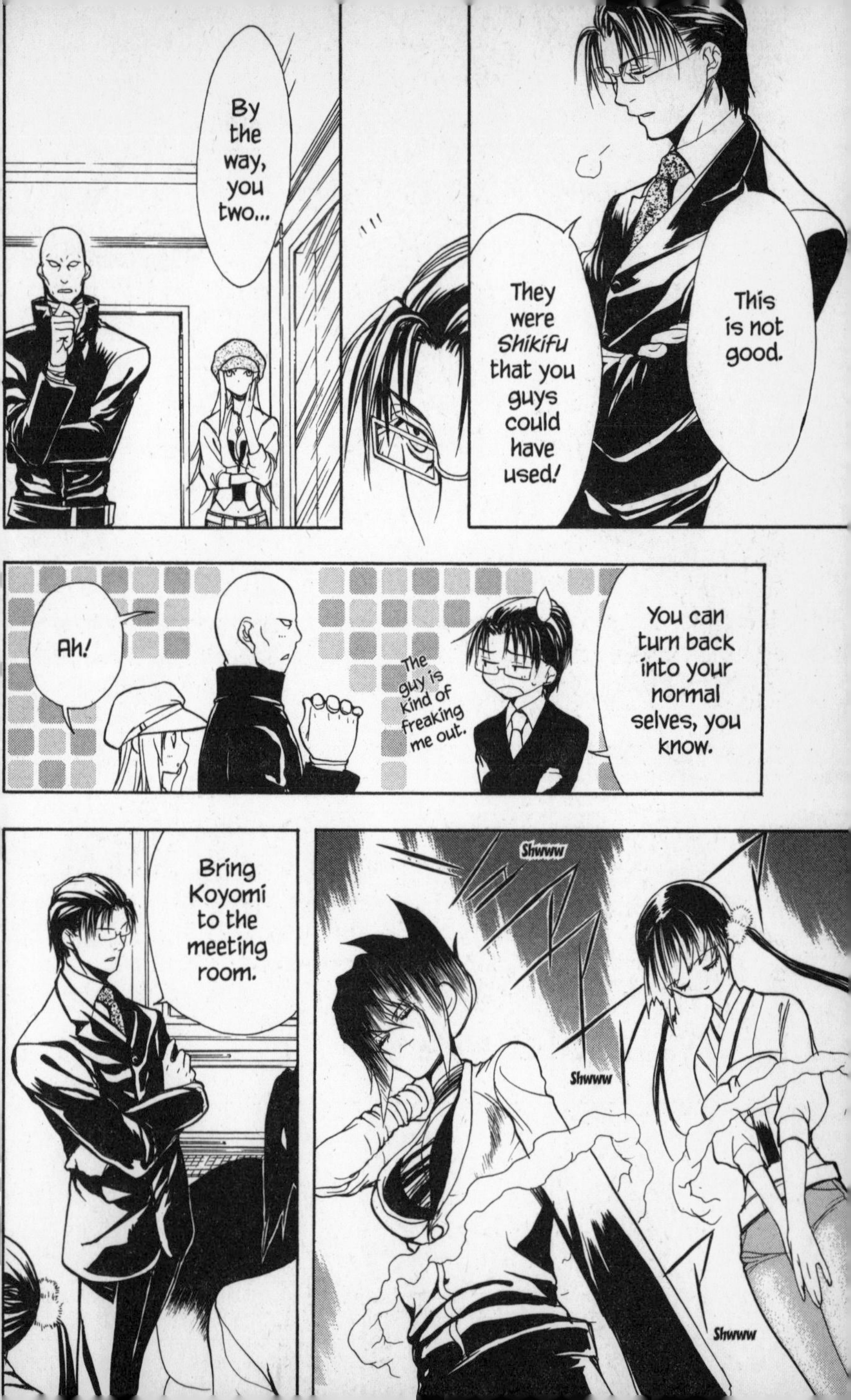
This is not good.
They were *Shikifu* that you guys could have used!
By the way, you two...
You can turn back into your normal selves, you know.
The guy is kind of freaking me out.
Ah!
Shwww
Shwww
Shwww
Bring Koyomi to the meeting room.

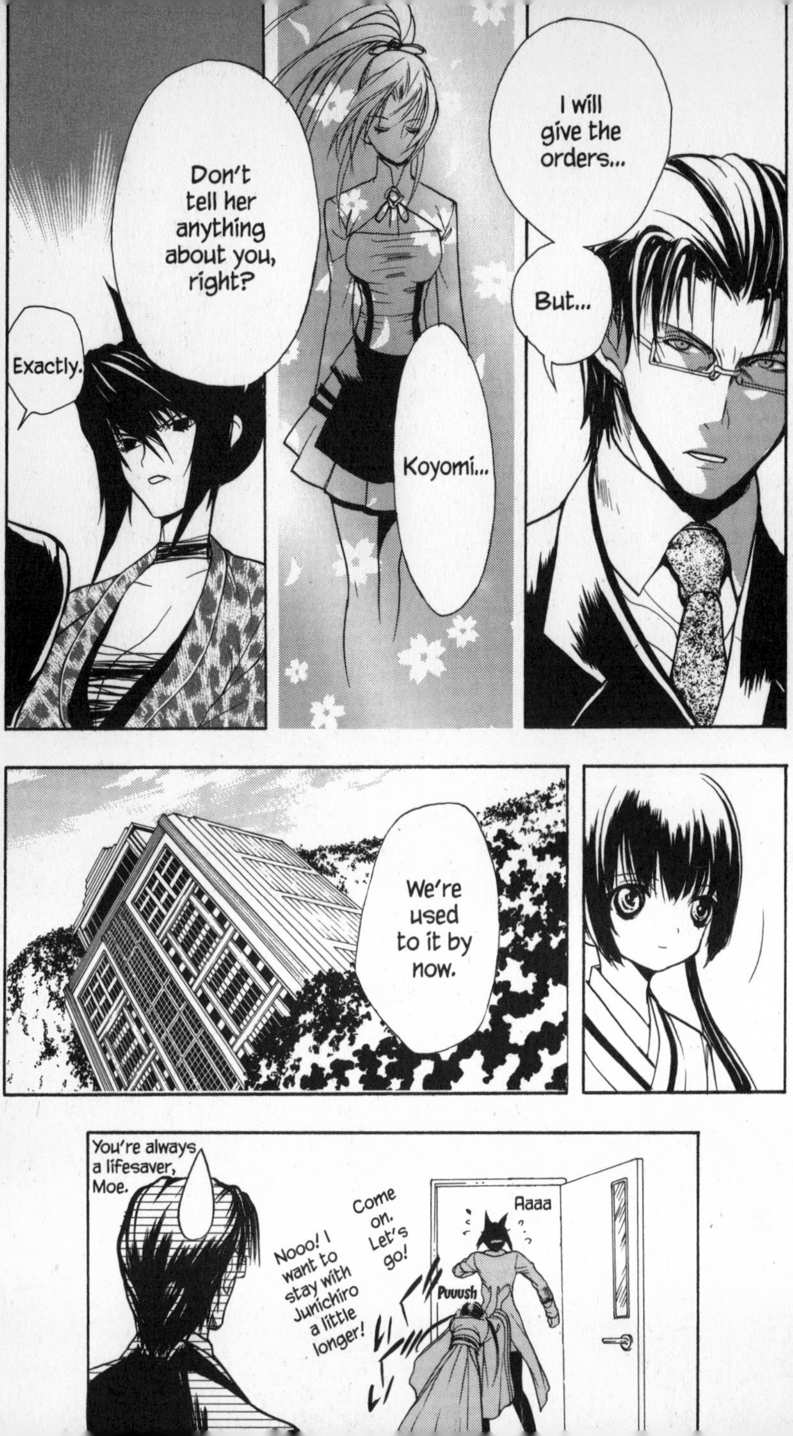
I will give the orders...
But...
Koyomi...
Don't tell her anything about you, right?
Exactly.
We're used to it by now.
Aaaa
Come on. Let's go!
You're always a lifesaver, Moe.
Puuush
Nooo! I want to stay with Junichiro a little longer!

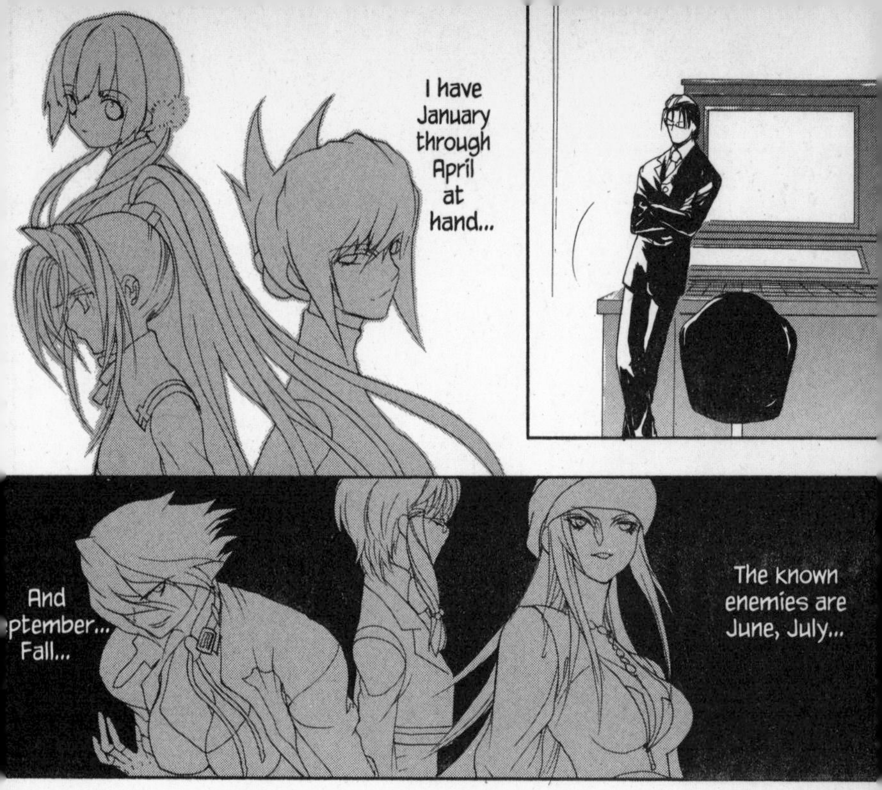
I have January through April at hand...
The known enemies are June, July...
And
ptember...
Fall...

***Shiki* Knowledge — the *Shiki Tsukai* groups —**

In general, the *Shiki Tsukai* are separated into twelve groups and usually do not oppose each other.

If they are grouped further, they are usually grouped by seasons: Spring, Summer, Fall, and Winter.

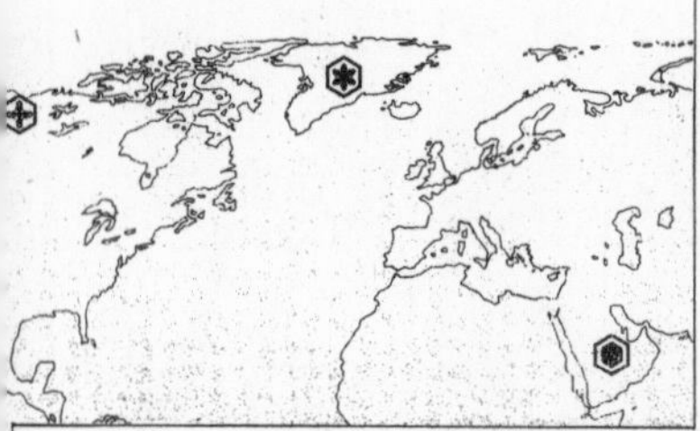

Each season is grouped as such:

[Spring: New Calendar March — May]

[Summer: New Calendar June — August]

[Fall: New Calendar September — November]

[Winter: New Calendar December — February]

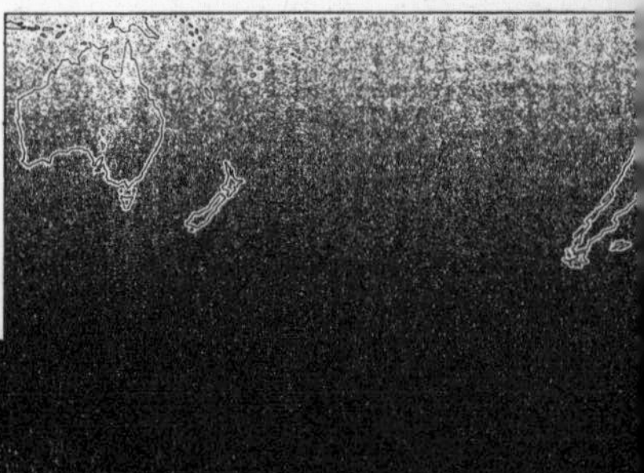

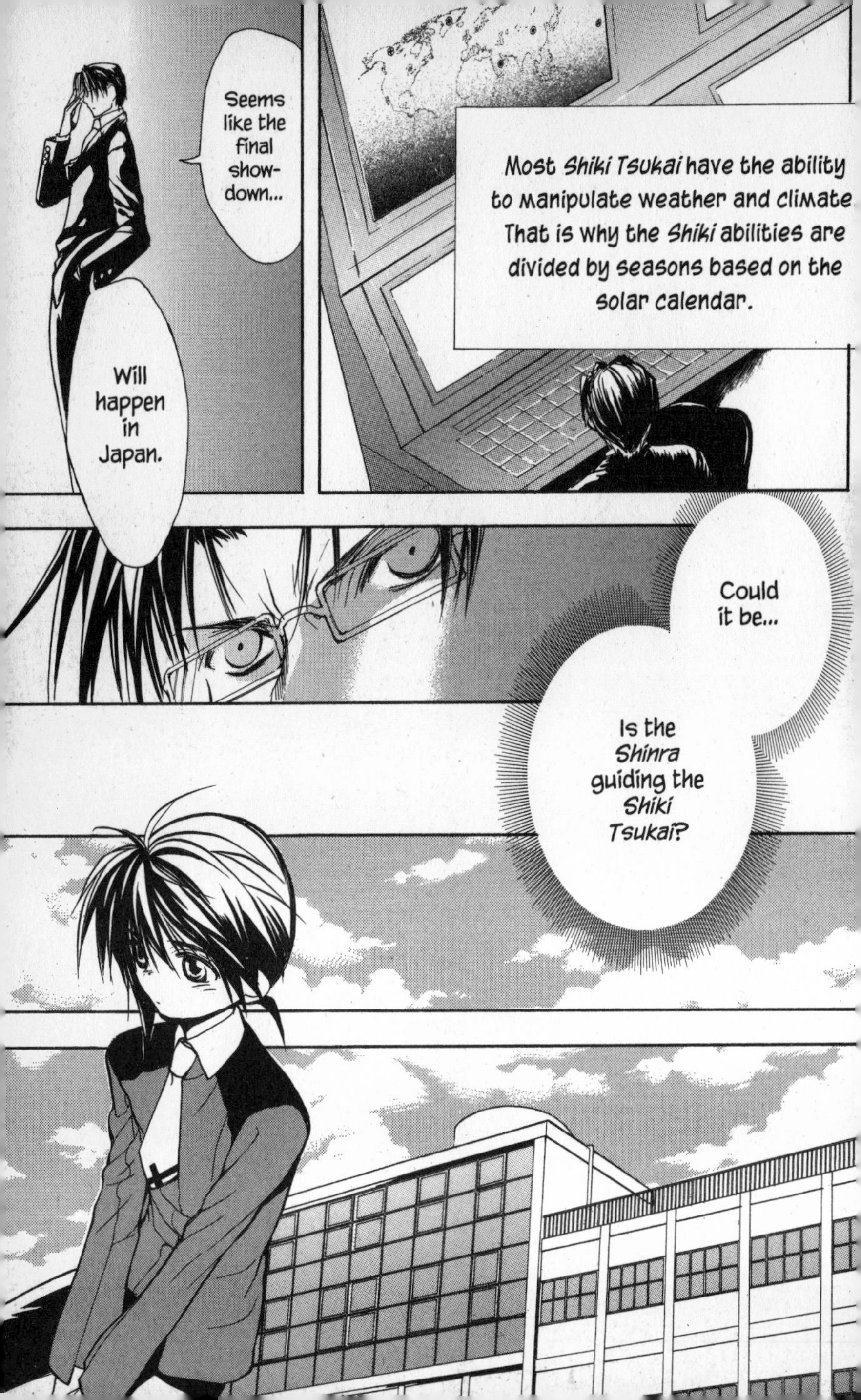
Most Shiki Tsukai have the ability to manipulate weather and climate That is why the Shiki abilities are divided by seasons based on the solar calendar.
Seems like the final show-down...
Will happen in Japan.
Could it be...
Is the Shinra guiding the Shiki Tsukai?

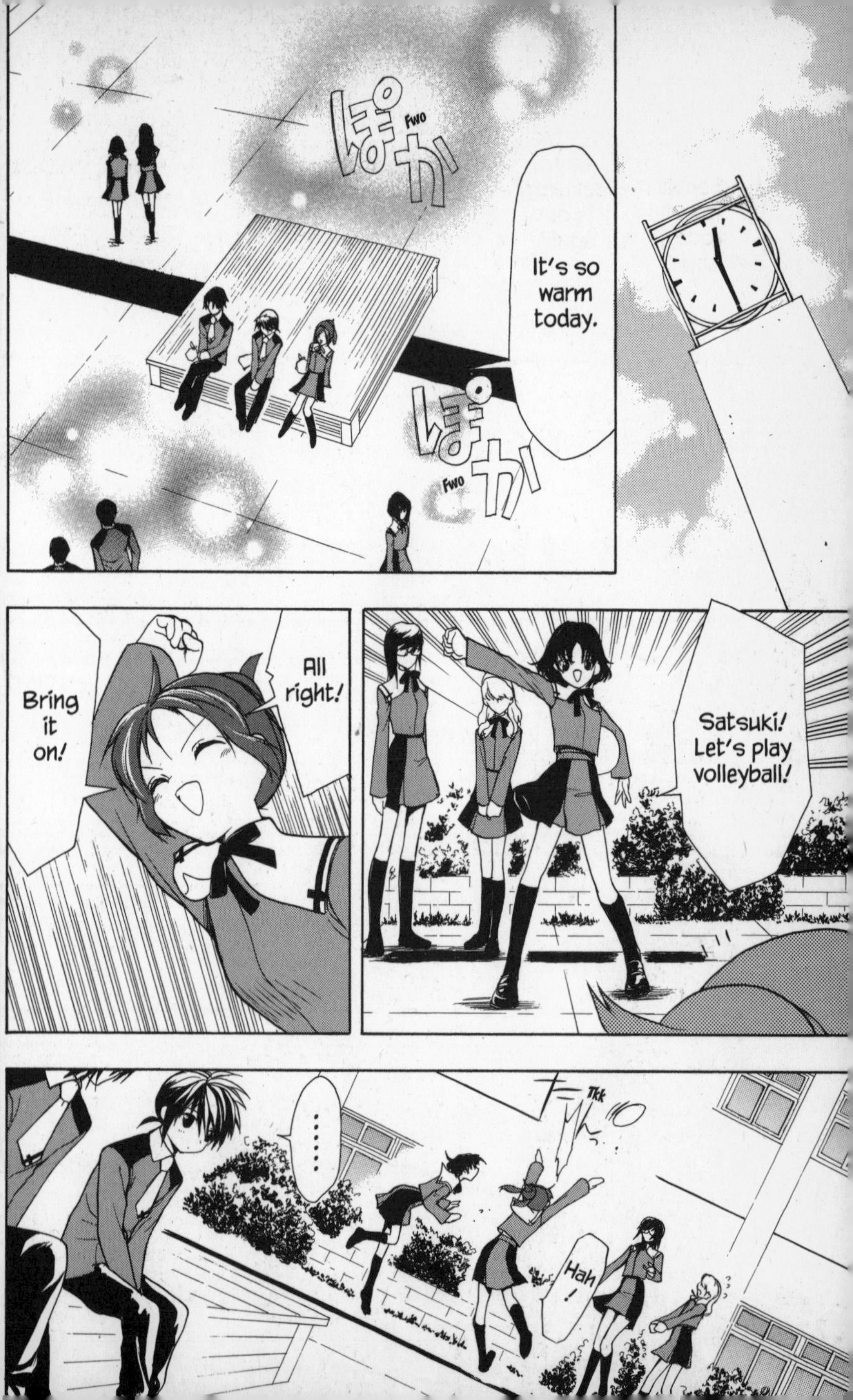
ぽか
Fwo
It's so warm today.
ぽか
Fwo
Satsuki! Let's play volleyball!
All right!
Bring it on!
Tkk
......
Hah!

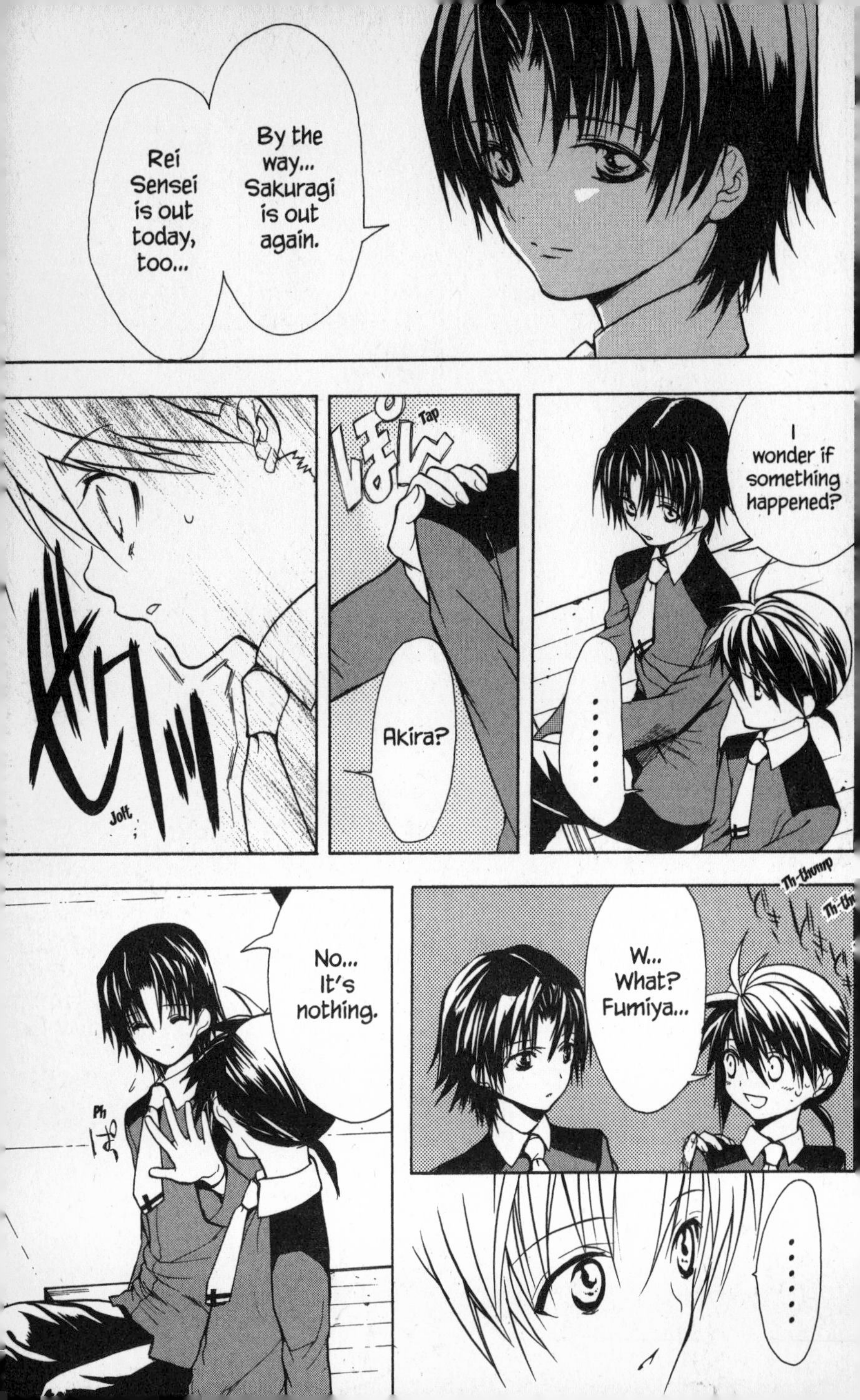
By the way... Sakuragi is out again.
Rei Sensei is out today, too...
I wonder if something happened?
......
Tap
Akira?
Jolt
Th-thump
Th-th
W... What? Fumiya...
......
No... It's nothing.
Ph

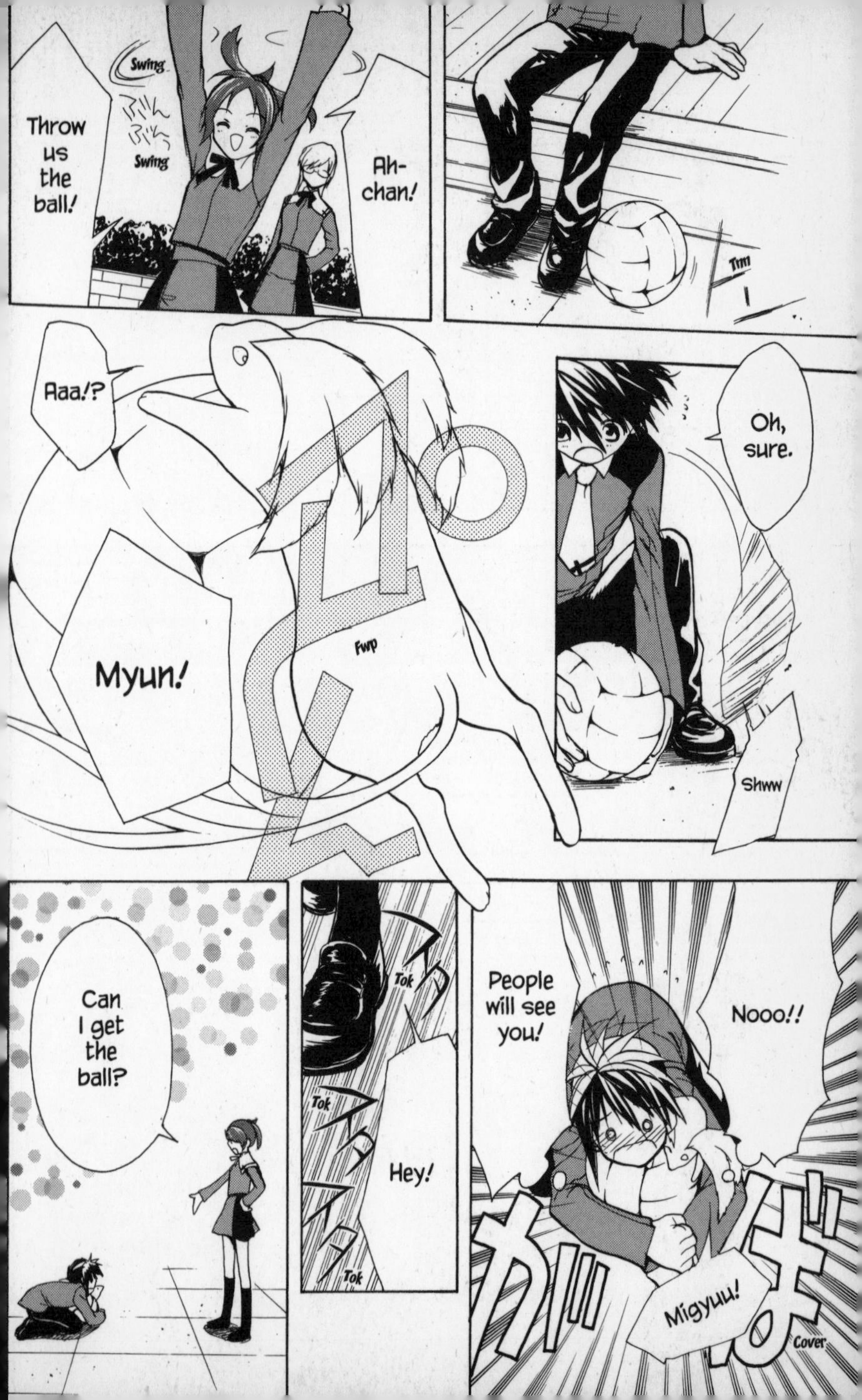

Tm
Ah-chan!
Swing
Swing
Throw us the ball!
Oh, sure.
Shww
Aaa!?
Fwp
Myun!
Nooo!!
People will see you!
Migyuu!
Cover
Tok
Tok
Hey!
Tok
Can I get the ball?

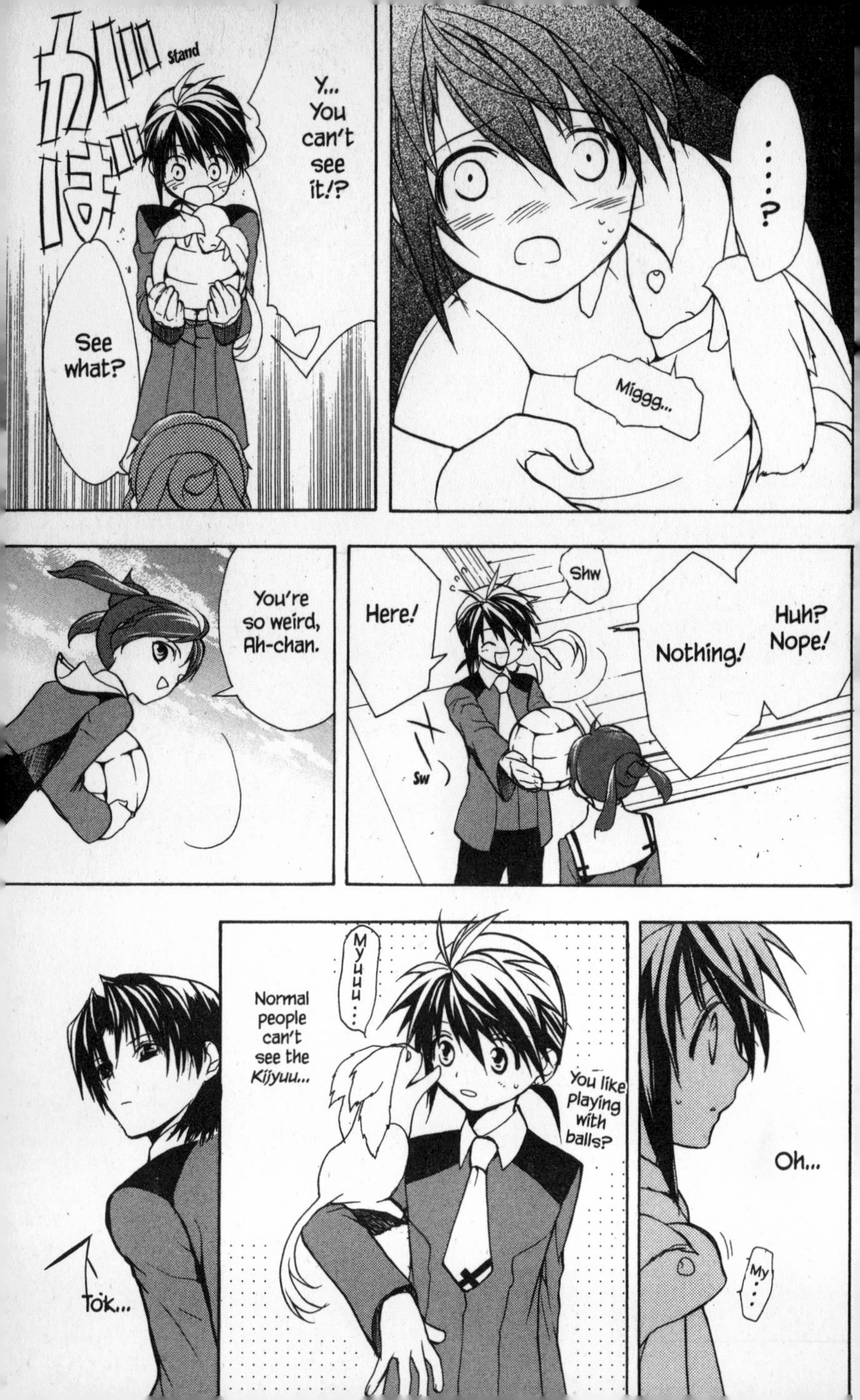

....?
Miggg...
Y... You can't see it!?
Stand
See what?
Shw
Huh? Nope!
Nothing!
Here!
Sw
You're so weird, Ah-chan.
Oh...
My...
Myuuu...
You like playing with balls?
Normal people can't see the Kijyuu...
Tok...

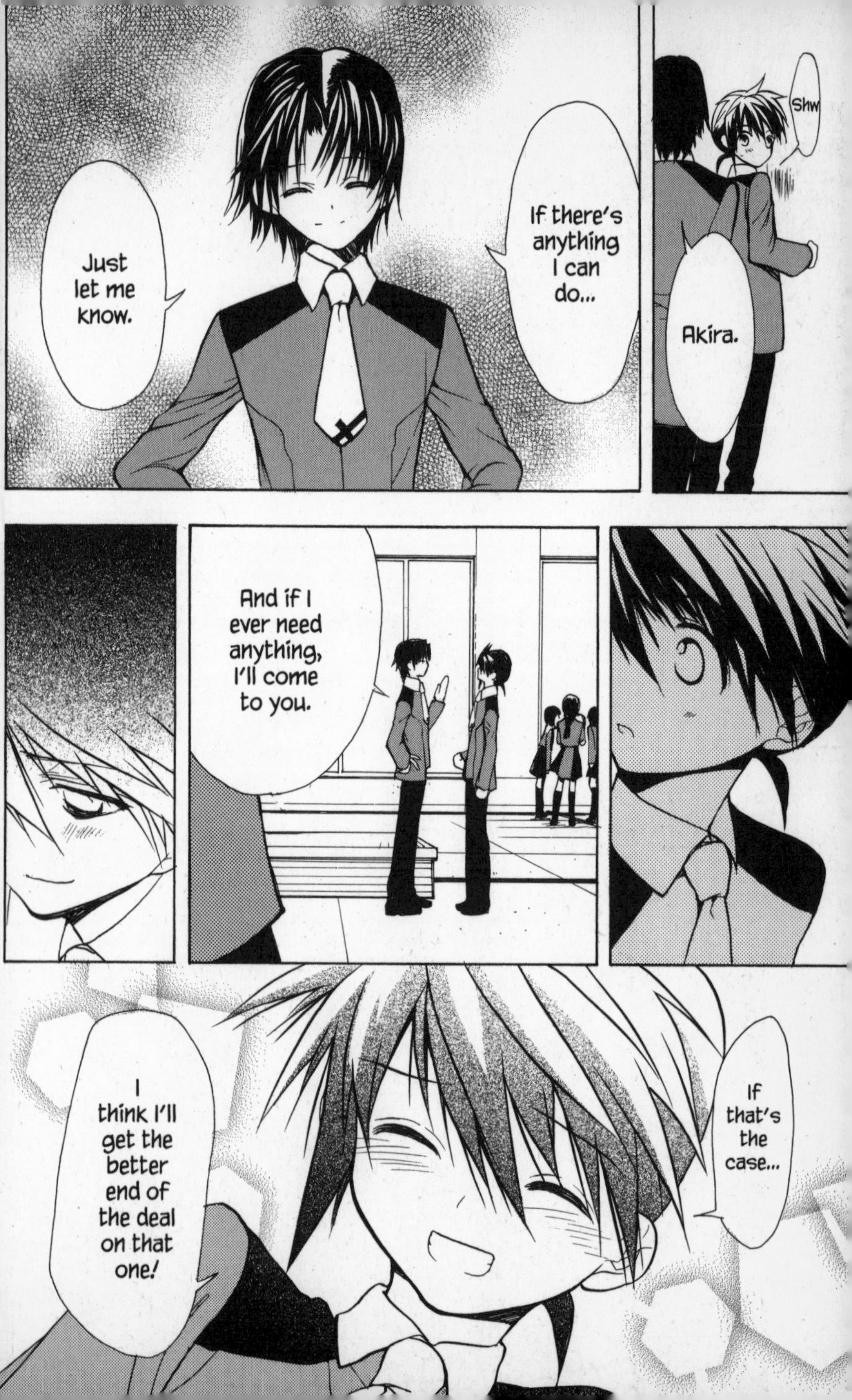
Shw
Akira.
If there's anything I can do...
Just let me know.
And if I ever need anything, I'll come to you.
If that's the case...
I think I'll get the better end of the deal on that one!

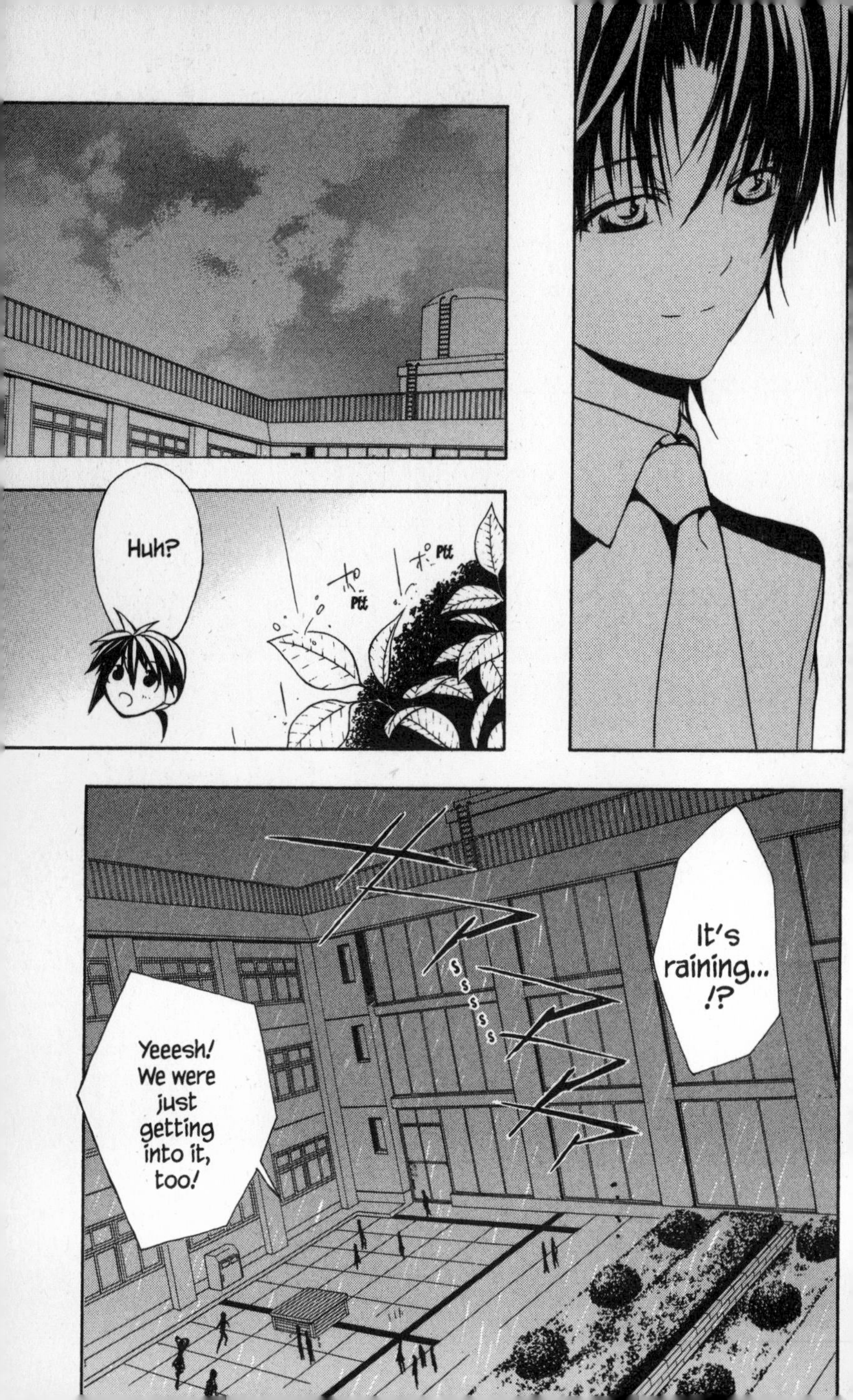
Huh?
ポ Ptt
ポ Ptt
It's raining...!?
sssss
Yeeesh! We were just getting into it, too!

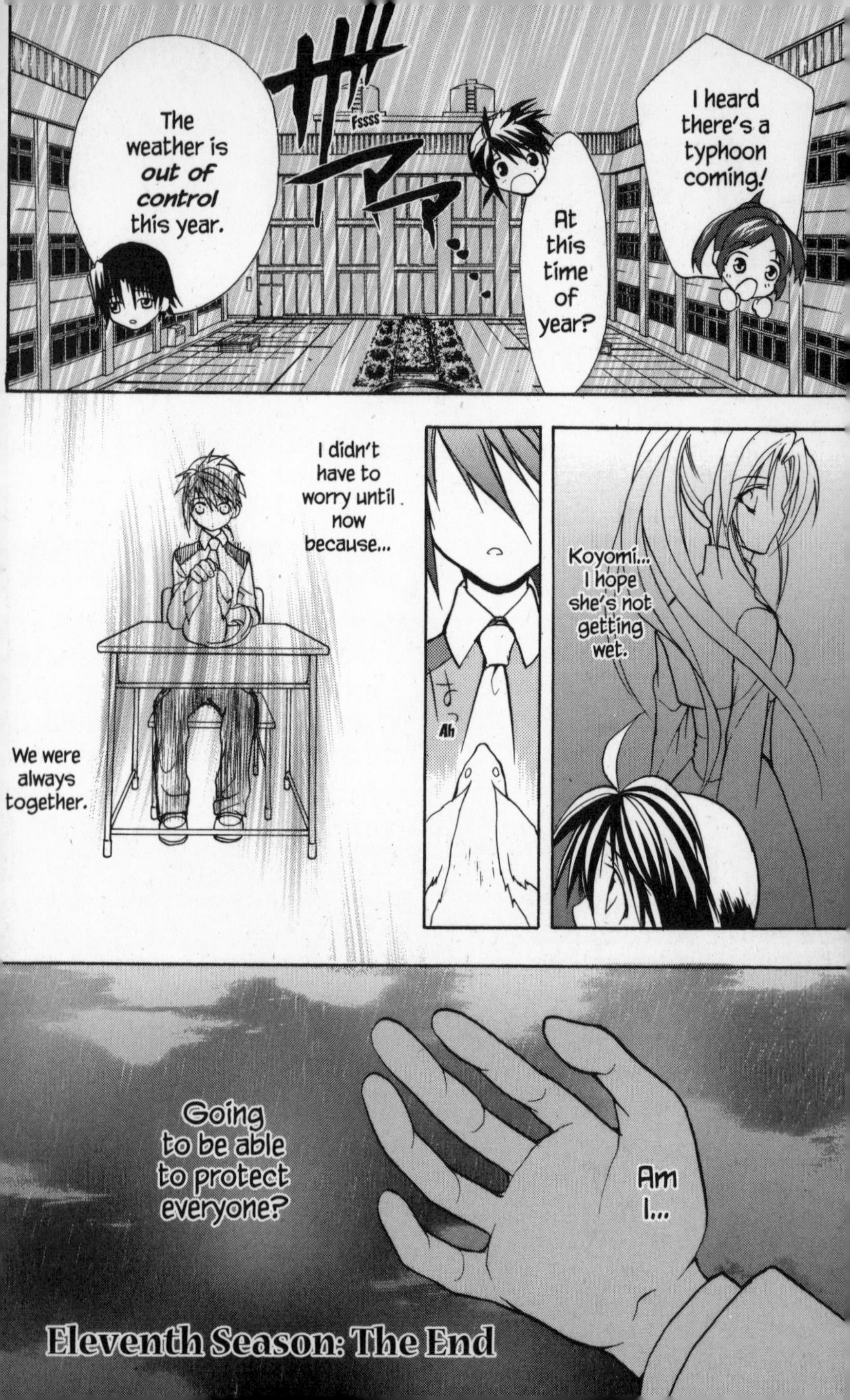
I heard there's a typhoon coming!
At this time of year?
Fssss
The weather is out of control this year.
Koyomi... I hope she's not getting wet.
Ah
I didn't have to worry until now because...
We were always together.
Am I...
Going to be able to protect everyone?
Eleventh Season: The End

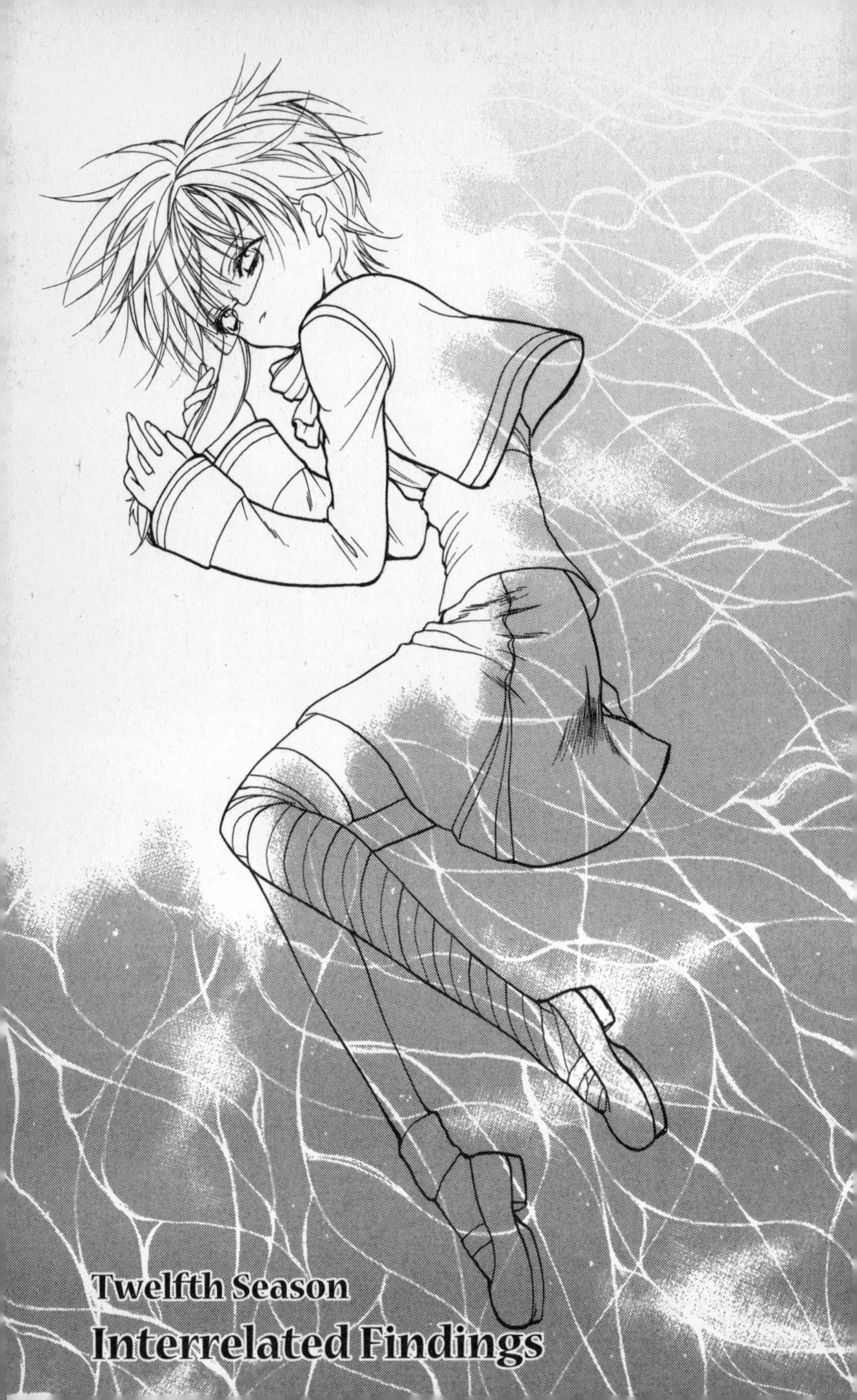

Twelfth Season

Interrelated Findings

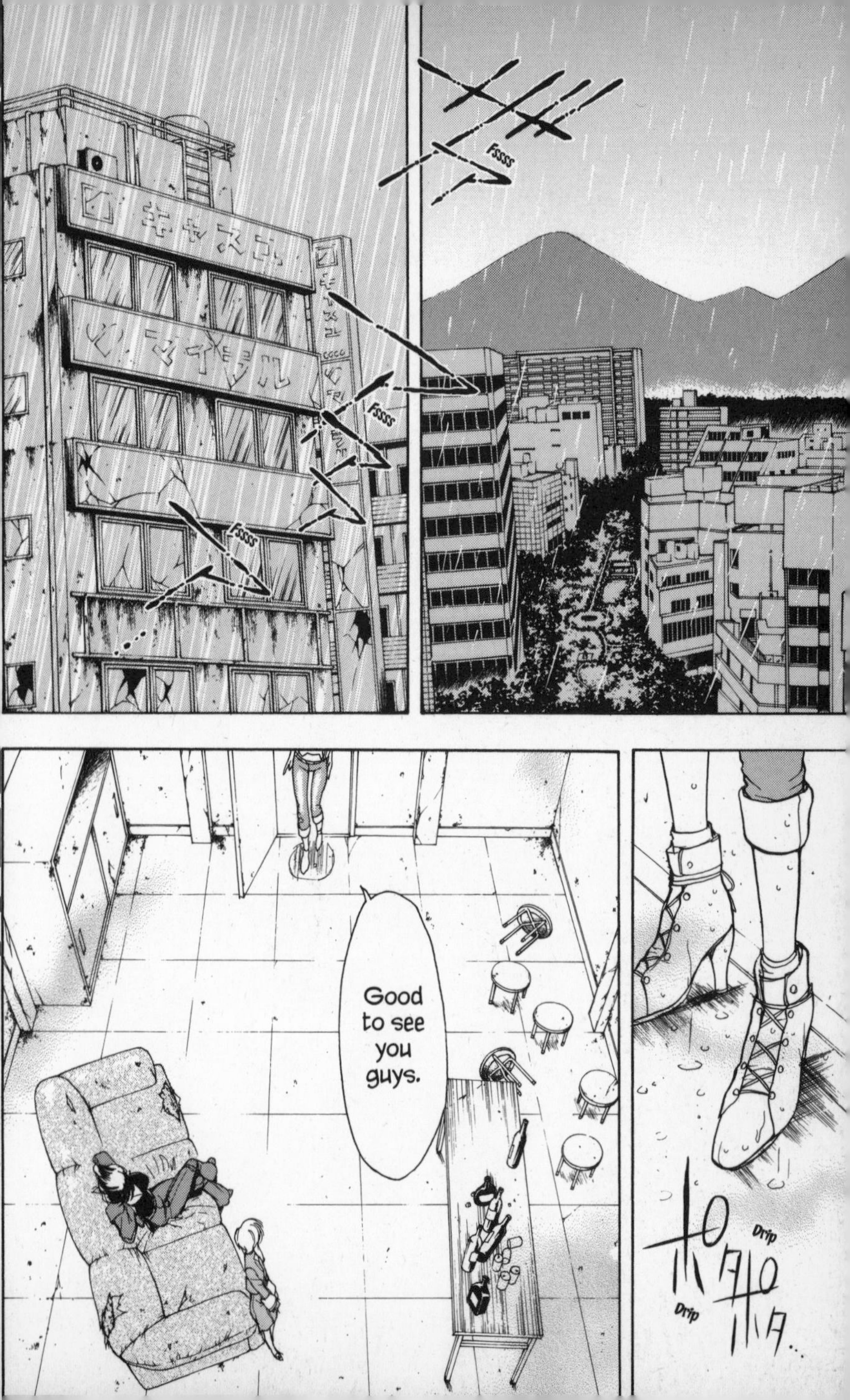
Fssss
Fssss
Fssss
Drip
Drip
Good to see you guys.

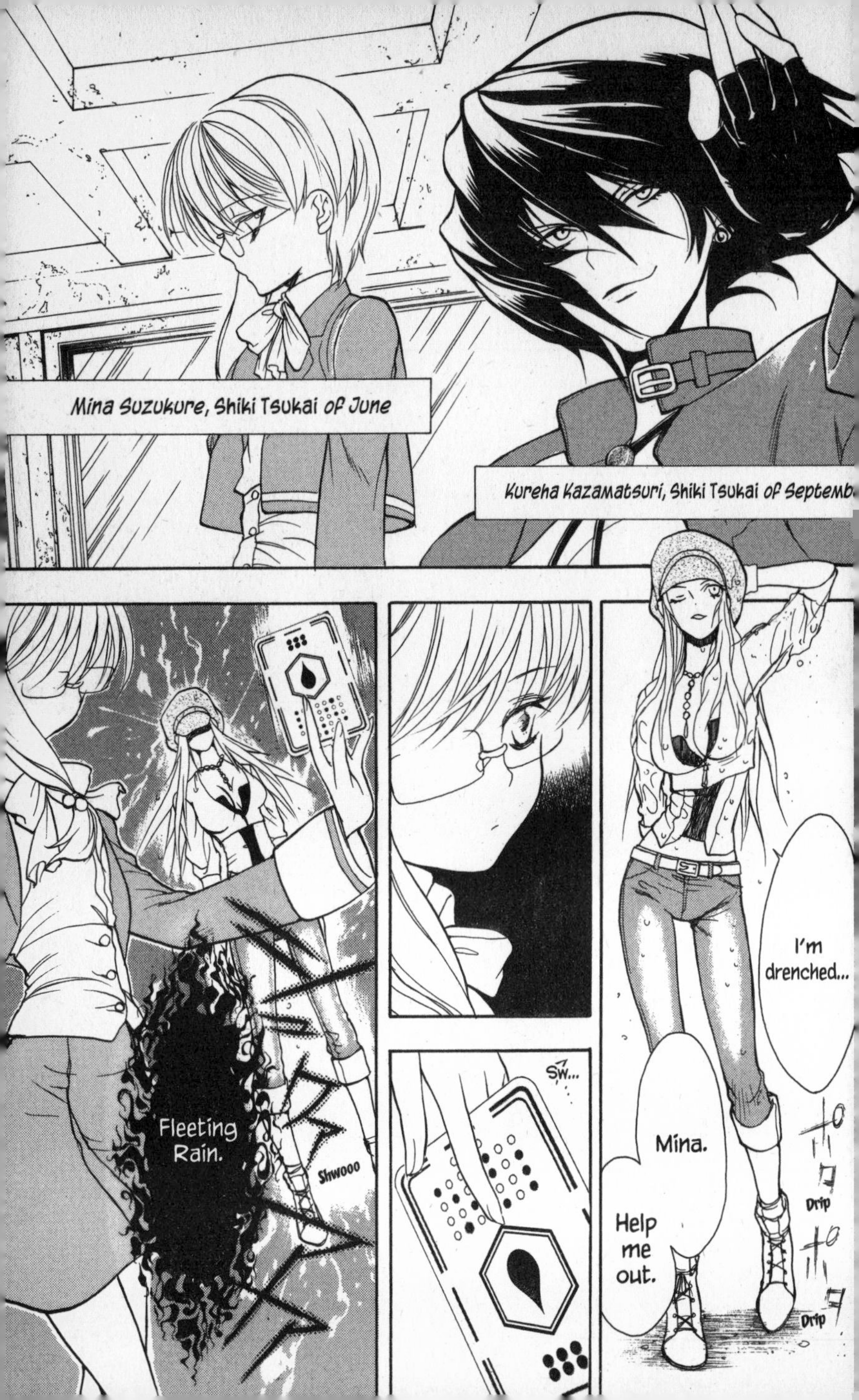
Kureha Kazamatsuri, Shiki Tsukai of Septemb
Mina Suzukure, Shiki Tsukai of June
I'm drenched...
Drip
Mina.
Help me out.
Drip
Sw...
Fleeting Rain.
Shwooo

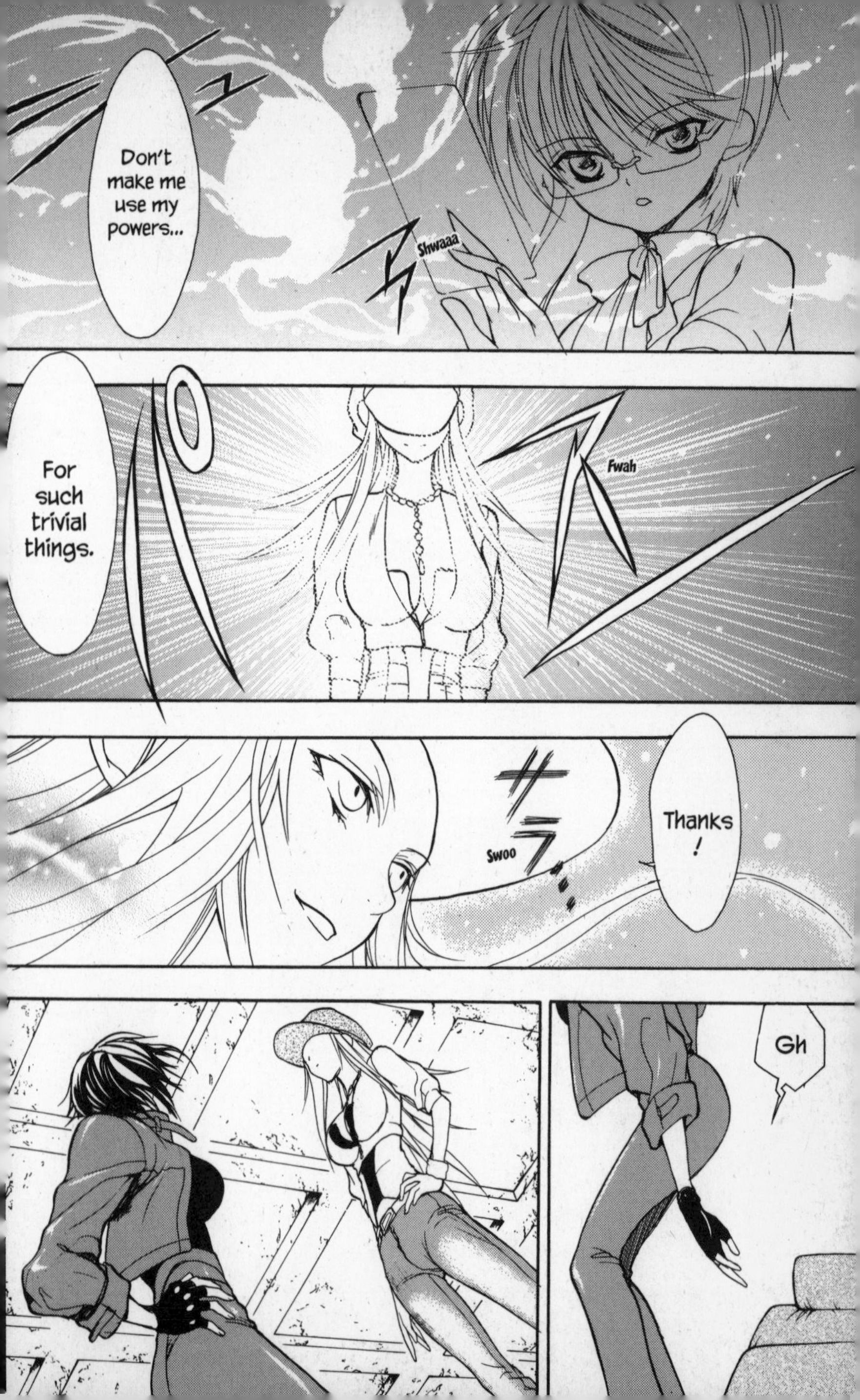
Shwaaa
Don't make me use my powers...
Fwah
For such trivial things.
Thanks!
Swoo
Gh

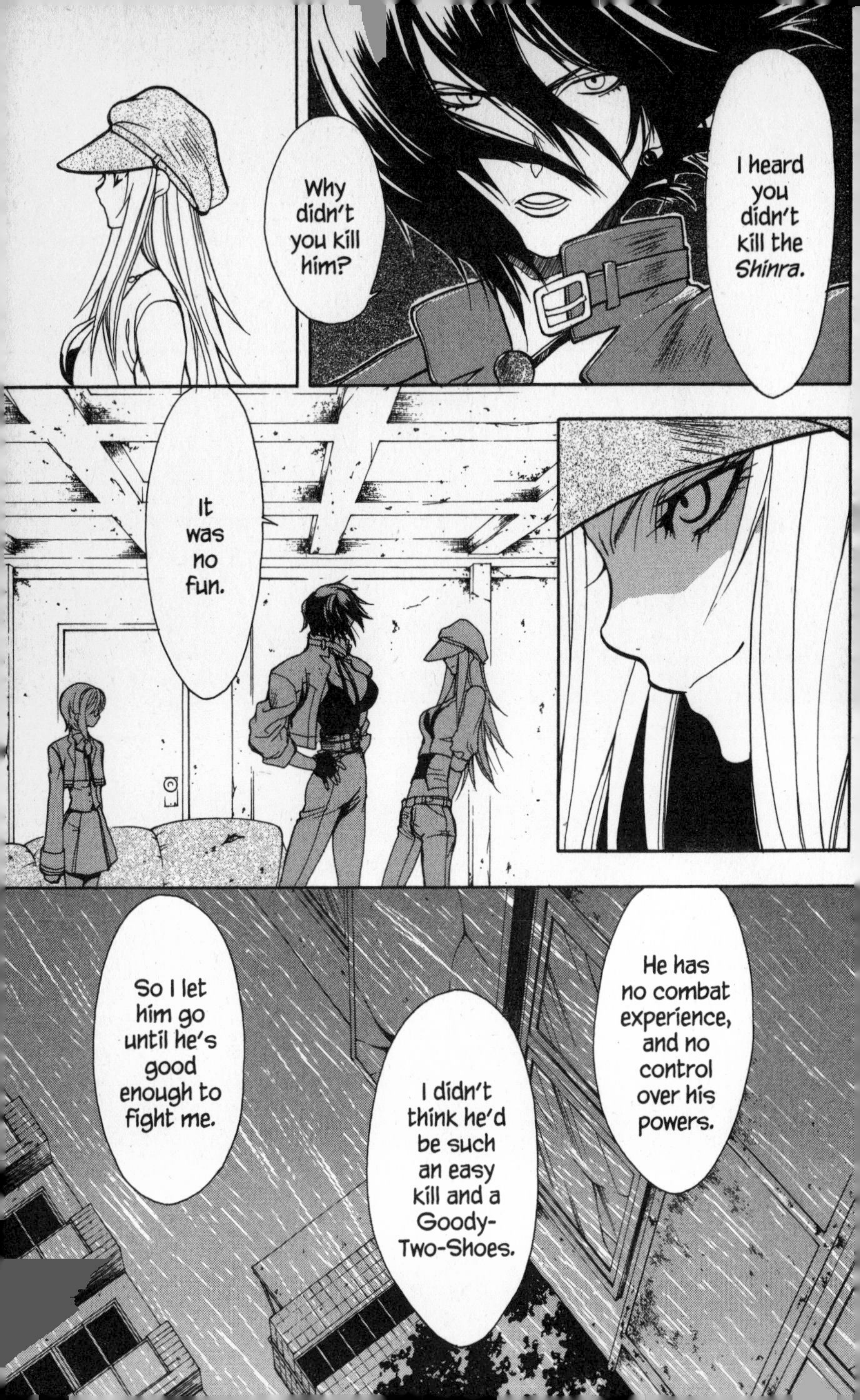
I heard you didn't kill the *Shinra*.
Why didn't you kill him?
It was no fun.
He has no combat experience, and no control over his powers.
I didn't think he'd be such an easy kill and a Goody-Two-Shoes.
So I let him go until he's good enough to fight me.

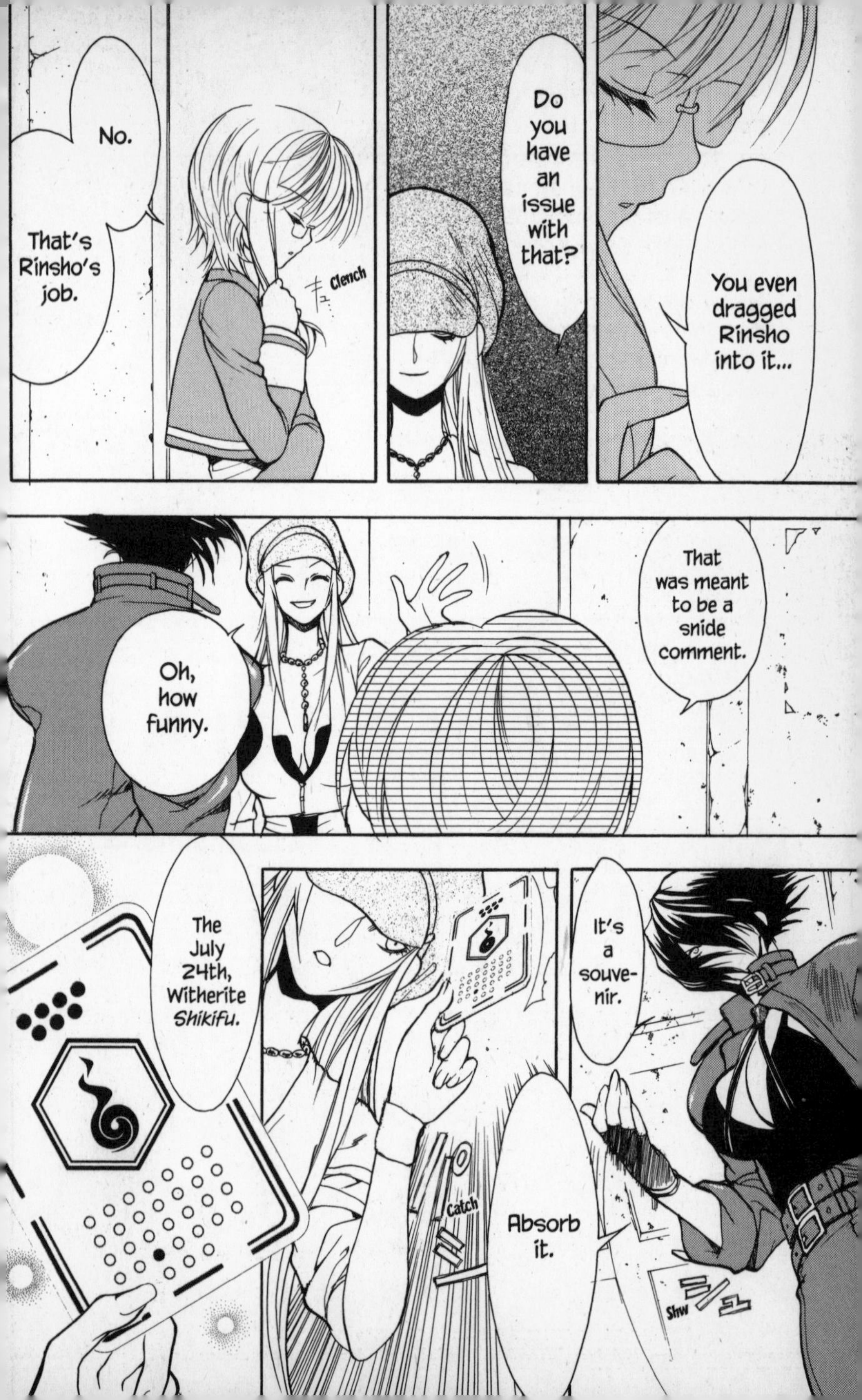
You even dragged Rinsho into it...
Do you have an issue with that?
No.
That's Rinsho's job.
Clench
That was meant to be a snide comment.
Oh, how funny.
It's a souvenir.
Absorb it.
Shw
Catch
The July 24th, Witherite Shikifu.

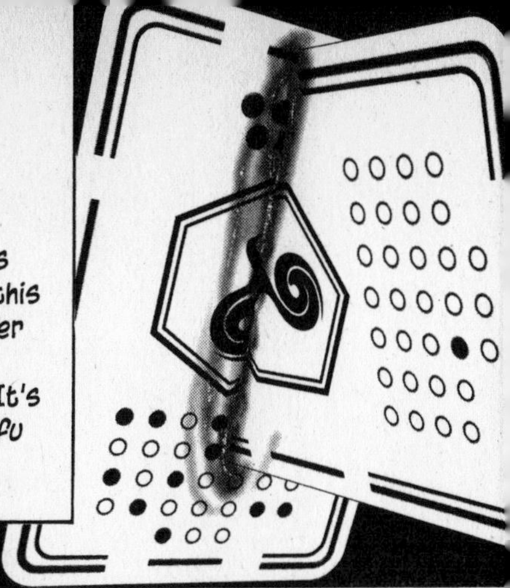

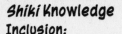

Shiki Knowledge

Inclusion:

The *Shiki Tsukai*'s *Shikifu* (made from their birthday stone) can absorb another *Shikifu* as long as it's from the same month. Doing this increases the *Shiki Tsukai*'s power and enables them to acquire additional season incantations. It's also possible to detach the *Shikifu* that was absorbed.

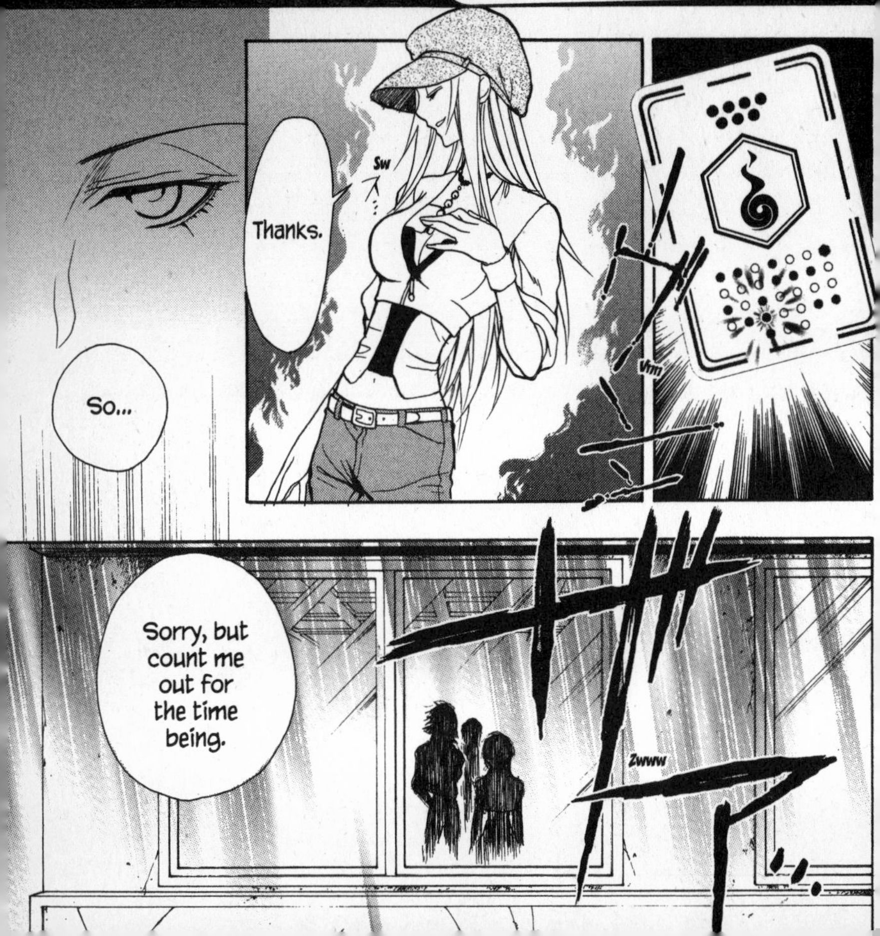
Vmm
Sw
Thanks.
So...
Sorry, but count me out for the time being.
Zwww

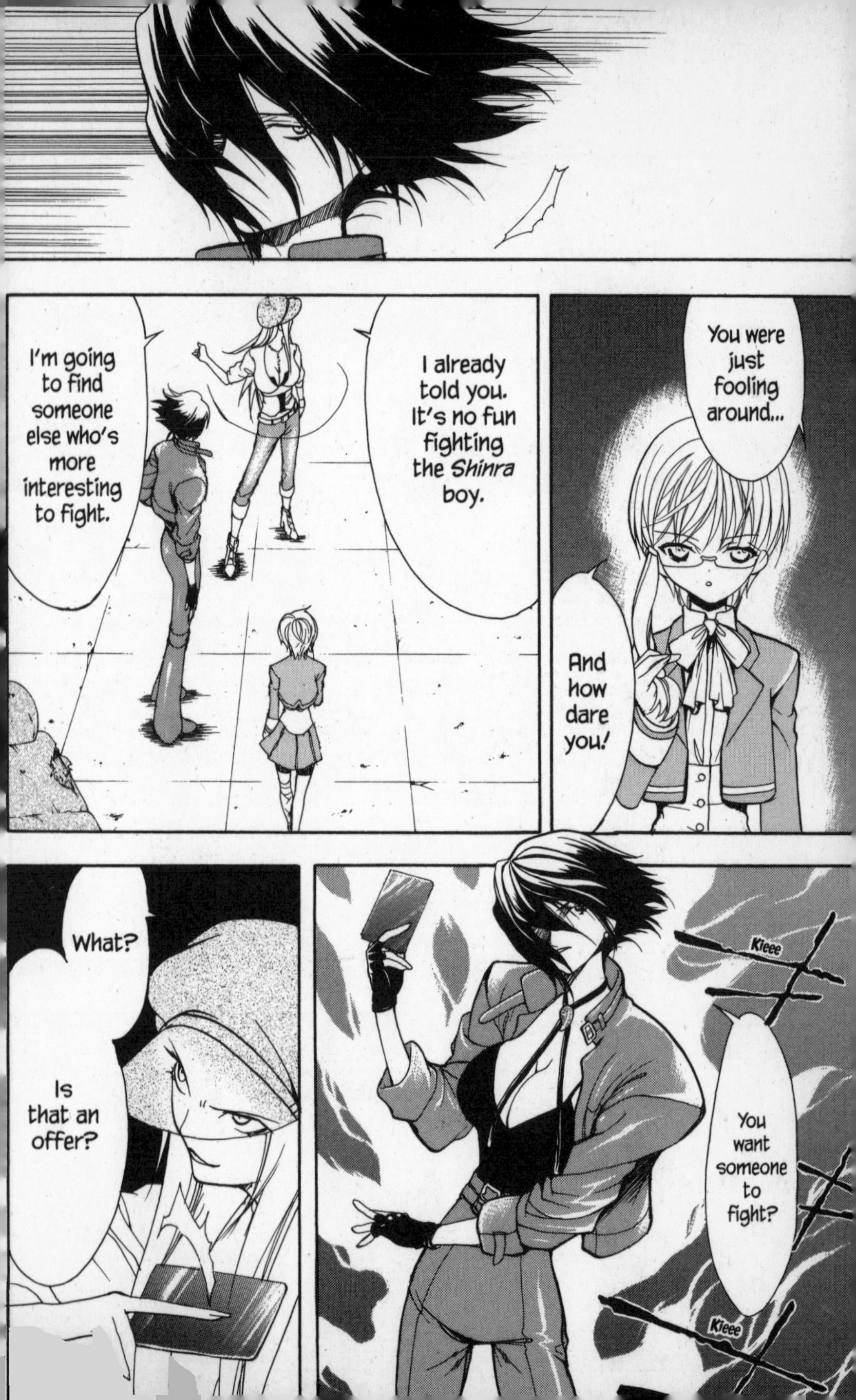
You were just fooling around...
And how dare you!
I already told you. It's no fun fighting the *Shinra* boy.
I'm going to find someone else who's more interesting to fight.
Kieee
You want someone to fight?
Kieee
What?
Is that an offer?

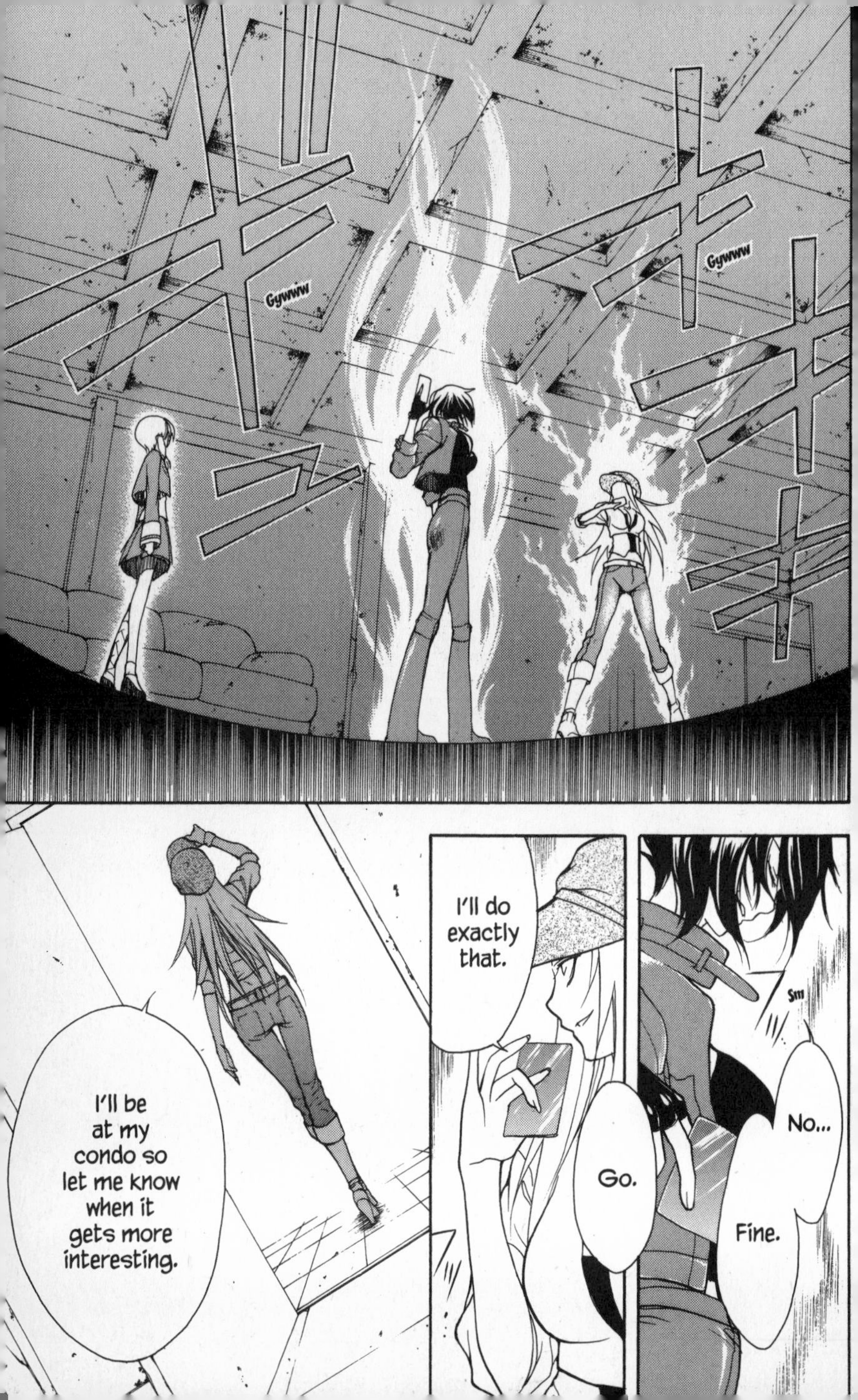
Gywww
Gywww
No...
Fine.
I'll do exactly that.
Go.
I'll be at my condo so let me know when it gets more interesting.

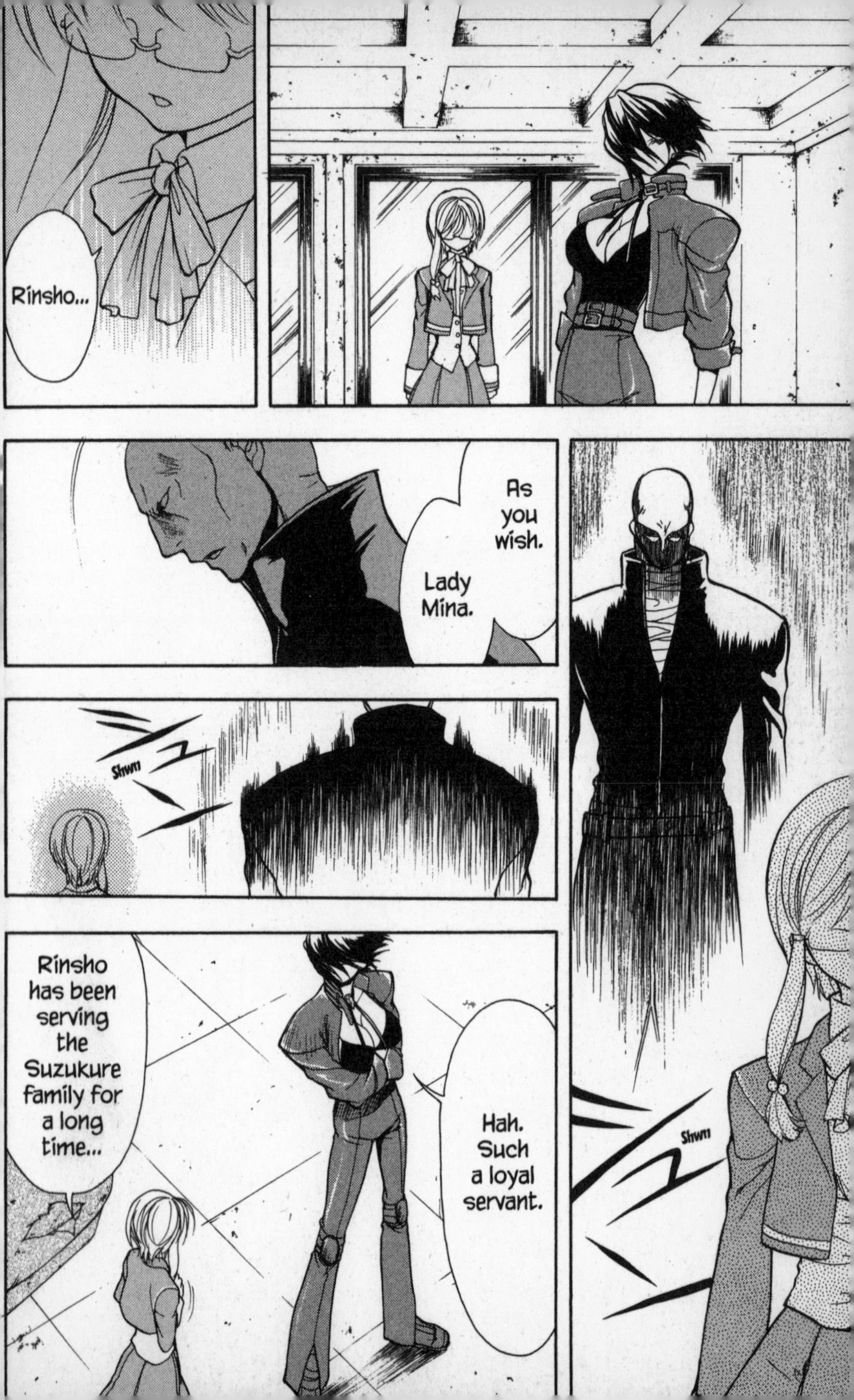
Rinsho...
Shwn
As you wish.
Lady Mina.
Shwn
Hah. Such a loyal servant.
Rinsho has been serving the Suzukure family for a long time...

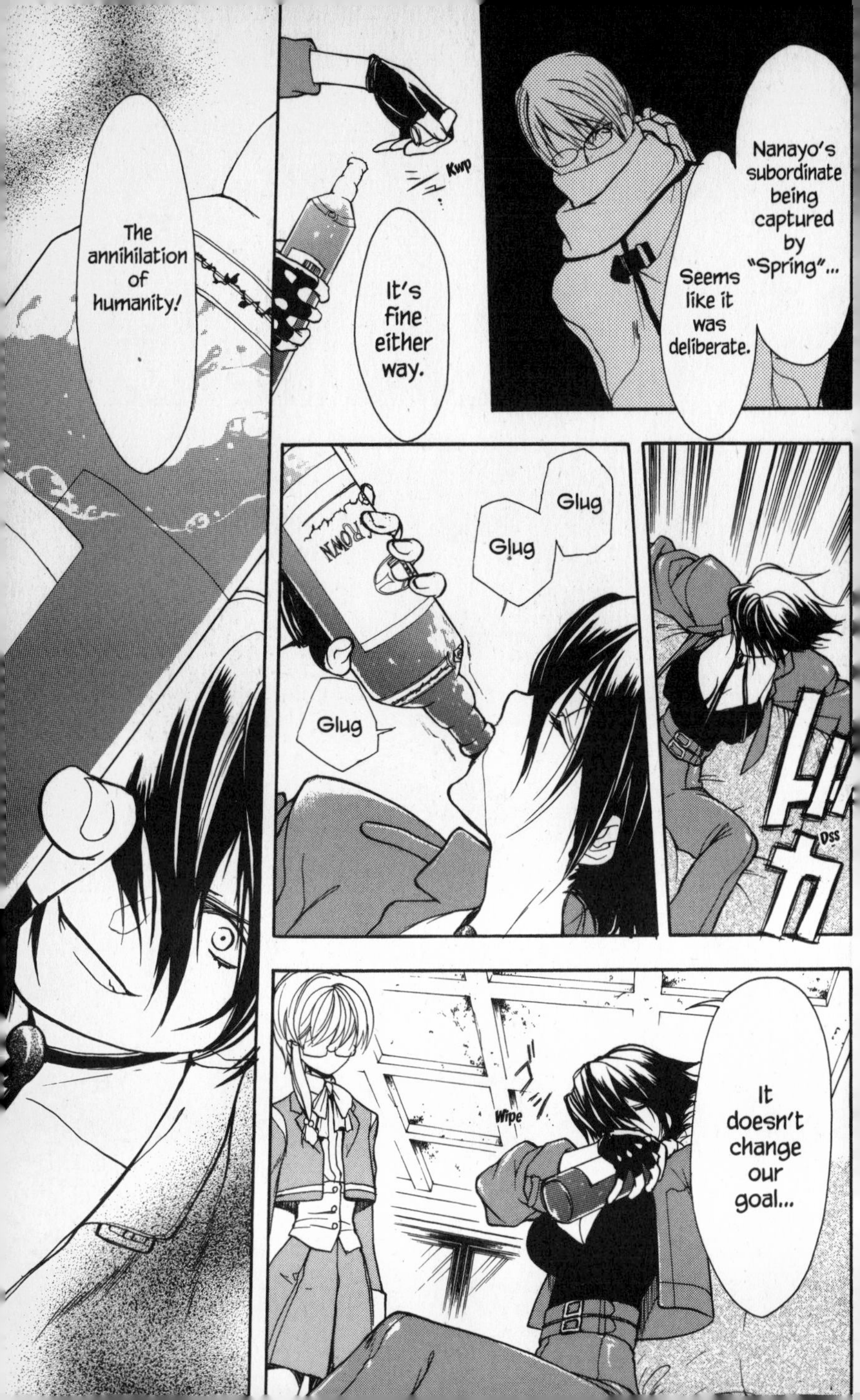
Nanayo's subordinate being captured by "Spring"...
Seems like it was deliberate.
Kwp
It's fine either way.
Dss
Glug
Glug
Glug
It doesn't change our goal...
Wipe
The annihilation of humanity!

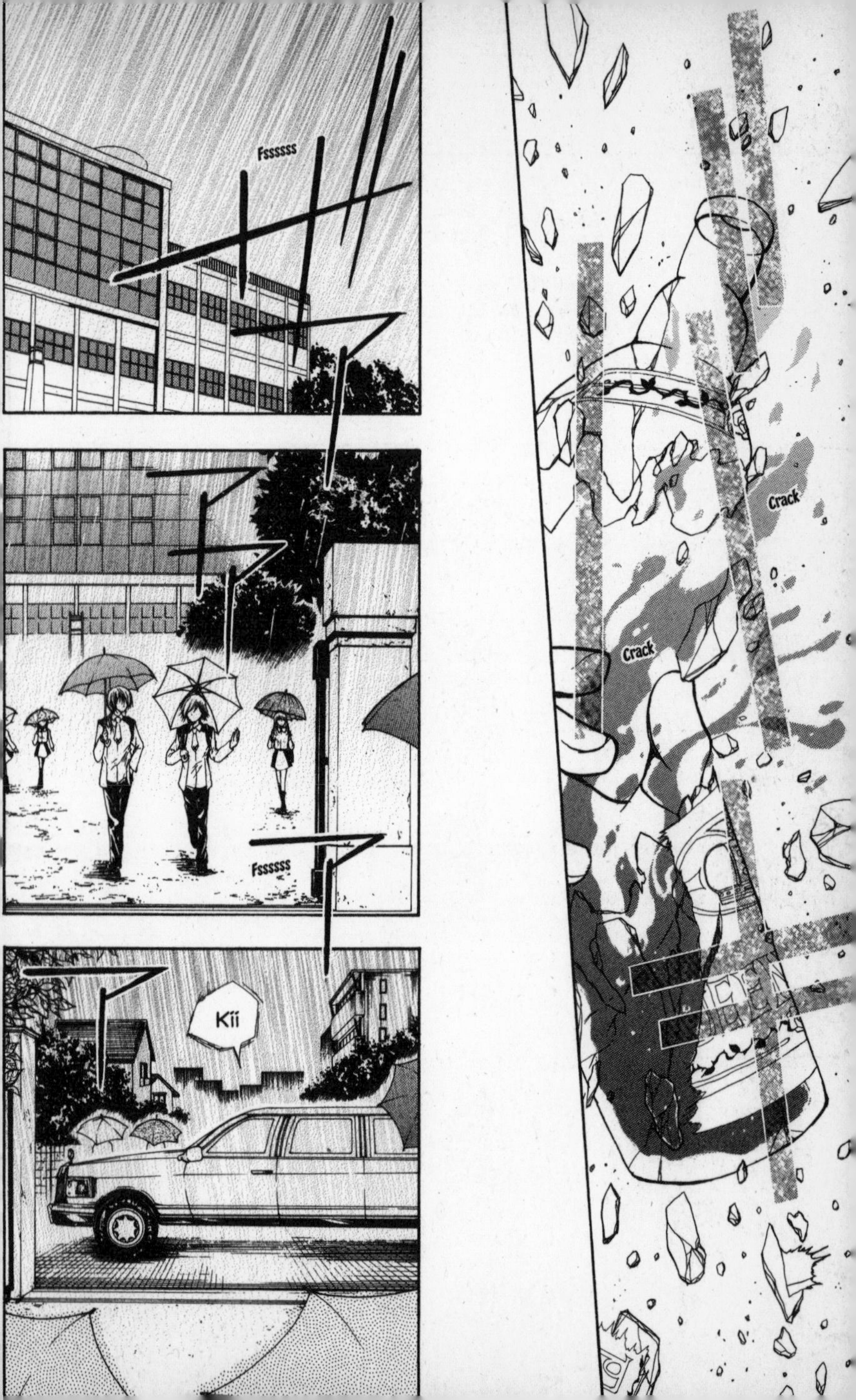
Crack
Crack
Fssssss
Fssssss
Kii

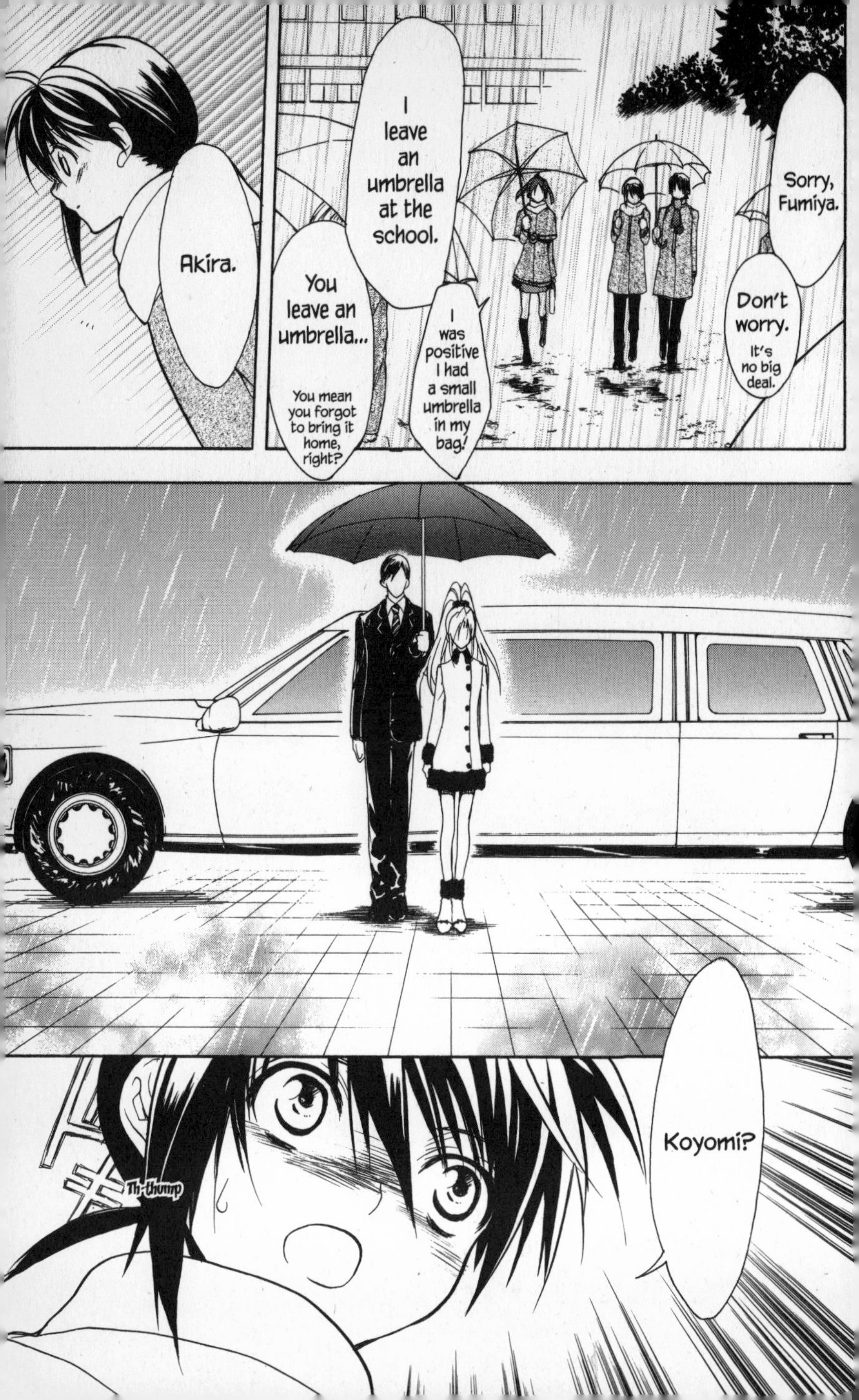
Sorry, Fumiya.
Don't worry.
It's no big deal.
I leave an umbrella at the school.
I was positive I had a small umbrella in my bag!
You leave an umbrella...
You mean you forgot to bring it home, right?
Akira.
Koyomi?
Th-thump

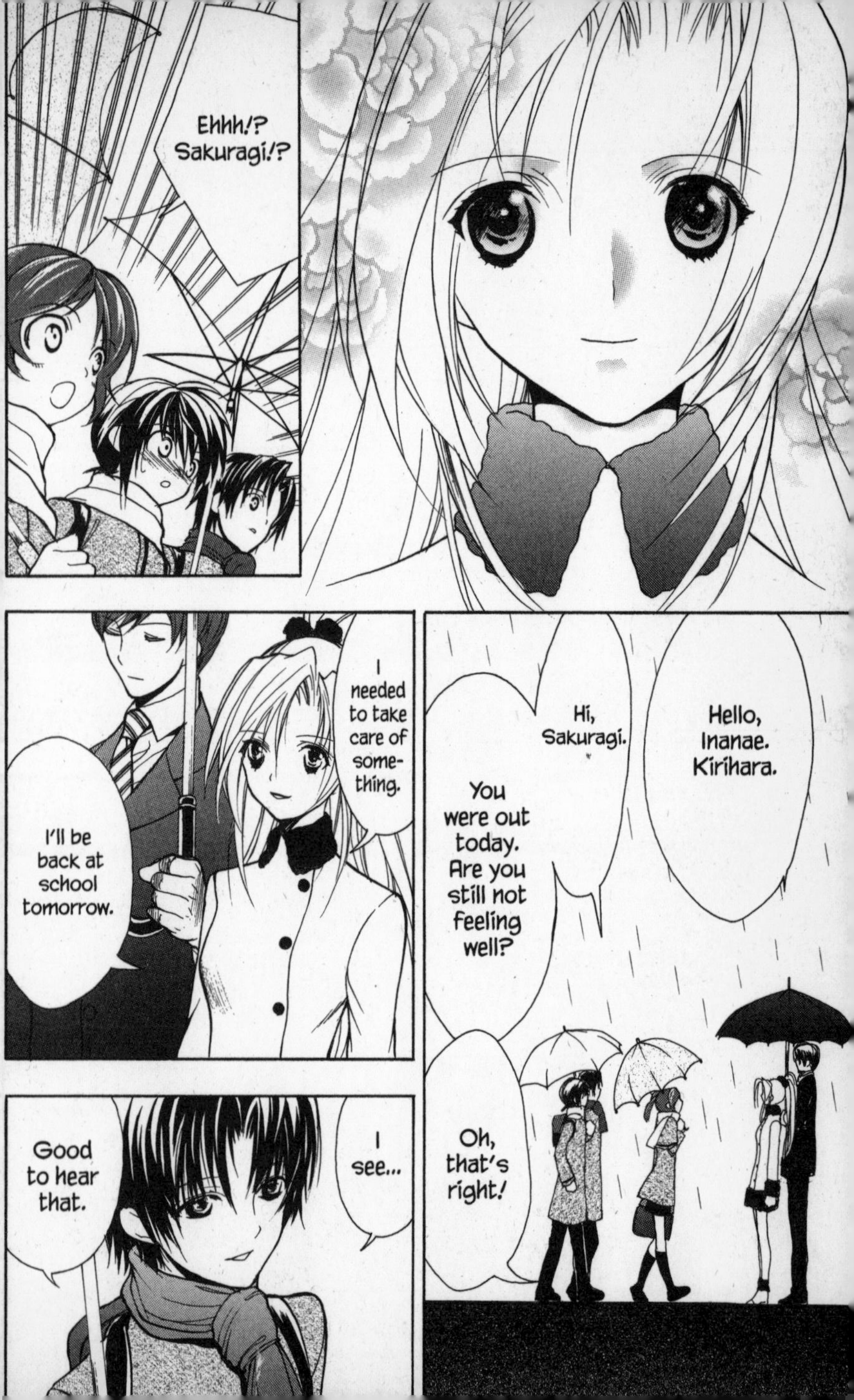

Ehhh!? Sakuragi!?
Hello, Inanae. Kirihara.
Hi, Sakuragi.
You were out today. Are you still not feeling well?
Oh, that's right!
I needed to take care of something.
I'll be back at school tomorrow.
I see...
Good to hear that.

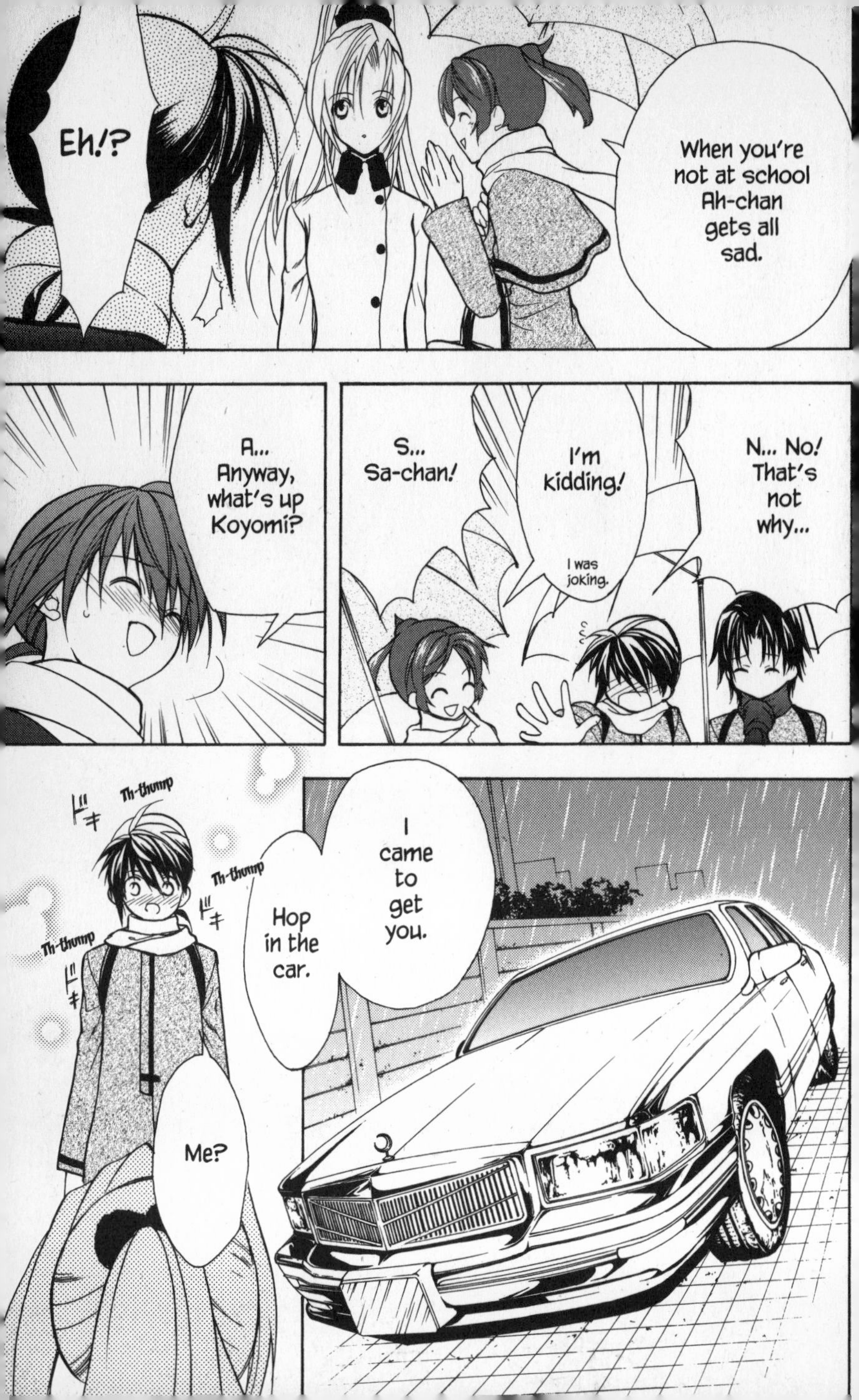
When you're not at school Ah-chan gets all sad.
Eh!?
N... No! That's not why...
I'm kidding!
I was joking.
S... Sa-chan!
A... Anyway, what's up Koyomi?
I came to get you.
Hop in the car.
Th-thump
ドキ
Th-thump
ドキ
Th-thump
ドキ
Me?

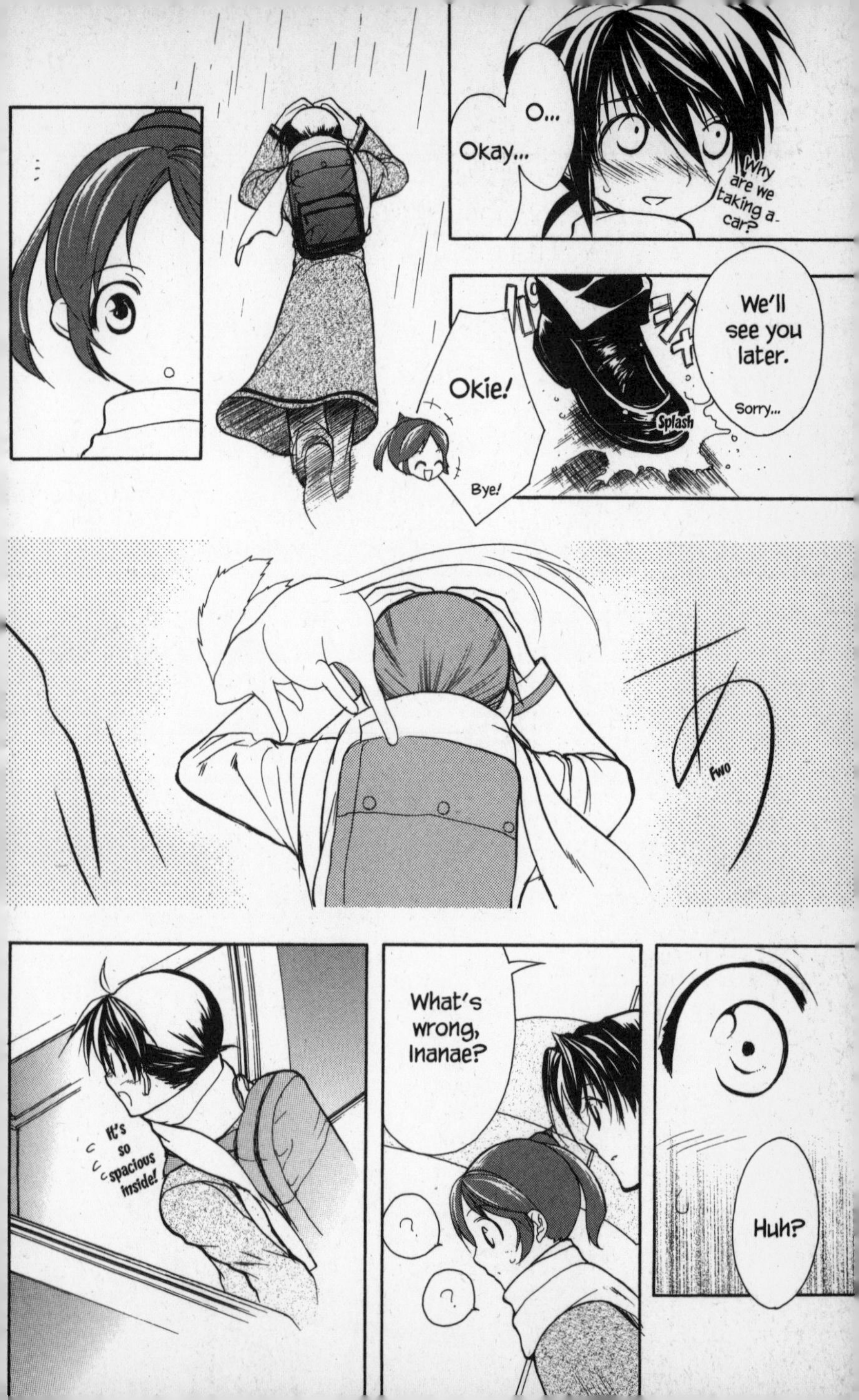

O...
Okay...
Why are we taking a car?
We'll see you later.
Sorry...
Splash
Okie!
Bye!
Fwo
Huh?
What's wrong, Inanae?
?
?
It's so spacious inside!

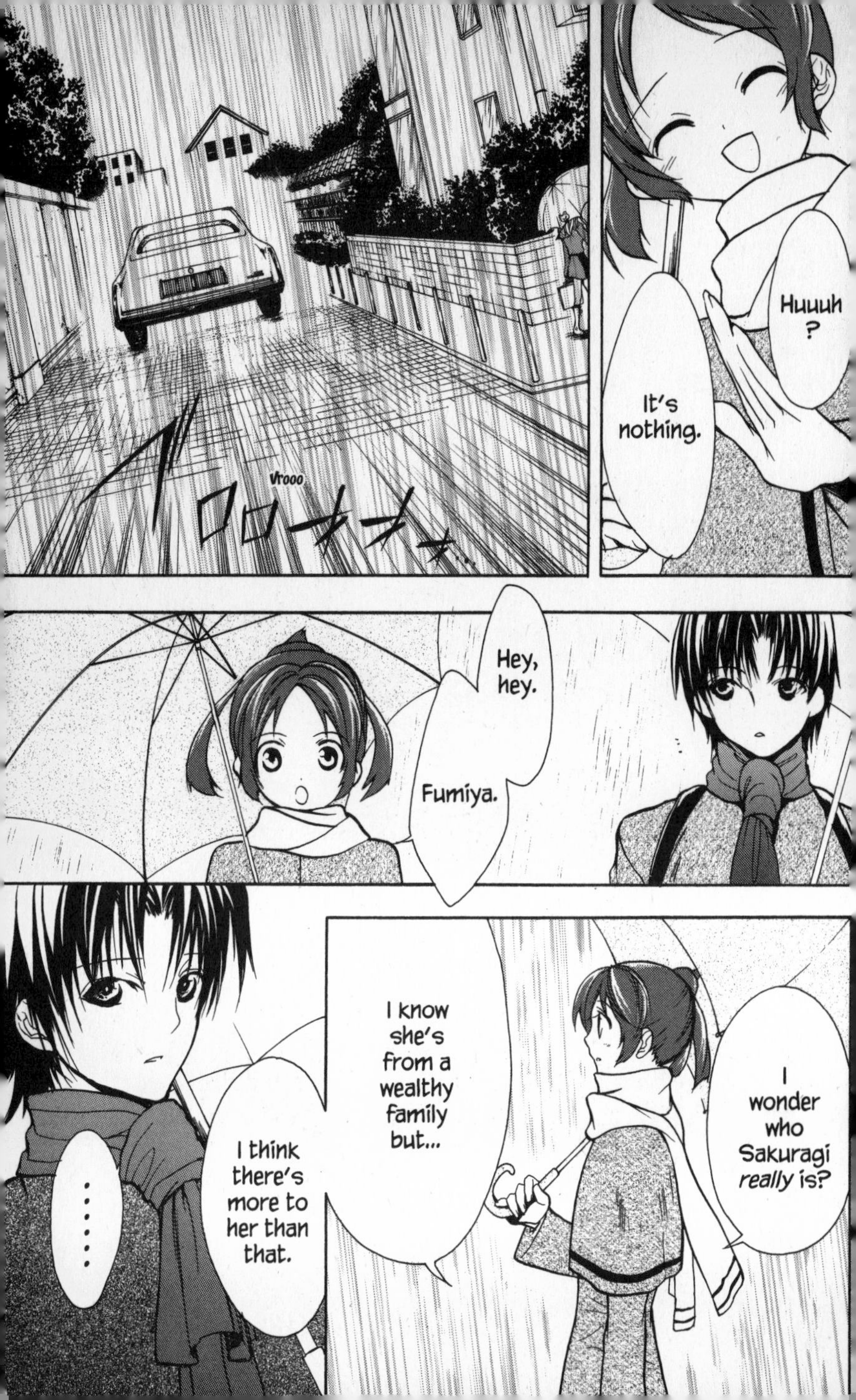
Huuuh?
It's nothing.
Vrooo
Hey, hey.
Fumiya.
I wonder who Sakuragi *really* is?
I know she's from a wealthy family but...
I think there's more to her than that.
......

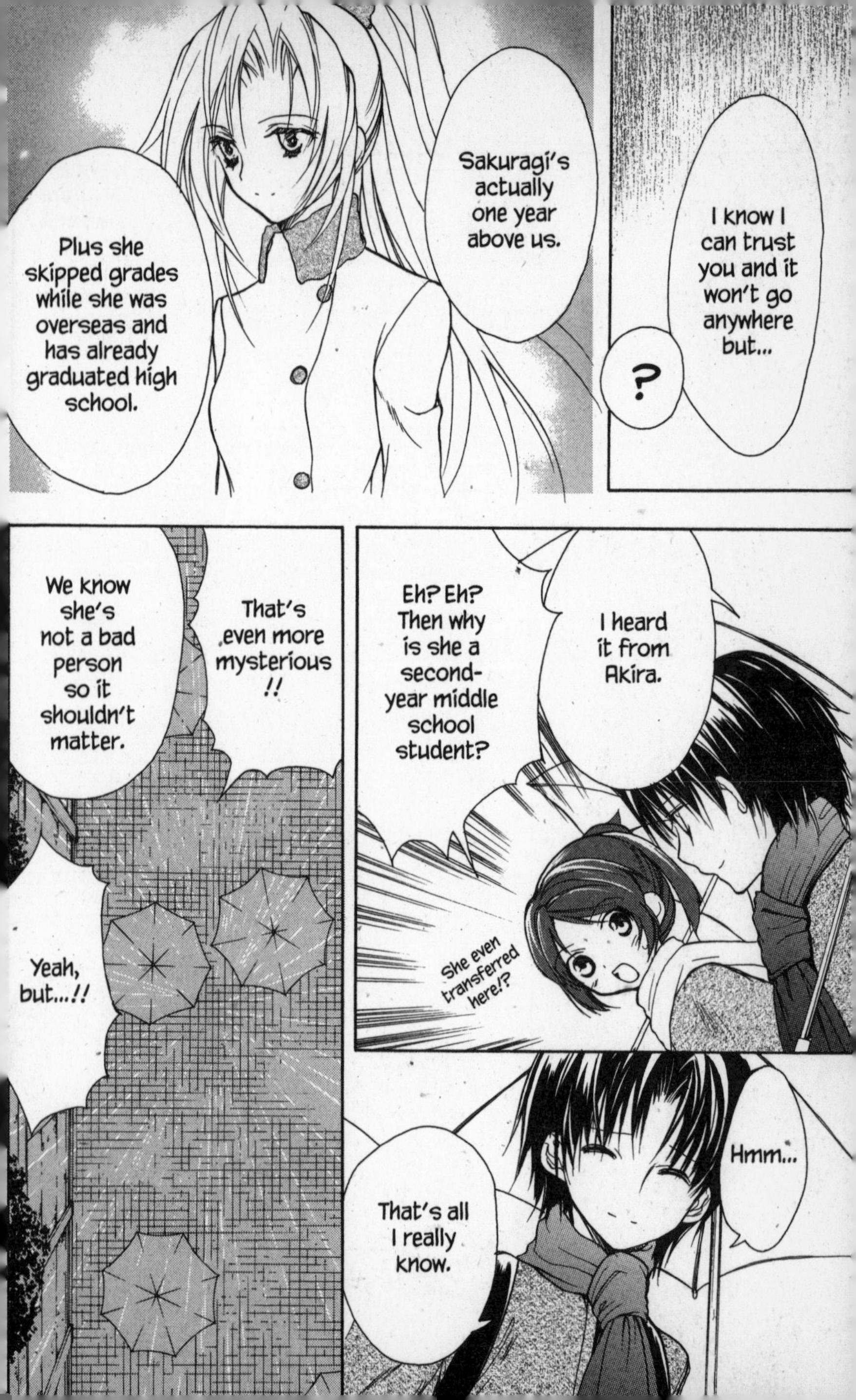
I know I can trust you and it won't go anywhere but...
?
Sakuragi's actually one year above us.
Plus she skipped grades while she was overseas and has already graduated high school.
I heard it from Akira.
Eh? Eh? Then why is she a second-year middle school student?
She even transferred here!?
Hmm...
That's all I really know.
That's even more mysterious!!
We know she's not a bad person so it shouldn't matter.
Yeah, but...!!

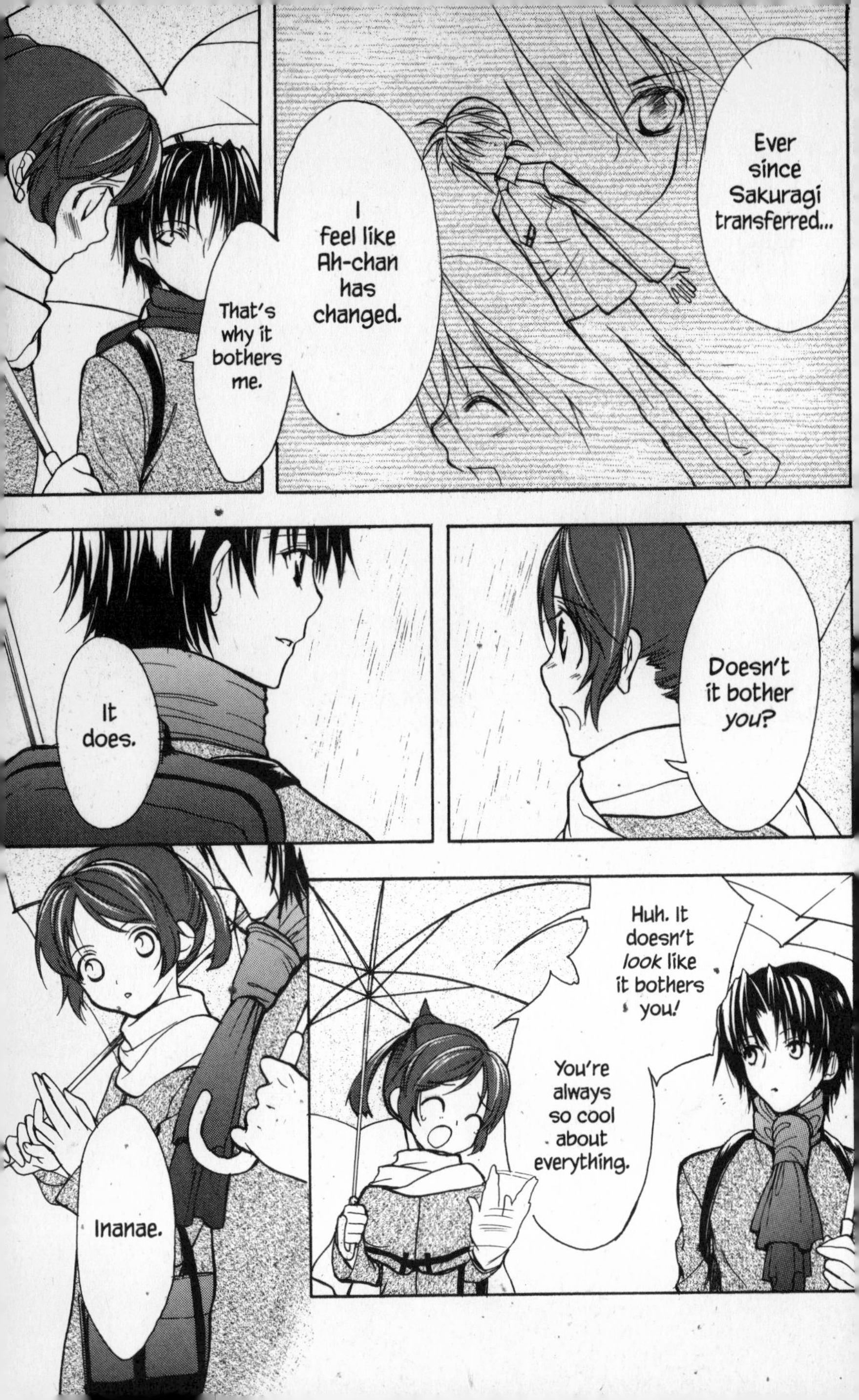
Ever since Sakuragi transferred...
I feel like Ah-chan has changed.
That's why it bothers me.
Doesn't it bother *you*?
It does.
Huh. It doesn't *look* like it bothers you!
You're always so cool about everything.
Inanae.

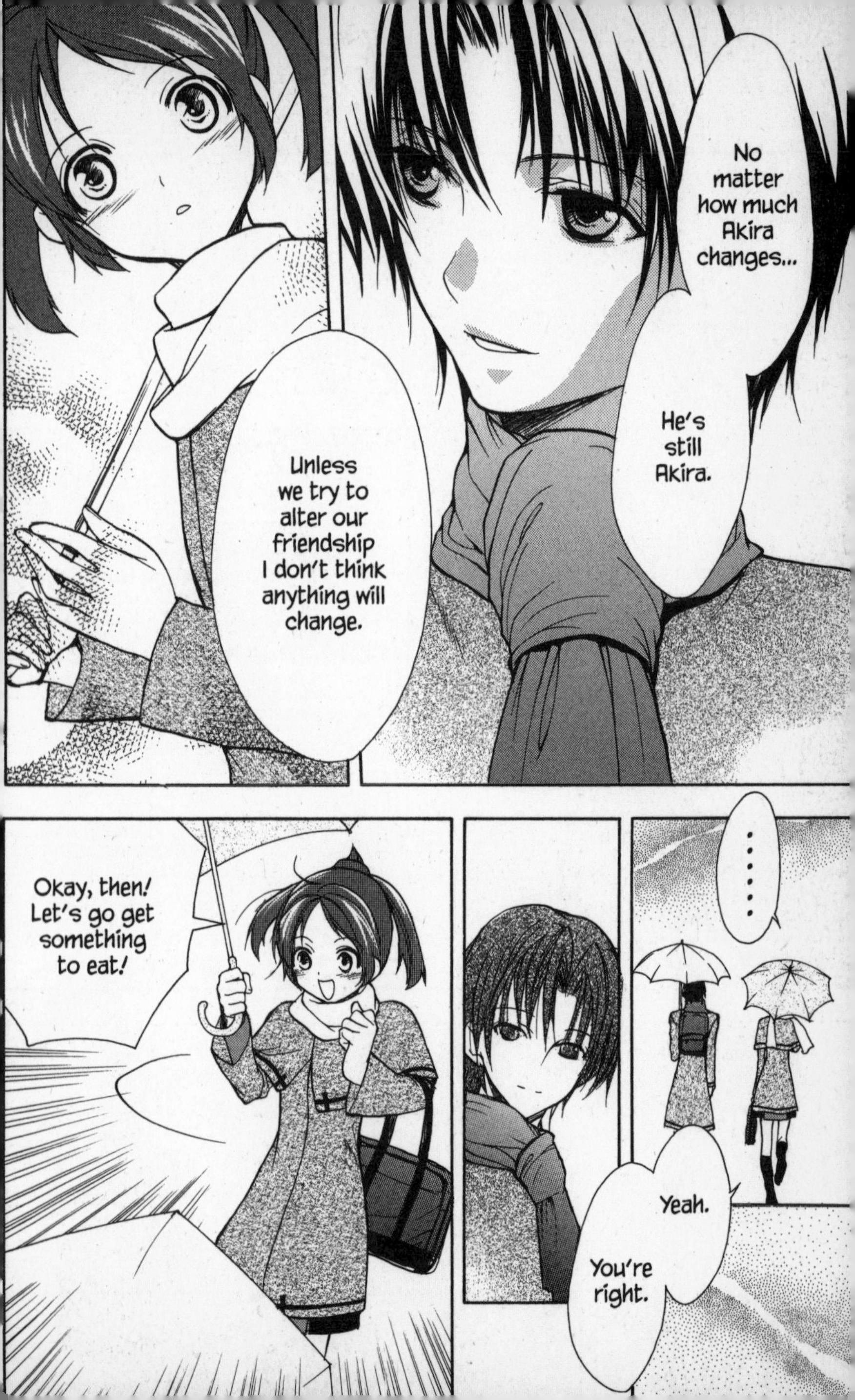
No matter how much Akira changes...
He's still Akira.
Unless we try to alter our friendship I don't think anything will change.
......
Yeah.
You're right.
Okay, then! Let's go get something to eat!

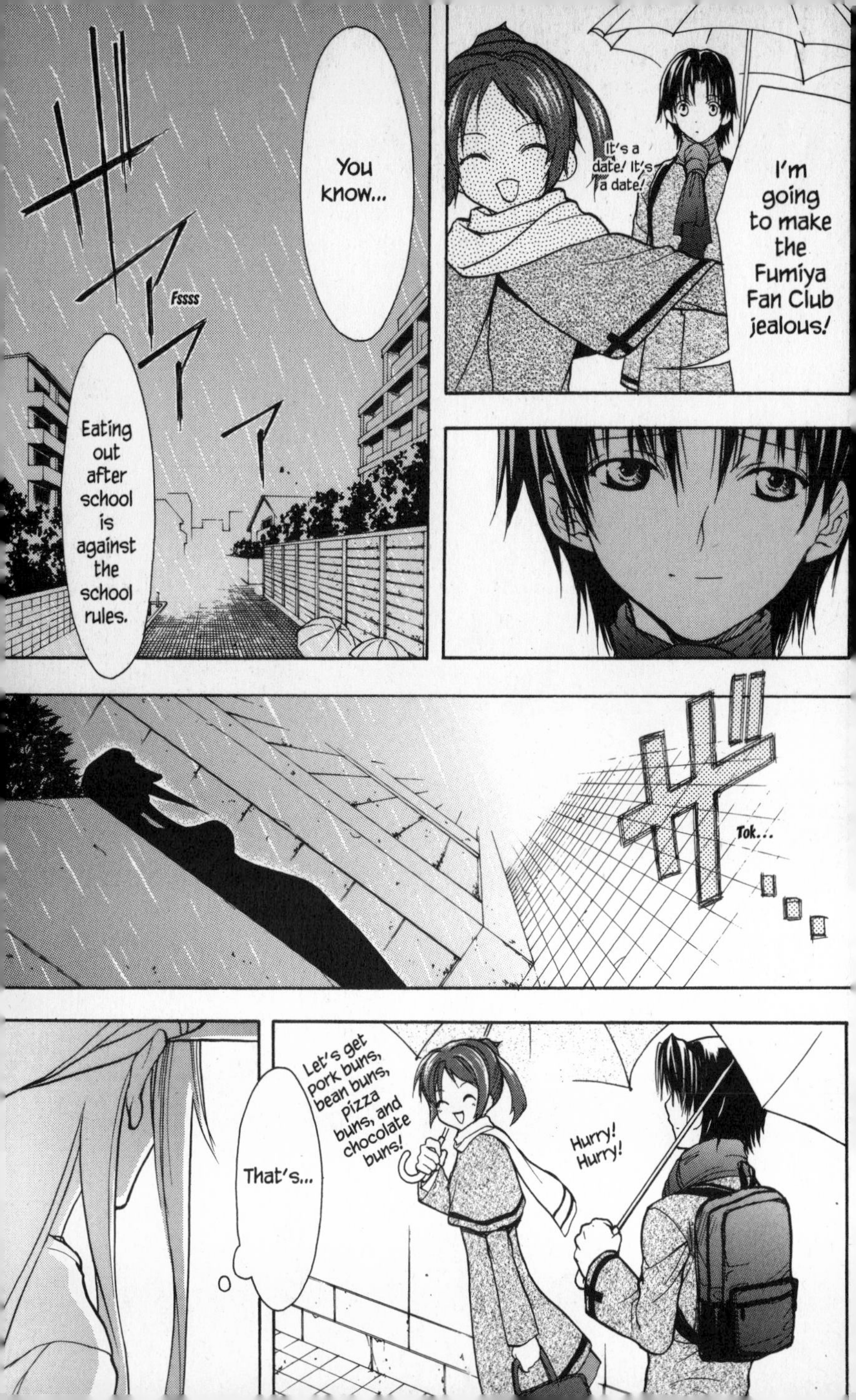
I'm going to make the Fumiya Fan Club jealous!
It's a date! It's a date!
You know...
Fssss
Eating out after school is against the school rules.
Tok...
Hurry! Hurry!
Let's get pork buns, bean buns, pizza buns, and chocolate buns!
That's...

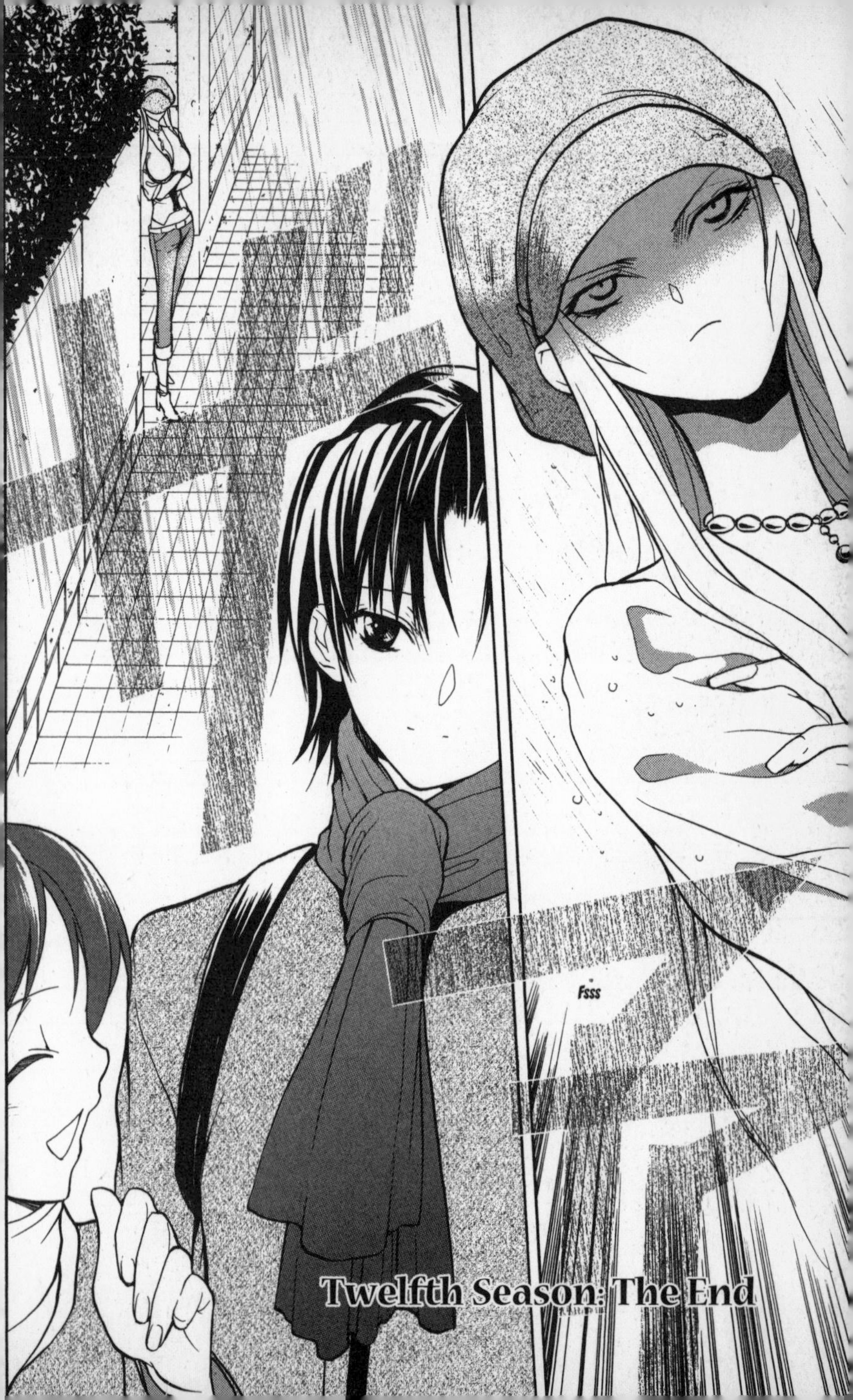
Fsss
Twelfth Season: The End

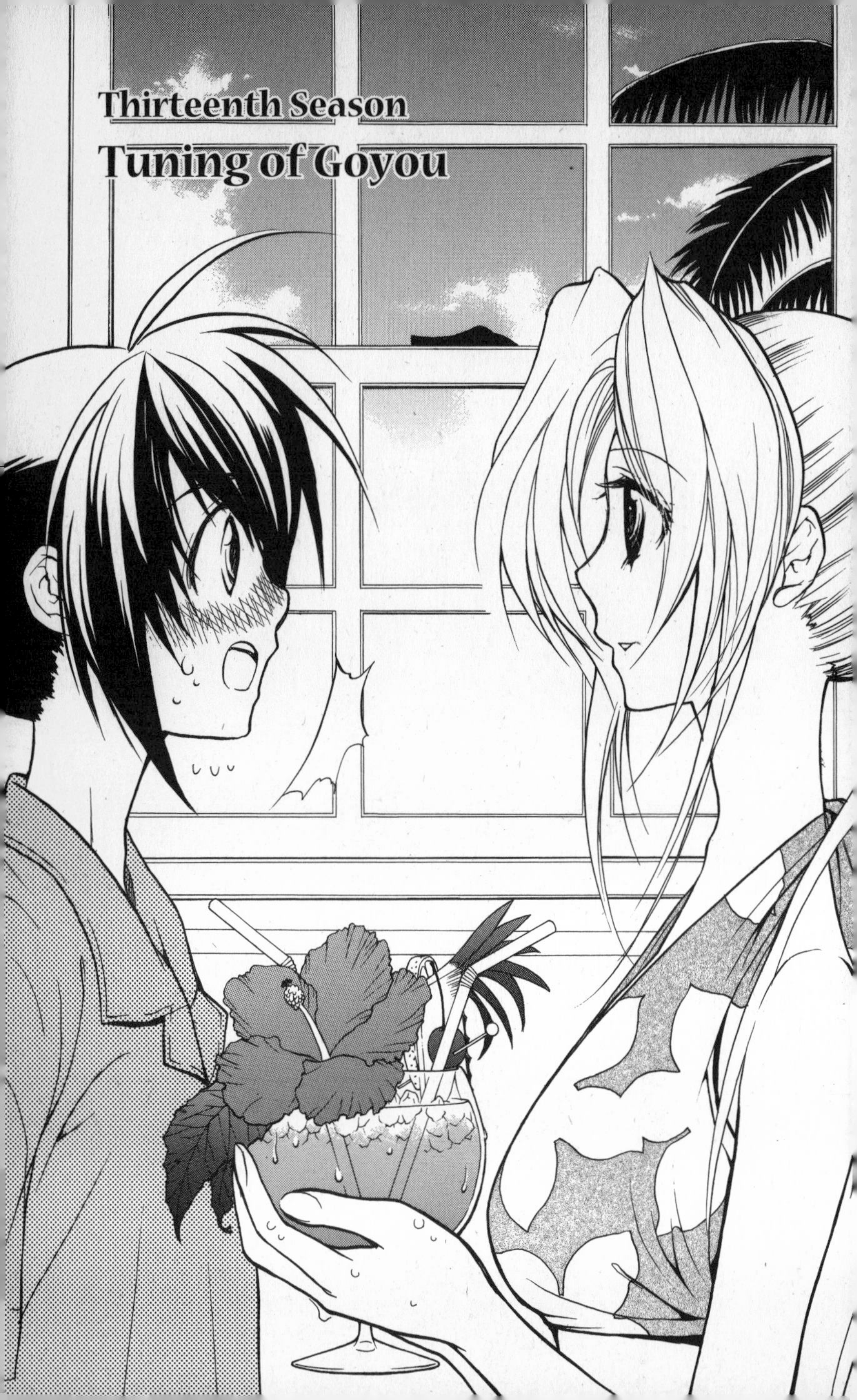
Thirteenth Season
Tuning of Goyou

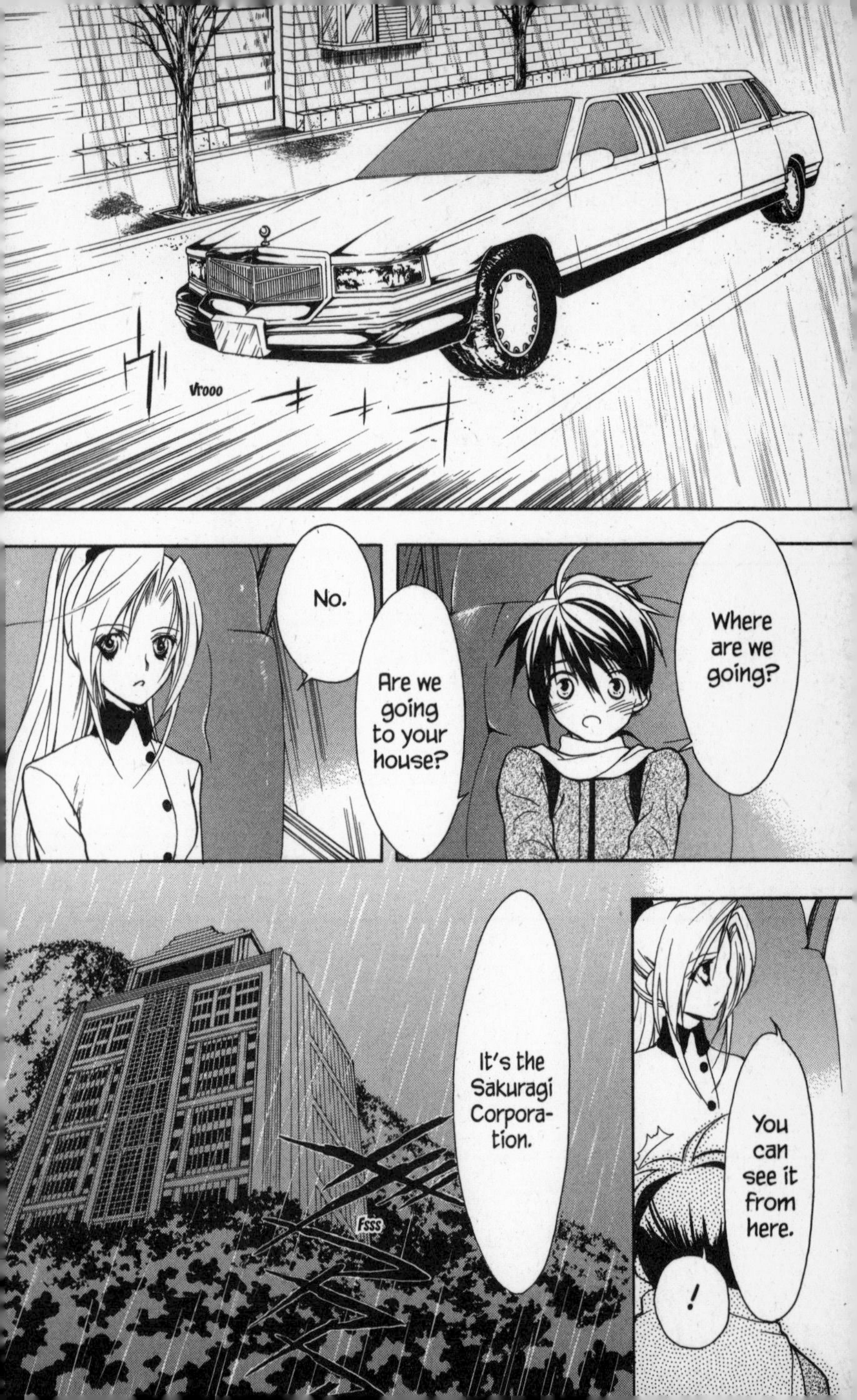
Vrooo
Where are we going?
Are we going to your house?
No.
You can see it from here.
!
It's the Sakuragi Corporation.
Fsss

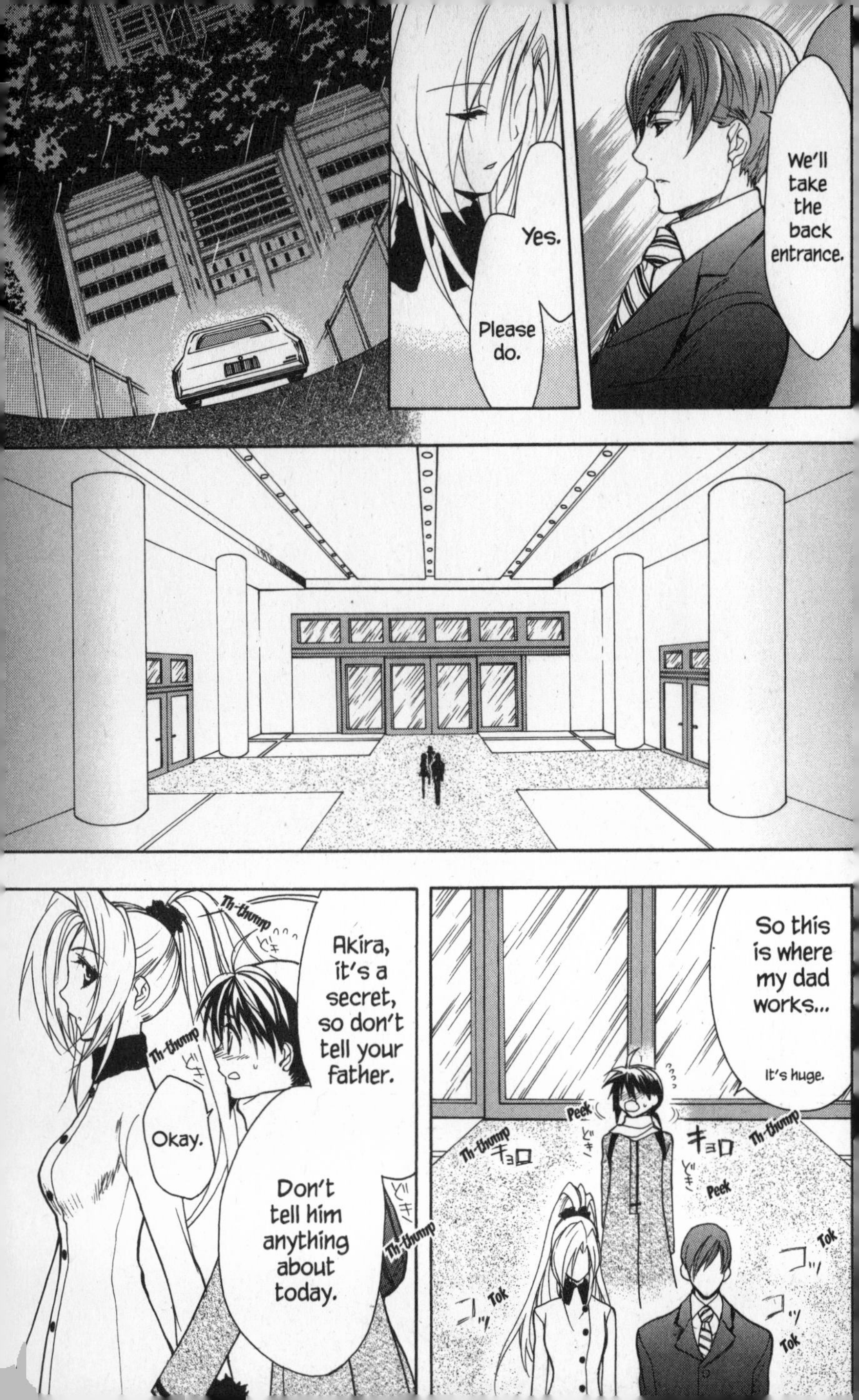
We'll take the back entrance.
Yes.
Please do.
So this is where my dad works...
It's huge.
Peek
どきっ
Th-thump
キョロ
Th-thump
キョロ
どきっ
Peek
Tok
ゴッ
Tok
ゴッ
Tok
ゴッ
Akira, it's a secret, so don't tell your father.
Th-thump
どきっ
Th-thump
どきっ
Okay.
Don't tell him anything about today.
どきっ
Th-thump

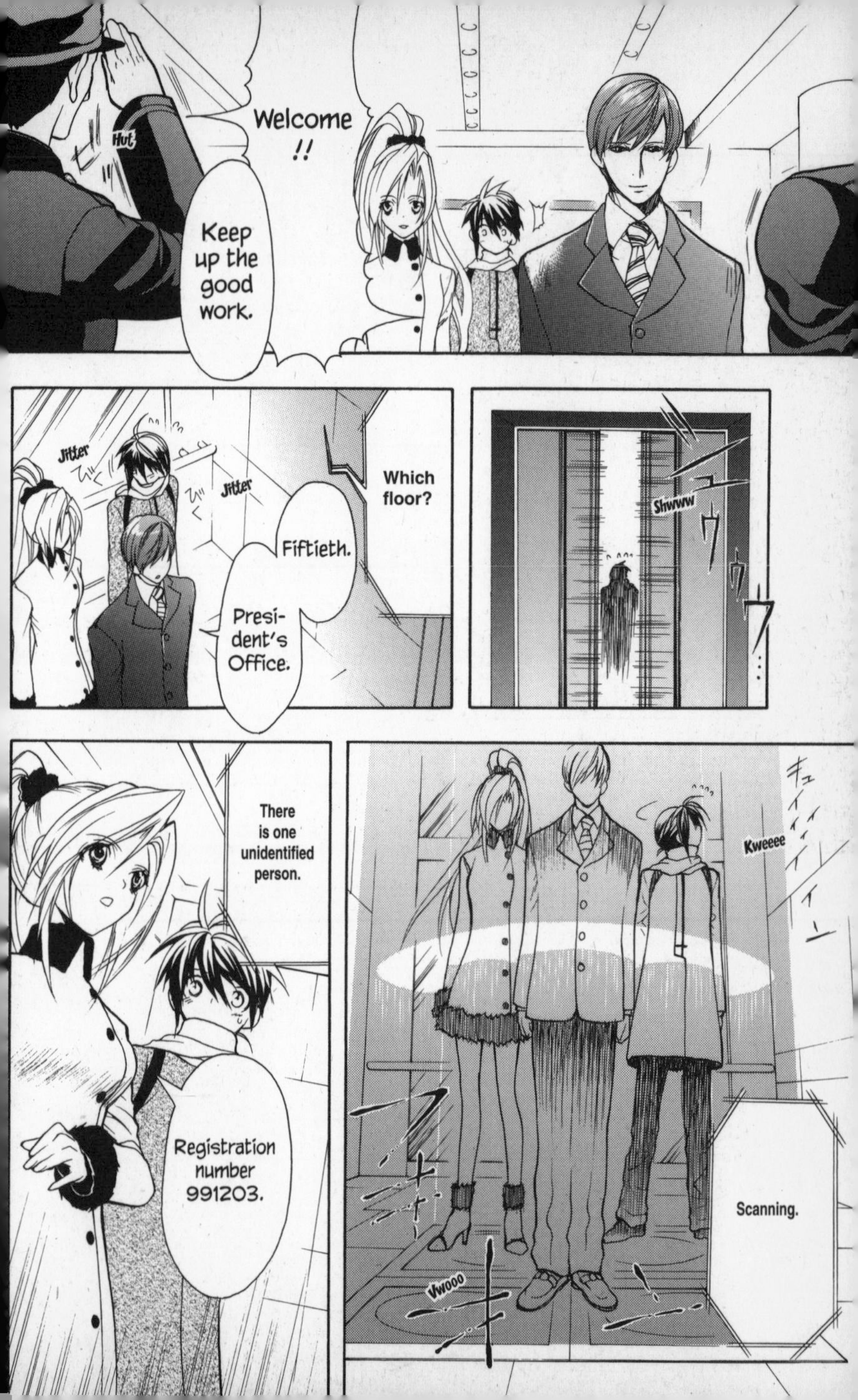
Welcome !!
Hut
Keep up the good work.
Shwww
Which floor?
Fiftieth.
Jitter
Jitter
President's Office.
Kweeee
Scanning.
Vwooo
There is one unidentified person.
Registration number 991203.

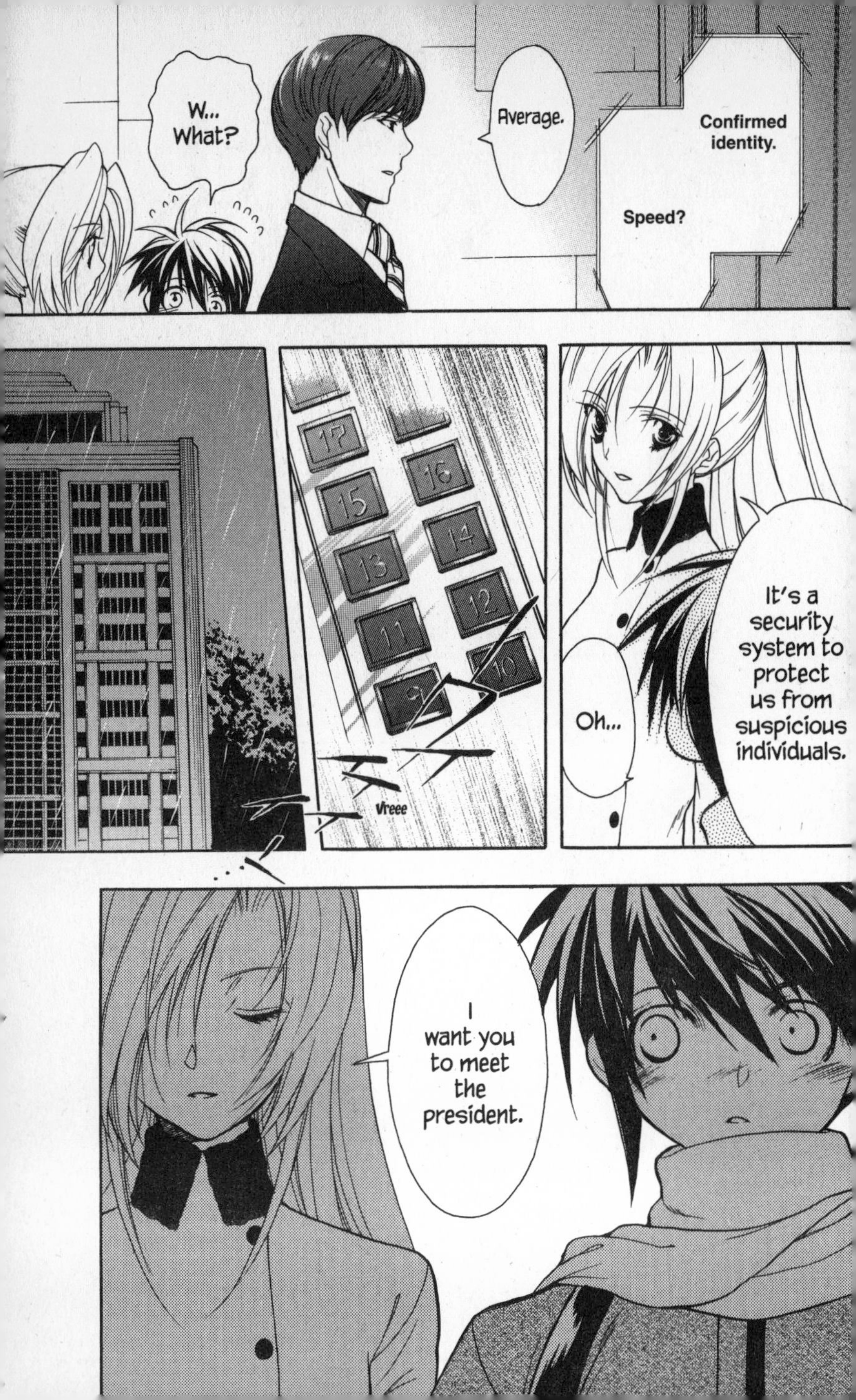
Confirmed identity.
Speed?
Average.
W... What?
It's a security system to protect us from suspicious individuals.
Oh...
Vreee
. . .
I want you to meet the president.

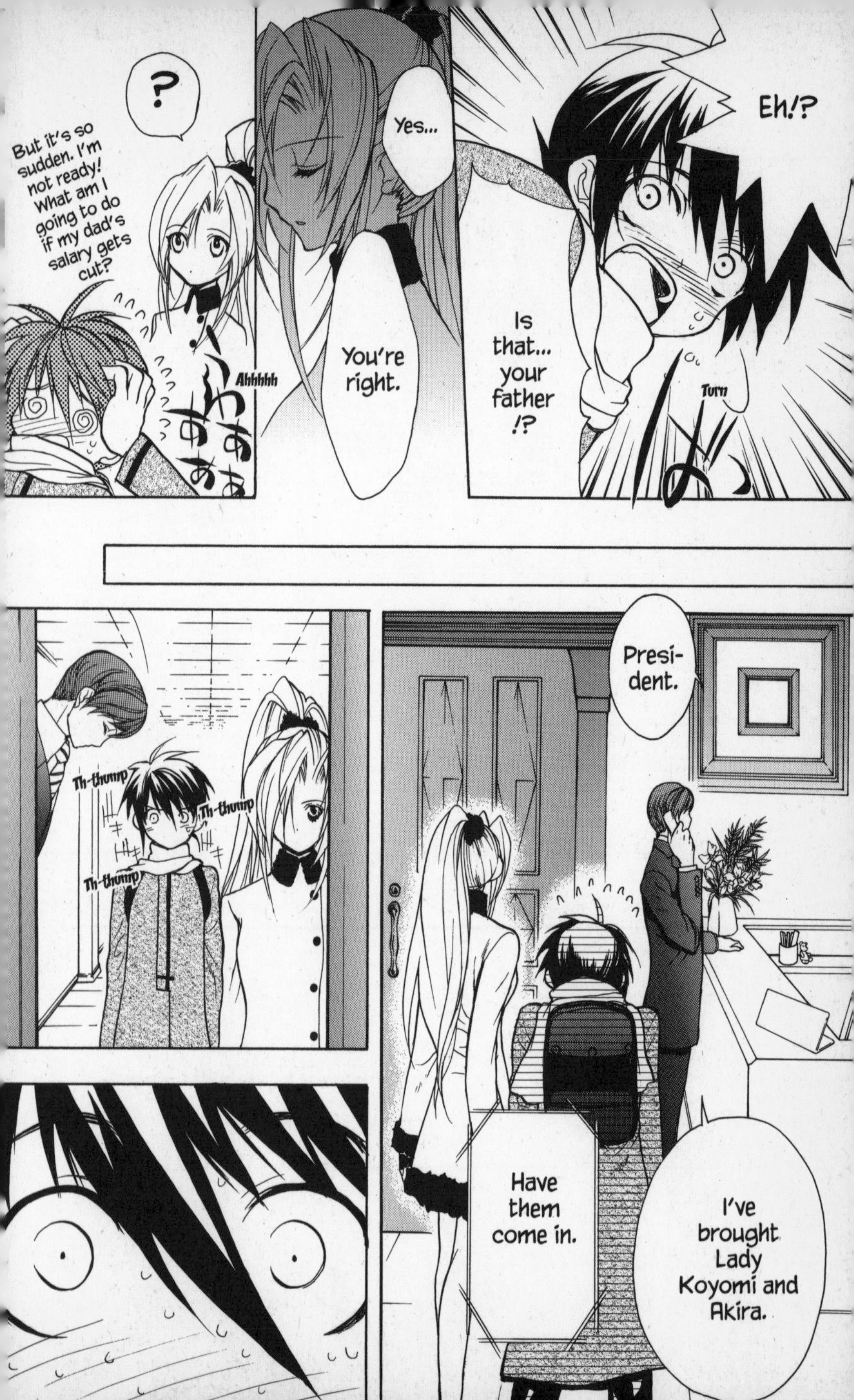
Eh!?
Is that... your father !?
Turn
Yes...
You're right.
?
But it's so sudden. I'm not ready! What am I going to do if my dad's salary gets cut?
Ahhhhh
わあああ
Presi-dent.
I've brought Lady Koyomi and Akira.
Have them come in.
Th-thump
Th-thump
Th-thump

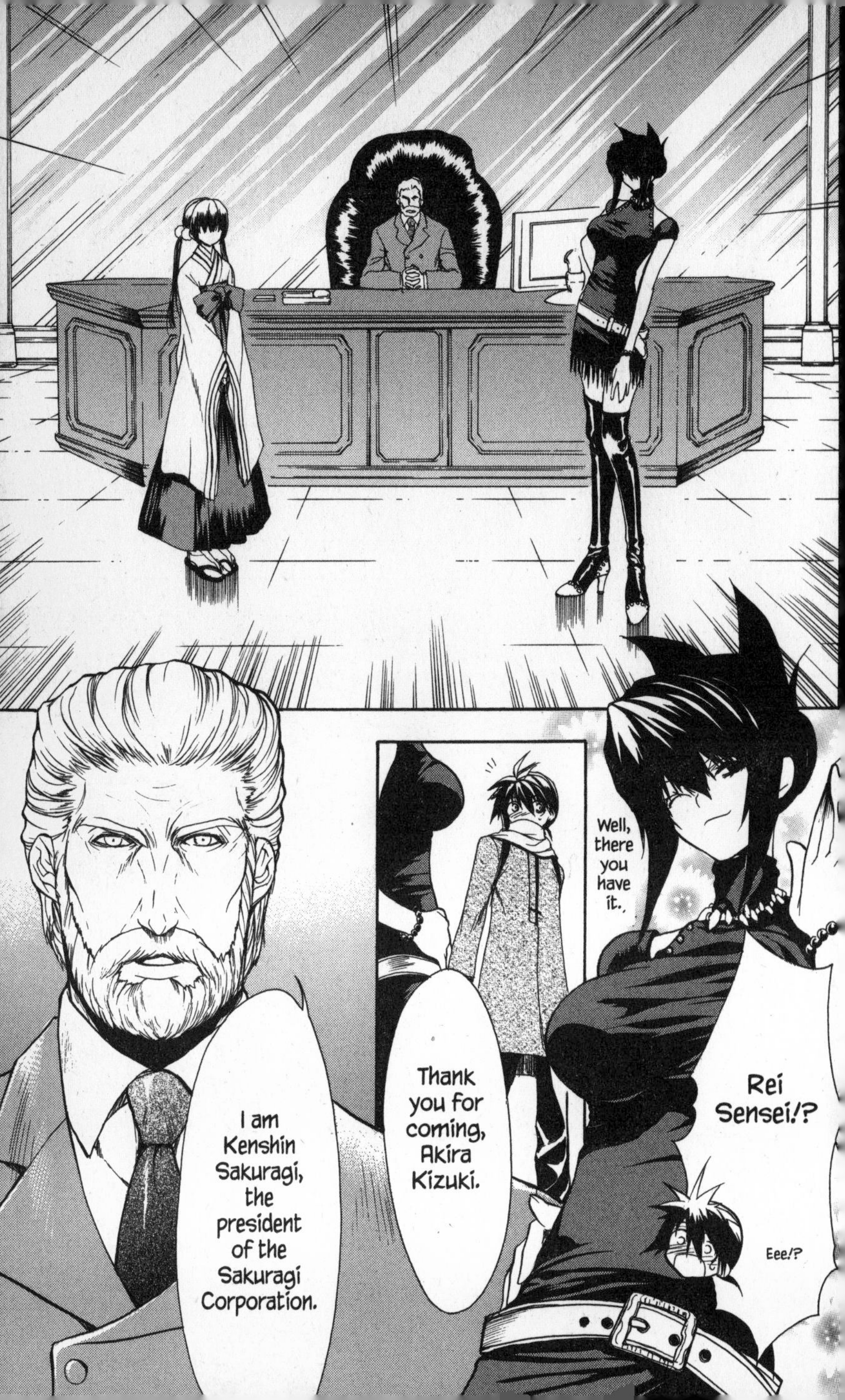
Well, there you have it.
Rei Sensei!?
Eee!?
Thank you for coming, Akira Kizuki.
I am Kenshin Sakuragi, the president of the Sakuragi Corporation.

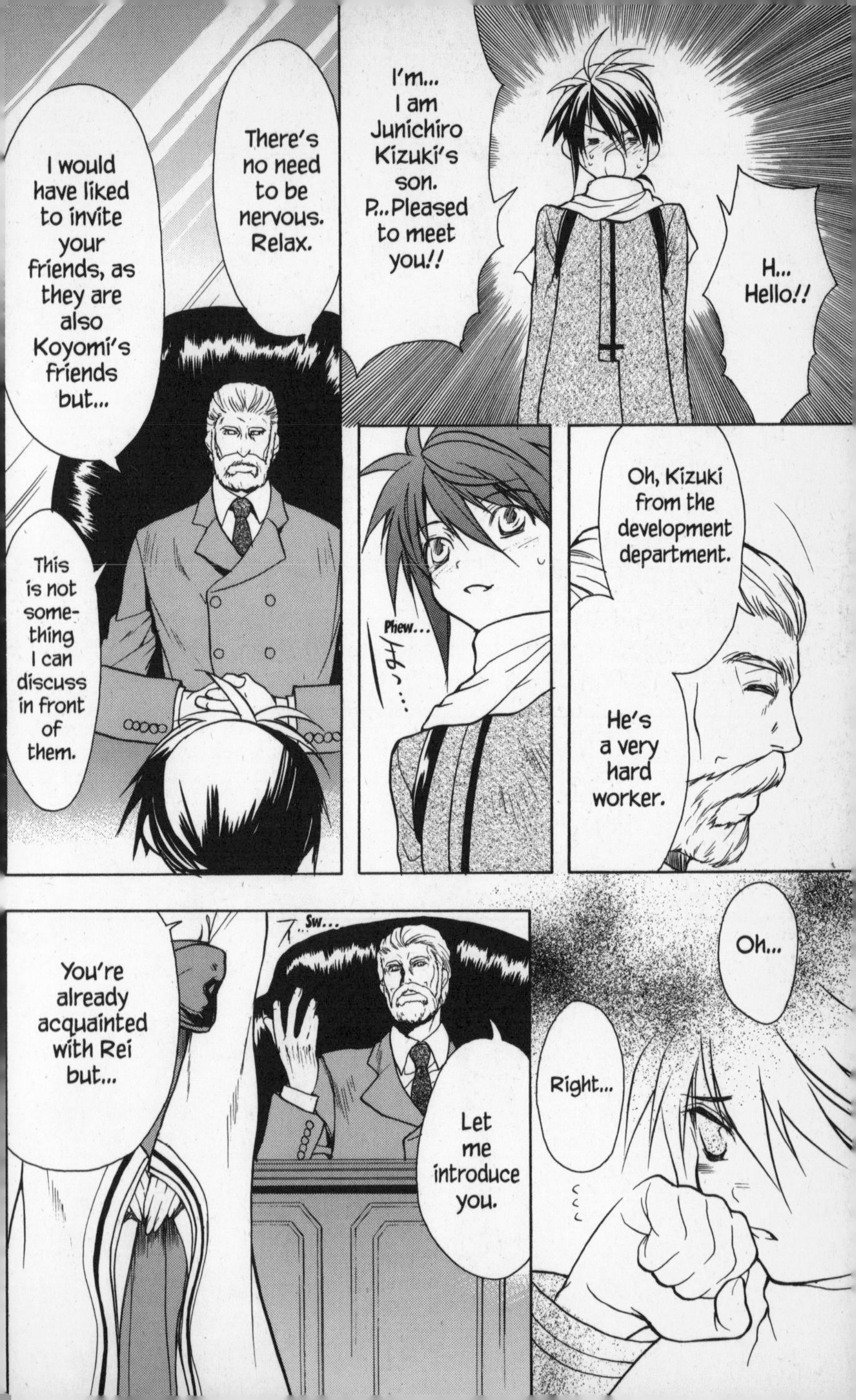
H... Hello!!
I'm... I am Junichiro Kizuki's son. P...Pleased to meet you!!
Oh, Kizuki from the development department.
He's a very hard worker.
Phew...
There's no need to be nervous. Relax.
I would have liked to invite your friends, as they are also Koyomi's friends but...
This is not something I can discuss in front of them.
Oh...
Right...
Sw...
You're already acquainted with Rei but...
Let me introduce you.

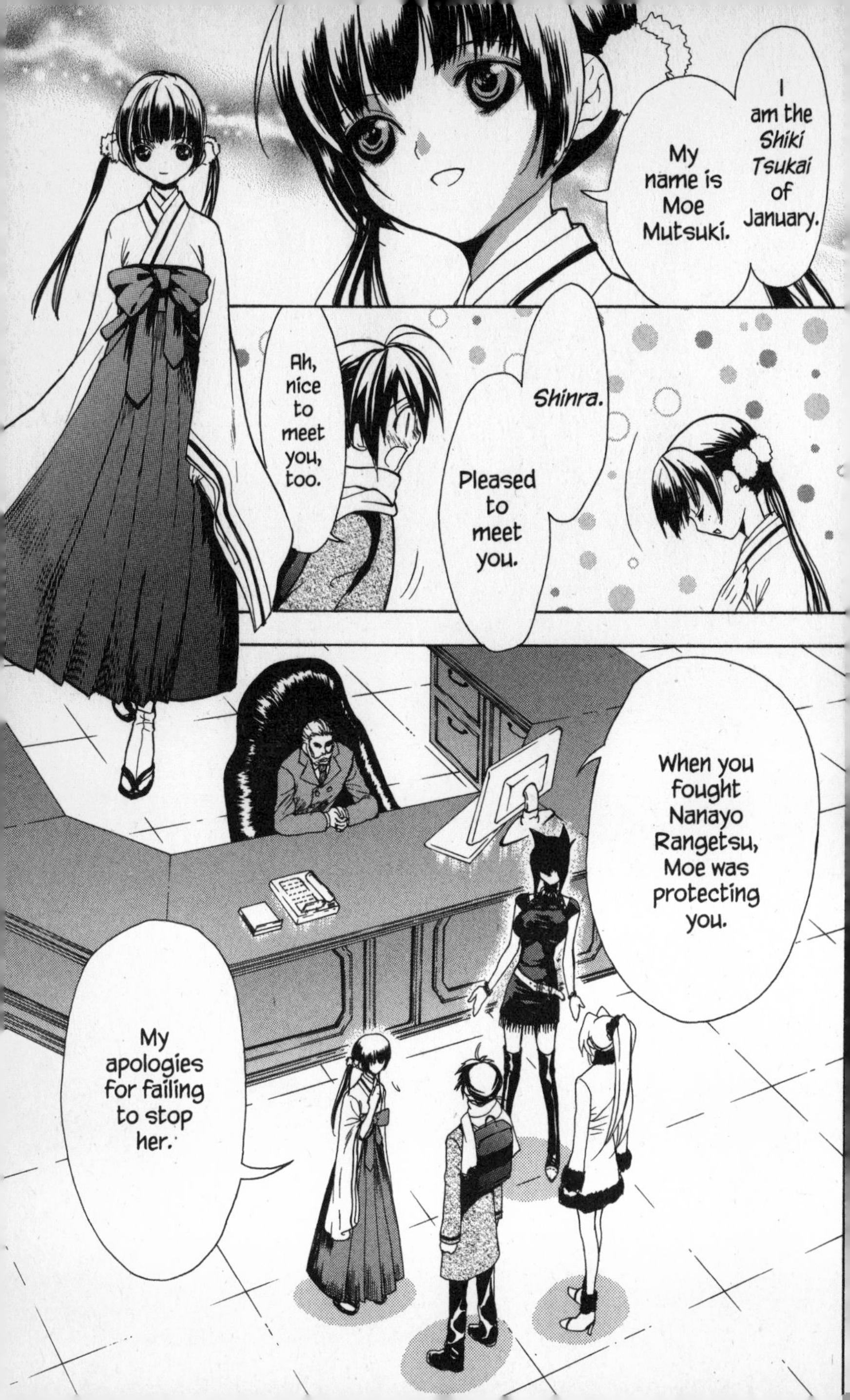
I am the Shiki Tsukai of January.
My name is Moe Mutsuki.
Shinra.
Pleased to meet you.
Ah, nice to meet you, too.
When you fought Nanayo Rangetsu, Moe was protecting you.
My apologies for failing to stop her.

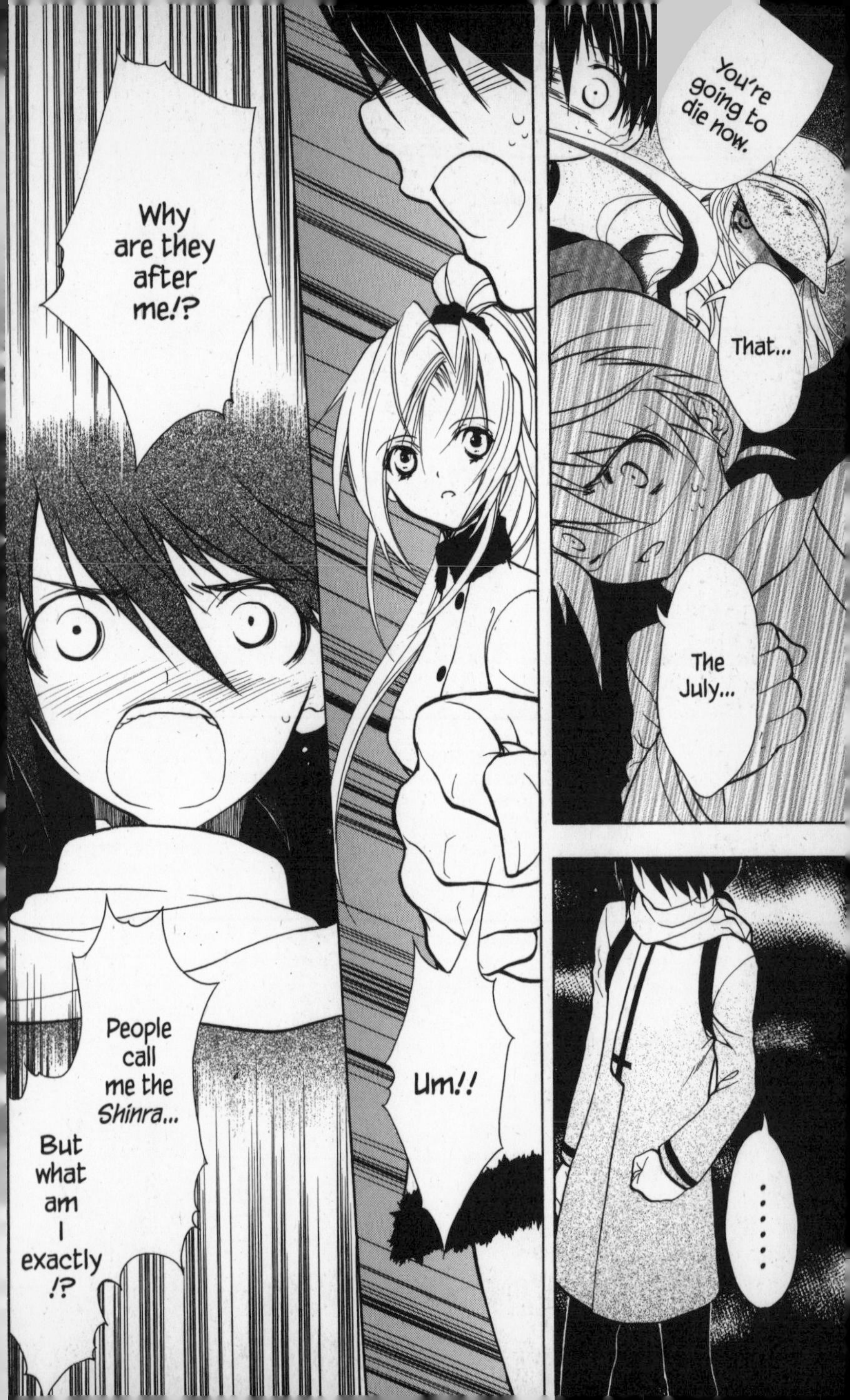
You're going to die now.
That...
The July...
......
Um!!
Why are they after me!?
People call me the *Shinra*...
But what am I exactly !?

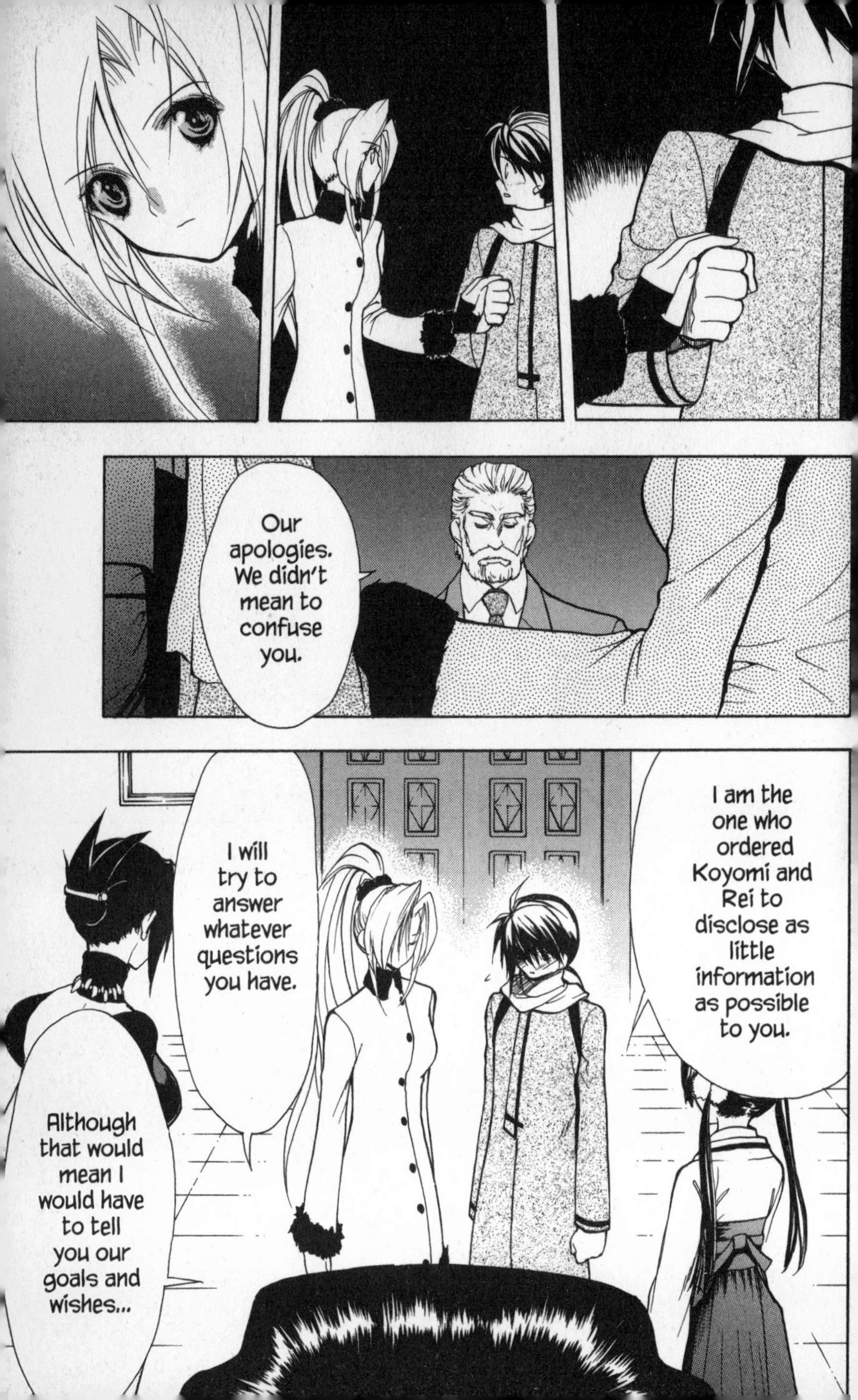
Our apologies. We didn't mean to confuse you.
I am the one who ordered Koyomi and Rei to disclose as little information as possible to you.
I will try to answer whatever questions you have.
Although that would mean I would have to tell you our goals and wishes...

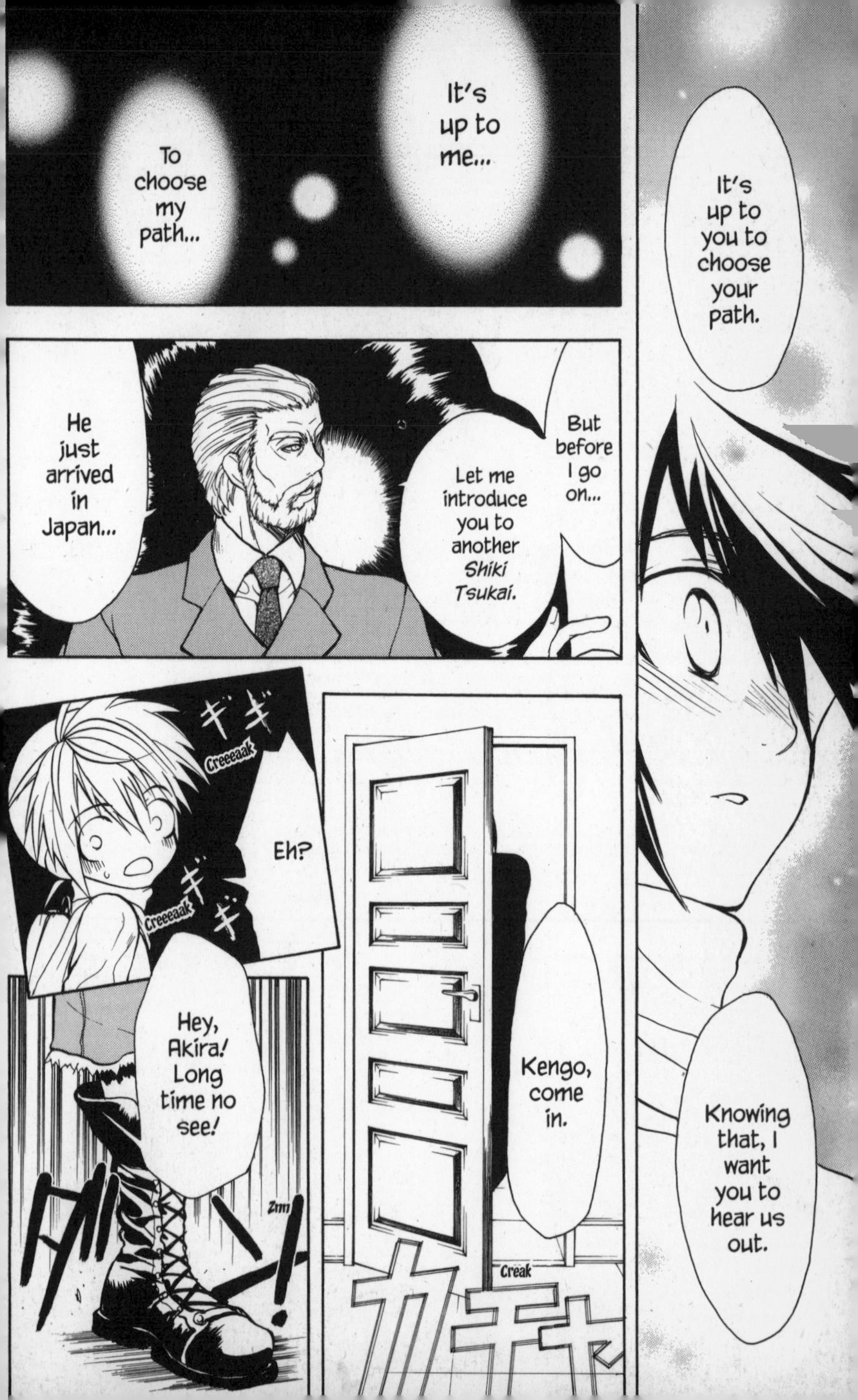

It's up to you to choose your path.
Knowing that, I want you to hear us out.
It's up to me...
To choose my path...
But before I go on...
Let me introduce you to another *Shiki Tsukai.*
He just arrived in Japan...
Kengo, come in.
カチャ
Creak
ギギ
Creeeaak
Eh?
ギギ
Creeeaak
Hey, Akira! Long time no see!
Zmm

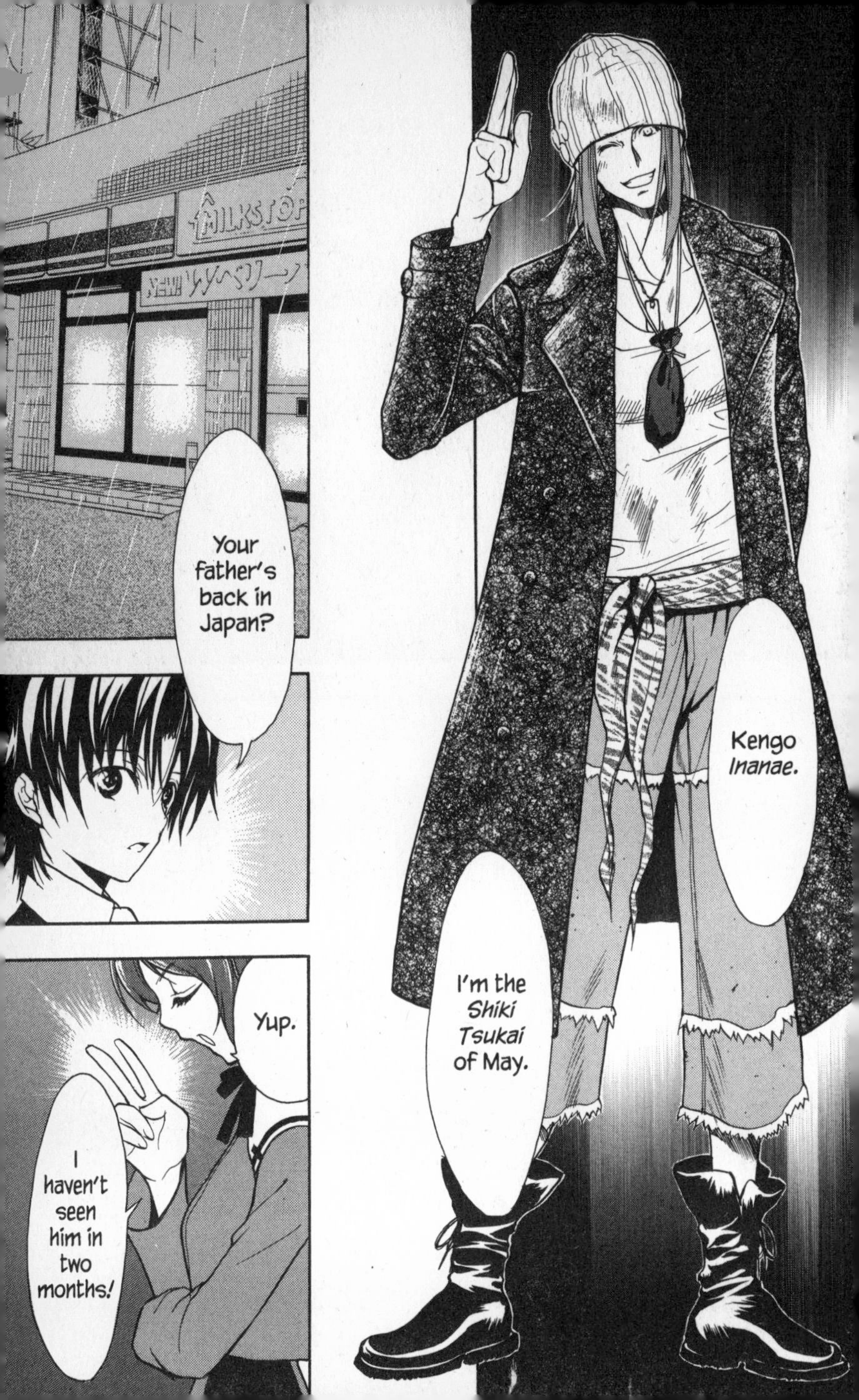
Kengo Inanae.
I'm the Shiki Tsukai of May.
Your father's back in Japan?
Yup.
I haven't seen him in two months!

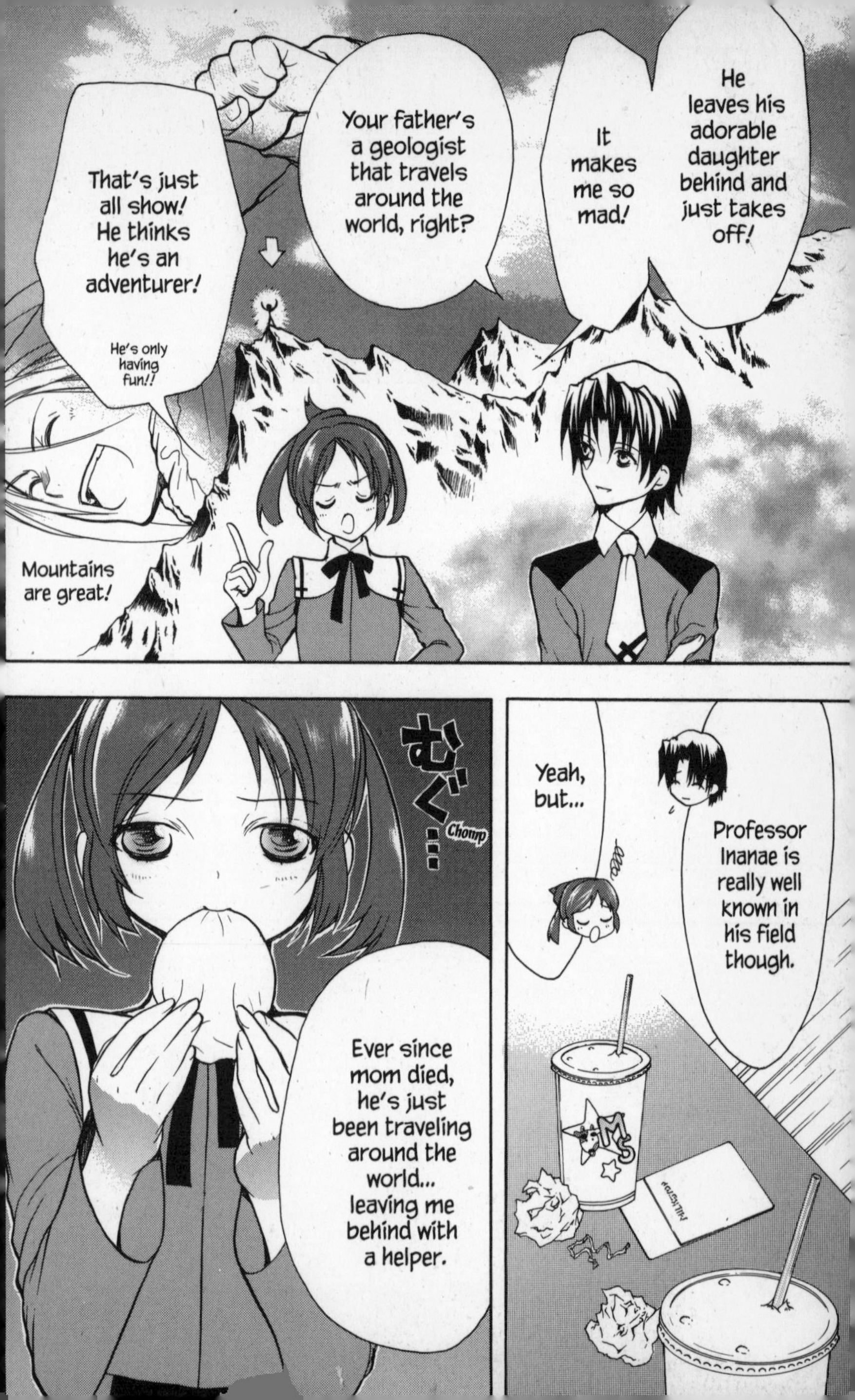

He leaves his adorable daughter behind and just takes off!
It makes me so mad!
Your father's a geologist that travels around the world, right?
That's just all show! He thinks he's an adventurer!
He's only having fun!!
Mountains are great!
Professor Inanae is really well known in his field though.
Yeah, but...
むぐ…
Chomp
Ever since mom died, he's just been traveling around the world... leaving me behind with a helper.

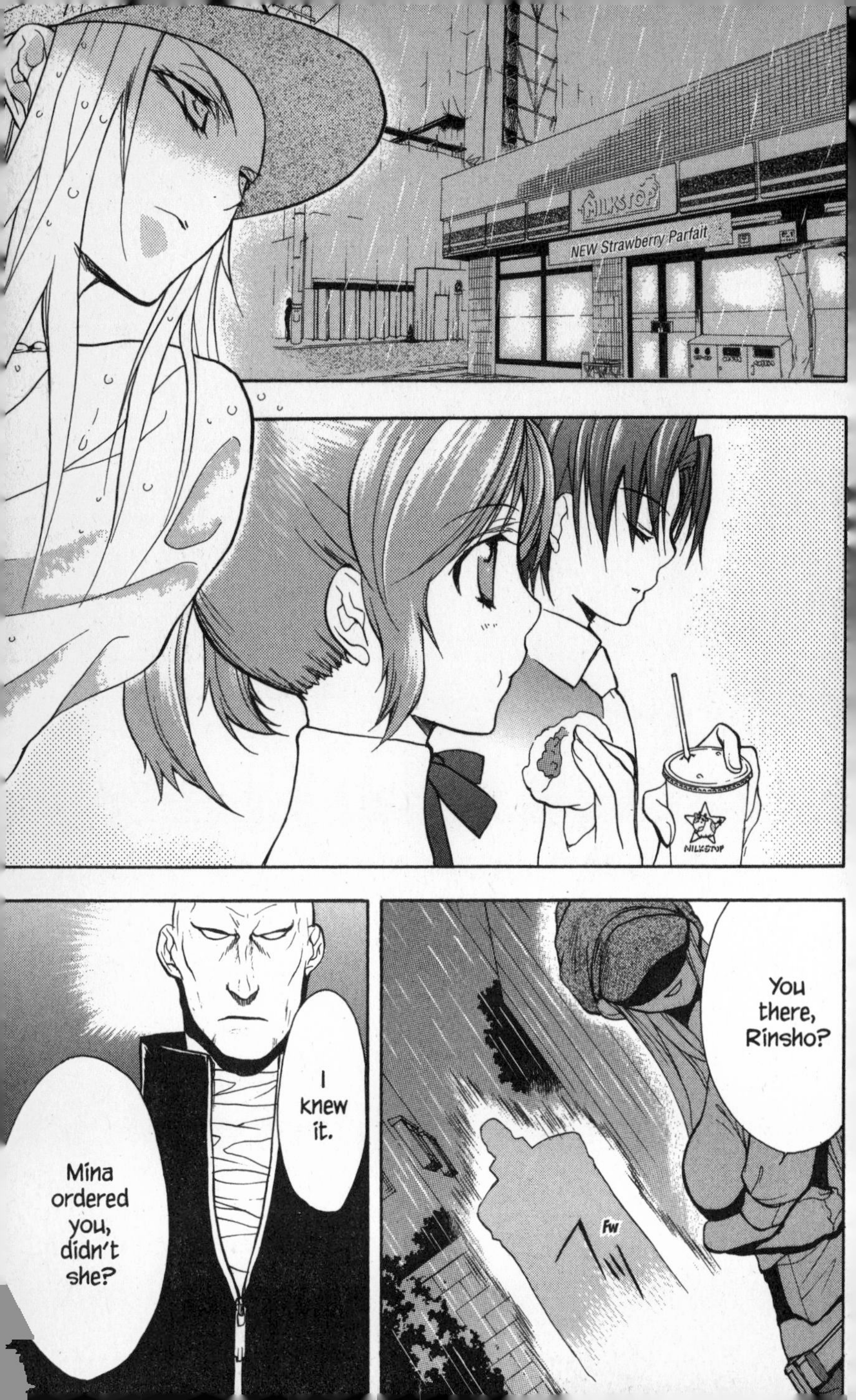
MILKSTOP
NEW Strawberry Parfait
MILKSTOP
You there, Rinsho?
Fw
I knew it.
Mina ordered you, didn't she?

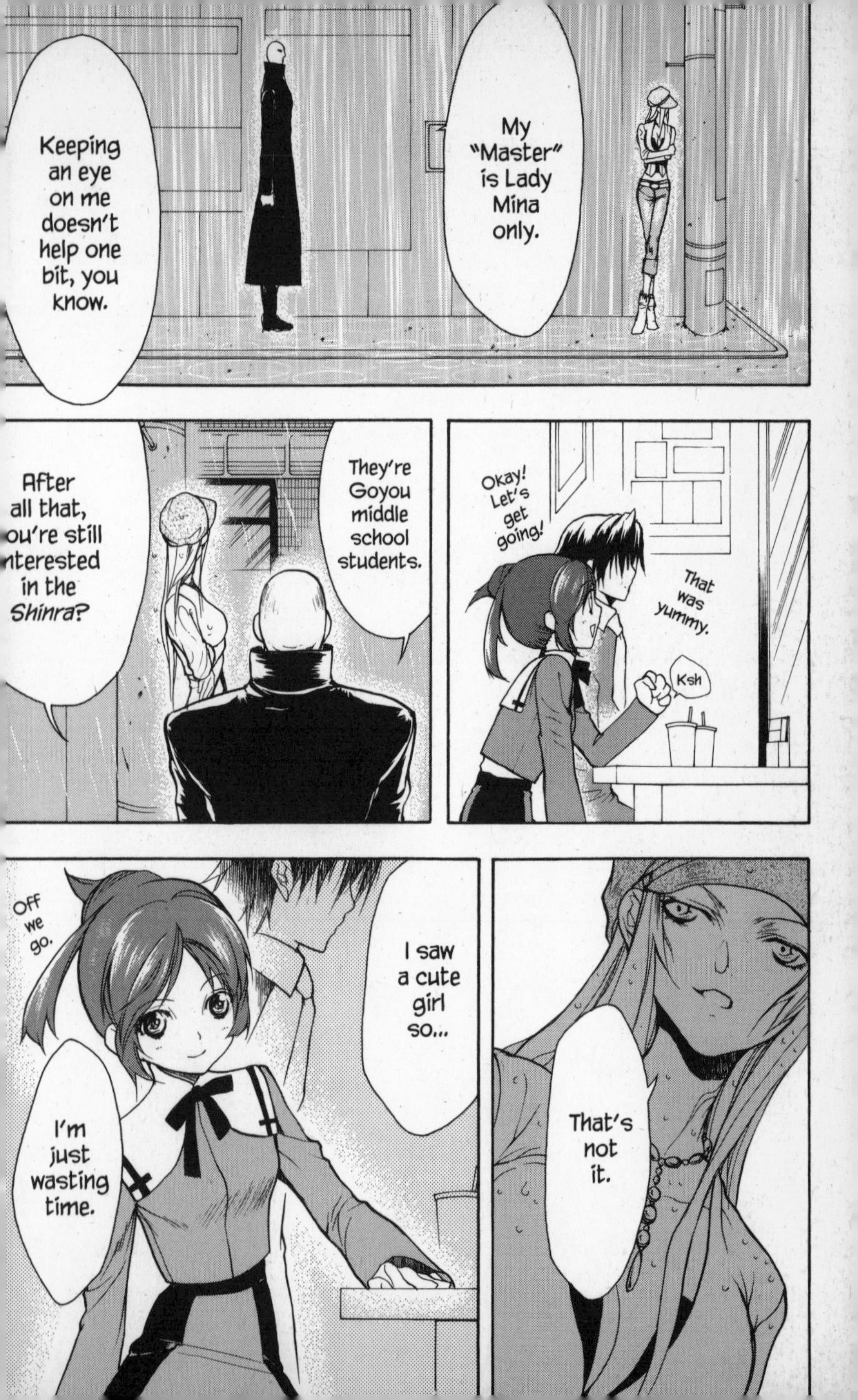

My "Master" is Lady Mina only.
Keeping an eye on me doesn't help one bit, you know.
Okay! Let's get going!
That was yummy.
Ksh
They're Goyou middle school students.
After all that, ou're still nterested in the Shinra?
That's not it.
I saw a cute girl so...
Off we go.
I'm just wasting time.

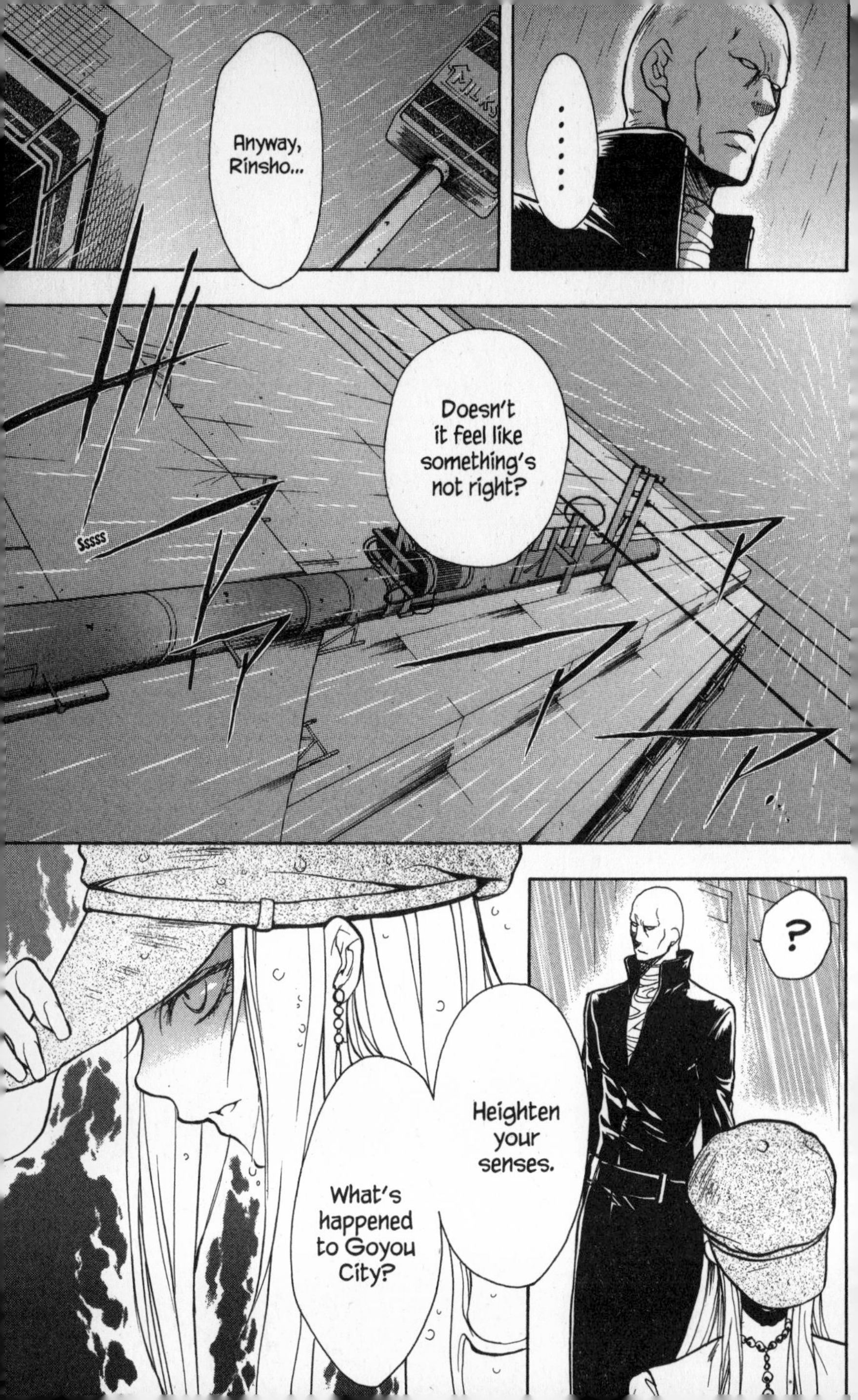
......
Anyway, Rinsho...
Doesn't it feel like something's not right?
Sssss
?
Heighten your senses.
What's happened to Goyou City?

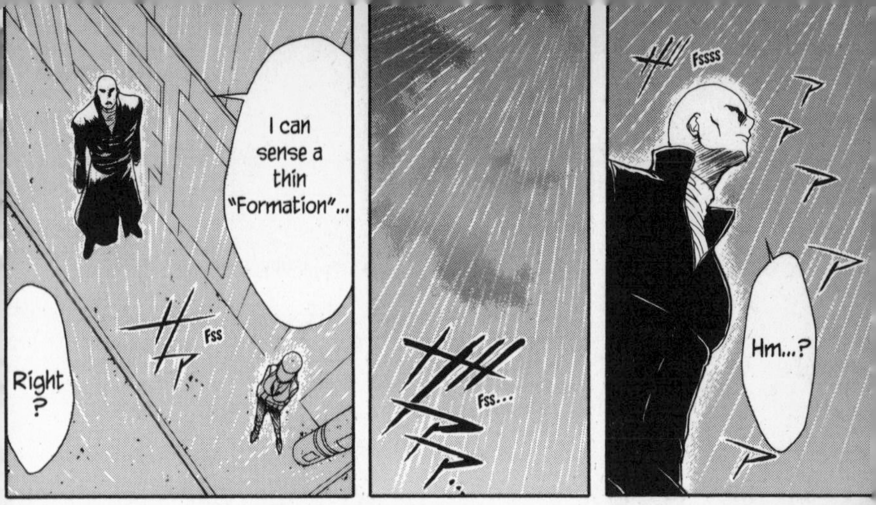
Fssss
Hm...?
Fss...
I can sense a thin "Formation"...
Fss
Right?

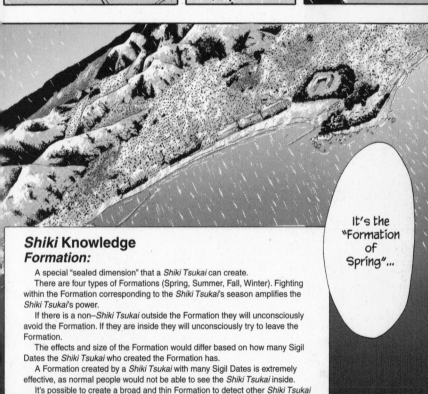

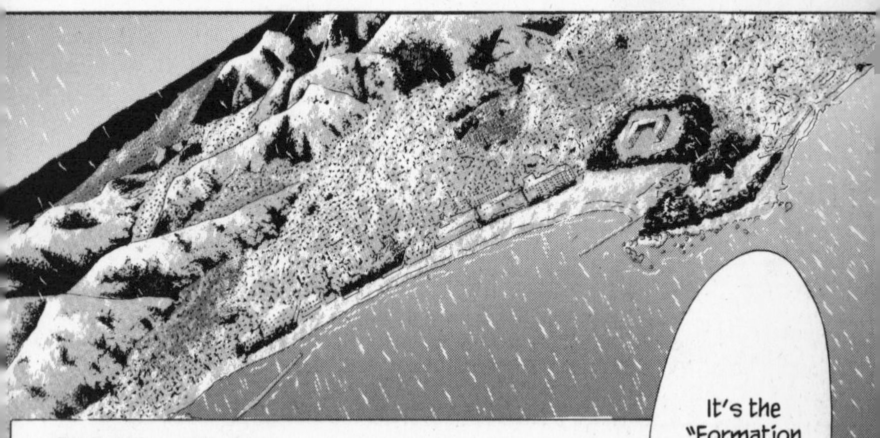
It's the "Formation of Spring"...

Shiki Knowledge
Formation:

A special "sealed dimension" that a *Shiki Tsukai* can create.

There are four types of Formations (Spring, Summer, Fall, Winter). Fighting within the Formation corresponding to the *Shiki Tsukai*'s season amplifies the *Shiki Tsukai*'s power.

If there is a non–*Shiki Tsukai* outside the Formation they will unconsciously avoid the Formation. If they are inside they will unconsciously try to leave the Formation.

The effects and size of the Formation would differ based on how many Sigil Dates the *Shiki Tsukai* who created the Formation has.

A Formation created by a *Shiki Tsukai* with many Sigil Dates is extremely effective, as normal people would not be able to see the *Shiki Tsukai* inside.

It's possible to create a broad and thin Formation to detect other *Shiki Tsukai* entering the sealed area without affecting the general public. If another *Shiki Tsukai* has more Sigil Dates than the *Shiki Tsukai* who originally created the Formation, it's possible to overwrite their Formation.

In general, a Formation is used to amplify a *Shiki Tsukai*'s power and to detect any suspicious movement. It's typically not used for battle.

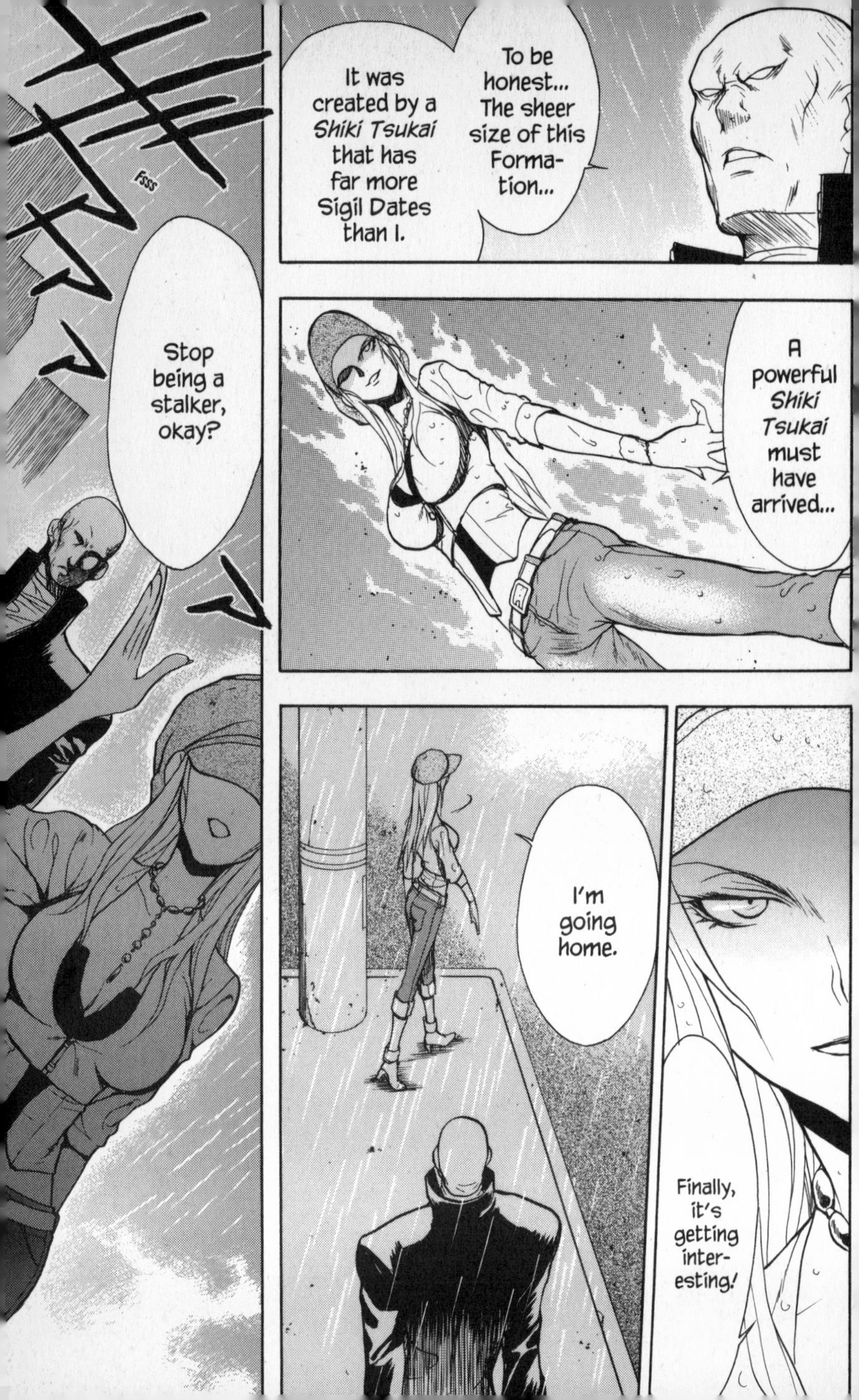
To be honest... The sheer size of this Forma-tion...
It was created by a Shiki Tsukai that has far more Sigil Dates than I.
A powerful Shiki Tsukai must have arrived...
Finally, it's getting inter-esting!
I'm going home.
Fsss
Stop being a stalker, okay?

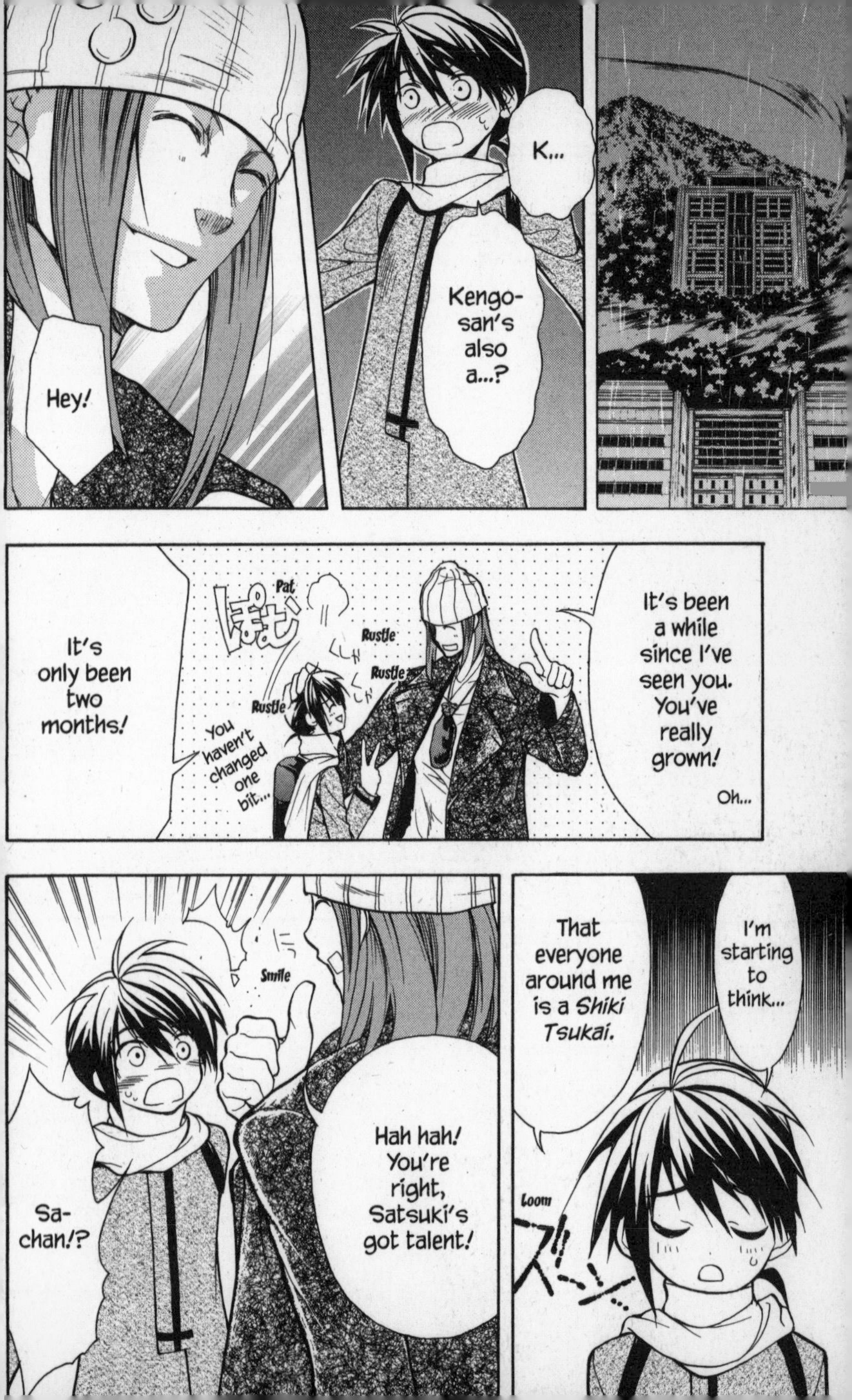
K...
Kengo-san's also a...?
Hey!
It's been a while since I've seen you. You've really grown!
Oh...
Pat
Rustle
Rustle
Rustle
You haven't changed one bit...
It's only been two months!
I'm starting to think...
That everyone around me is a *Shiki Tsukai.*
Loom
Smile
Hah hah! You're right, Satsuki's got talent!
Sa-chan!?

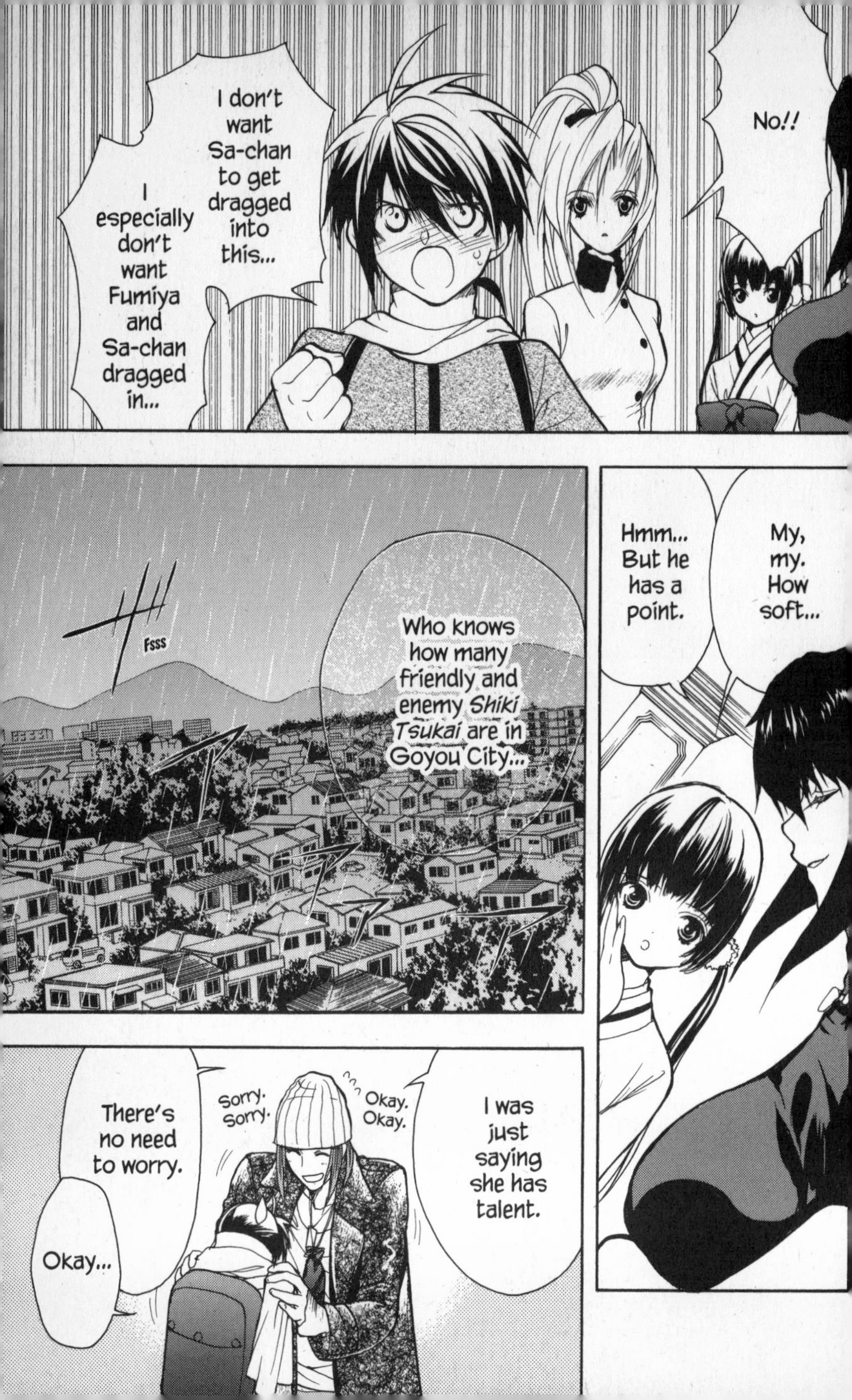
No!!
I don't want Sa-chan to get dragged into this...
I especially don't want Fumiya and Sa-chan dragged in...
My, my. How soft...
Hmm... But he has a point.
Fsss
Who knows how many friendly and enemy *Shiki Tsukai* are in Goyou City...
I was just saying she has talent.
Okay. Okay.
Sorry. Sorry.
There's no need to worry.
Okay...

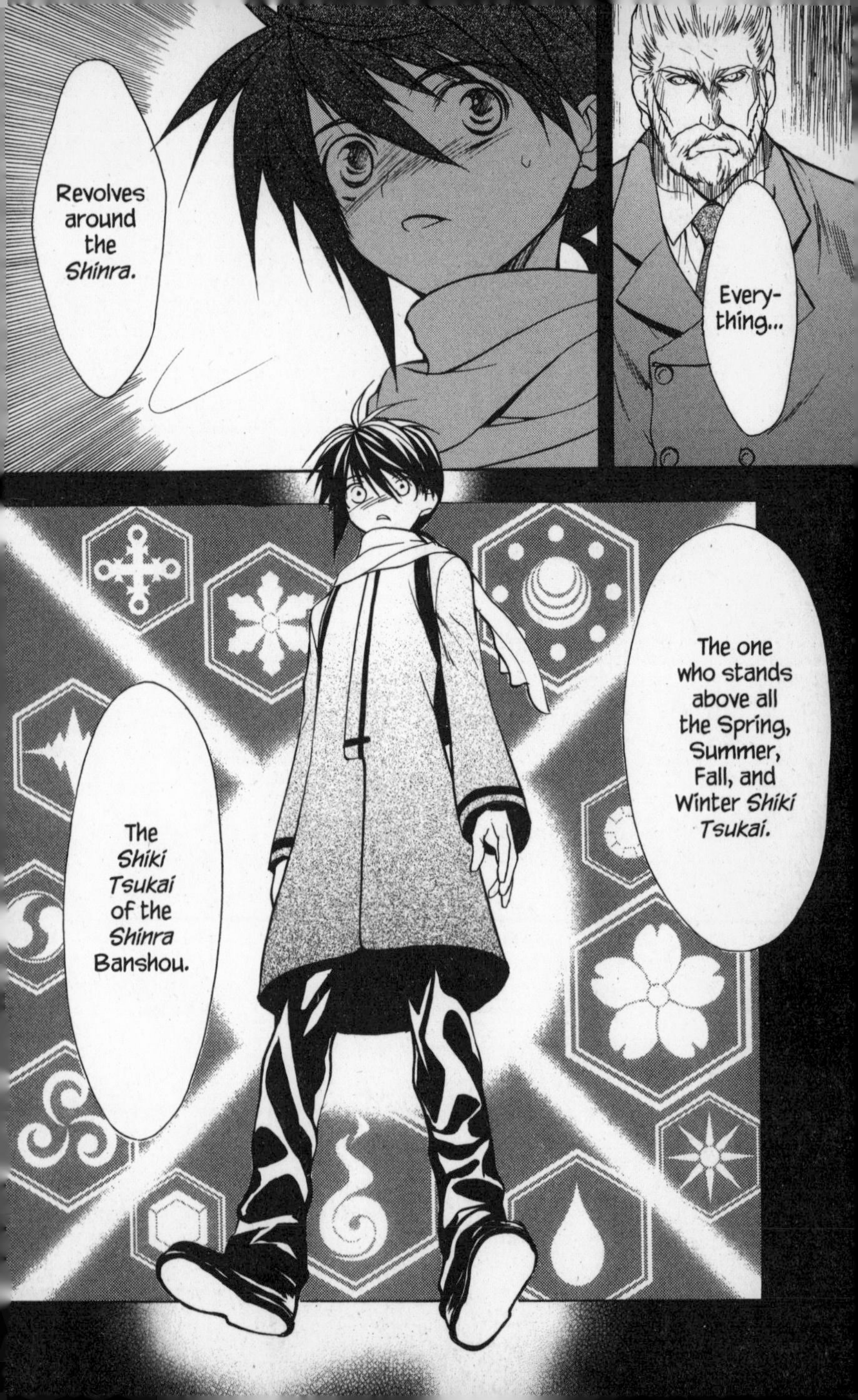
Every-thing...
Revolves around the *Shinra*.
The one who stands above all the Spring, Summer, Fall, and Winter *Shiki Tsukai*.
The *Shiki Tsukai* of the *Shinra* Banshou.

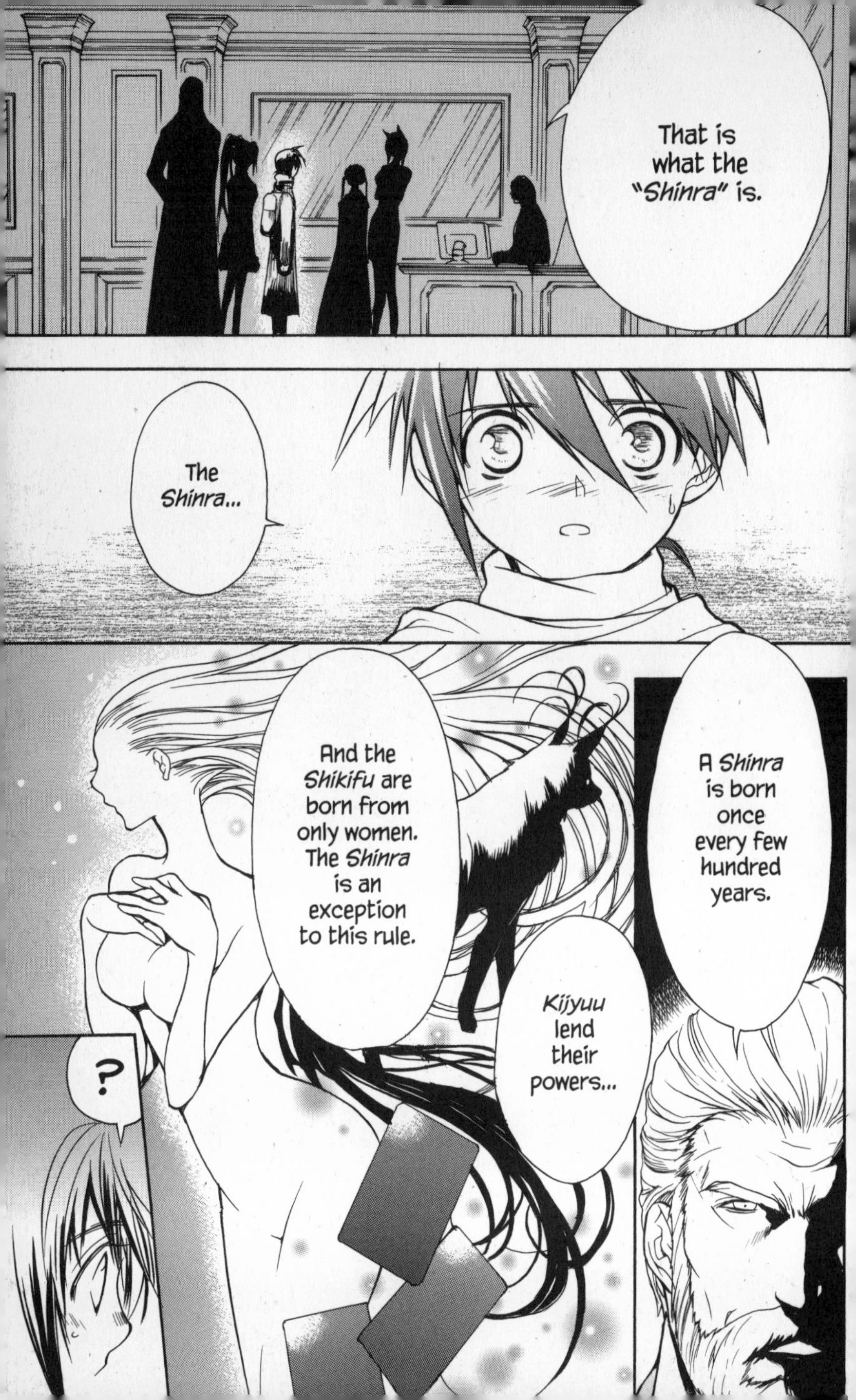
That is what the "Shinra" is.
The Shinra...
A Shinra is born once every few hundred years.
And the Shikifu are born from only women. The Shinra is an exception to this rule.
Kijyuu lend their powers...
?

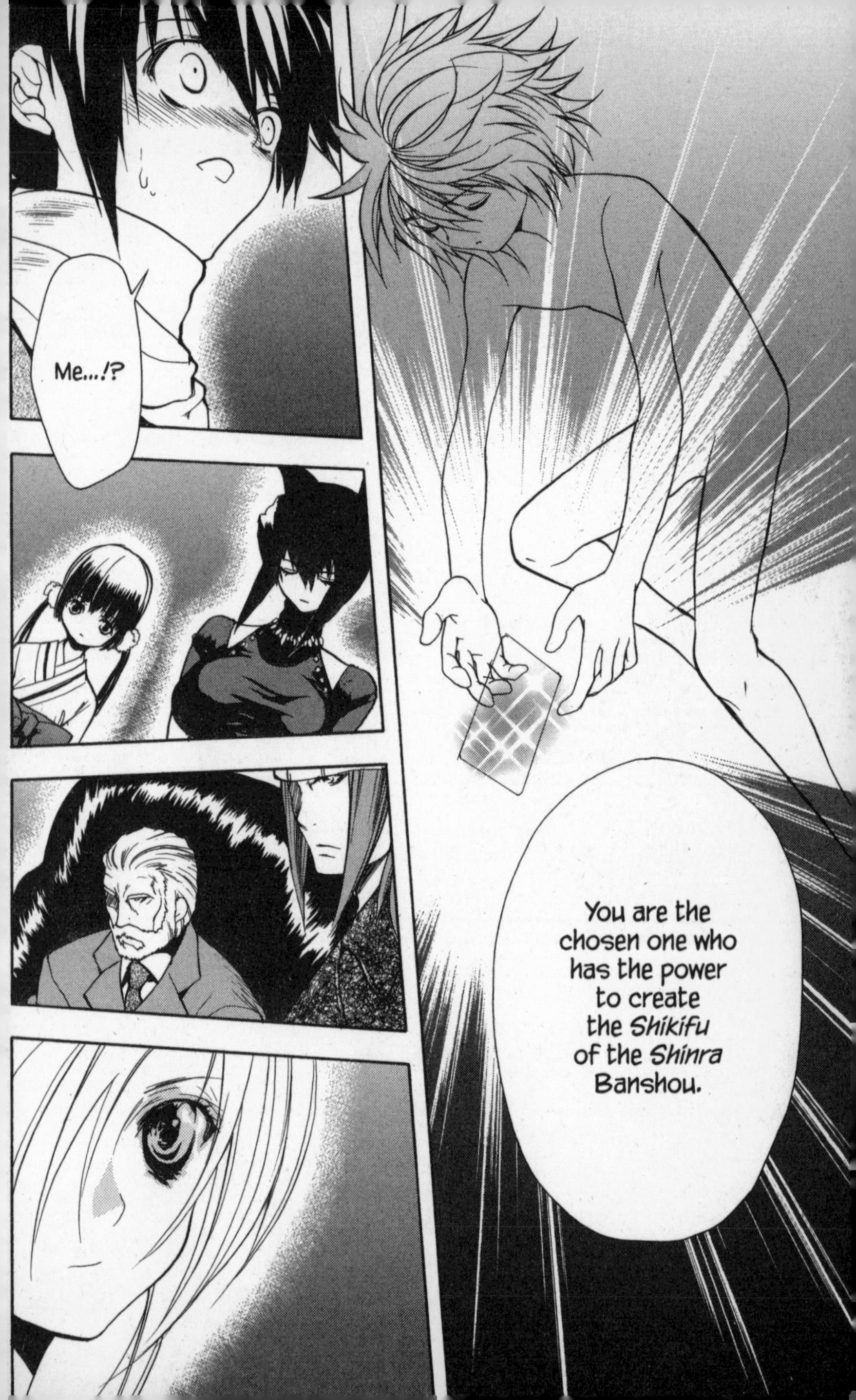
You are the chosen one who has the power to create the *Shikifu* of the *Shinra Banshou.*
Me...!?

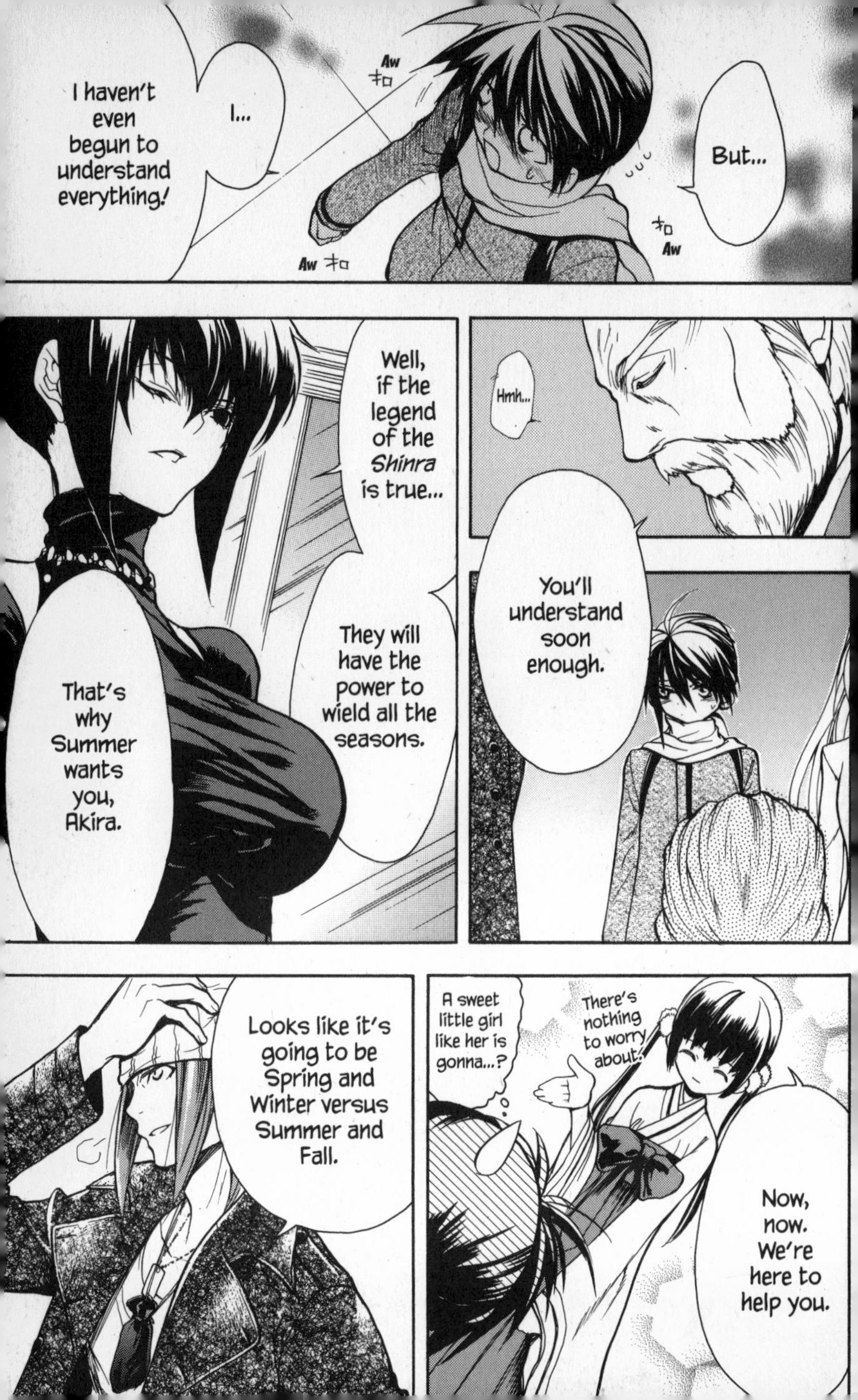
But...
Aw
キロ
Aw キロ
I...
Aw キロ
I haven't even begun to understand everything!
Hmh...
You'll understand soon enough.
Well, if the legend of the *Shinra* is true...
They will have the power to wield all the seasons.
That's why Summer wants you, Akira.
There's nothing to worry about.
Now, now. We're here to help you.
A sweet little girl like her is gonna...?
Looks like it's going to be Spring and Winter versus Summer and Fall.

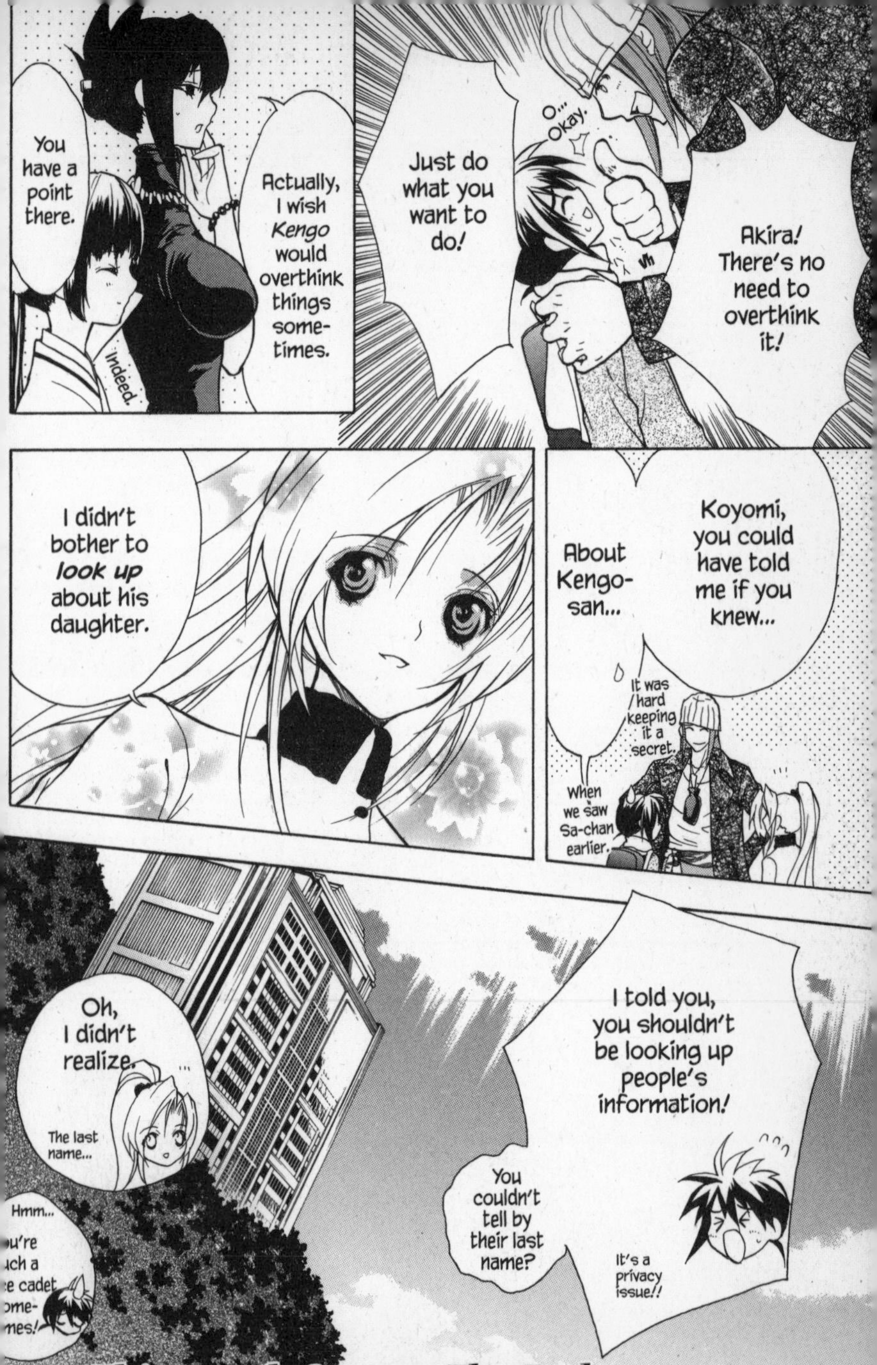
Akira! There's no need to overthink it!
O... Okay.
Just do what you want to do!
Actually, I wish *Kengo* would overthink things some-times.
You have a point there.
Indeed.
Koyomi, you could have told me if you knew...
About Kengo-san...
It was hard keeping it a secret.
When we saw Sa-chan earlier.
I didn't bother to ***look up*** about his daughter.
I told you, you shouldn't be looking up people's information!
You couldn't tell by their last name?
It's a privacy issue!!
Oh, I didn't realize.
The last name...
Hmm...
u're ich a e cadet ome- mes!

Thirteenth Season: The End

Fourteenth Season

Suite of the Storm

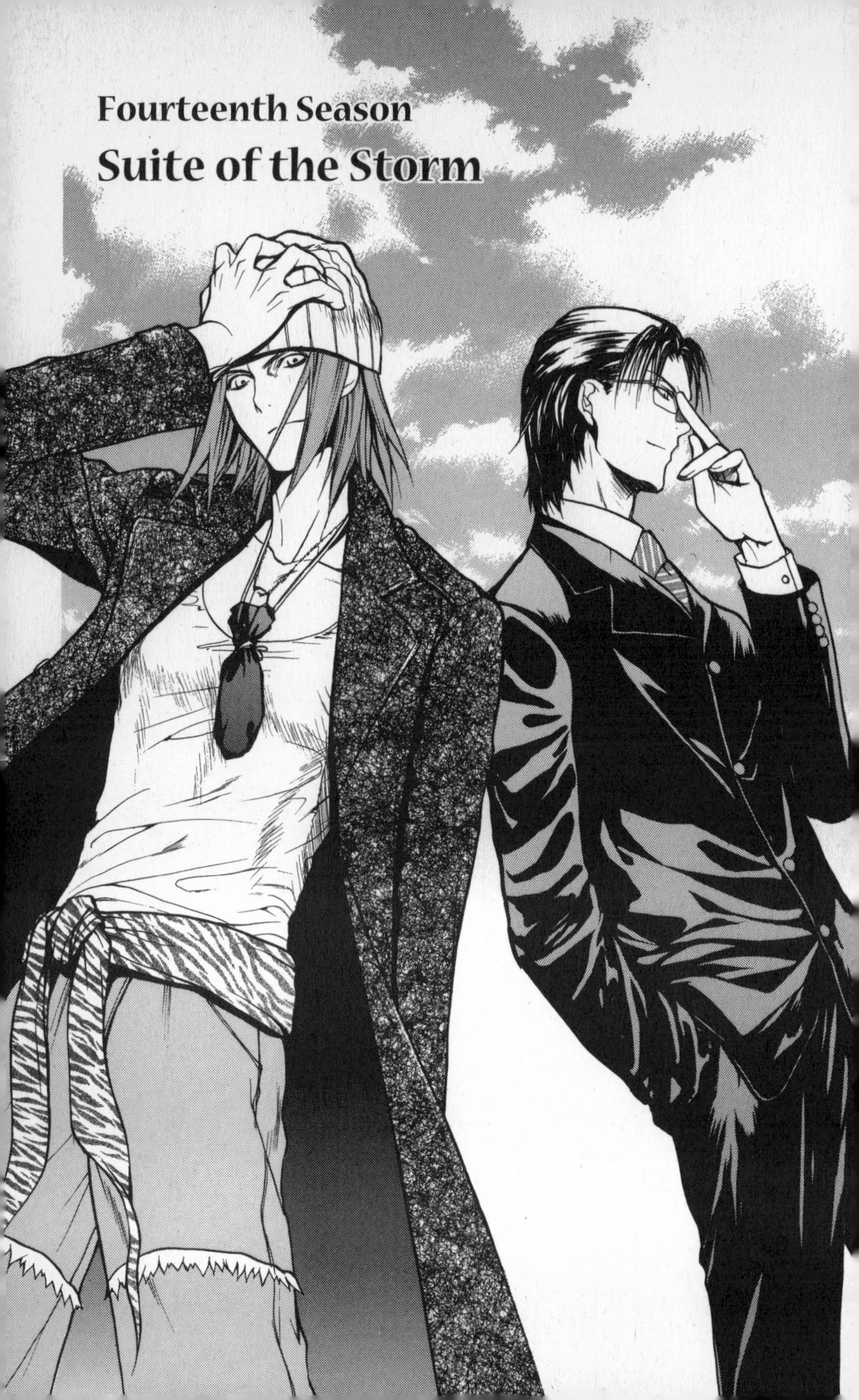

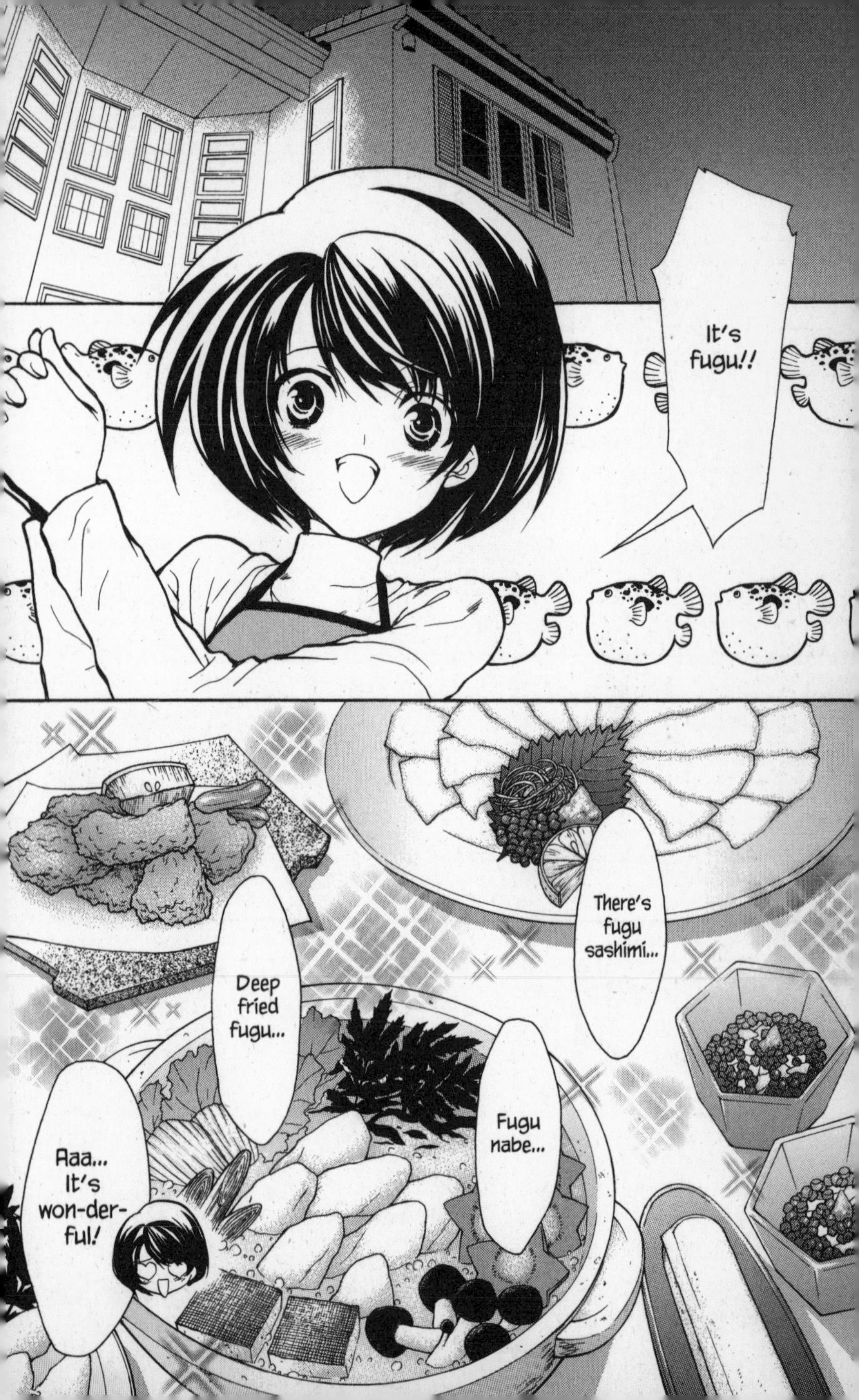
It's fugu!!
There's fugu sashimi...
Deep fried fugu...
Fugu nabe...
Aaa... It's won-der-ful!

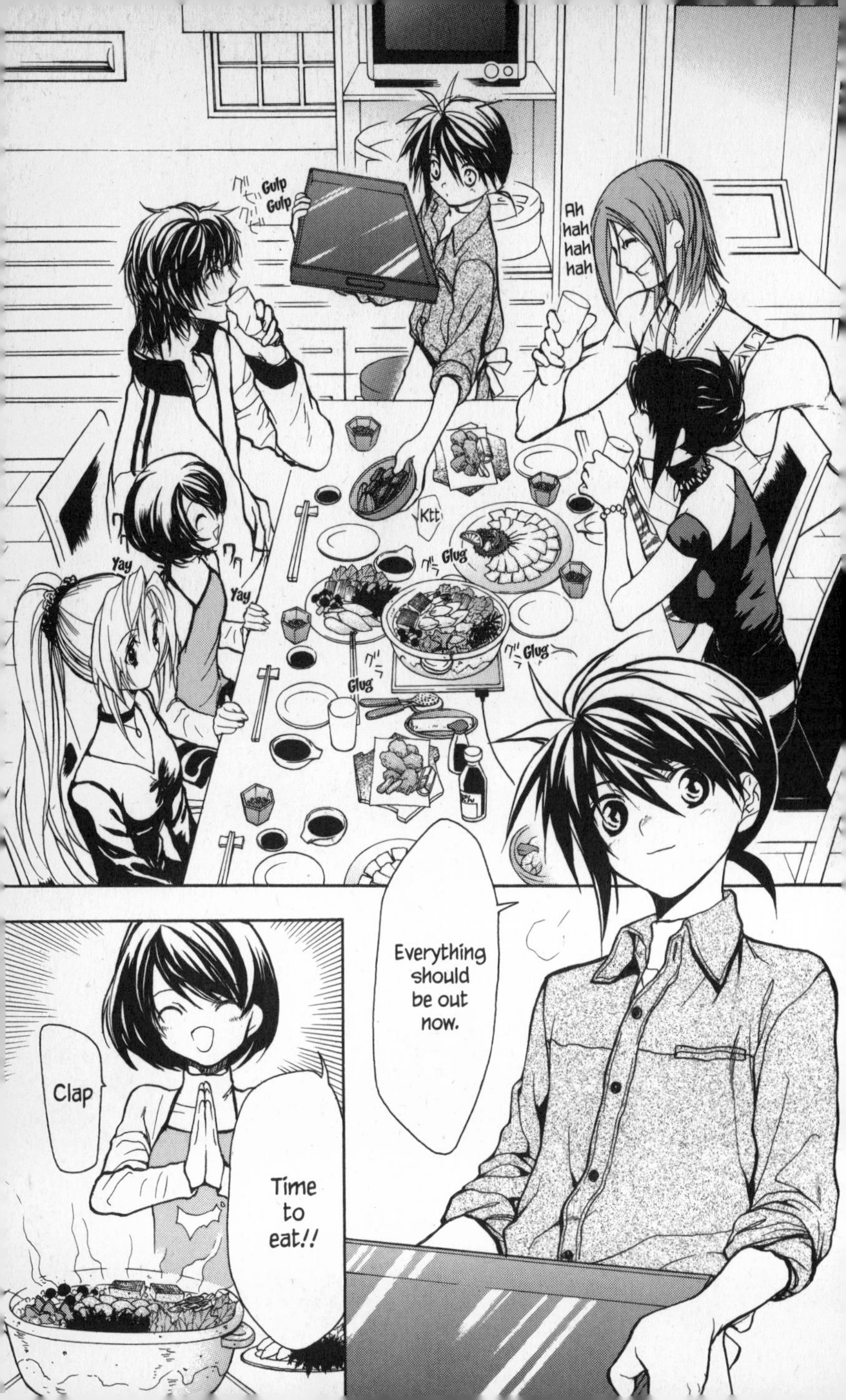
Ah hah hah hah
Gulp Gulp
Ktt
Glug
Glug
Yay
Yay
Glug
Everything should be out now.
Clap
Time to eat!!

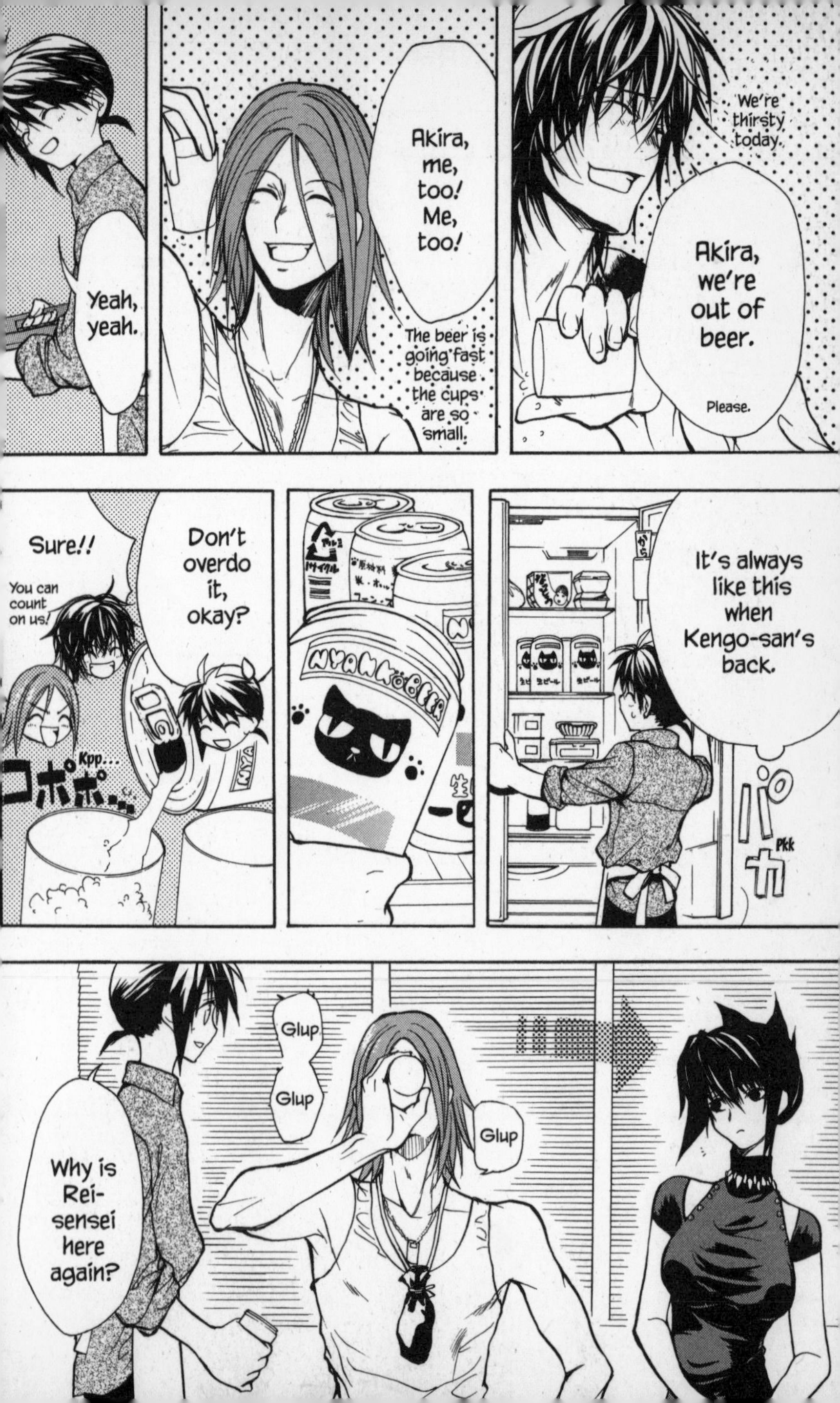
We're thirsty today.
Akira, we're out of beer.
Please.
Akira, me, too! Me, too!
The beer is going fast because the cups are so small.
Yeah, yeah.
It's always like this when Kengo-san's back.
パカ
Pkk
NYANKO BEER
Don't overdo it, okay?
Sure!!
You can count on us!
コポポ...
Kpp...
Glup
Glup
Glup
Why is Rei-sensei here again?

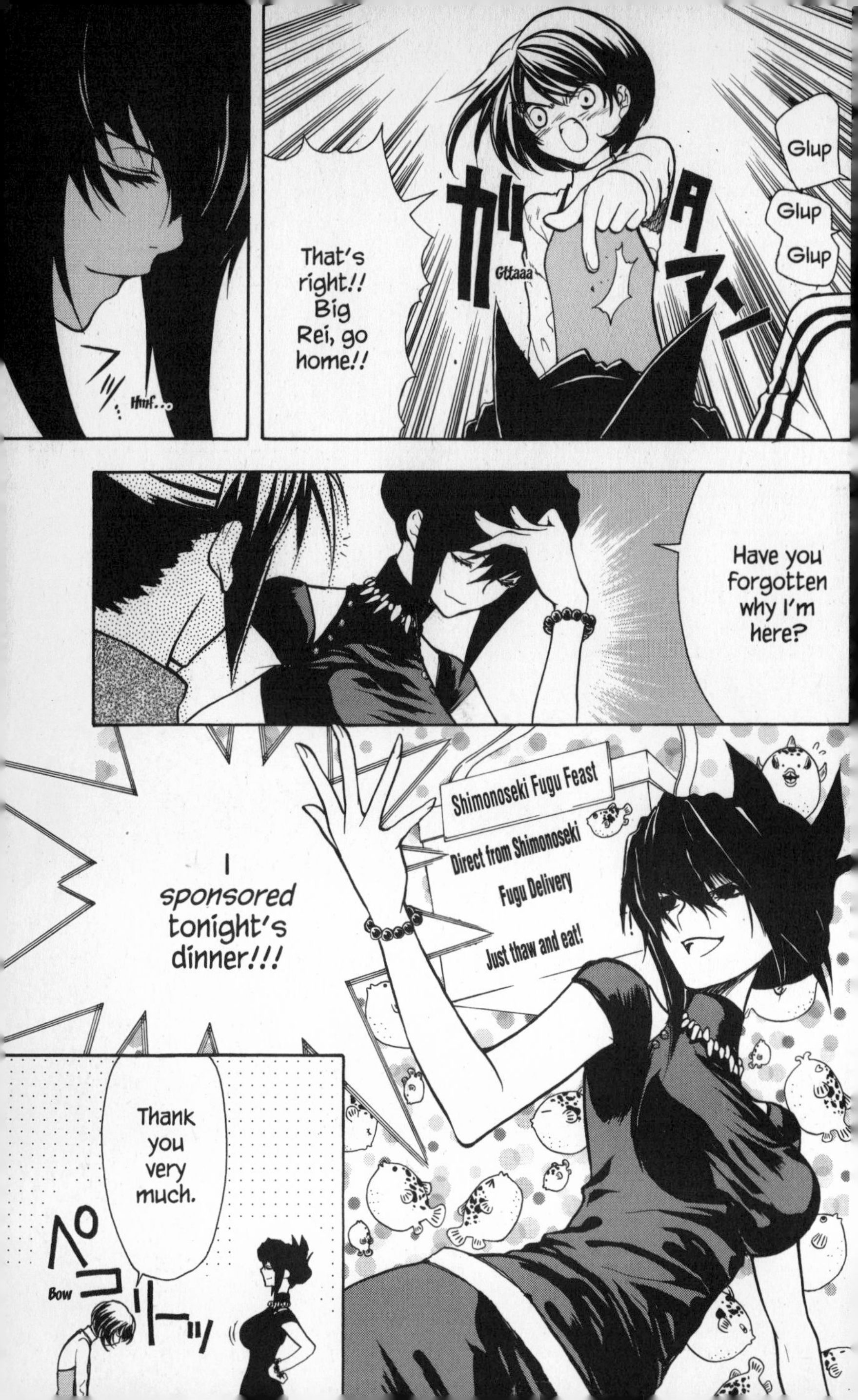
Glup
Glup
Glup
That's right!! Big Rei, go home!!
Gttaaa
Hmf...
Have you forgotten why I'm here?
Shimonoseki Fugu Feast
Direct from Shimonoseki
Fugu Delivery
Just thaw and eat!
I sponsored tonight's dinner!!!
Thank you very much.
Bow

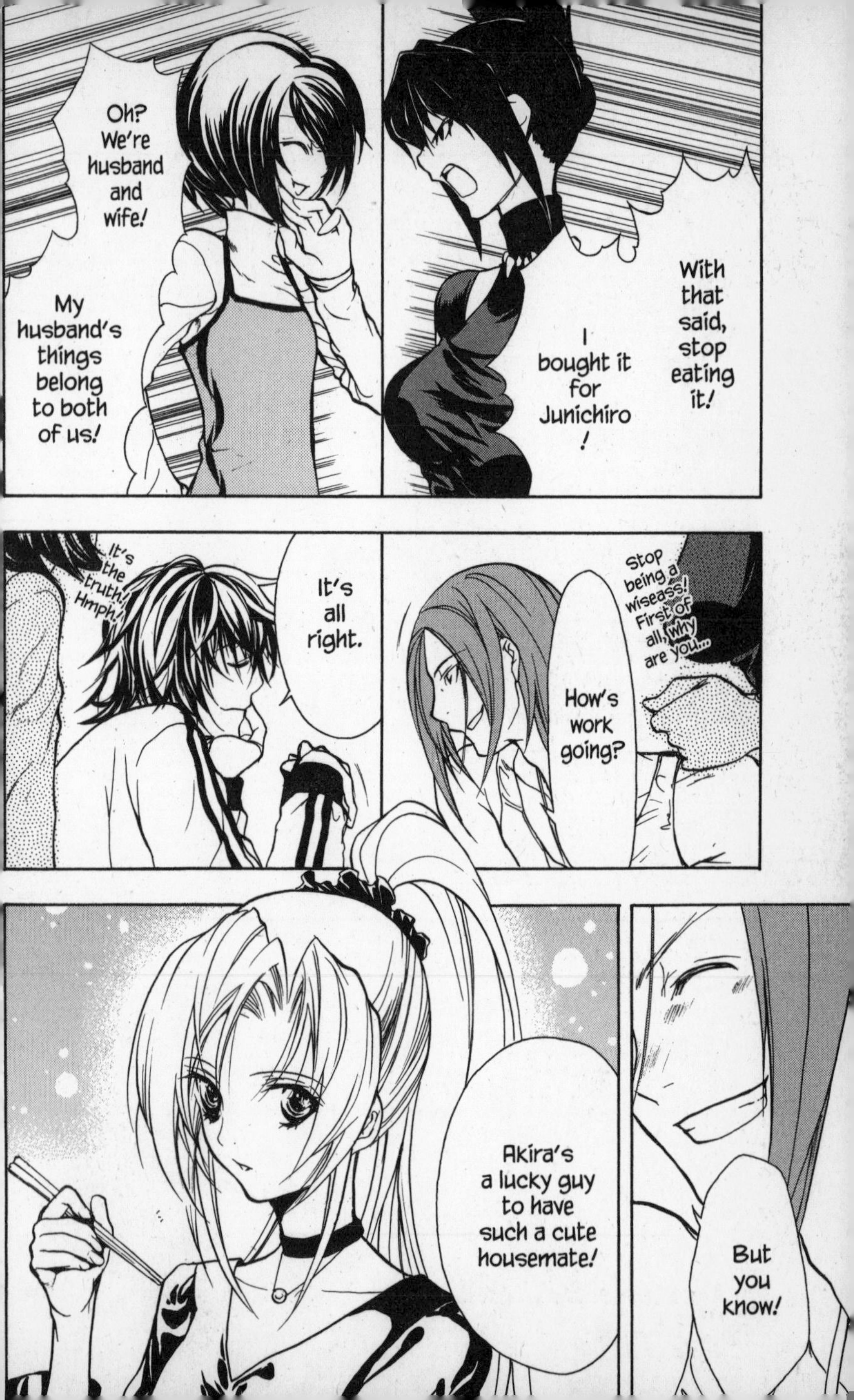
With that said, stop eating it!
I bought it for Junichiro!
Oh? We're husband and wife!
My husband's things belong to both of us!
Stop being a wiseass! First of all, why are you...
How's work going?
It's all right.
It's the truth! Hmph!
But you know!
Akira's a lucky guy to have such a cute housemate!

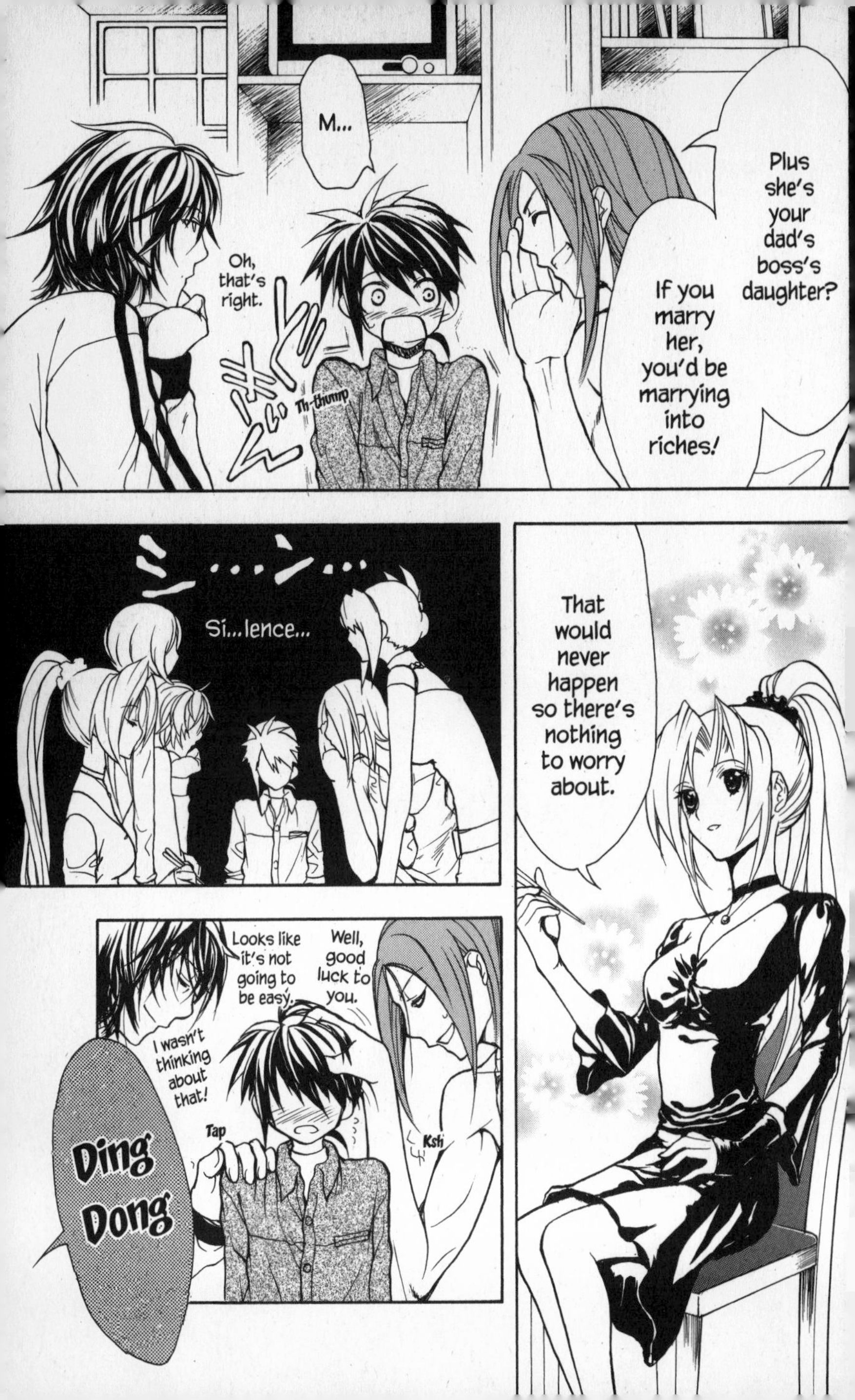
Plus she's your dad's boss's daughter?
If you marry her, you'd be marrying into riches!
M...
Oh, that's right.
Th-thump
That would never happen so there's nothing to worry about.
Si...lence...
Well, good luck to you.
Looks like it's not going to be easy.
I wasn't thinking about that!
Ksh
Tap
Ding Dong

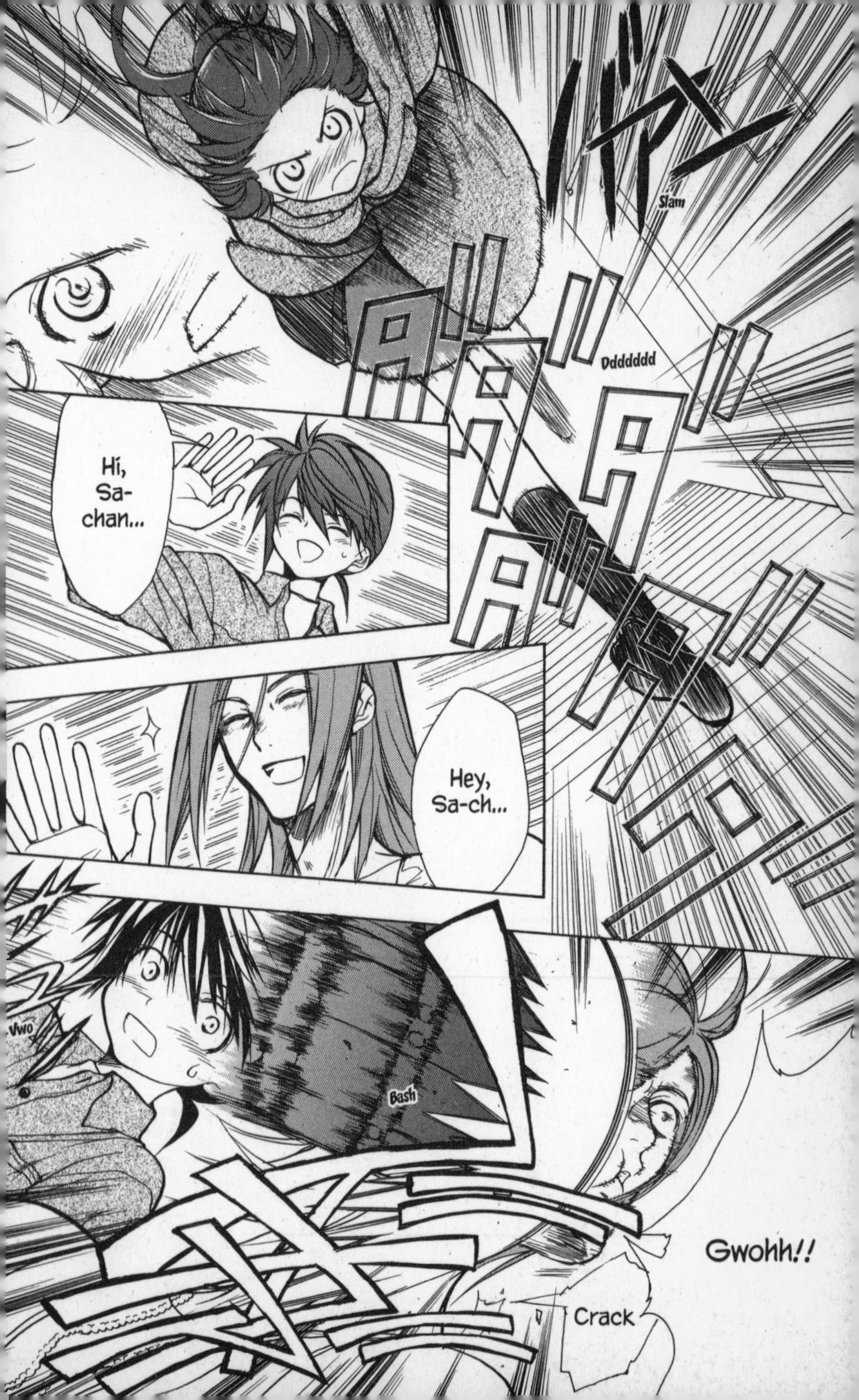
Slam
Ddddddd
Hi, Sa-chan...
Hey, Sa-ch...
Gwohh!!
Crack
Bash
Vwo

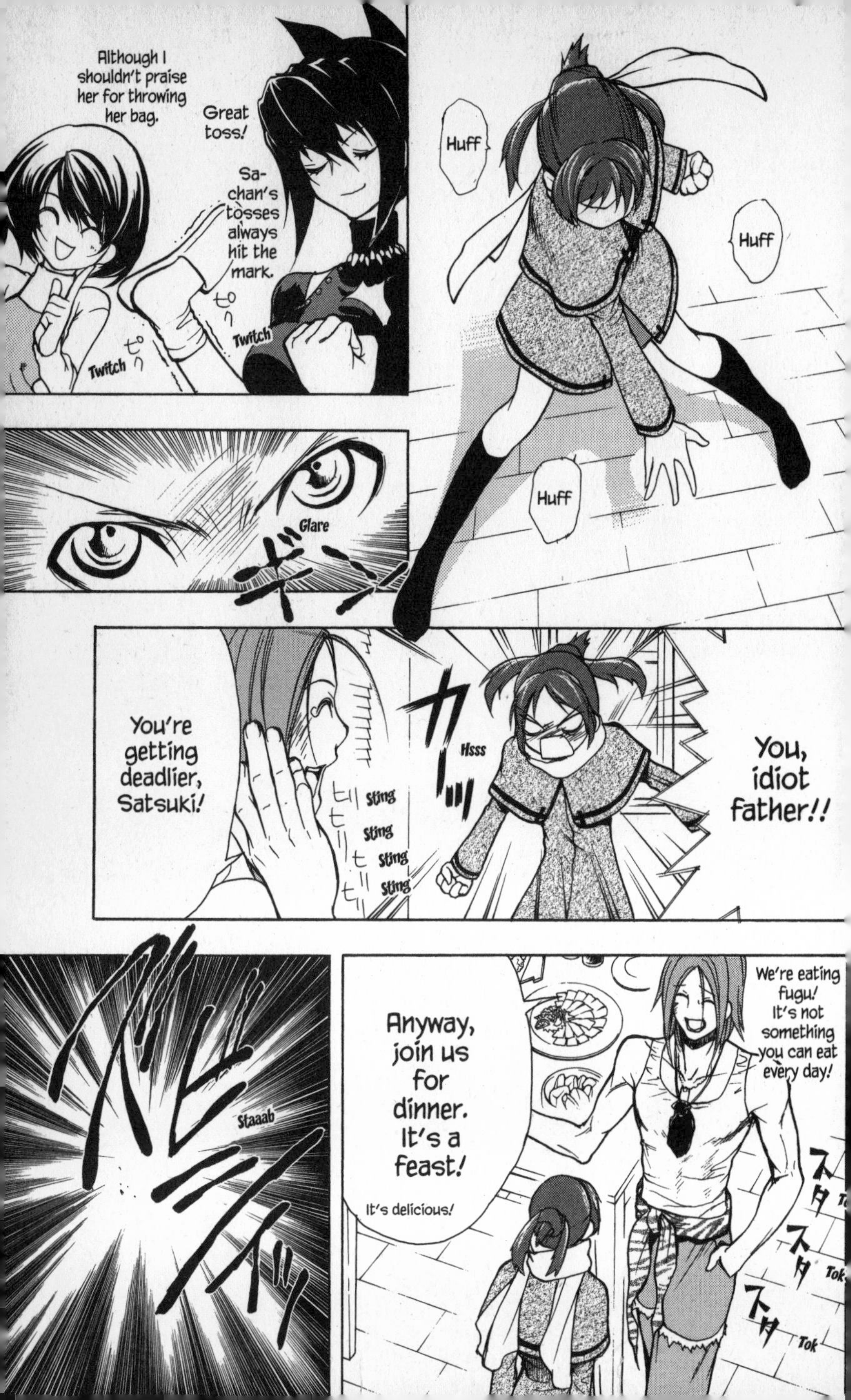

Huff
Huff
Huff
Great toss!
Although I shouldn't praise her for throwing her bag.
Sa-chan's tosses always hit the mark.
Twitch
Twitch
Glare
You, idiot father!!
Hsss
You're getting deadlier, Satsuki!
Sting
Sting
Sting
Sting
We're eating fugu! It's not something you can eat every day!
Anyway, join us for dinner. It's a feast!
It's delicious!
Tok
Tok
Tok
Staaab

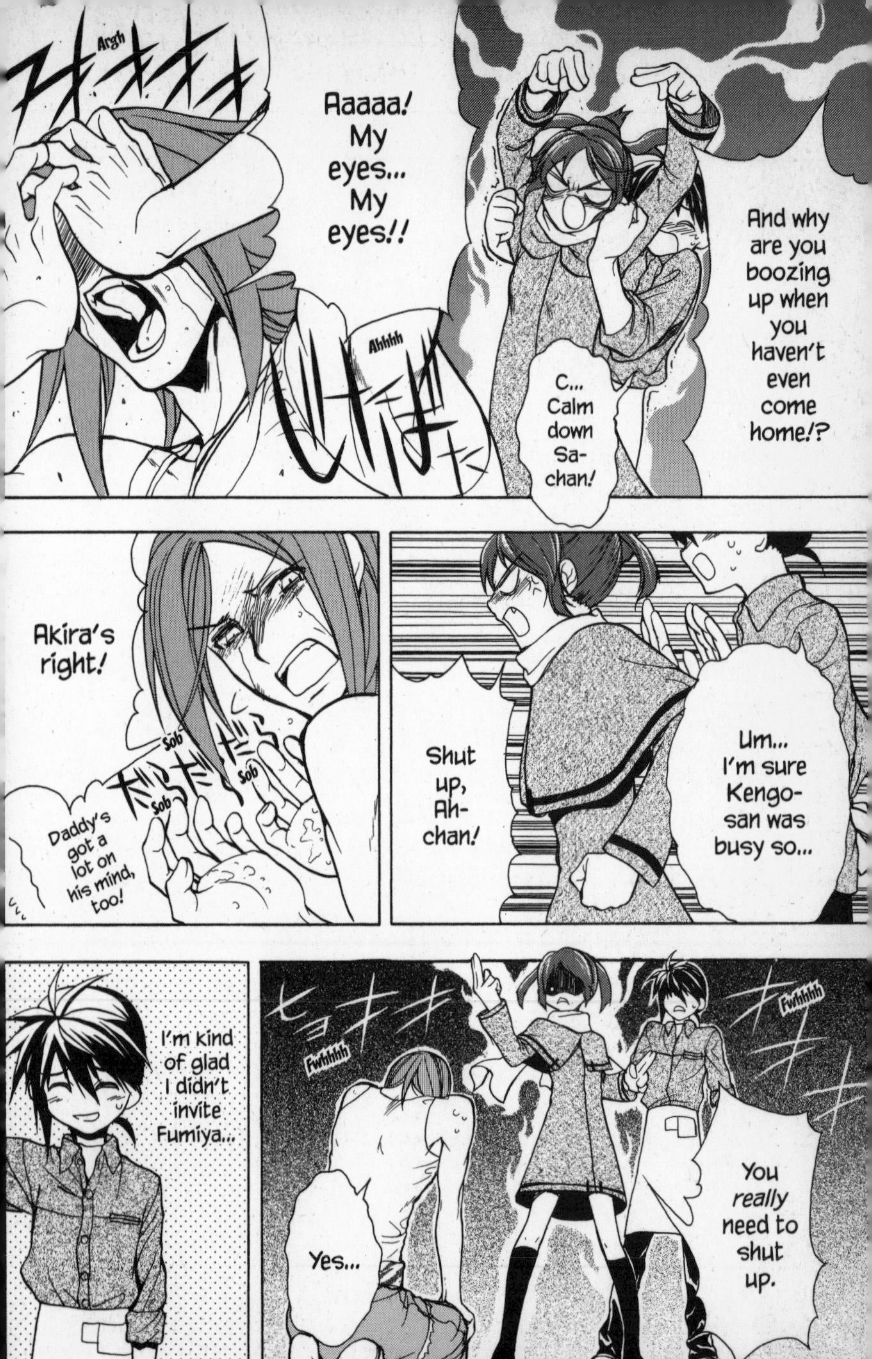
And why are you boozing up when you haven't even come home!?
C... Calm down Sa-chan!
Aaaaa! My eyes... My eyes!!
Argh
Ahhhh
Um... I'm sure Kengo-san was busy so...
Shut up, Ah-chan!
Akira's right!
Sob
Sob
Sob
Daddy's got a lot on his mind, too!
Fwhhhh
You *really* need to shut up.
Fwhhhh
Yes...
I'm kind of glad I didn't invite Fumiya...

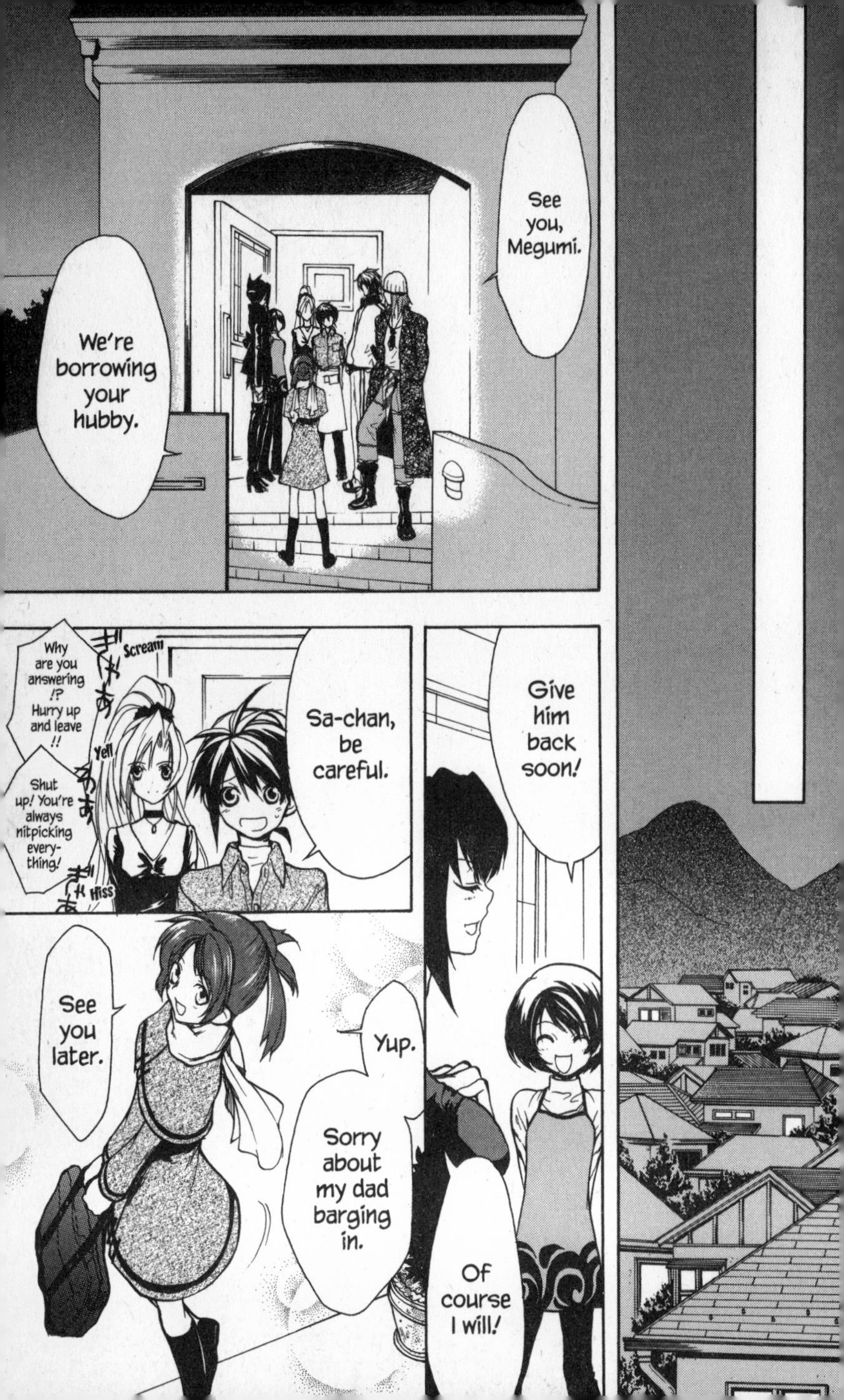
See you, Megumi.
We're borrowing your hubby.
Give him back soon!
Sa-chan, be careful.
Scream
Why are you answering !? Hurry up and leave !!
Yell
Shut up! You're always nitpicking every-thing!
Hiss
Yup.
See you later.
Sorry about my dad barging in.
Of course I will!

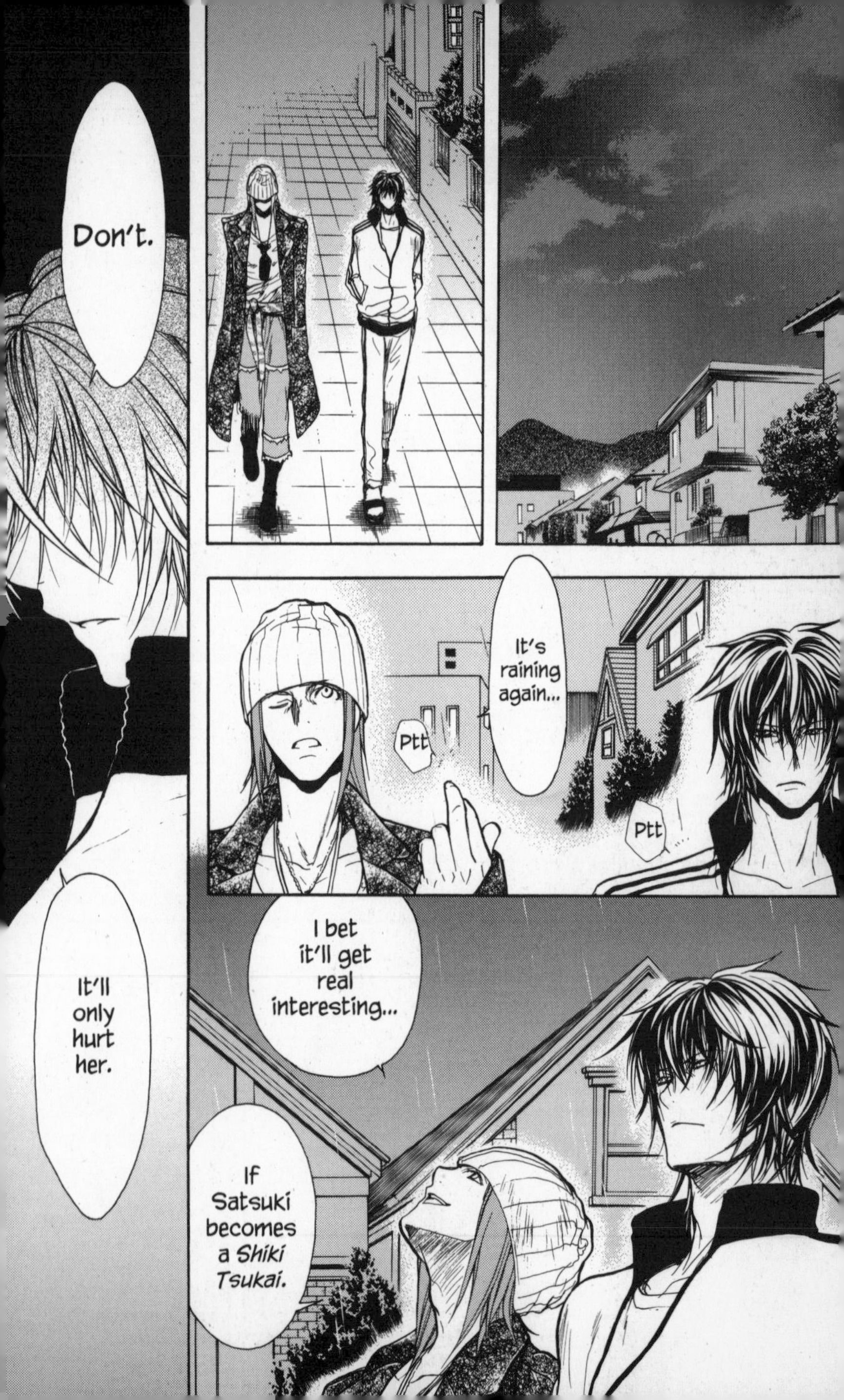
It's raining again...
Ptt
Ptt
I bet it'll get real interesting...
If Satsuki becomes a Shiki Tsukai.
Don't.
It'll only hurt her.

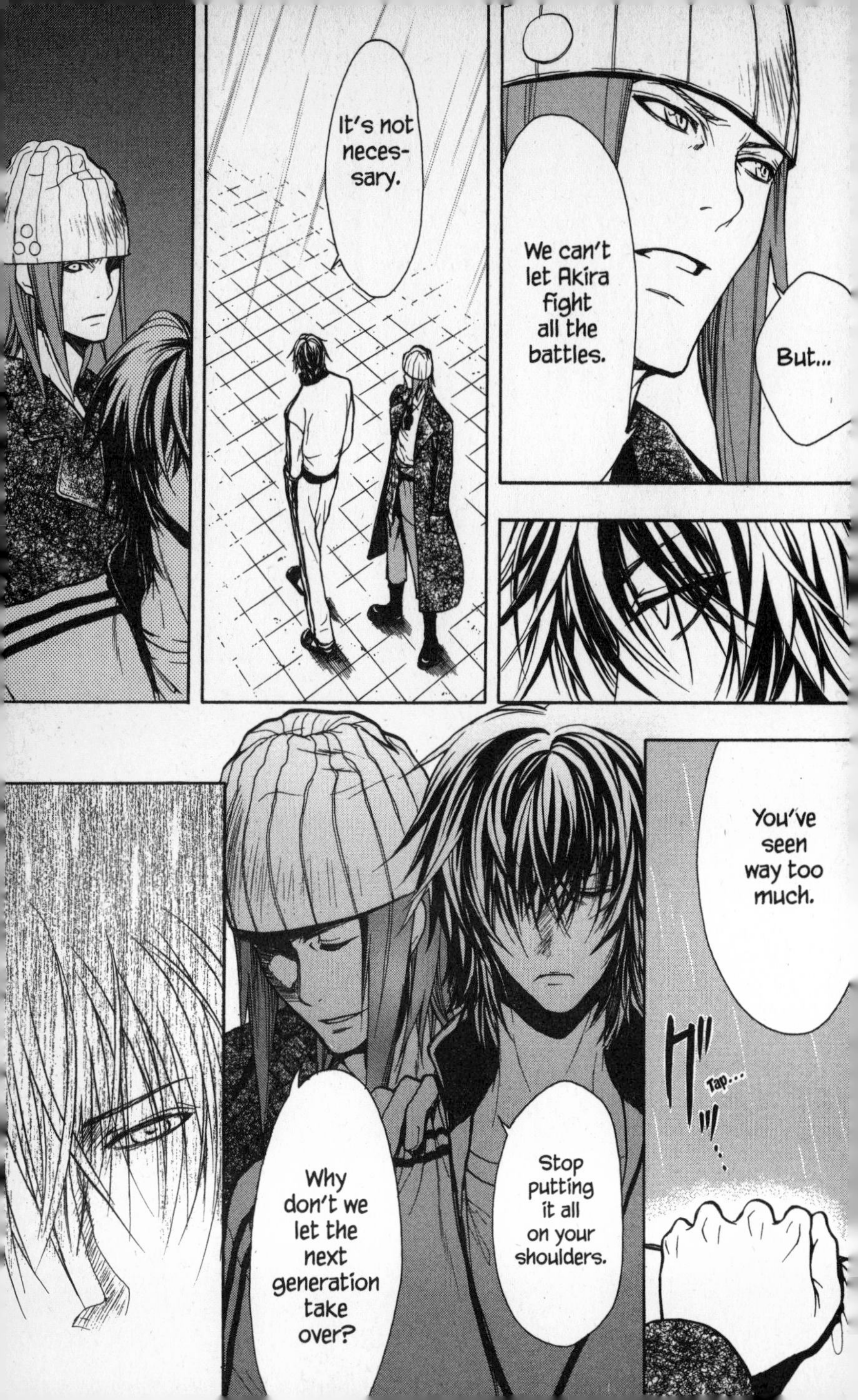

But...
We can't let Akira fight all the battles.
It's not neces-sary.
You've seen way too much.
Tap...
Stop putting it all on your shoulders.
Why don't we let the next generation take over?

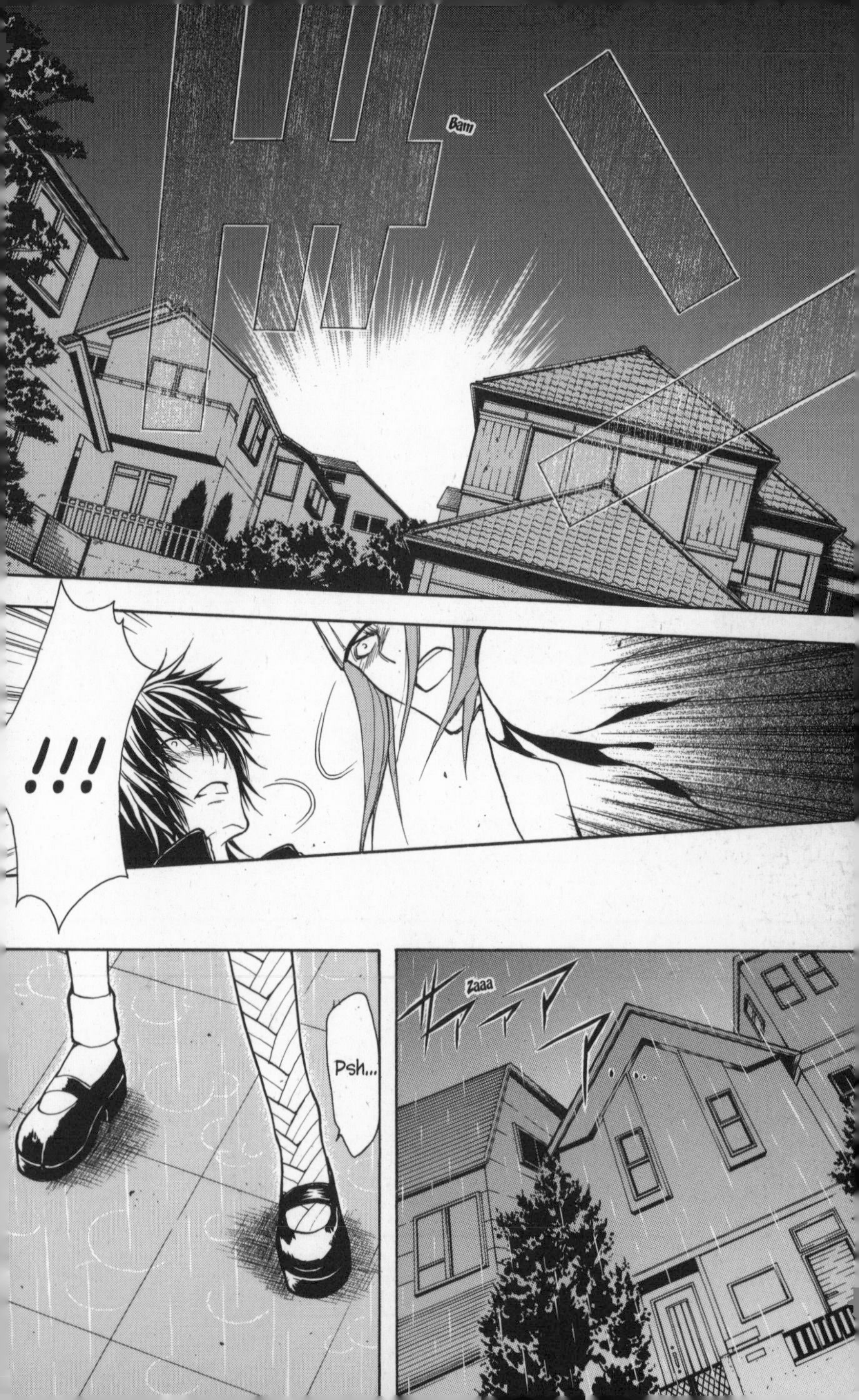
Bam
!!!
Zaaa
Psh...

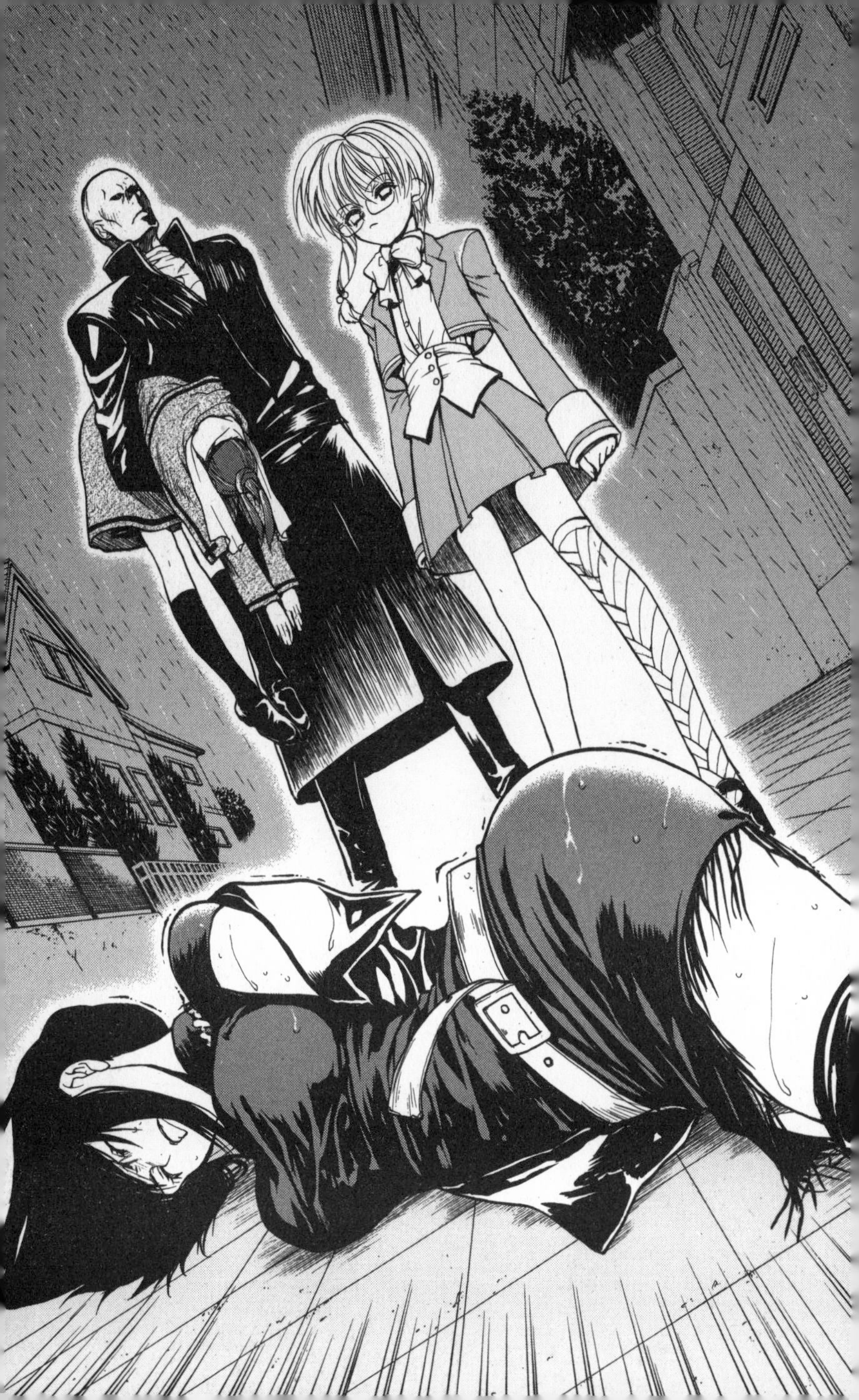

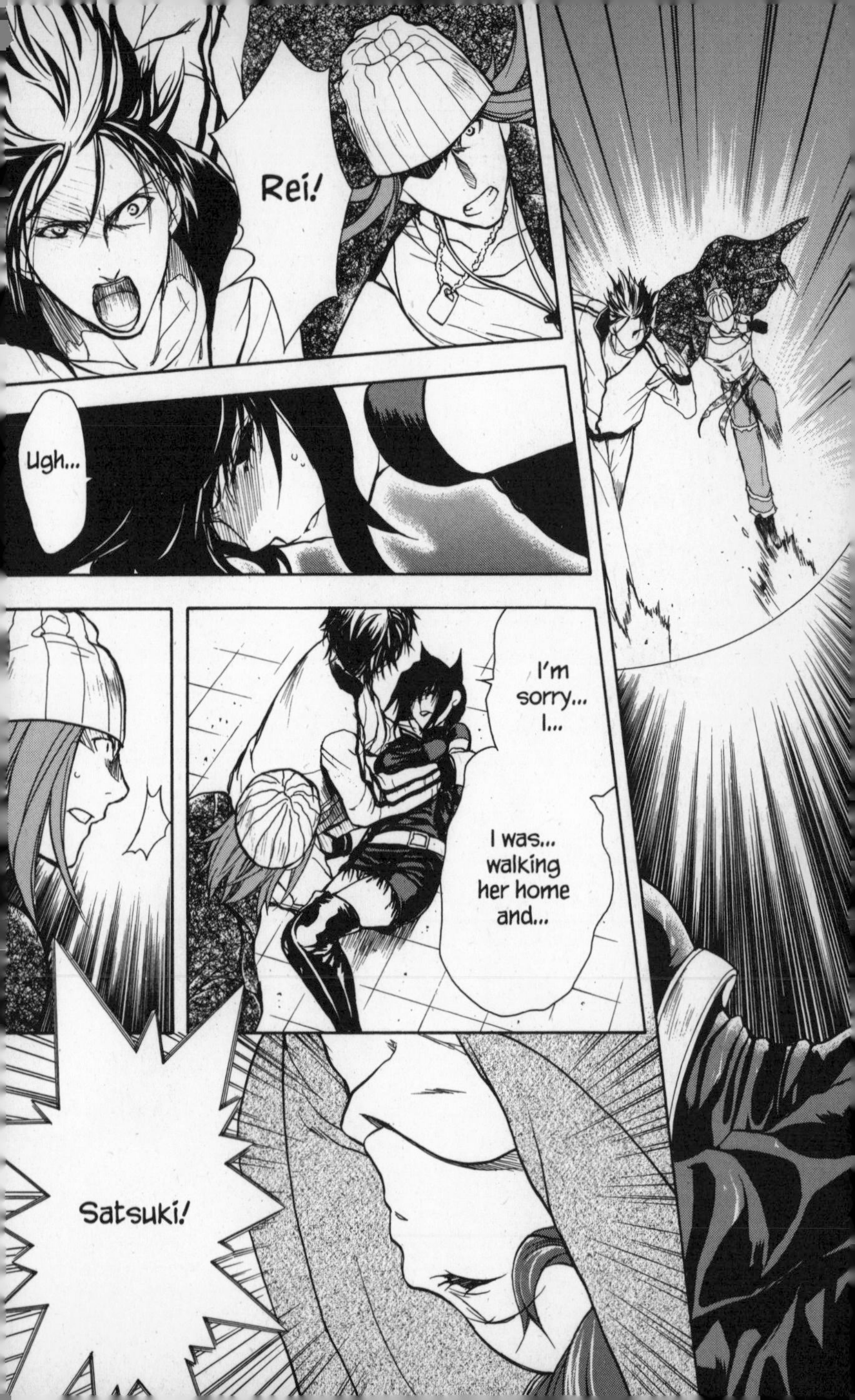
Rei!
Ugh...
I'm sorry... I...
I was... walking her home and...
Satsuki!

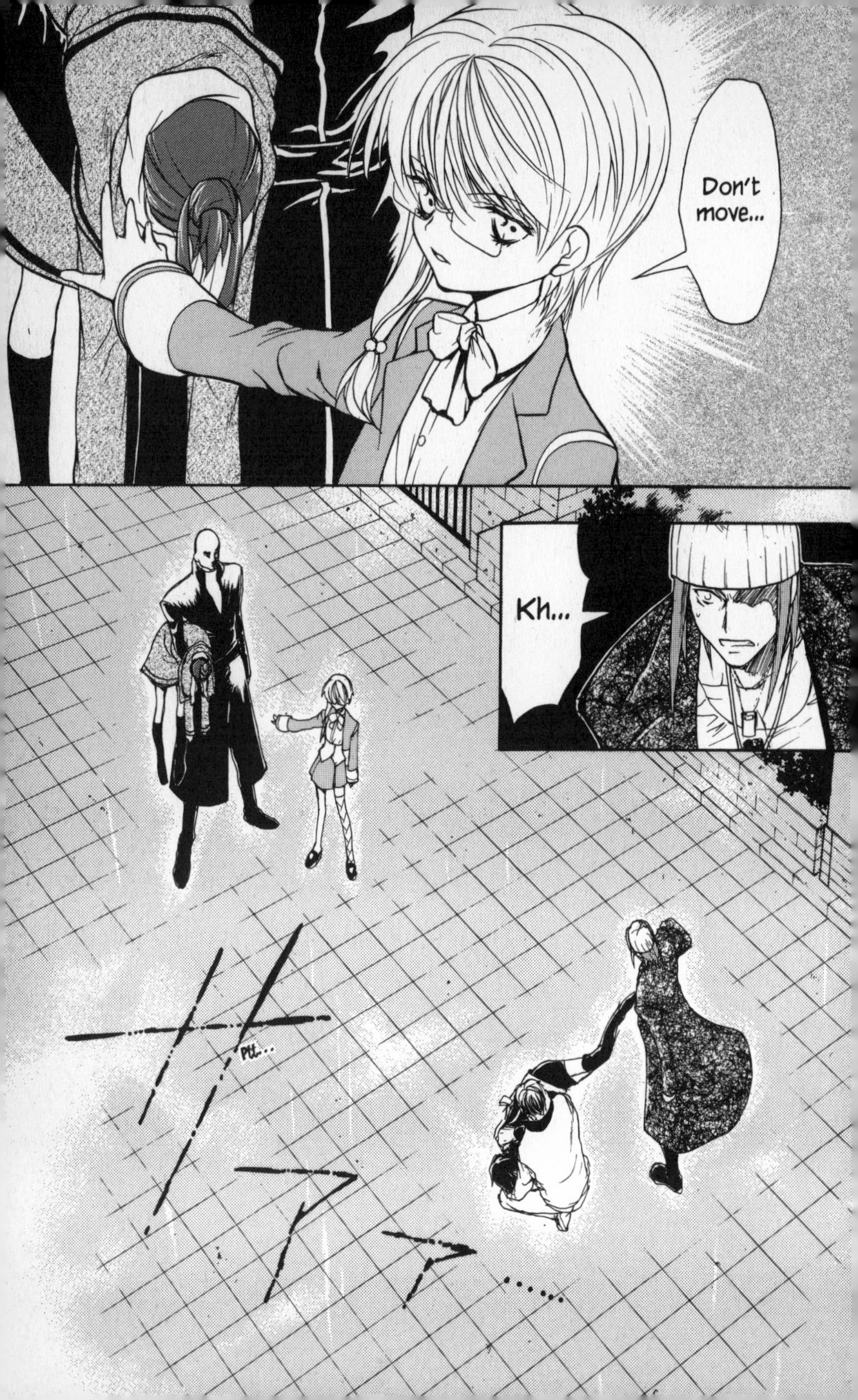
Don't move...
Kh...
Ptt...

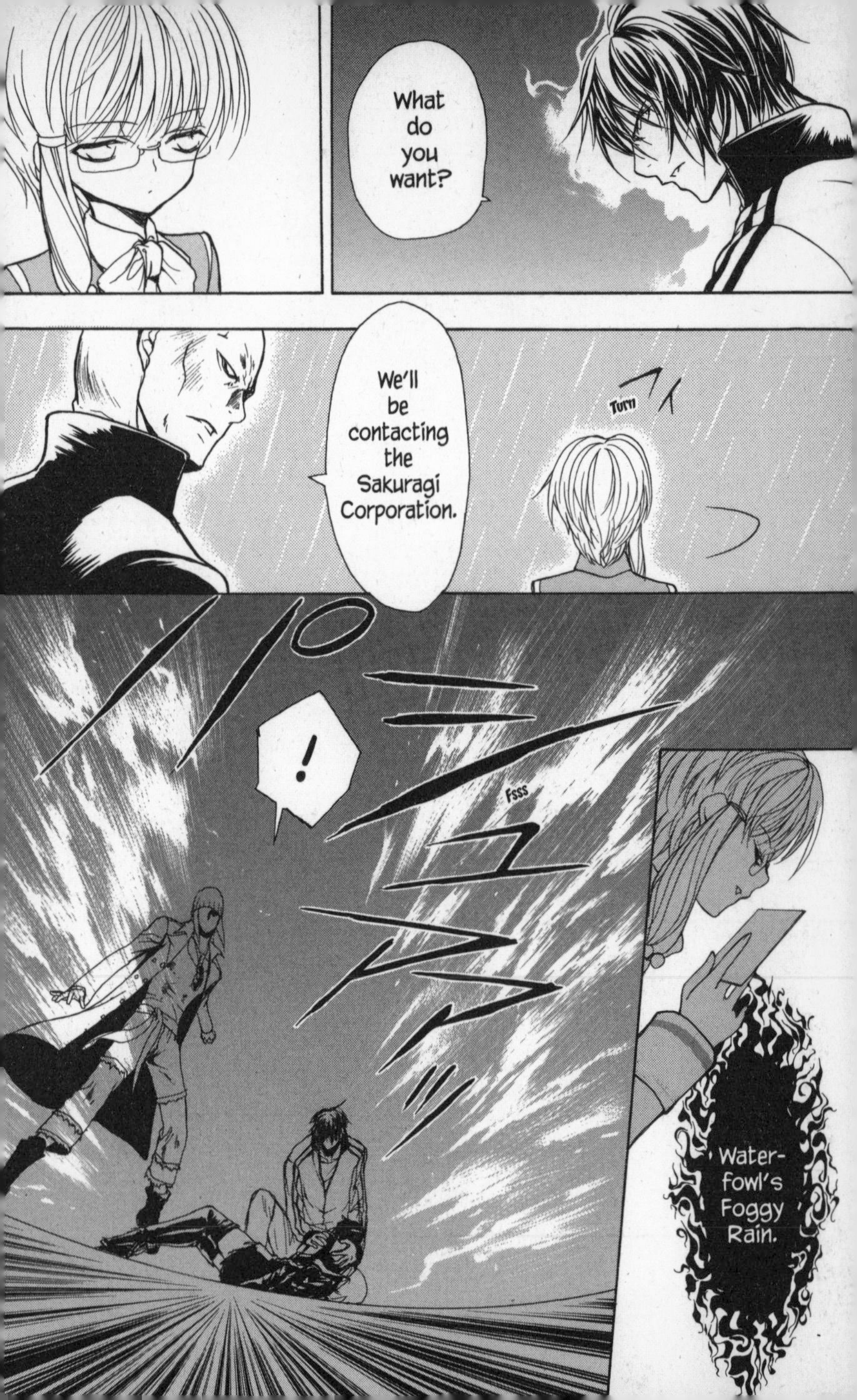
What do you want?
We'll be contacting the Sakuragi Corporation.
Turn
Water-fowl's Foggy Rain.
!
Fsss

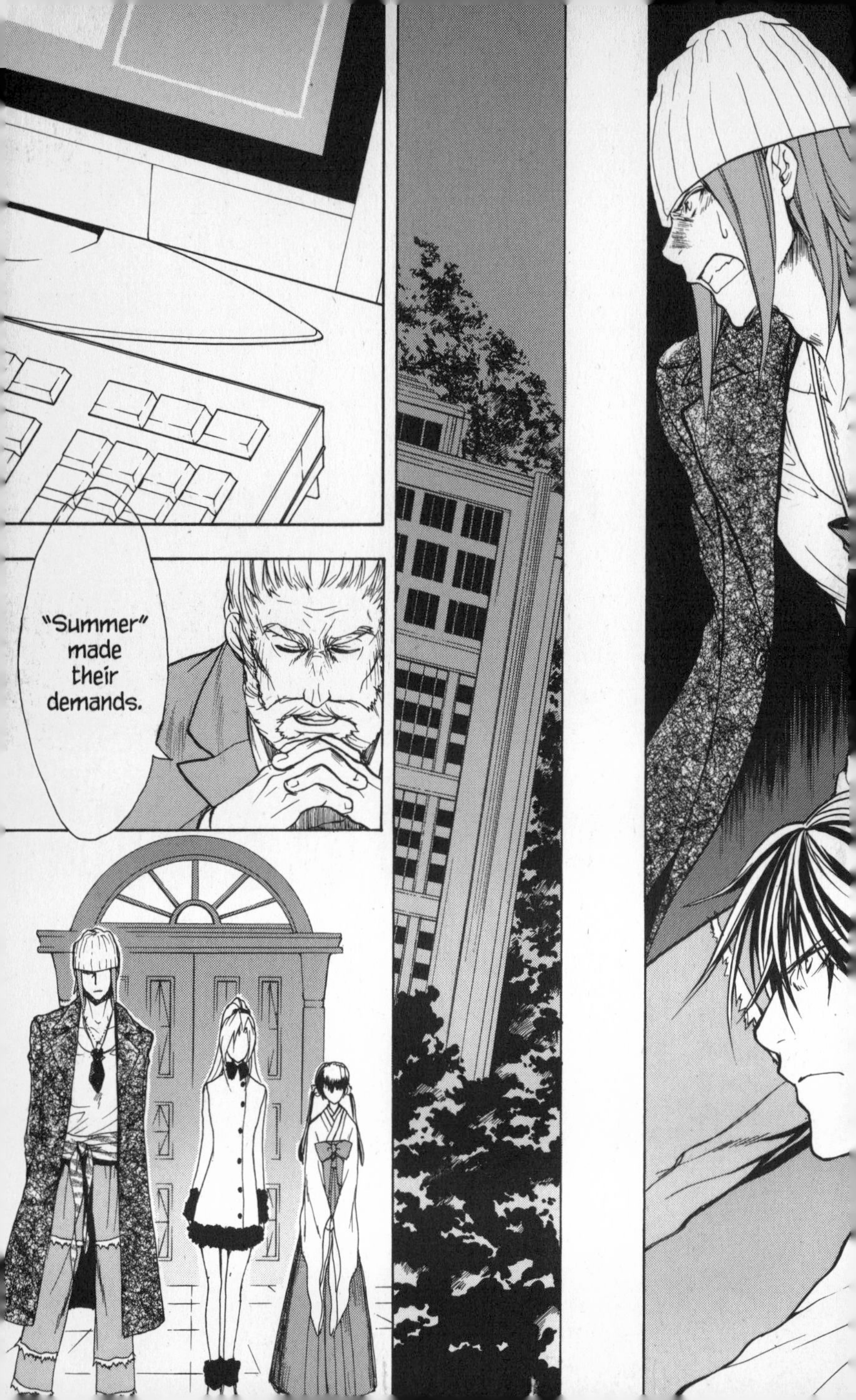
"Summer" made their demands.

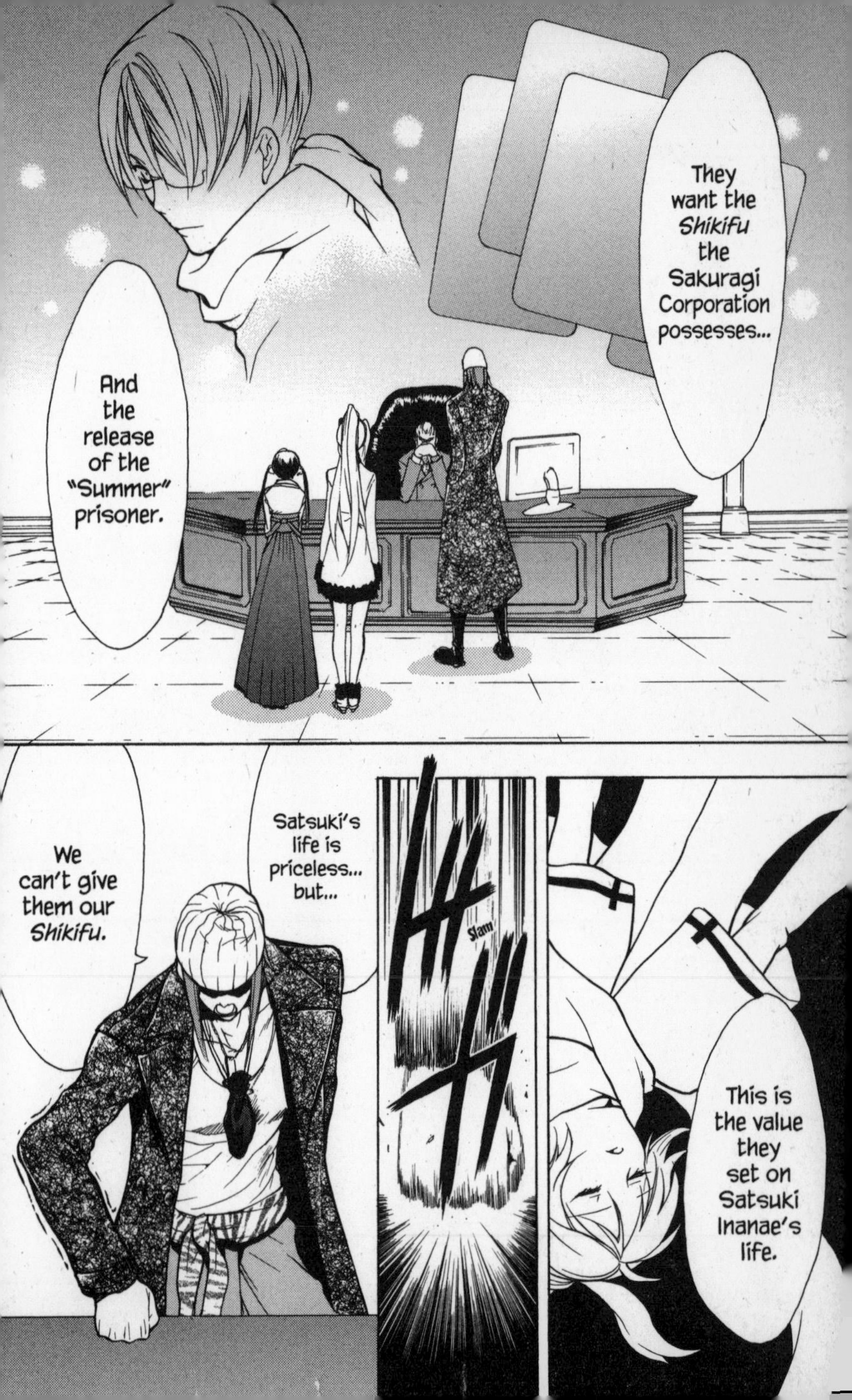
They want the *Shikifu* the Sakuragi Corporation possesses...
And the release of the "Summer" prisoner.
This is the value they set on Satsuki Inanae's life.
Slam
Satsuki's life is priceless... but...
We can't give them our *Shikifu*.

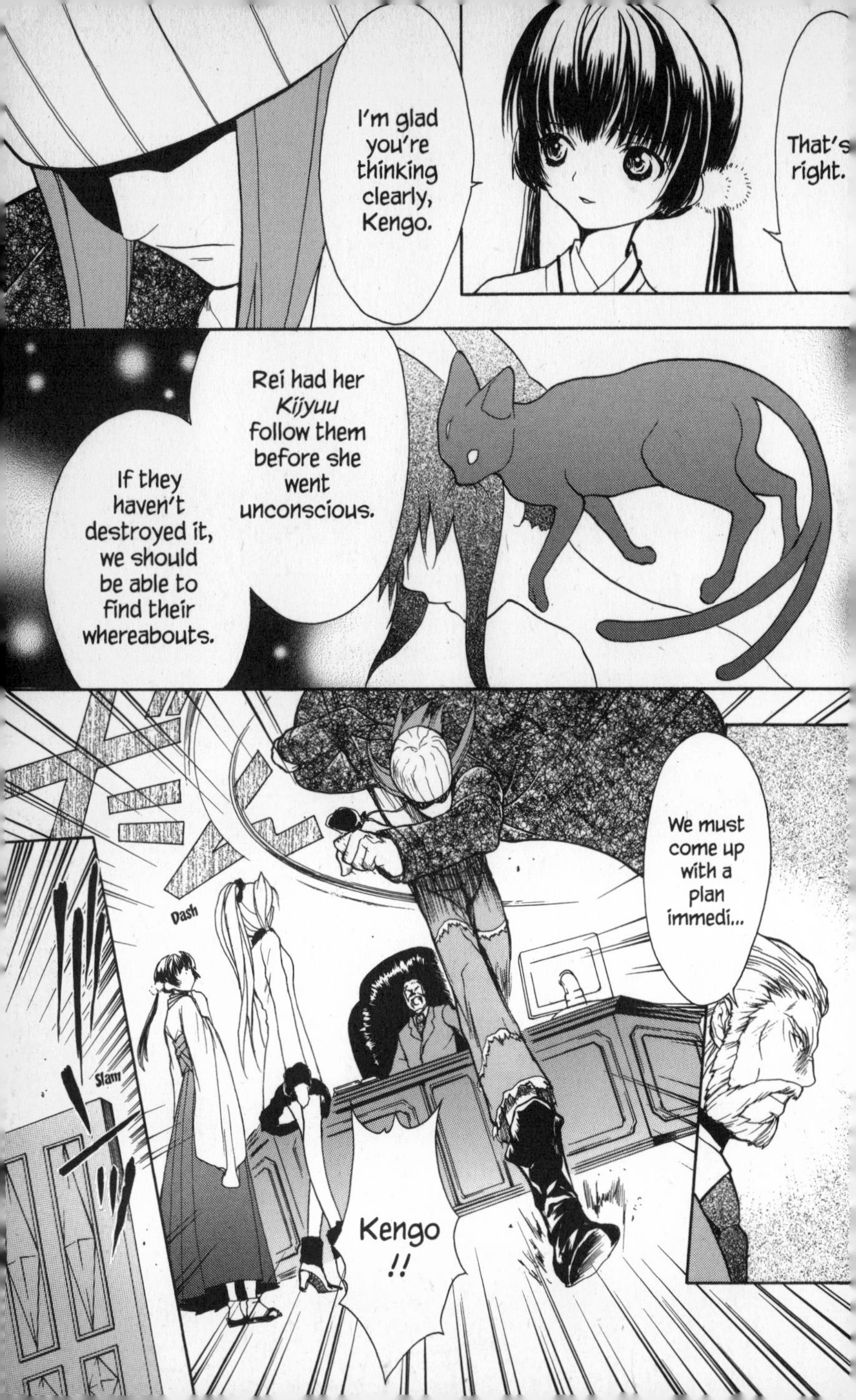
That's right.
I'm glad you're thinking clearly, Kengo.
Rei had her *Kijyuu* follow them before she went unconscious.
If they haven't destroyed it, we should be able to find their whereabouts.
We must come up with a plan immedi...
Dash
Slam
Kengo !!

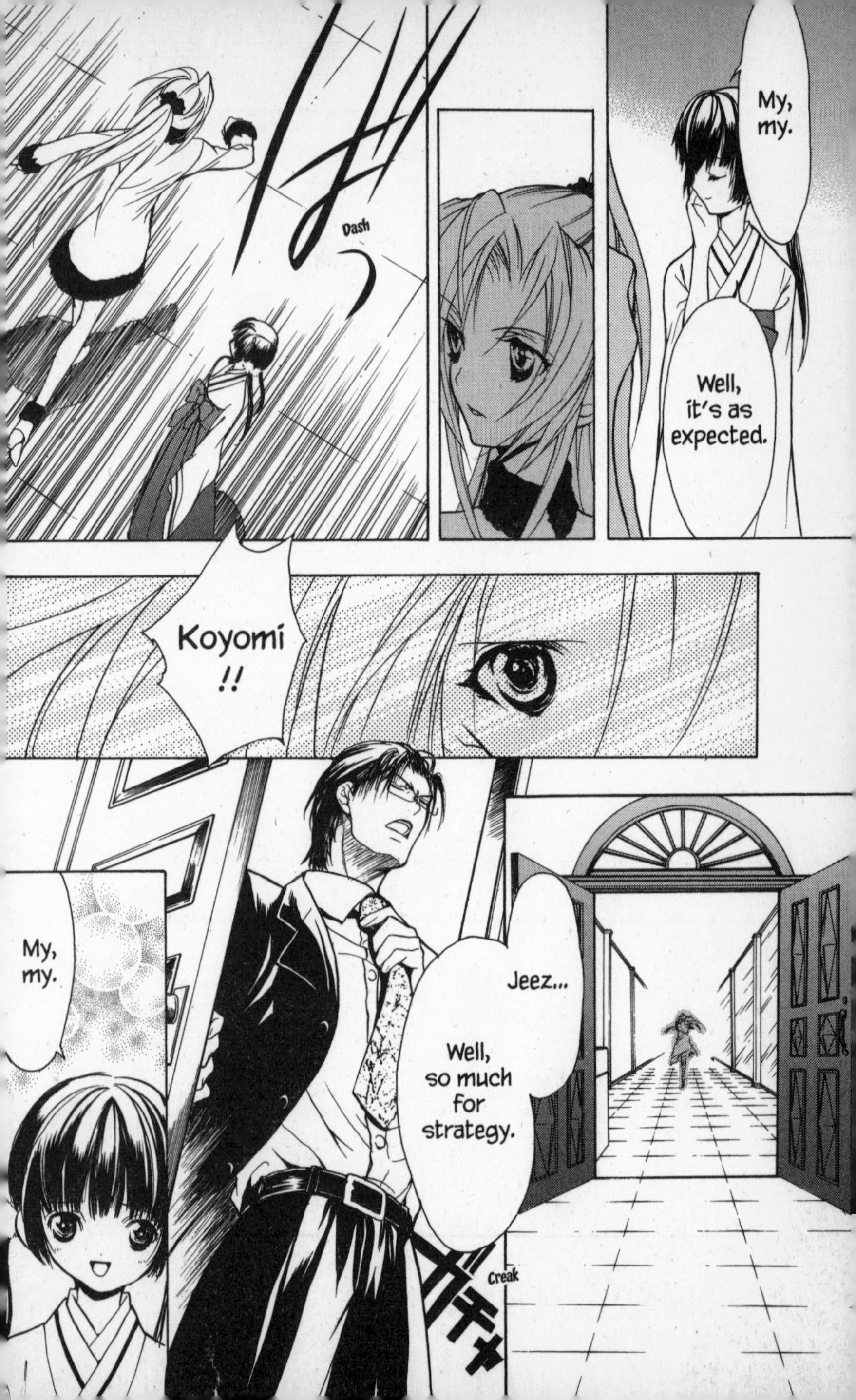
My, my.
Well, it's as expected.
Dash
Koyomi !!
Jeez...
Well, so much for strategy.
Creak
My, my.

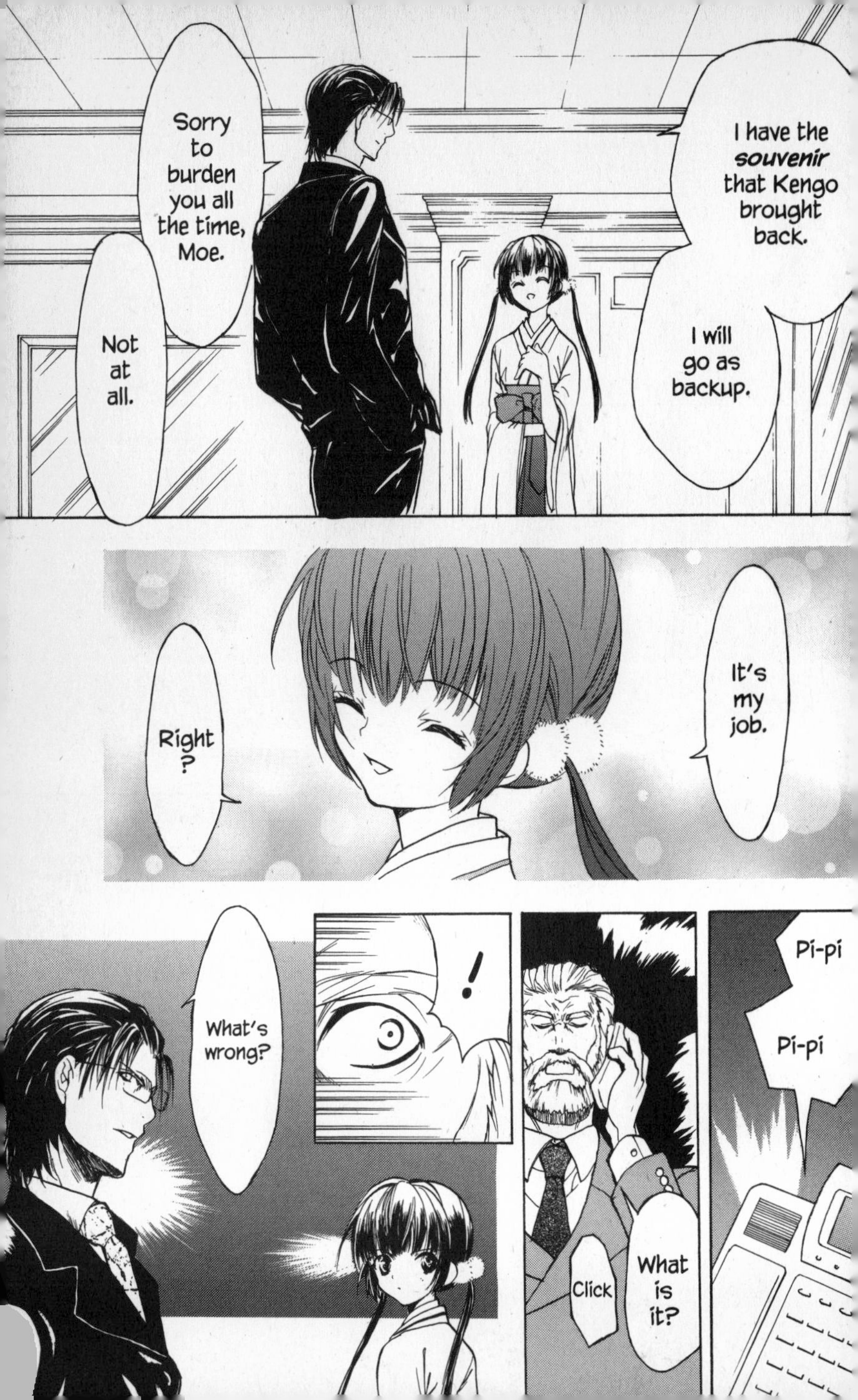
I have the *souvenir* that Kengo brought back.
I will go as backup.
Sorry to burden you all the time, Moe.
Not at all.
It's my job.
Right?
Pi-pi
Pi-pi
What is it?
Click
!
What's wrong?

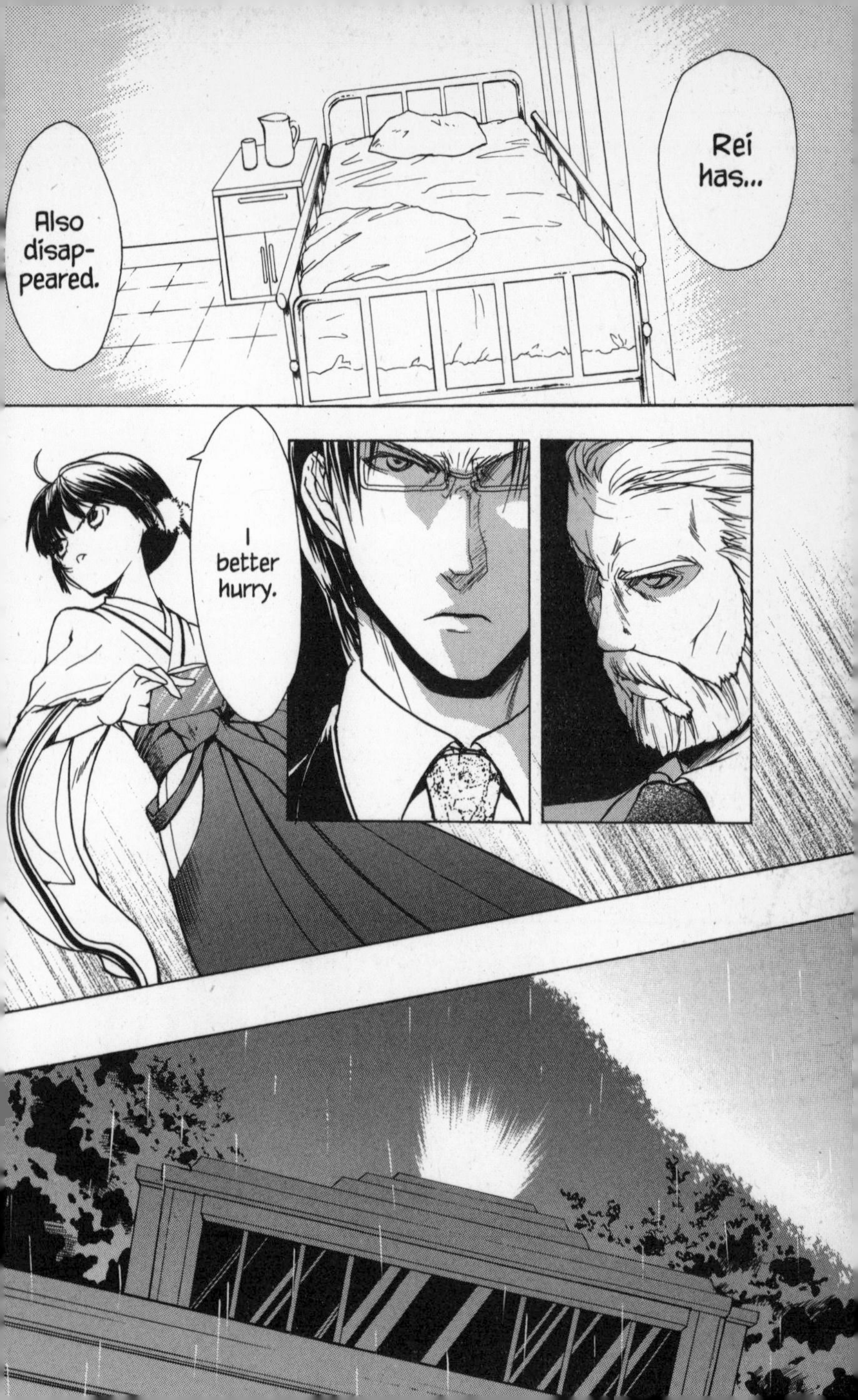
Rei has...
Also disappeared.
I better hurry.

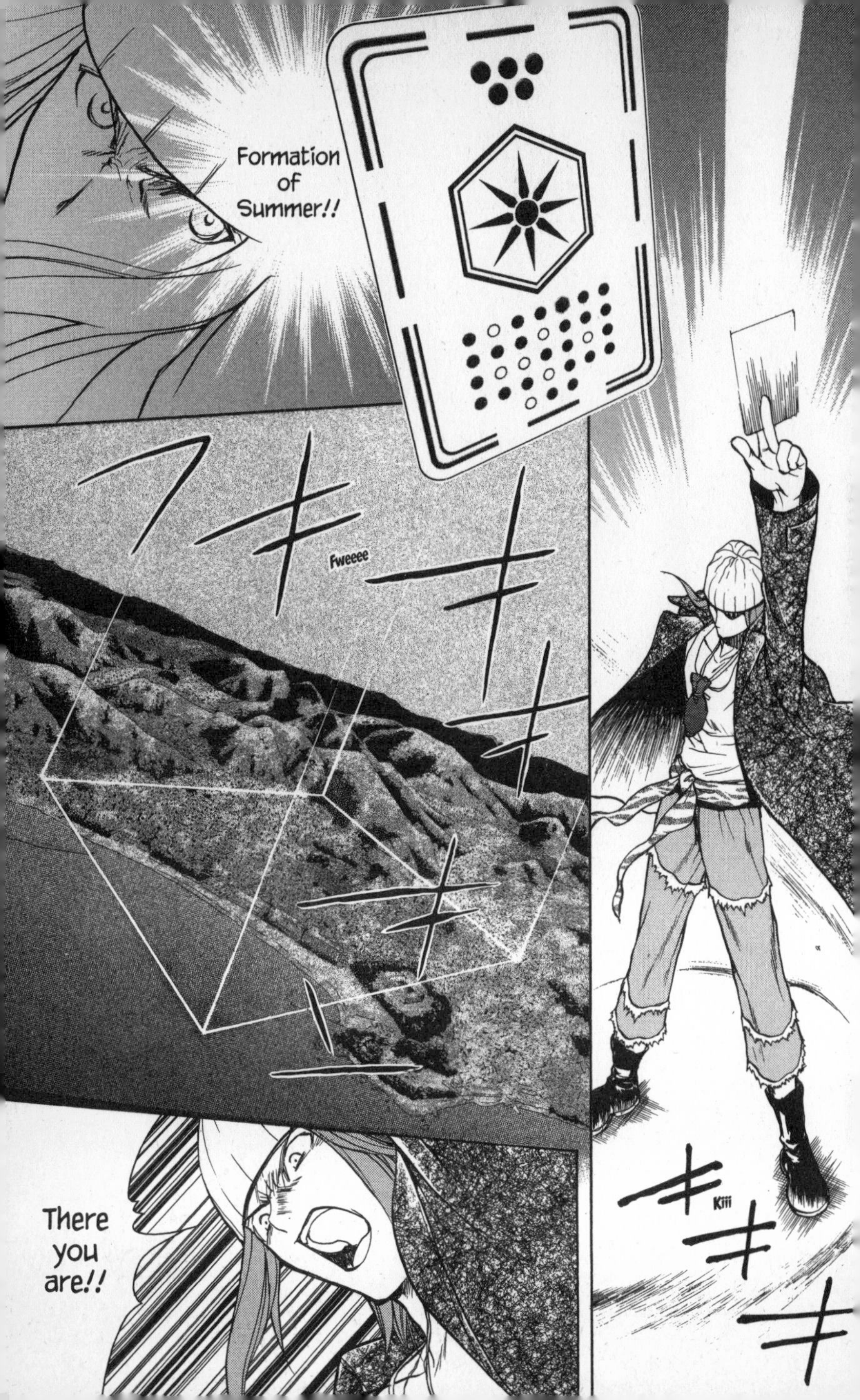
Formation of Summer!!
Kiii
Fweeee
There you are!!

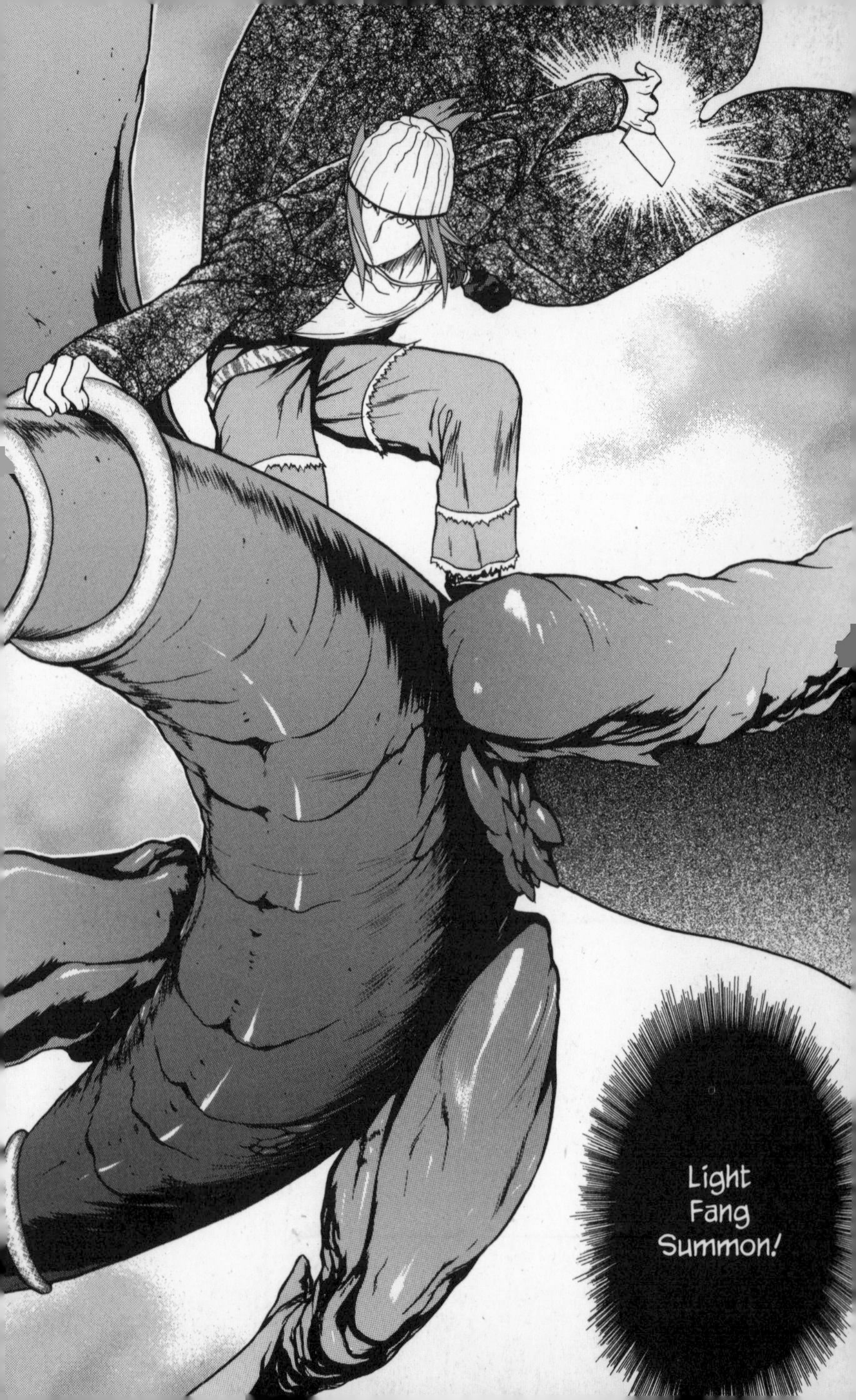
Light Fang Summon!

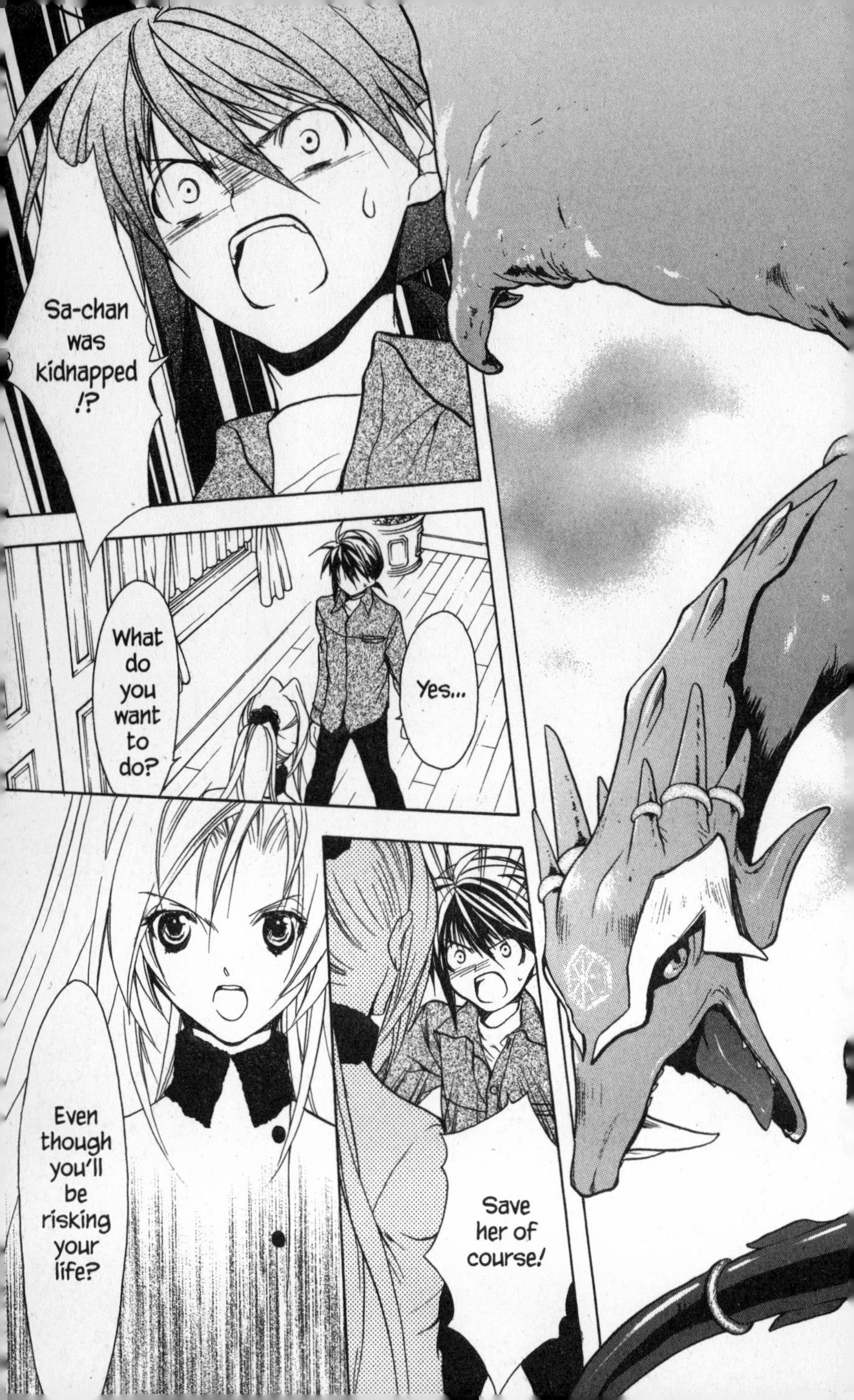
Sa-chan was kidnapped!?
Yes...
What do you want to do?
Save her of course!
Even though you'll be risking your life?

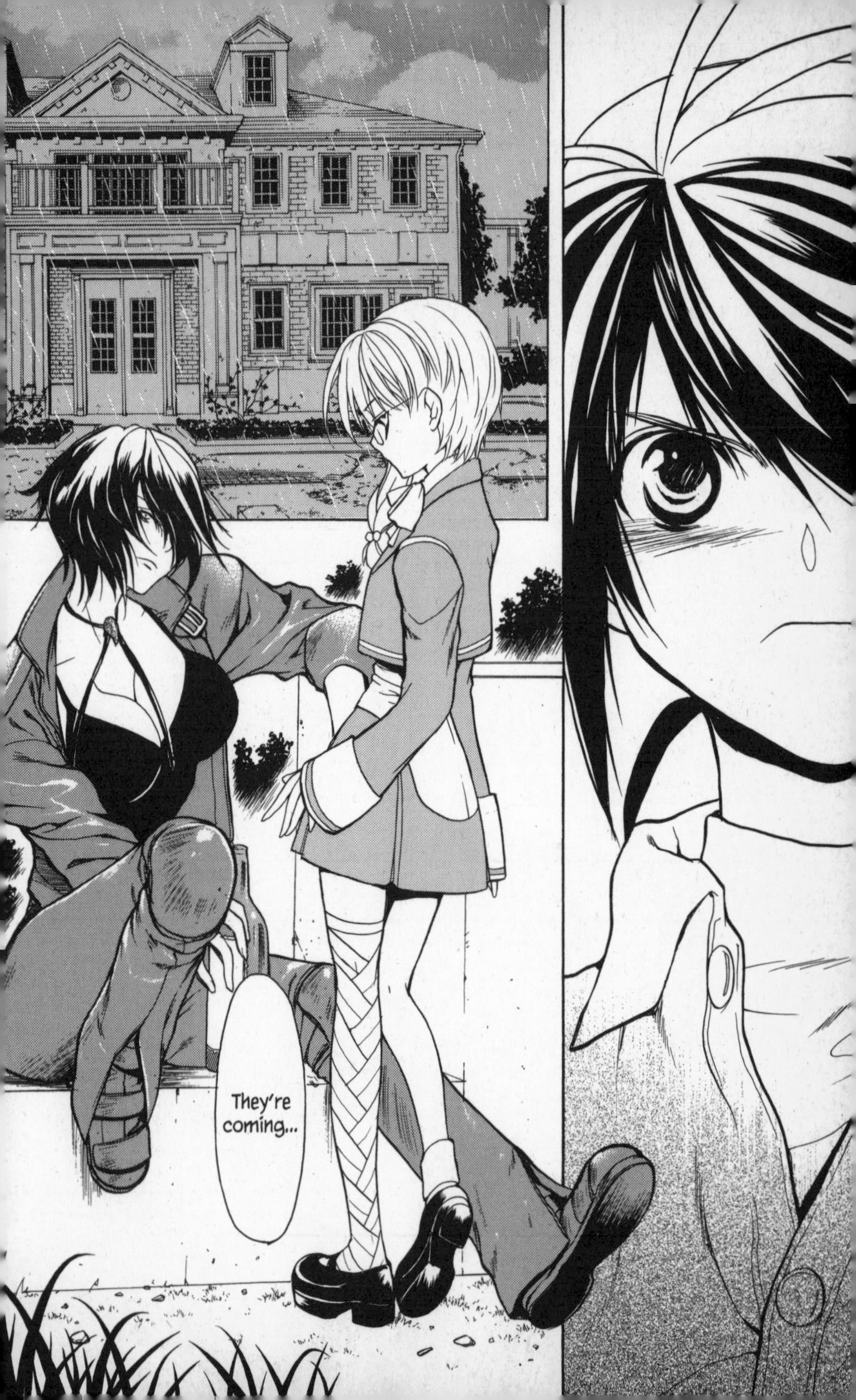
They're coming...

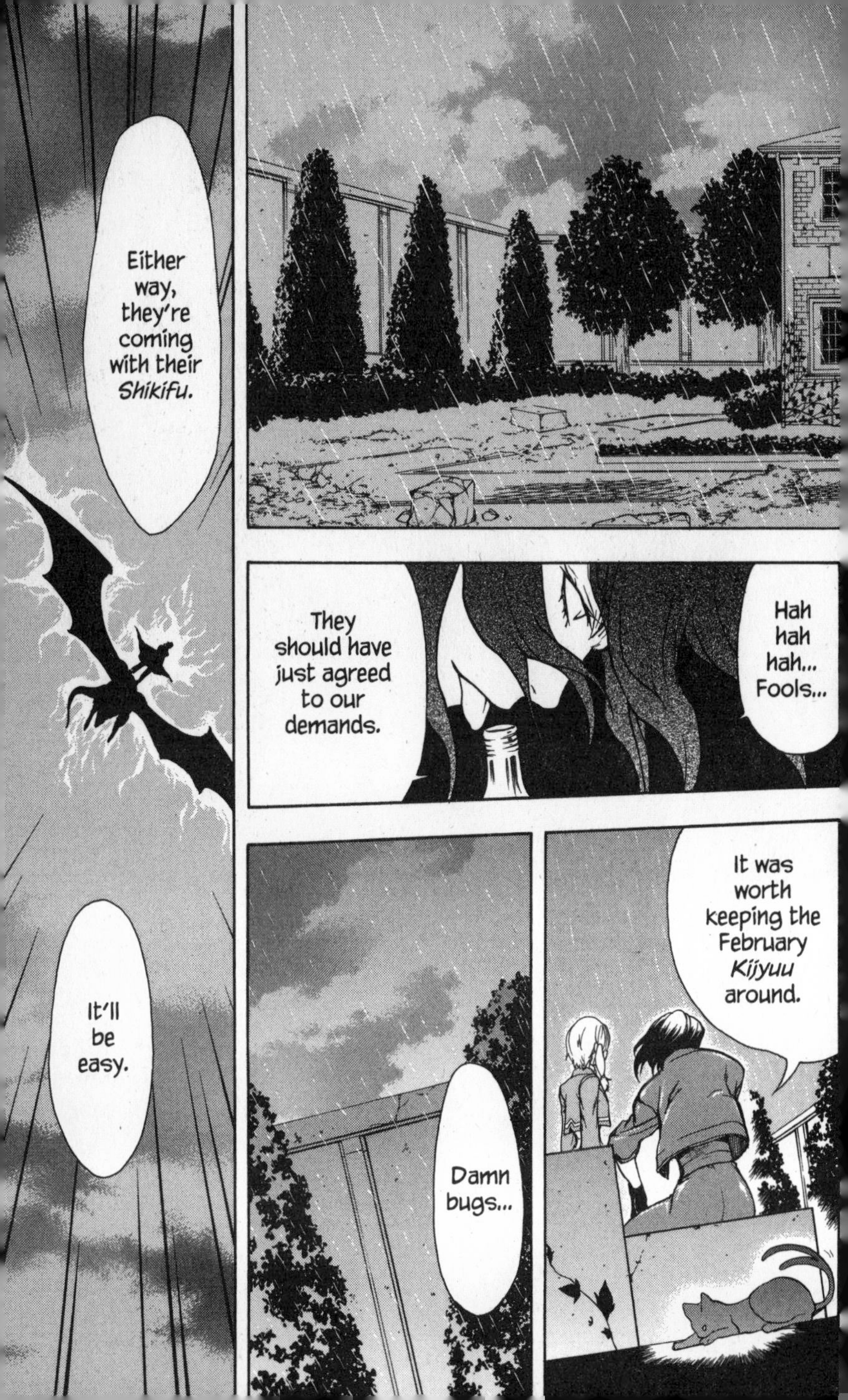
Hah hah hah... Fools...
They should have just agreed to our demands.
It was worth keeping the February Kijyuu around.
Damn bugs...
Either way, they're coming with their Shikifu.
It'll be easy.

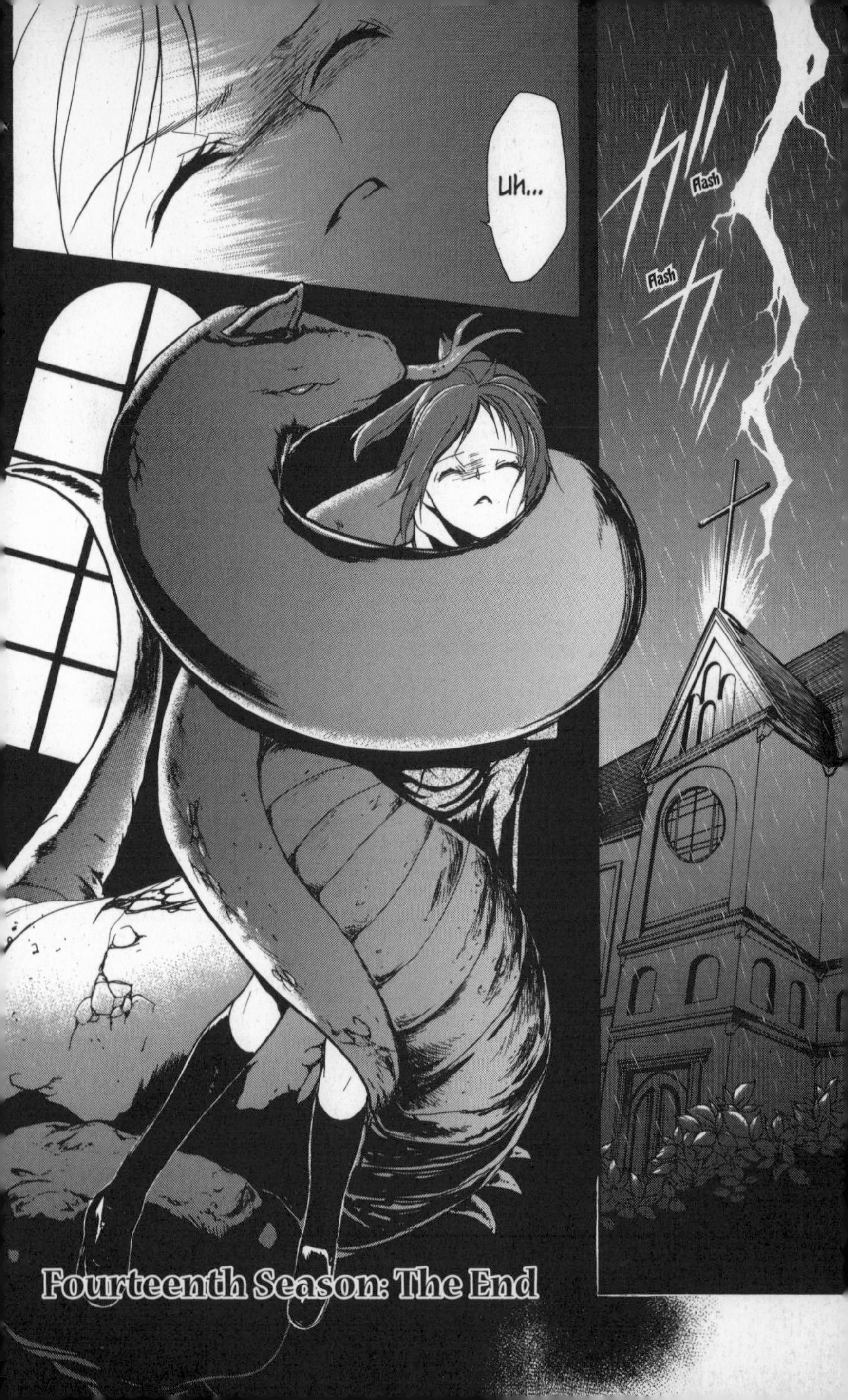
Flash
Flash
Uh...
Fourteenth Season: The End

Fifteenth Season

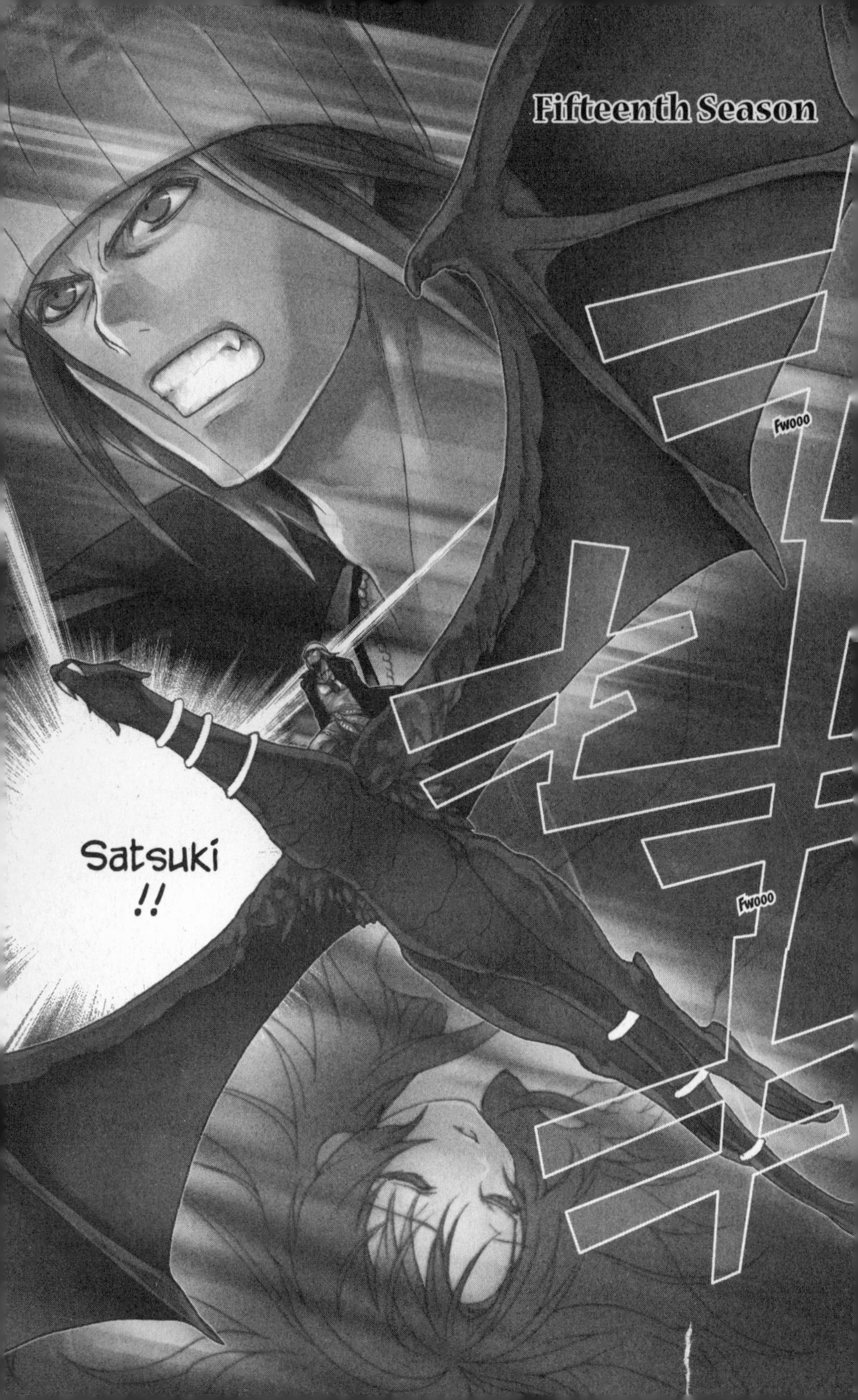
Fwooo
Fwooo
Satsuki !!

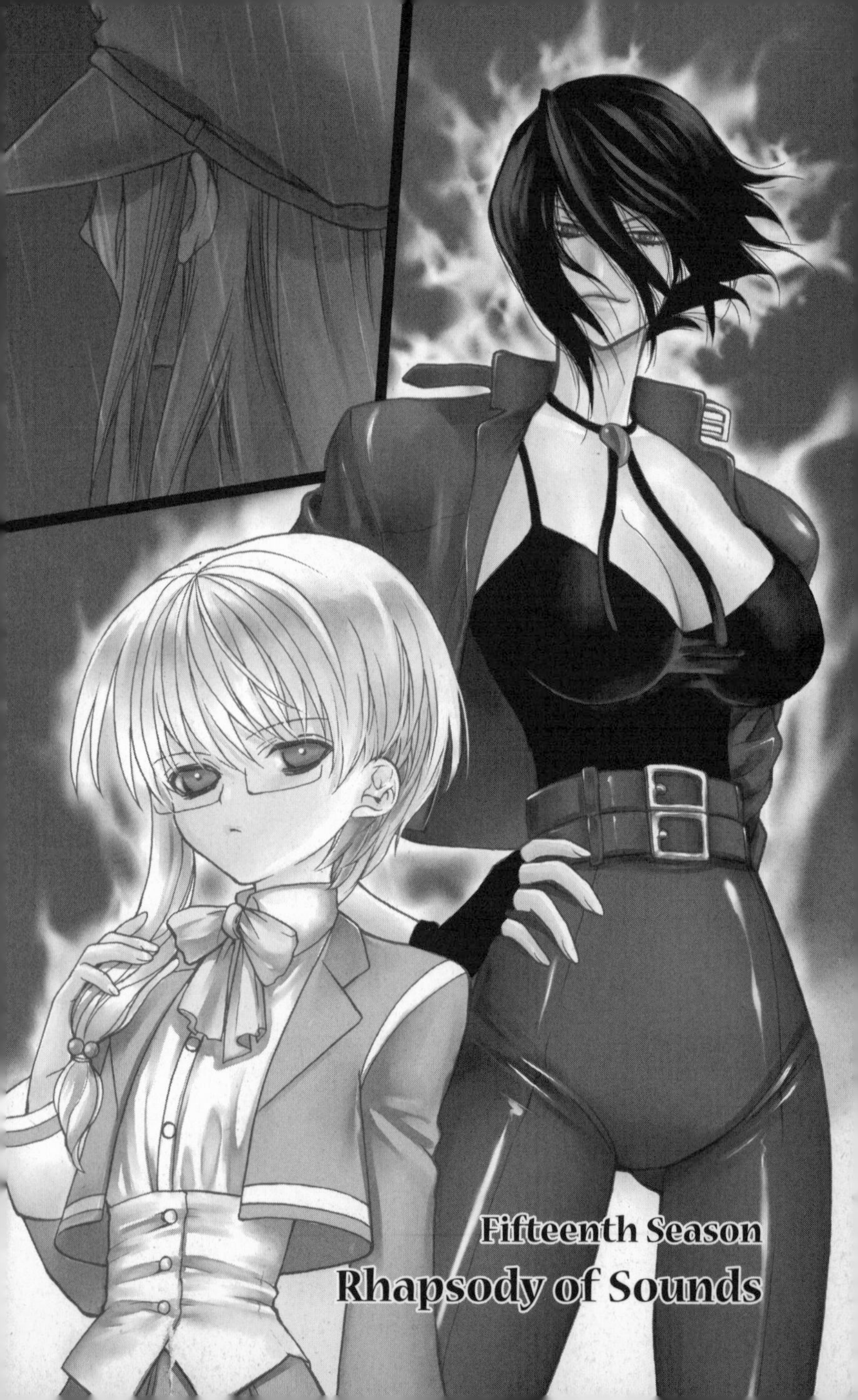
Fifteenth Season
Rhapsody of Sounds

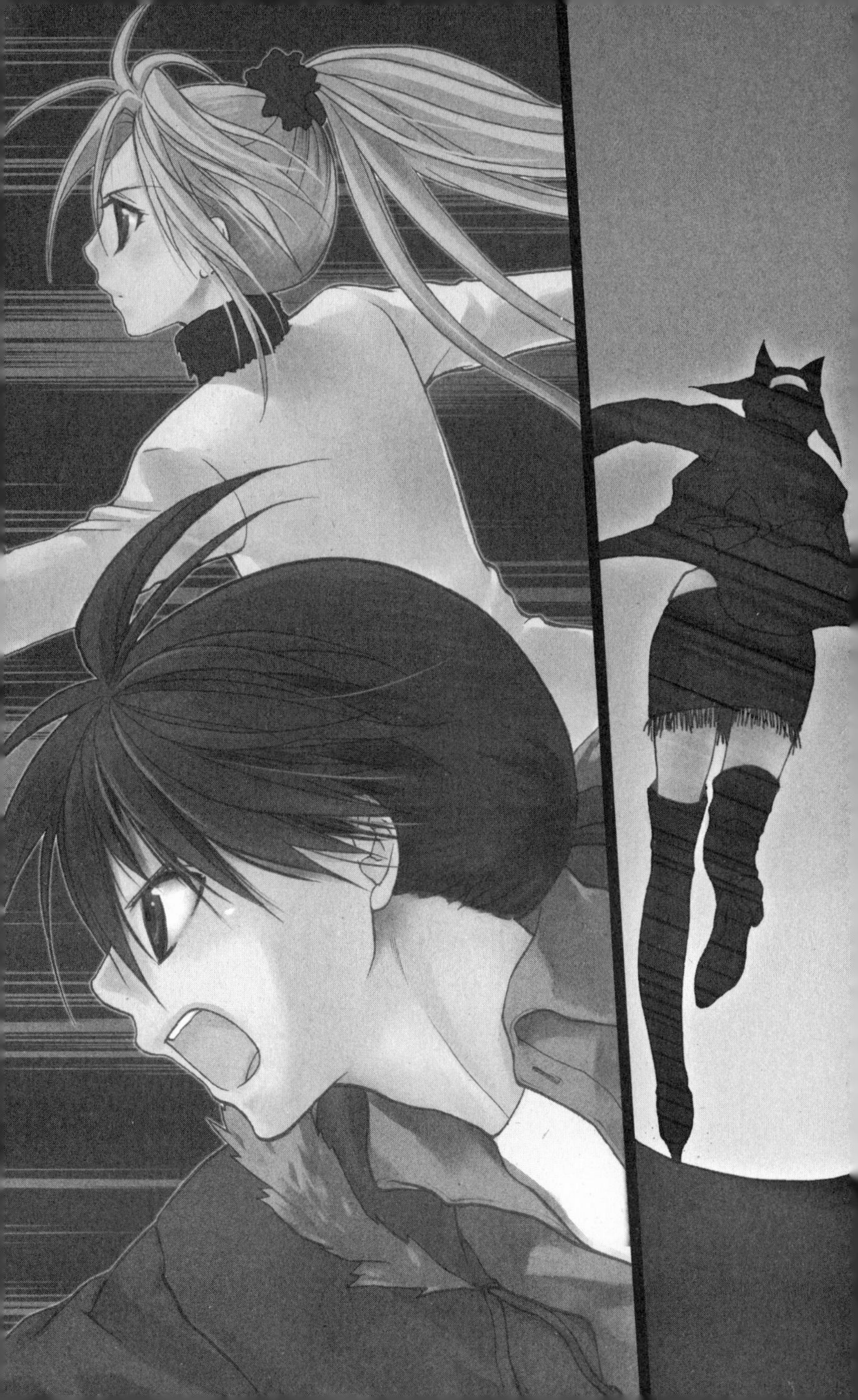

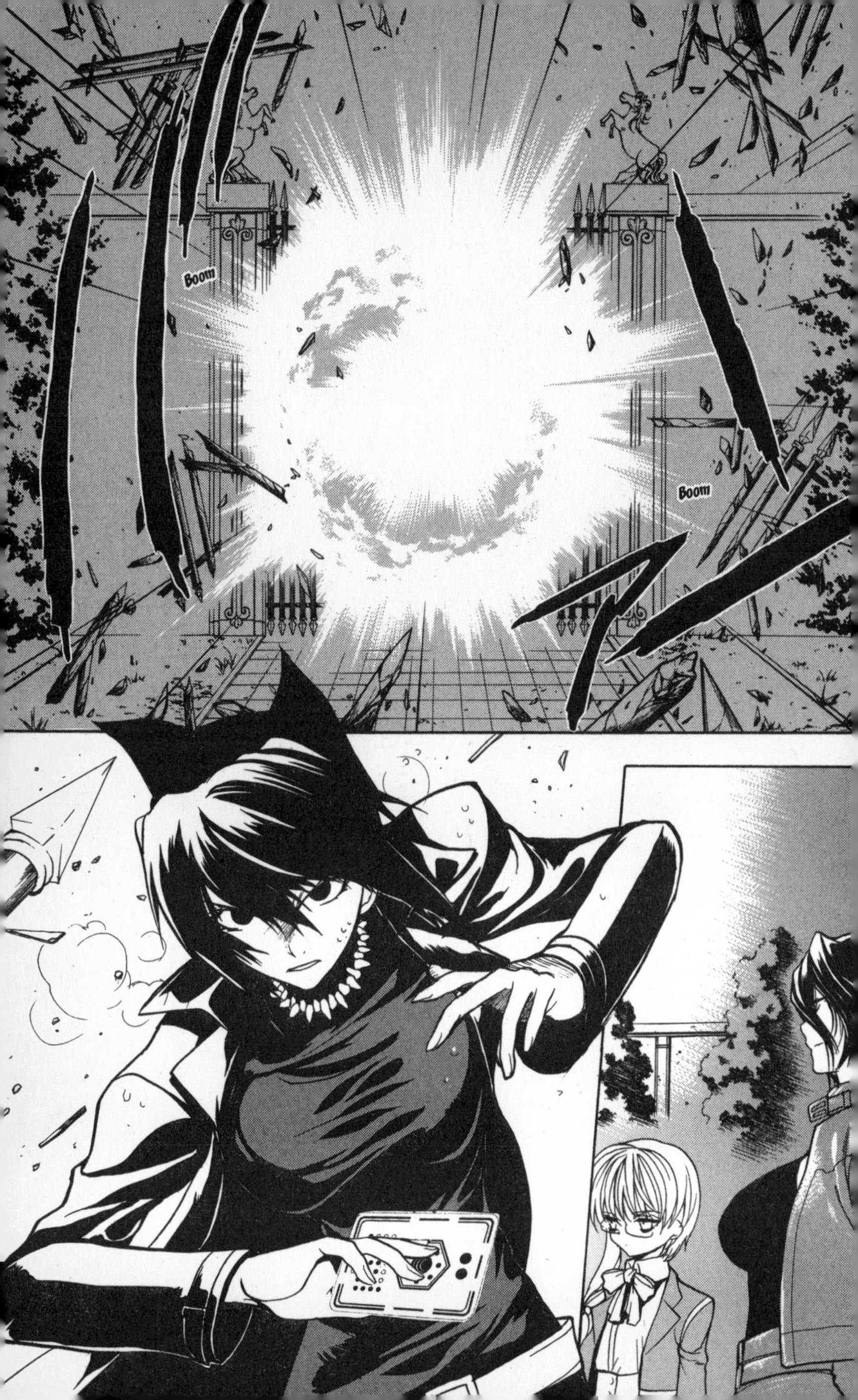
Boom
Boom

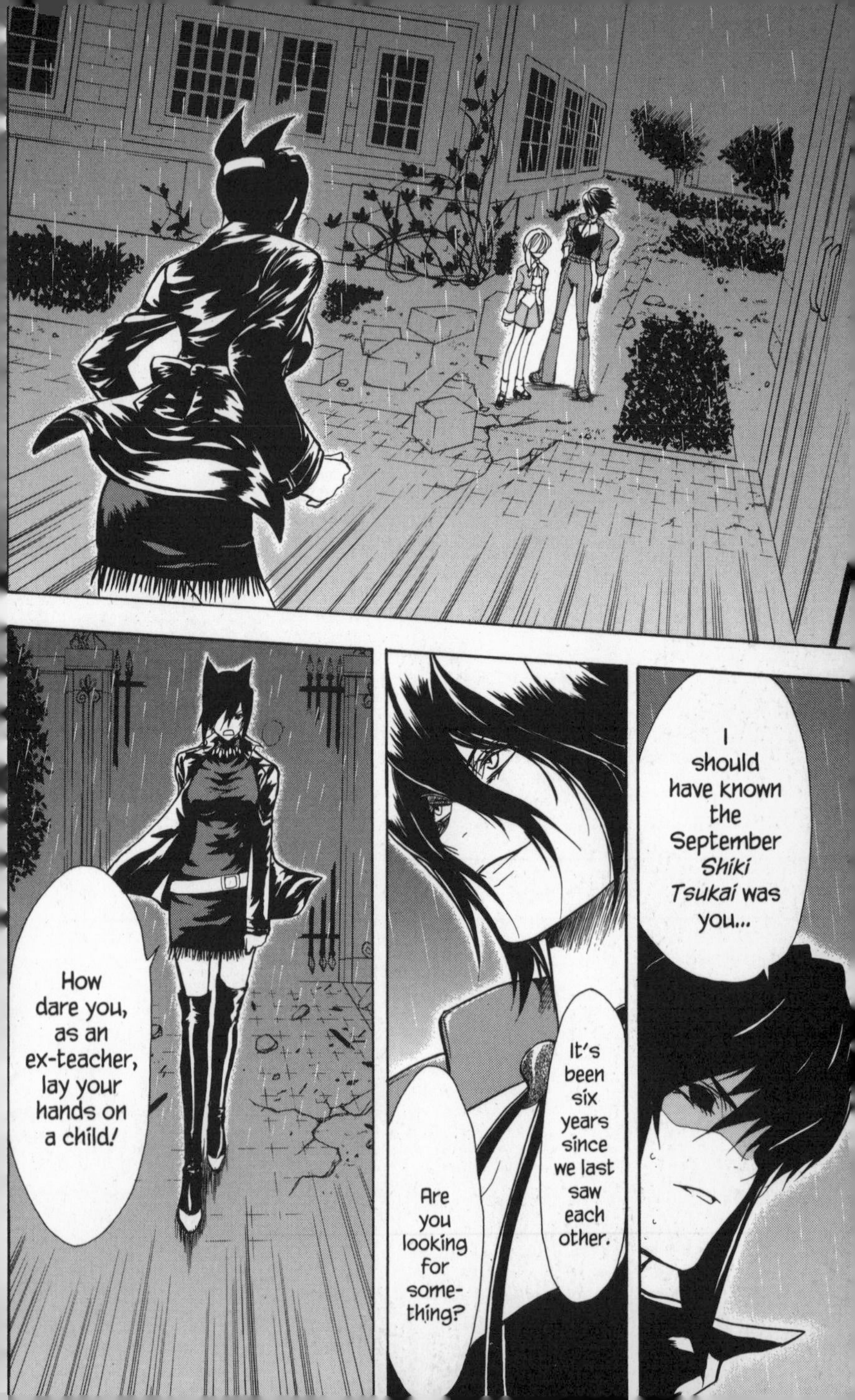
I should have known the September *Shiki Tsukai* was you...
It's been six years since we last saw each other.
Are you looking for something?
How dare you, as an ex-teacher, lay your hands on a child!

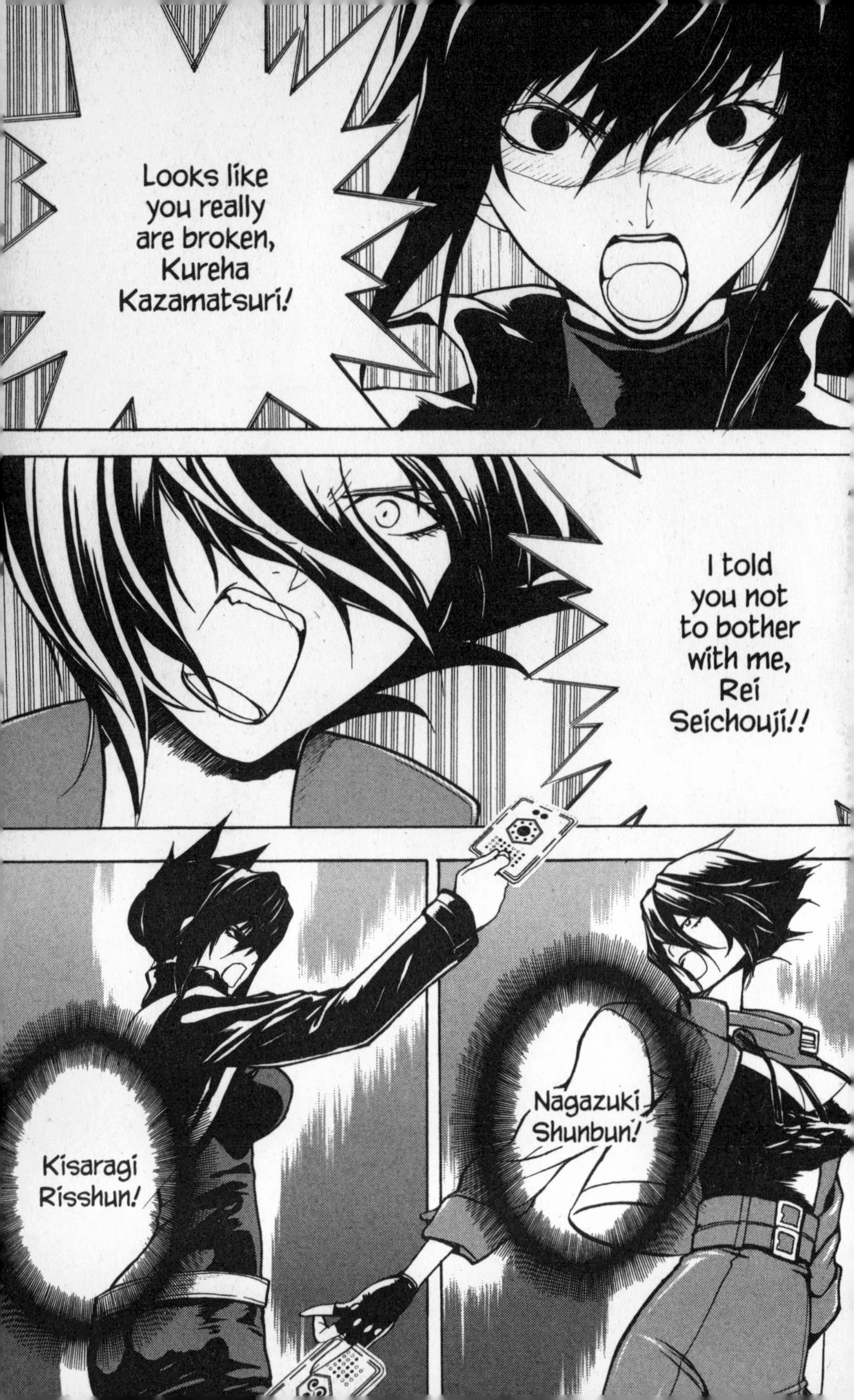
Looks like you really are broken, Kureha Kazamatsuri!
I told you not to bother with me, Rei Seichouji!!
Nagazuki Shunbun!
Kisaragi Risshun!

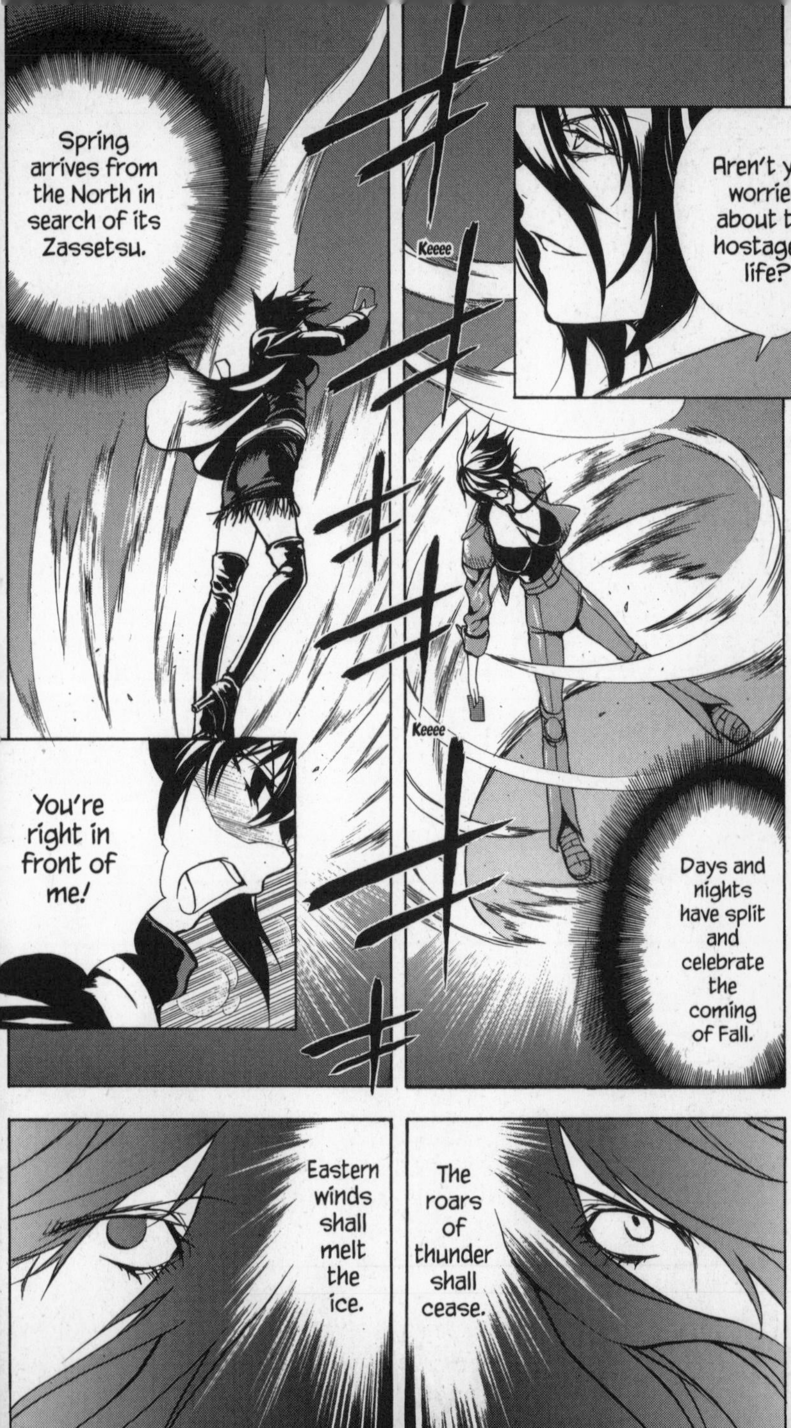
Aren't you worried about the hostage's life?
Keeee
Spring arrives from the North in search of its Zassetsu.
Keeee
Days and nights have split and celebrate the coming of Fall.
You're right in front of me!
The roars of thunder shall cease.
Eastern winds shall melt the ice.

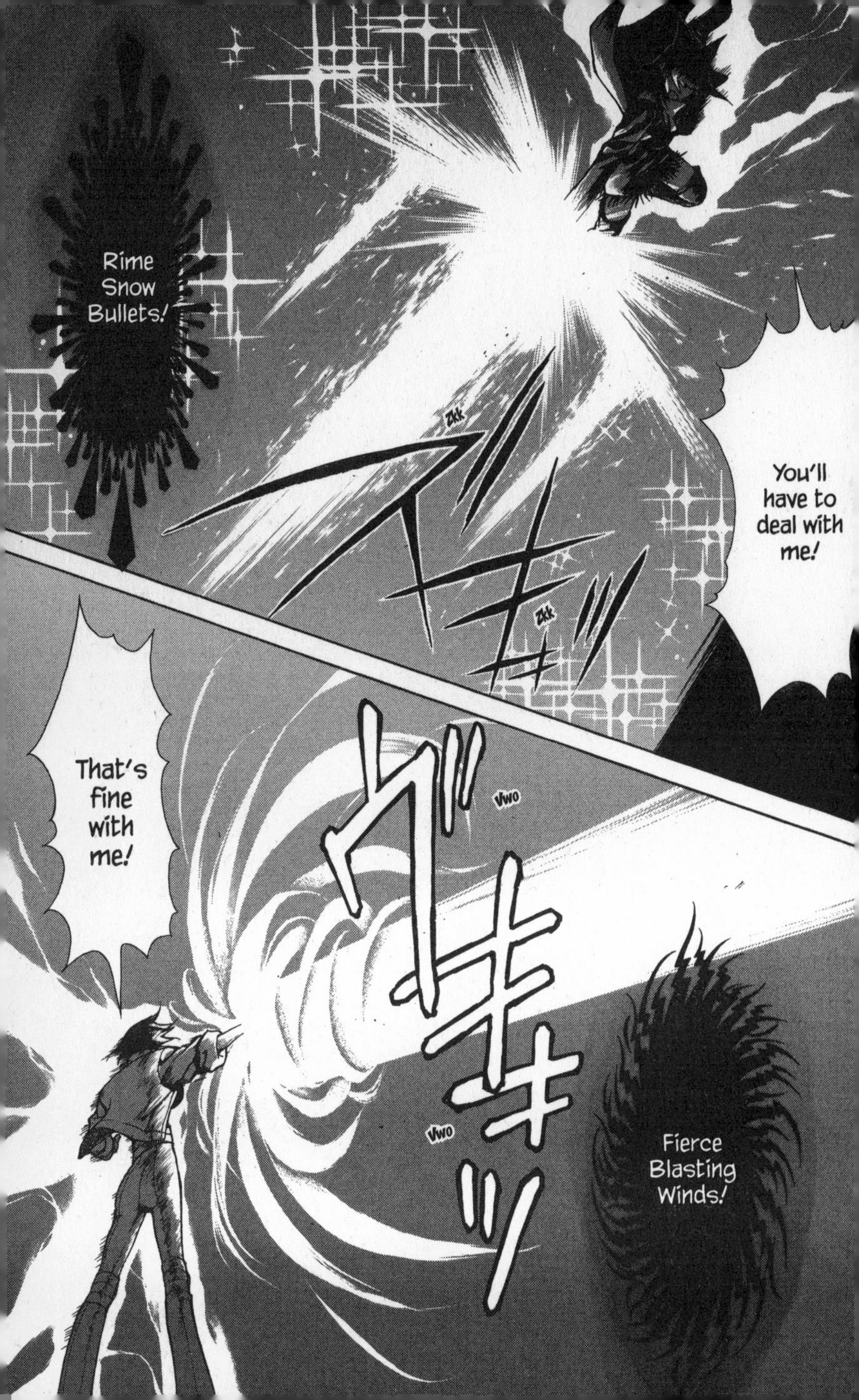
Rime Snow Bullets!
Zkk
Zkk
You'll have to deal with me!
Vwo
That's fine with me!
Vwo
Fierce Blasting Winds!

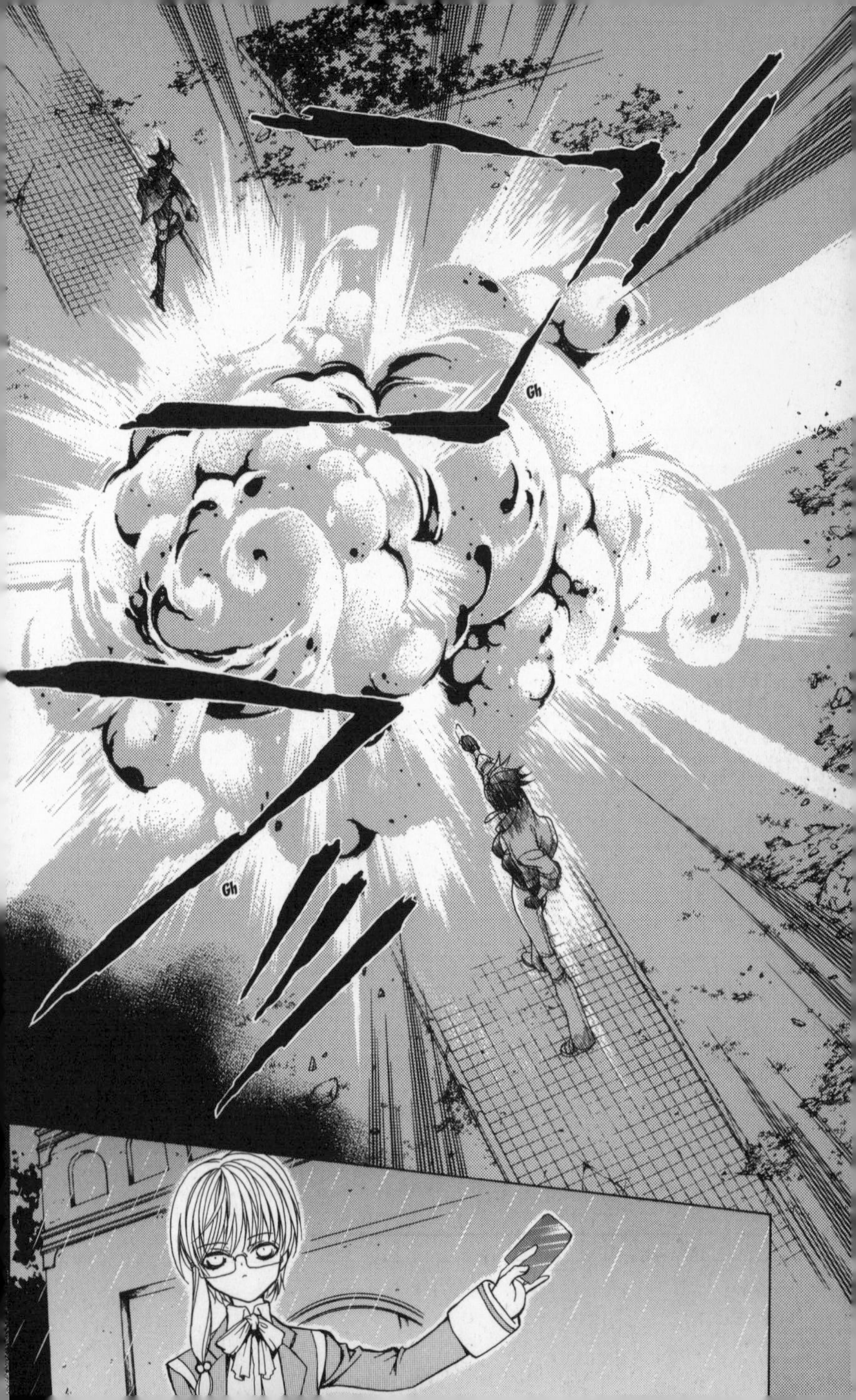
Gh
Gh

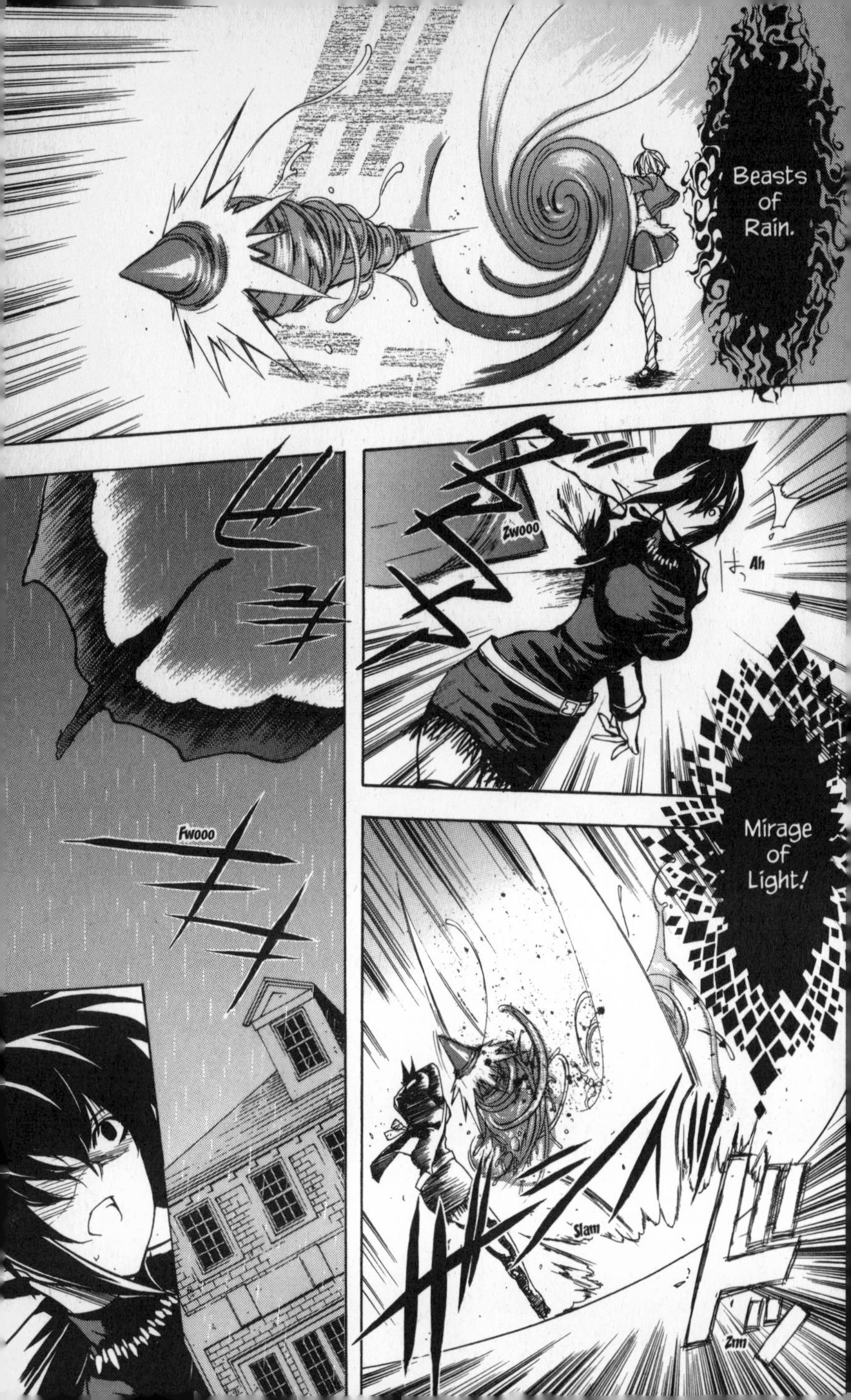
Beasts of Rain.
Zwooo
Ah
Mirage of Light!
Slam
Zm
Fwooo

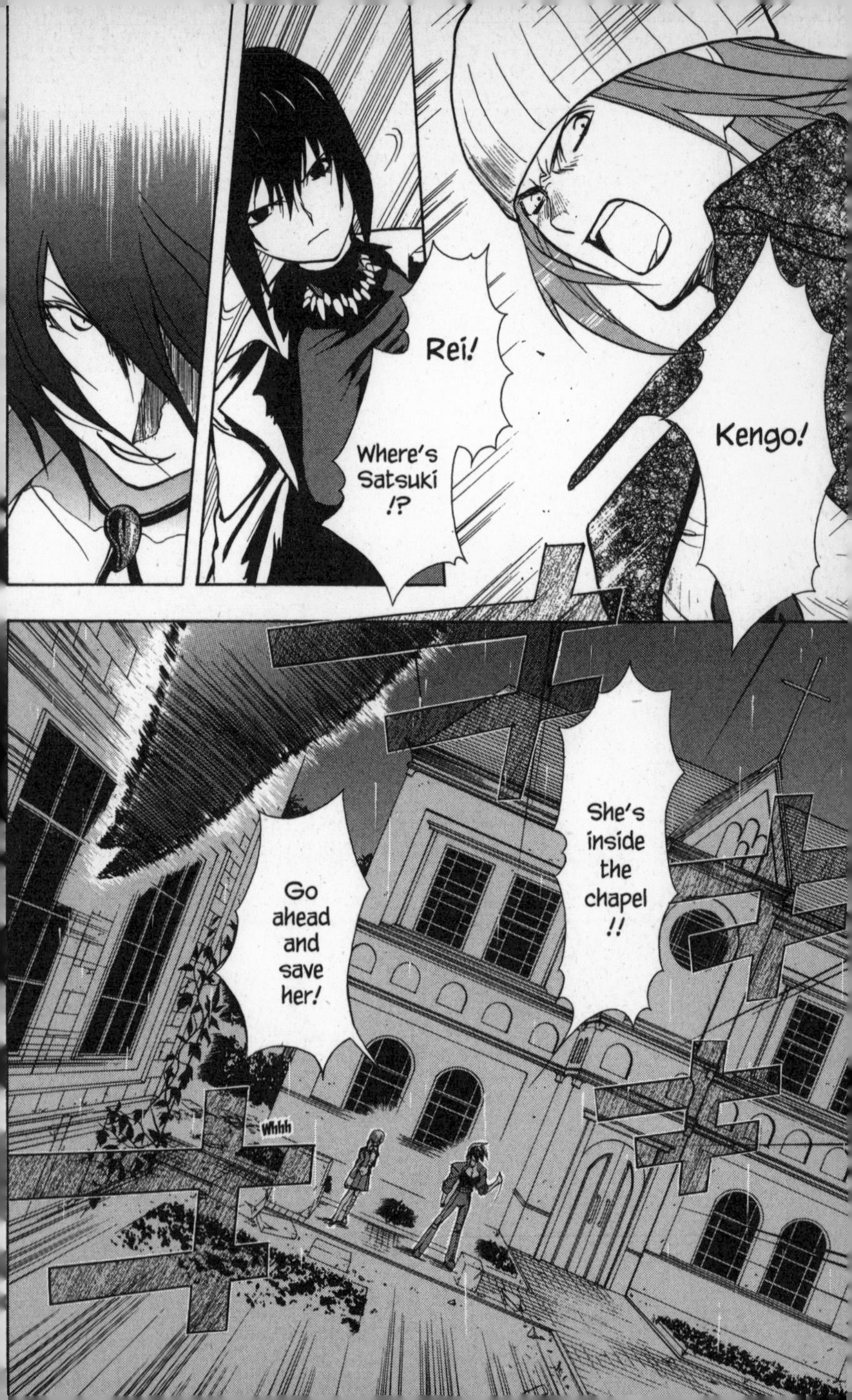
Kengo!
Rei!
Where's Satsuki !?
She's inside the chapel !!
Go ahead and save her!
Whhh

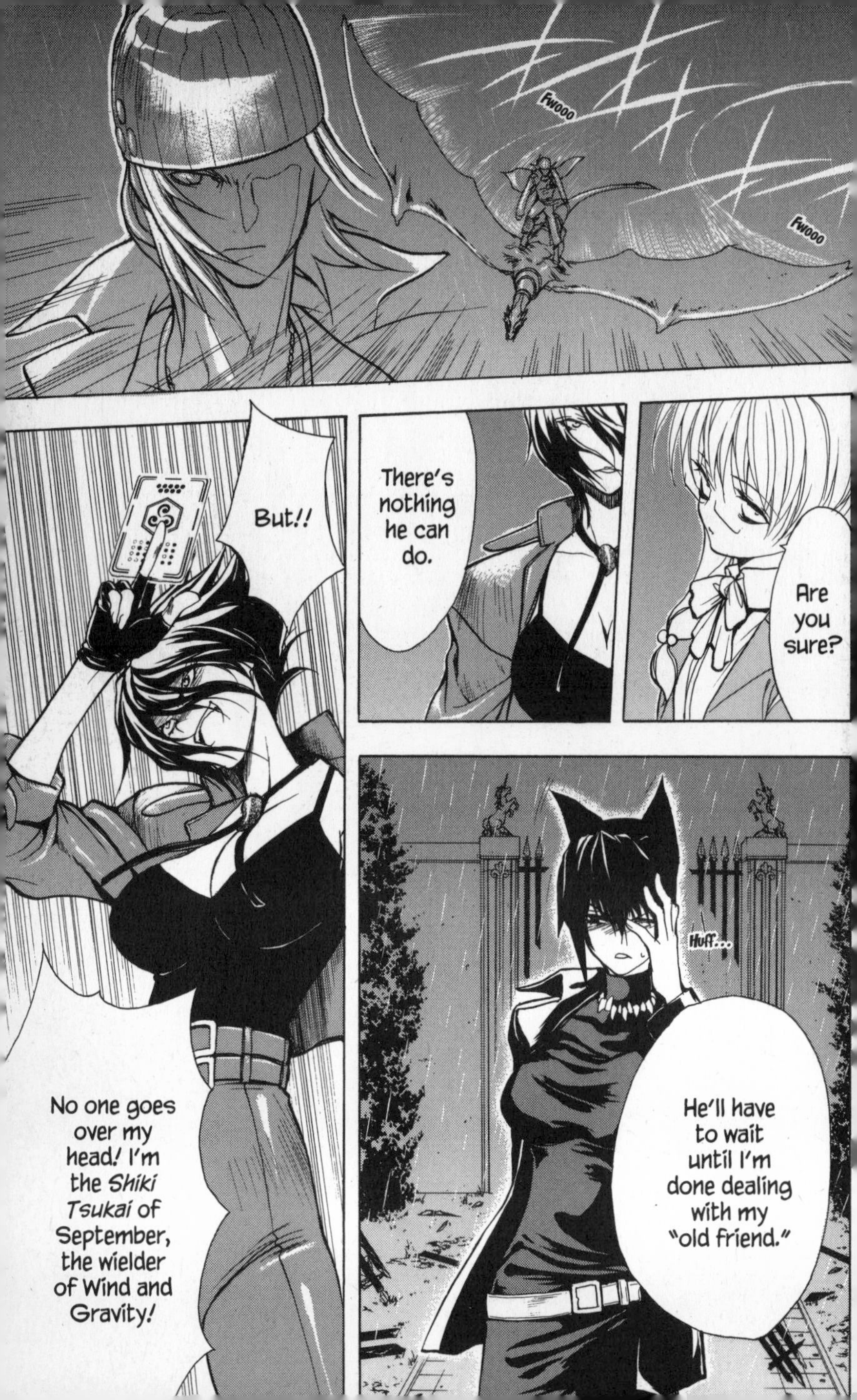

Fwooo
Fwooo
Are you sure?
There's nothing he can do.
Huff...
He'll have to wait until I'm done dealing with my "old friend."
But!!
No one goes over my head! I'm the *Shiki Tsukai* of September, the wielder of Wind and Gravity!

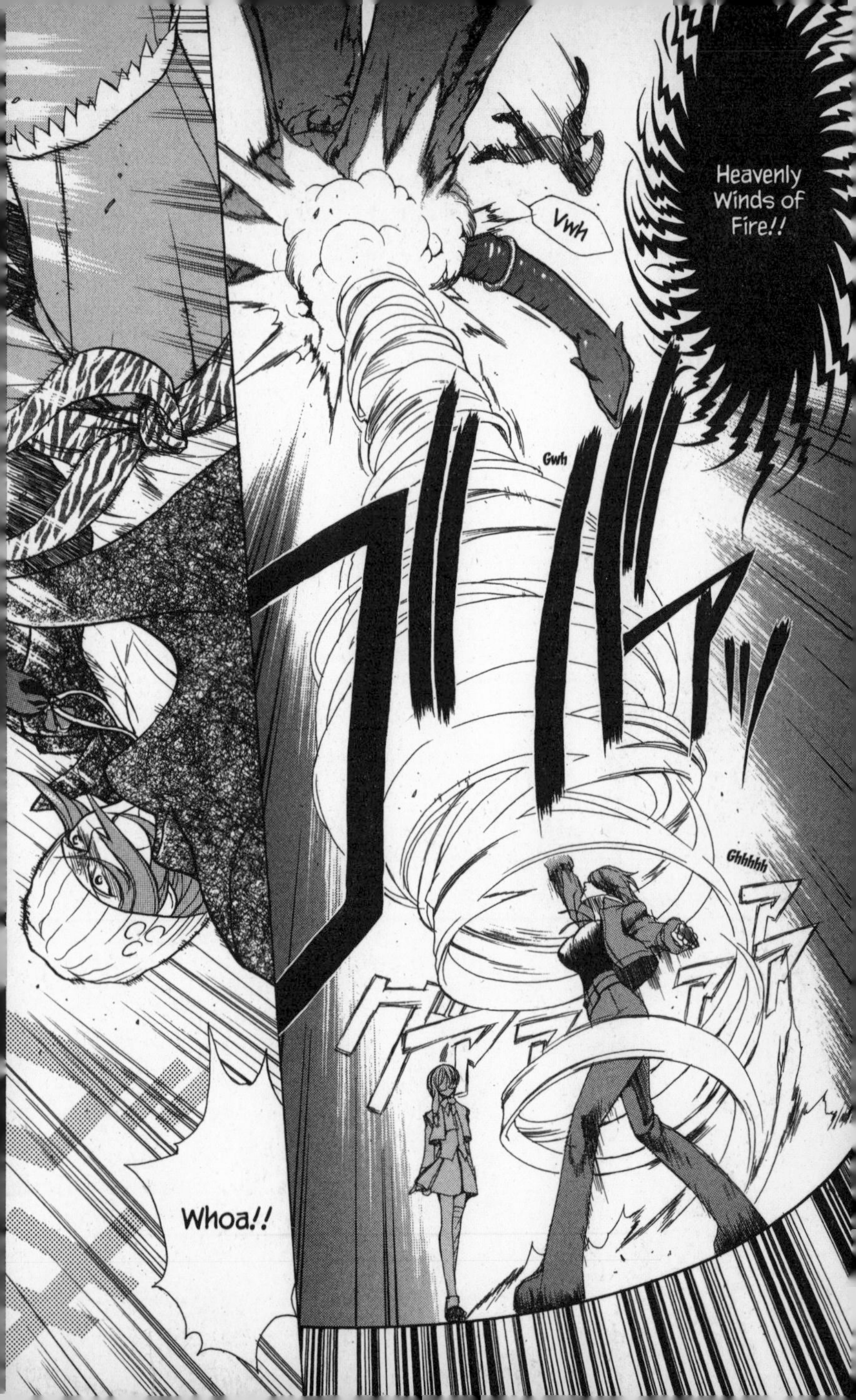
Heavenly Winds of Fire!!
Vwh
Gwh
Ghhhhh
Whoa!!

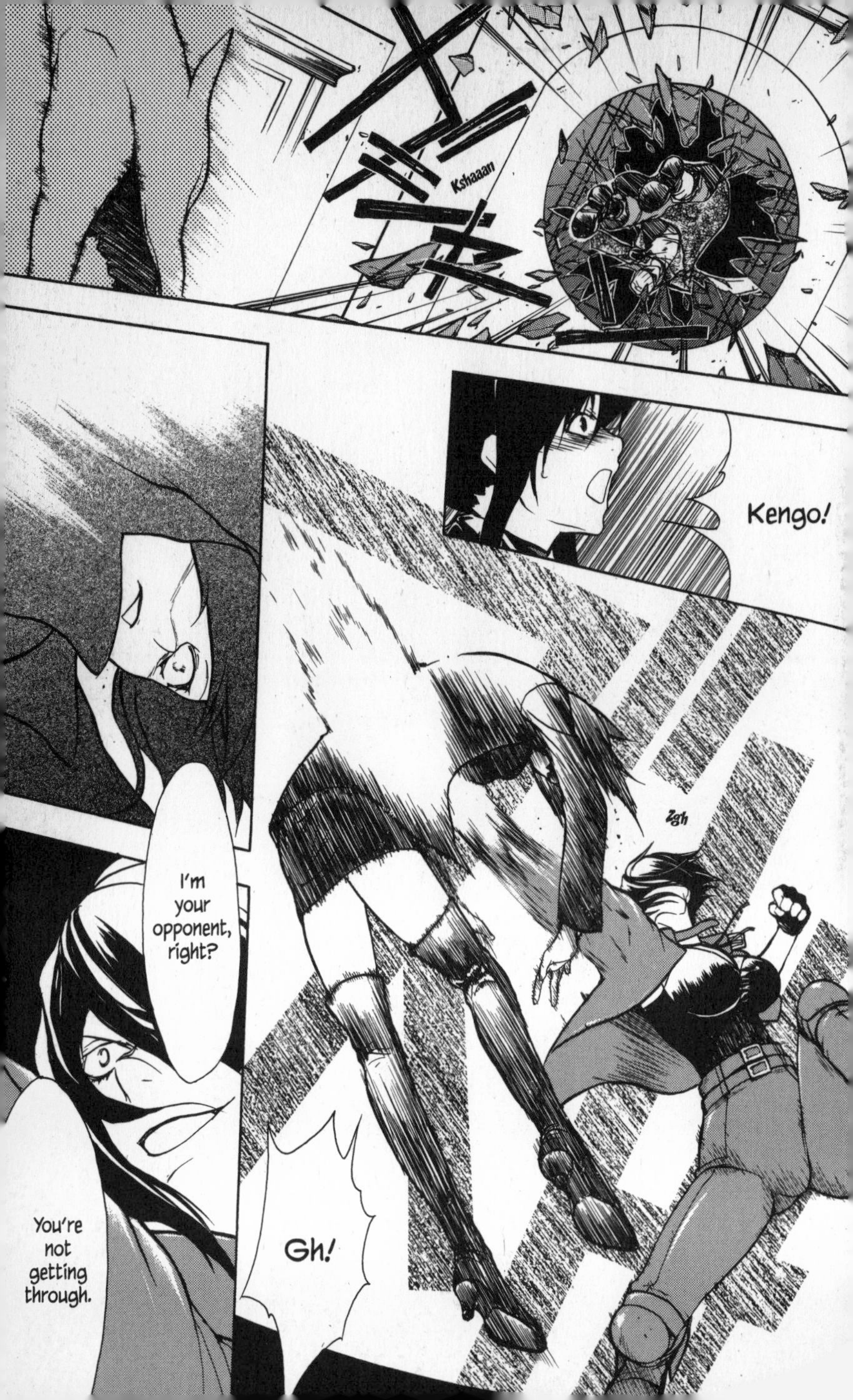
Kshaaan
Kengo!
Zgh
Gh!
I'm your opponent, right?
You're not getting through.

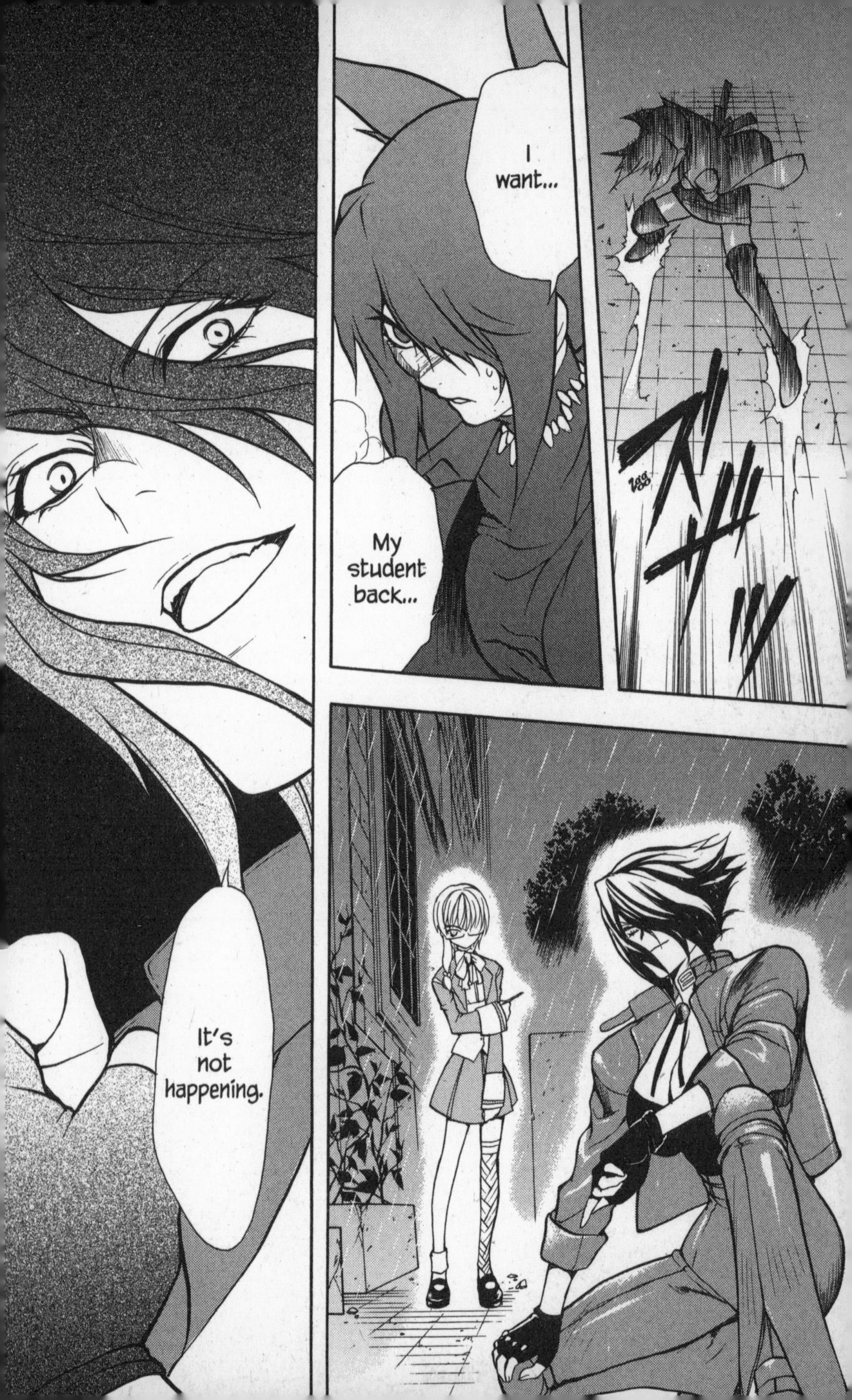
I want...
My student back...
It's not happening.

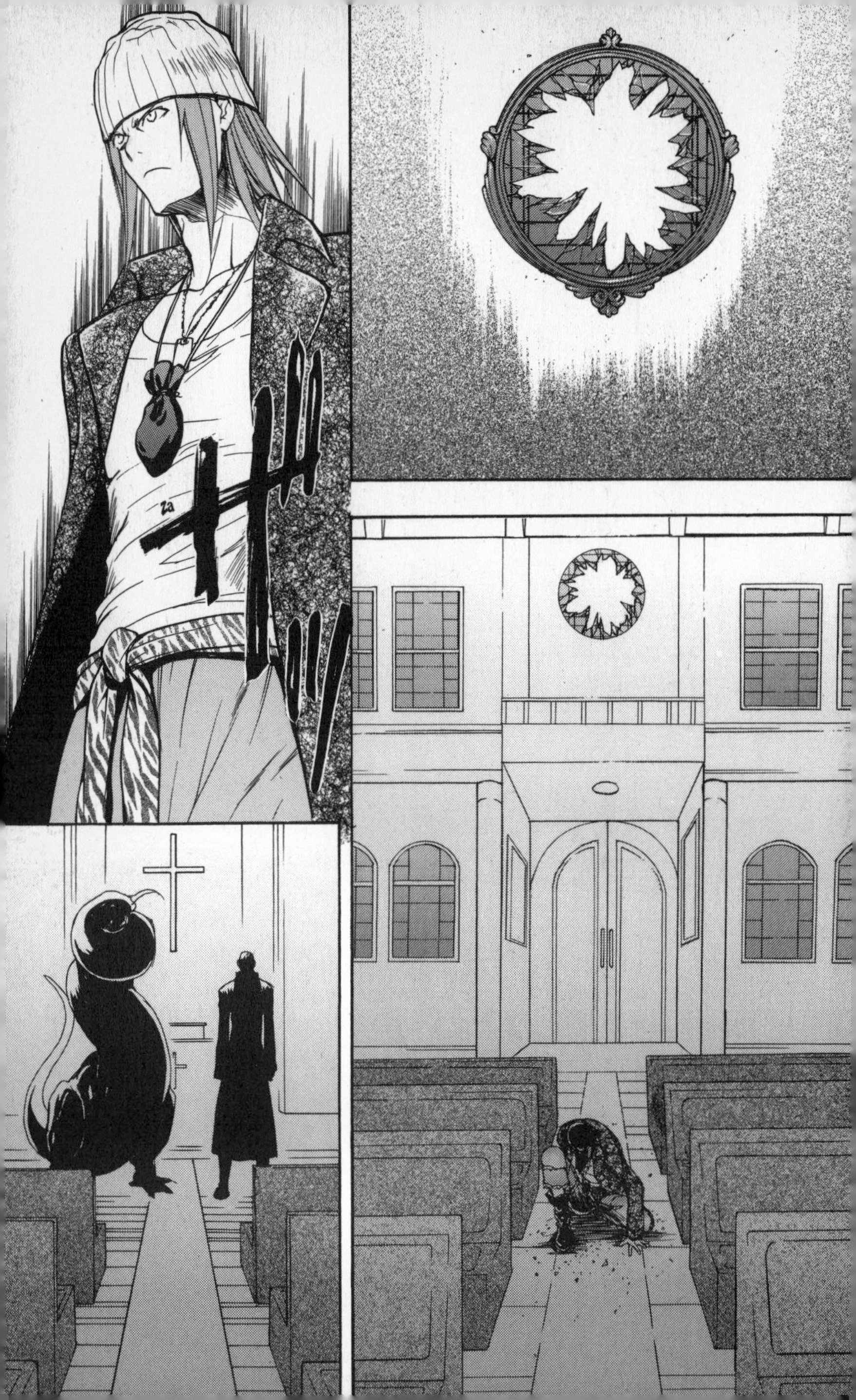
za

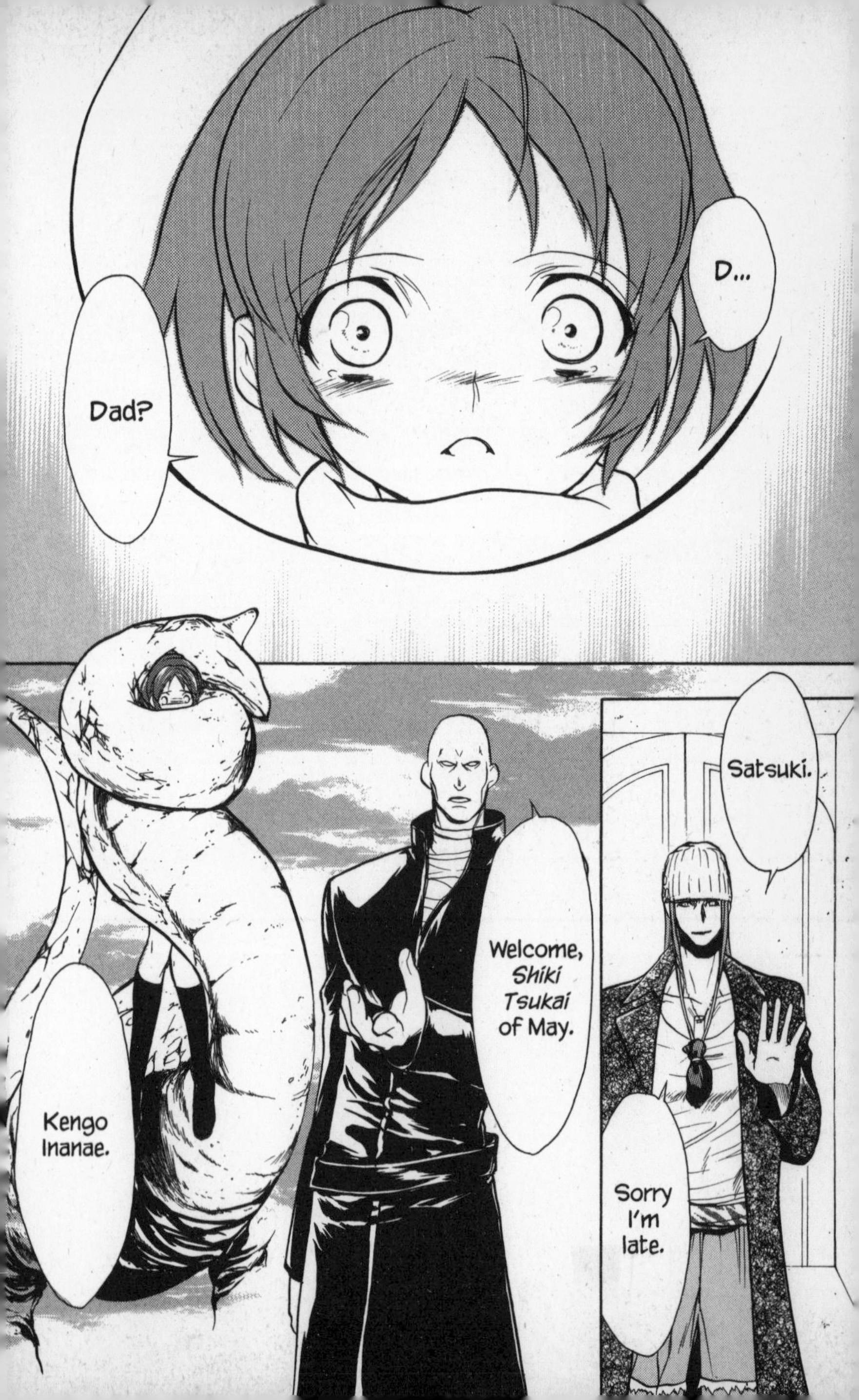
D...
Dad?
Satsuki.
Sorry I'm late.
Welcome, Shiki Tsukai of May.
Kengo Inanae.

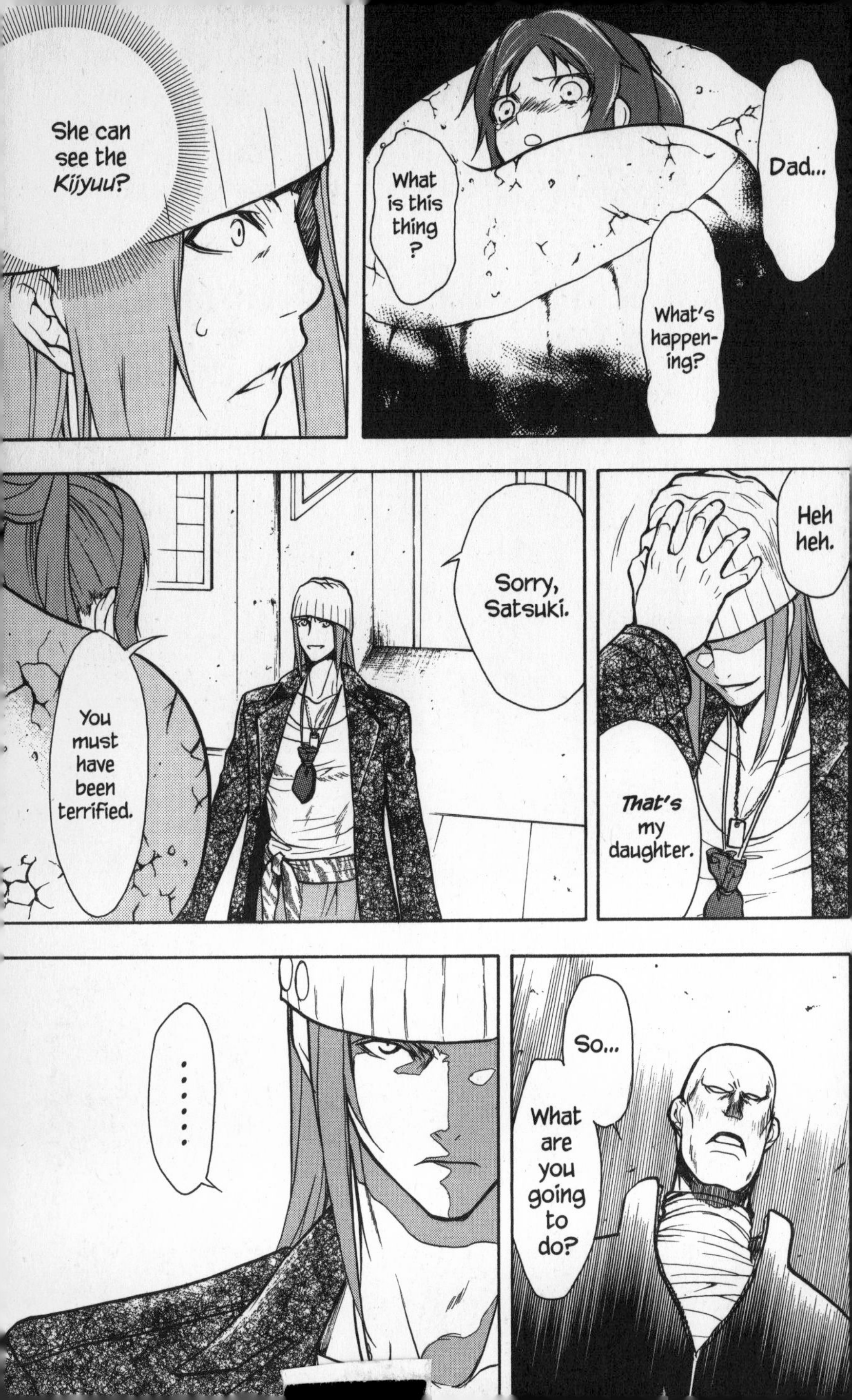
Dad...
What is this thing?
What's happening?
She can see the *Kijyuu*?
Heh heh.
That's my daughter.
Sorry, Satsuki.
You must have been terrified.
So...
What are you going to do?
......

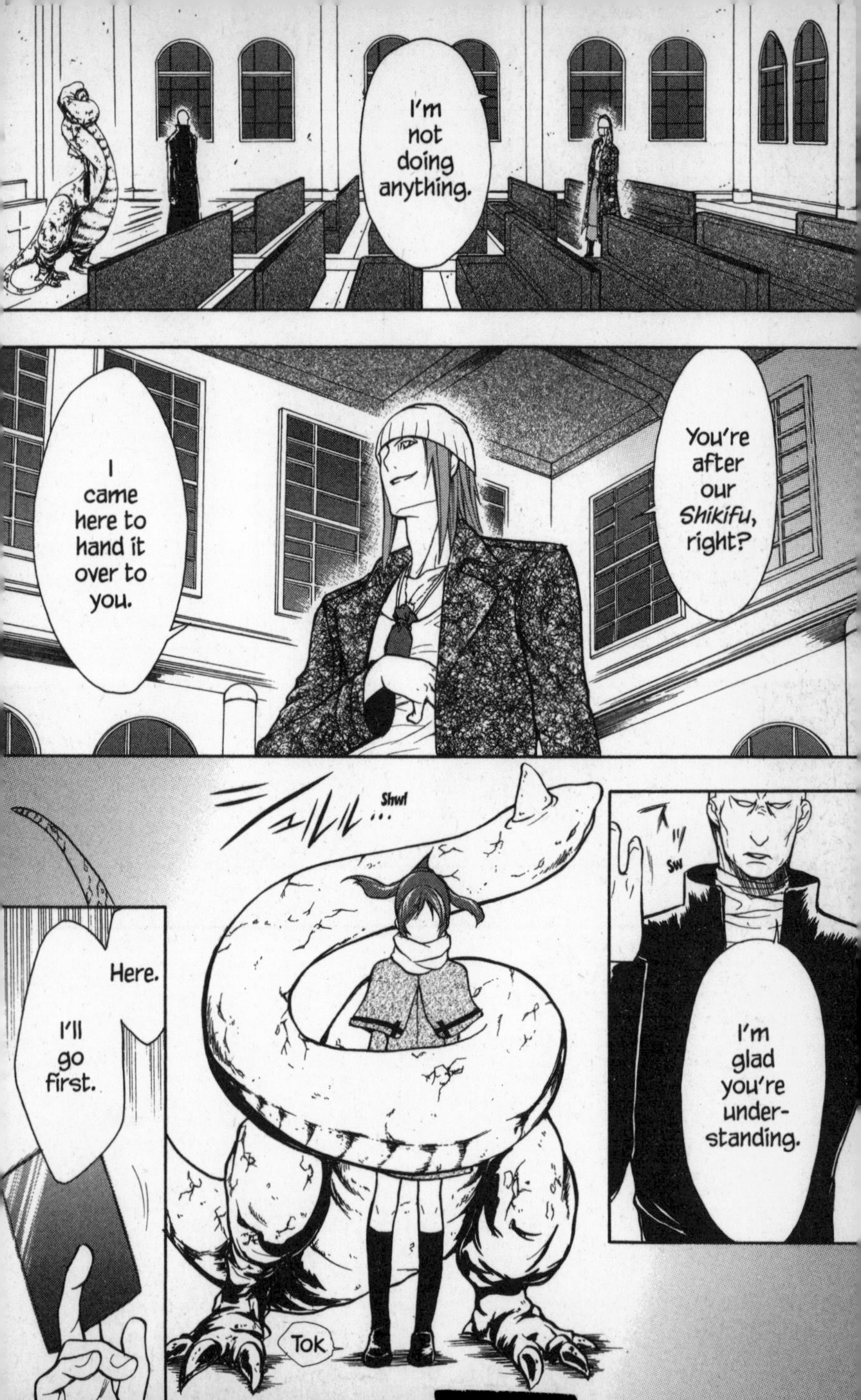
I'm not doing anything.
You're after our *Shikifu*, right?
I came here to hand it over to you.
Sw
I'm glad you're under-standing.
Shwl...
TOK
Here.
I'll go first.

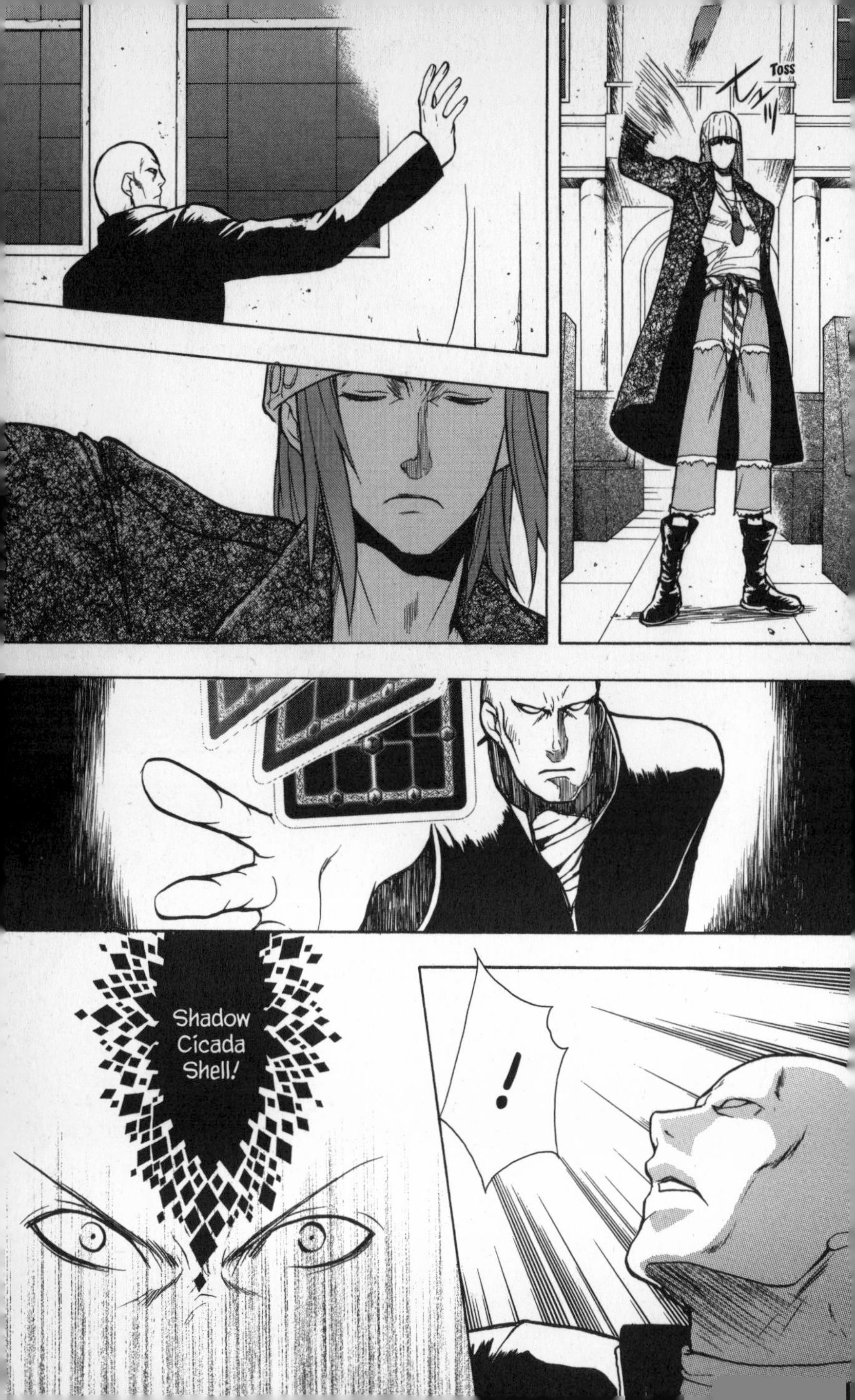
Toss
!
Shadow Cicada Shell!

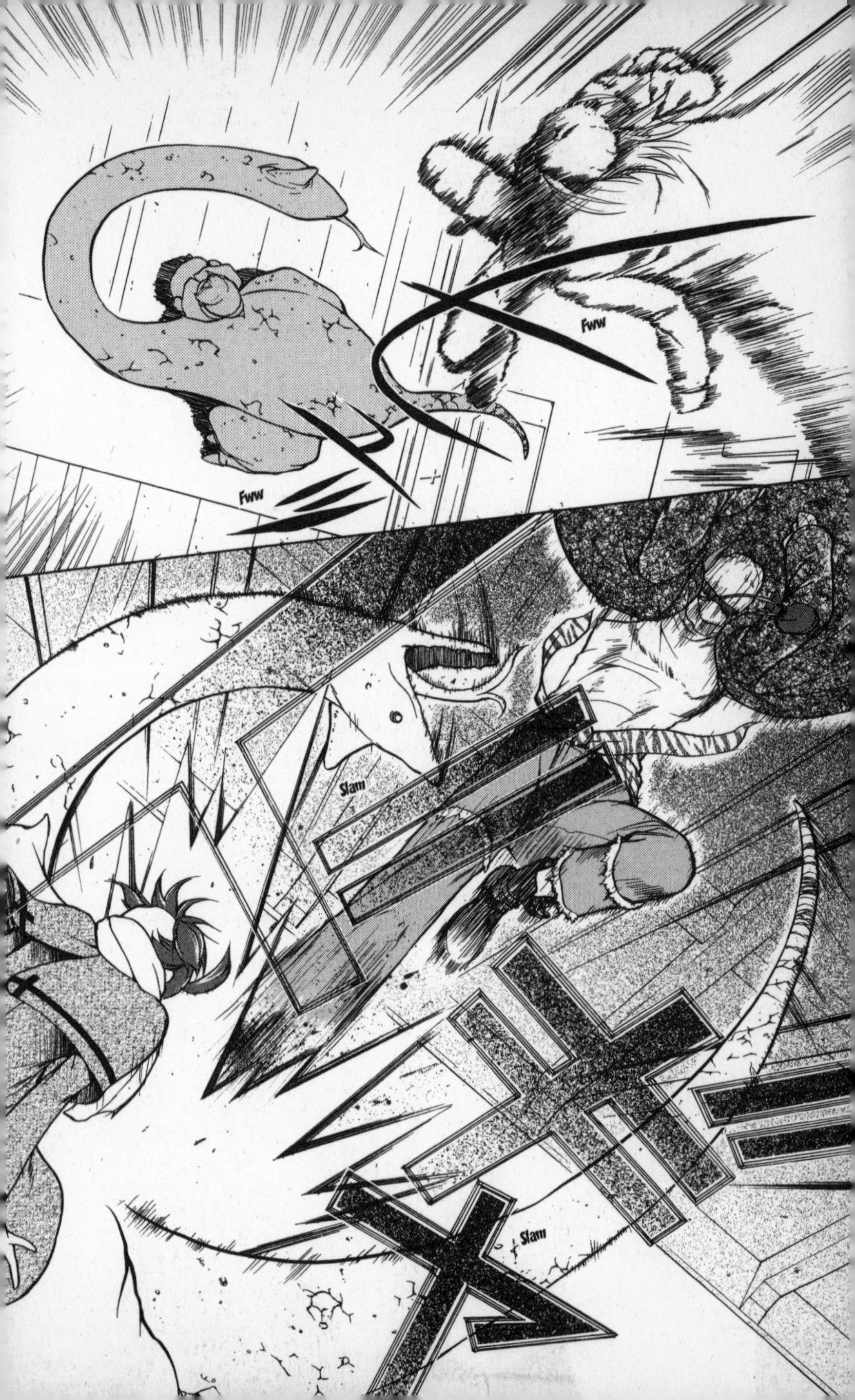
Fww
Fww
Slam
Slam

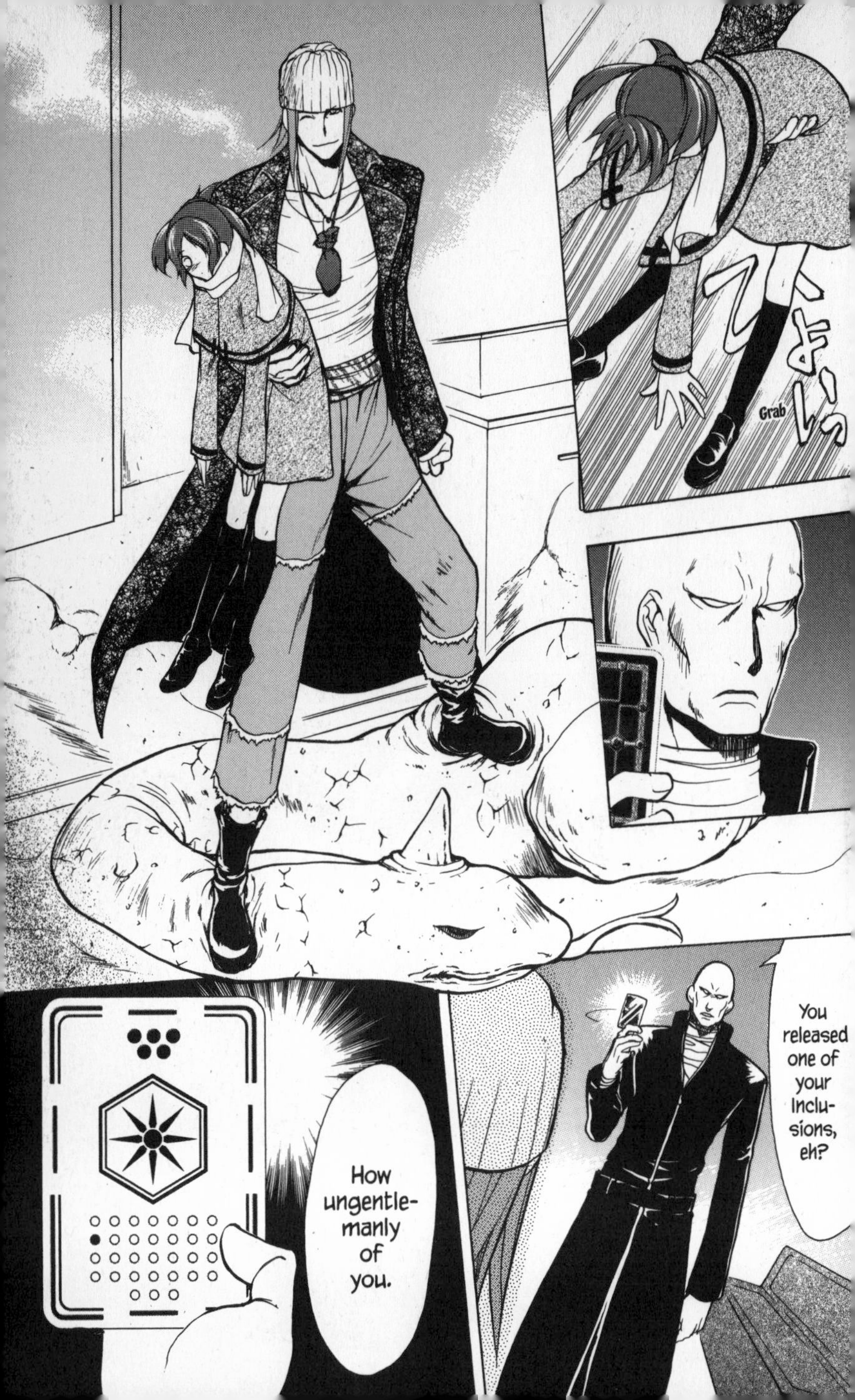
Grab
You released one of your Inclusions, eh?
How ungentlemanly of you.

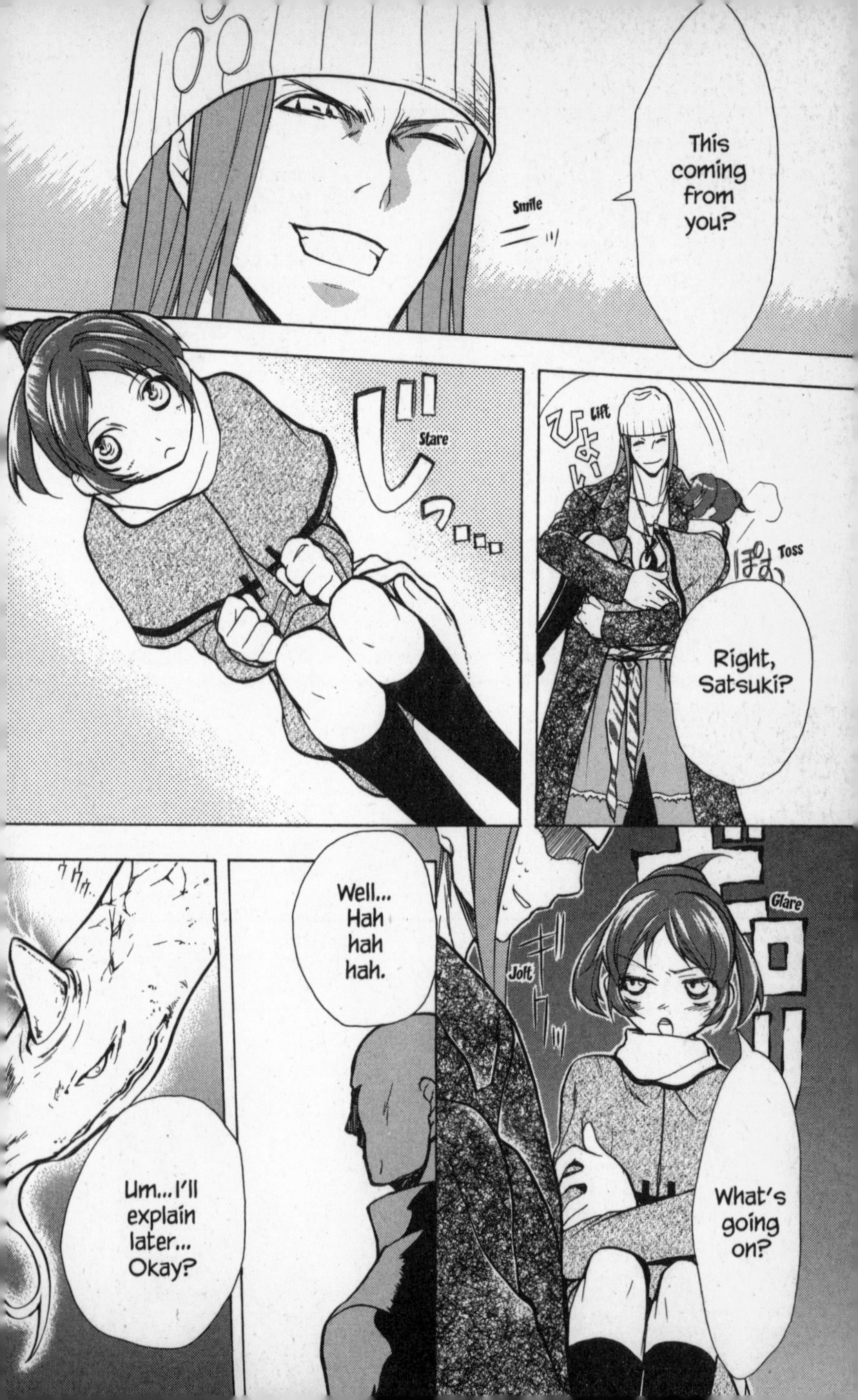
This coming from you?
Smile
Lift
Toss
Right, Satsuki?
Stare
Glare
Jolt
What's going on?
Well... Hah hah hah.
Um...I'll explain later... Okay?

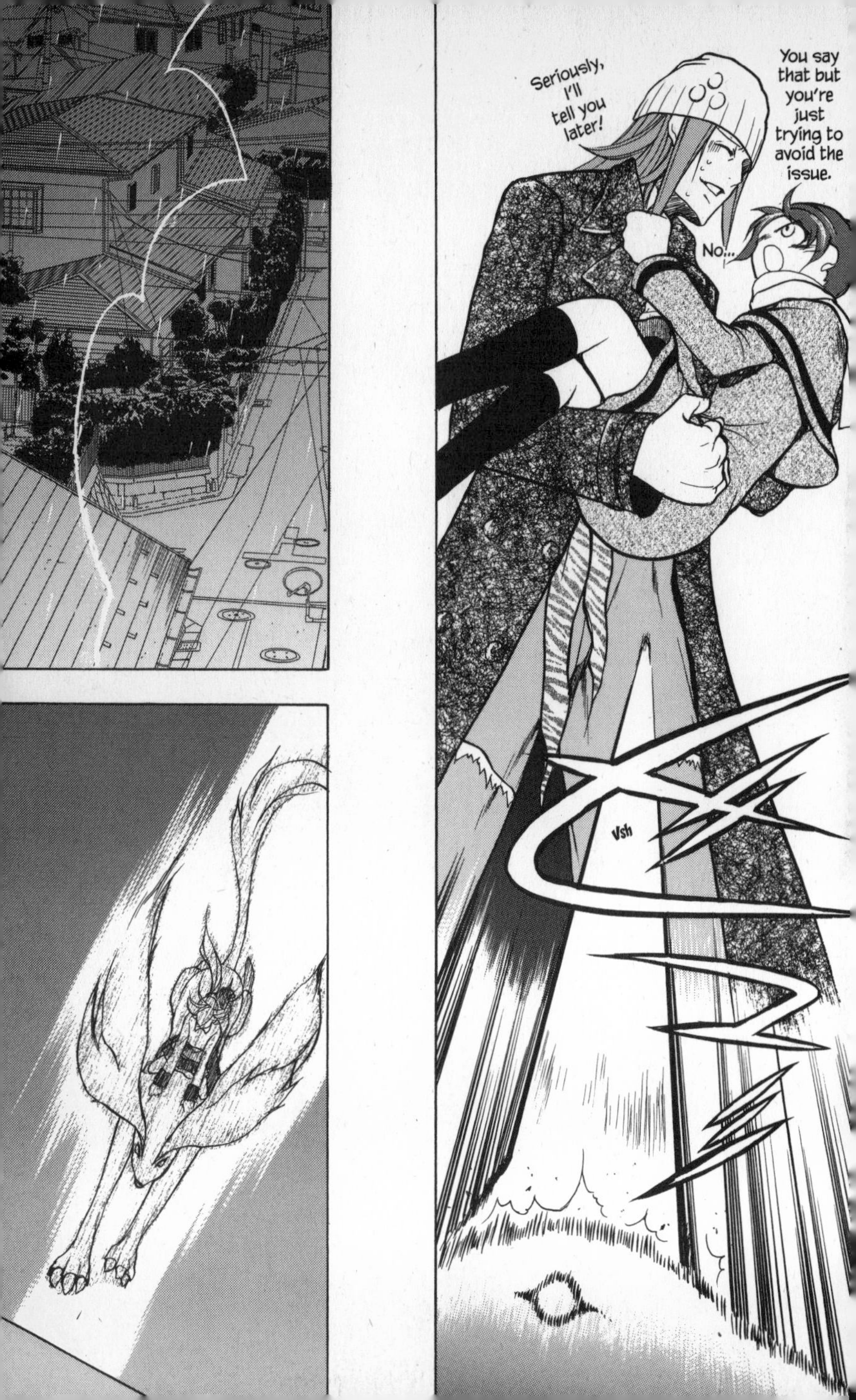
You say that but you're just trying to avoid the issue.
Seriously, I'll tell you later!
No...
Vsh

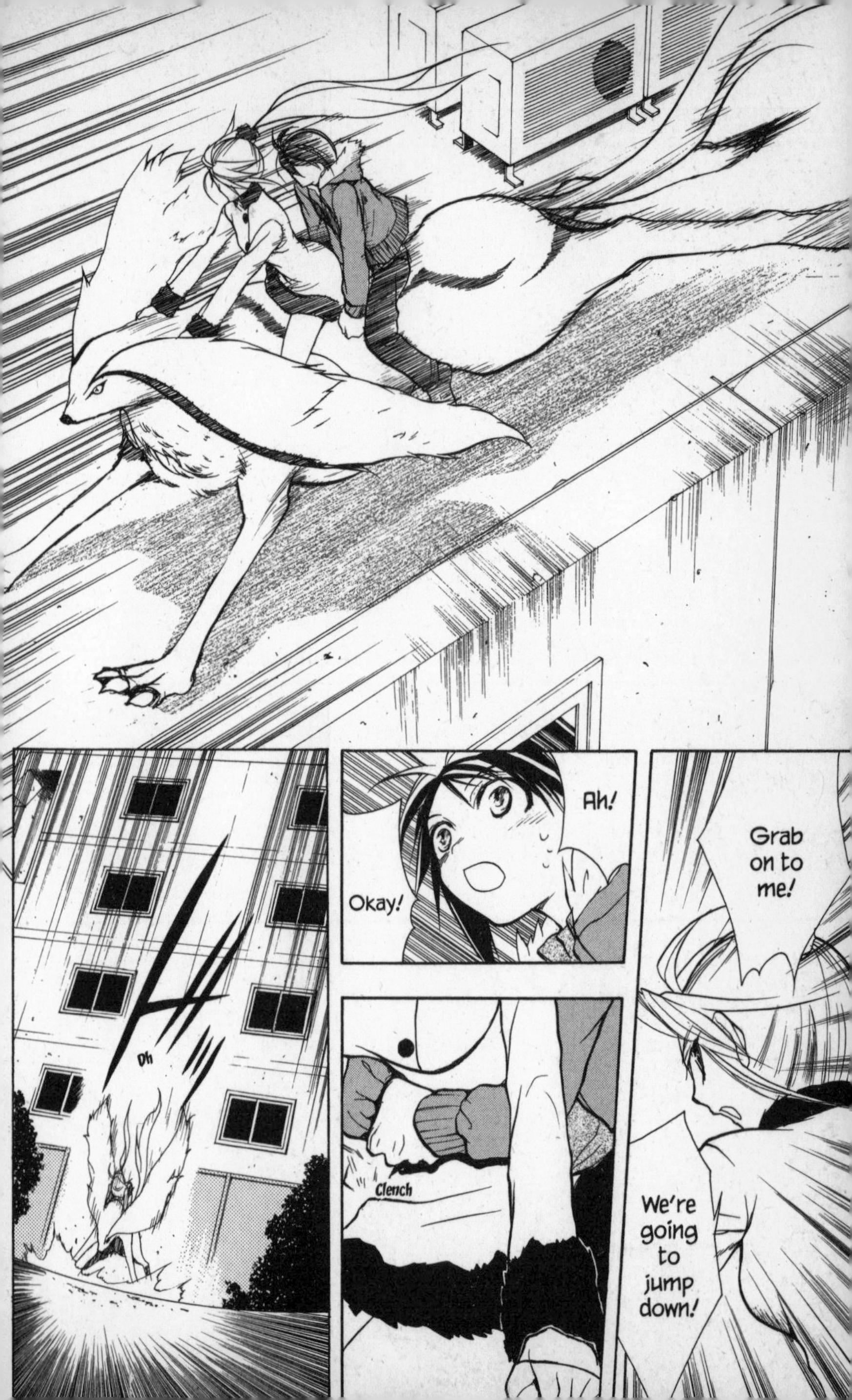

Grab on to me!
We're going to jump down!
Ah!
Okay!
Clench
Dh

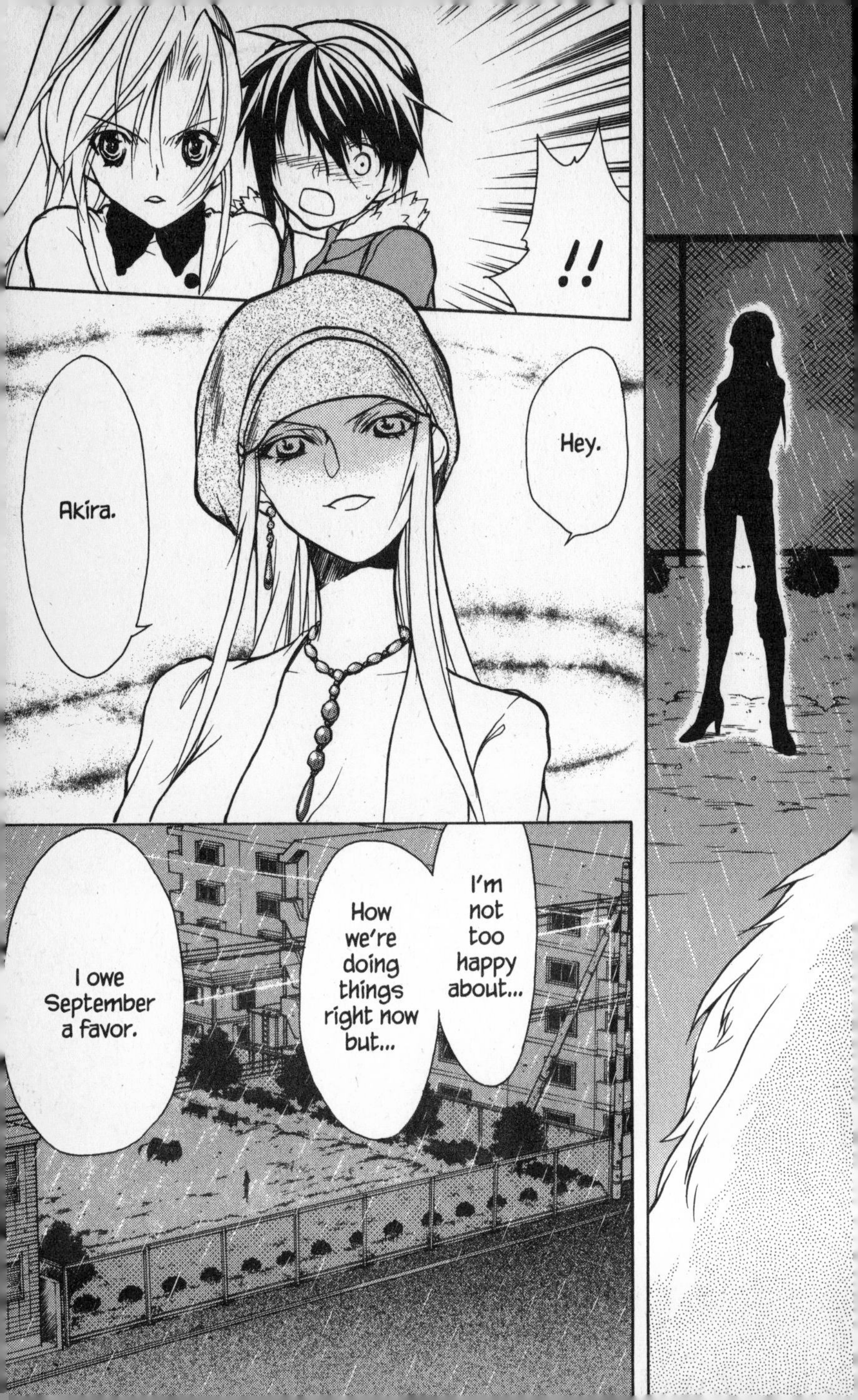
!!
Hey.
Akira.
I'm not too happy about...
How we're doing things right now but...
I owe September a favor.

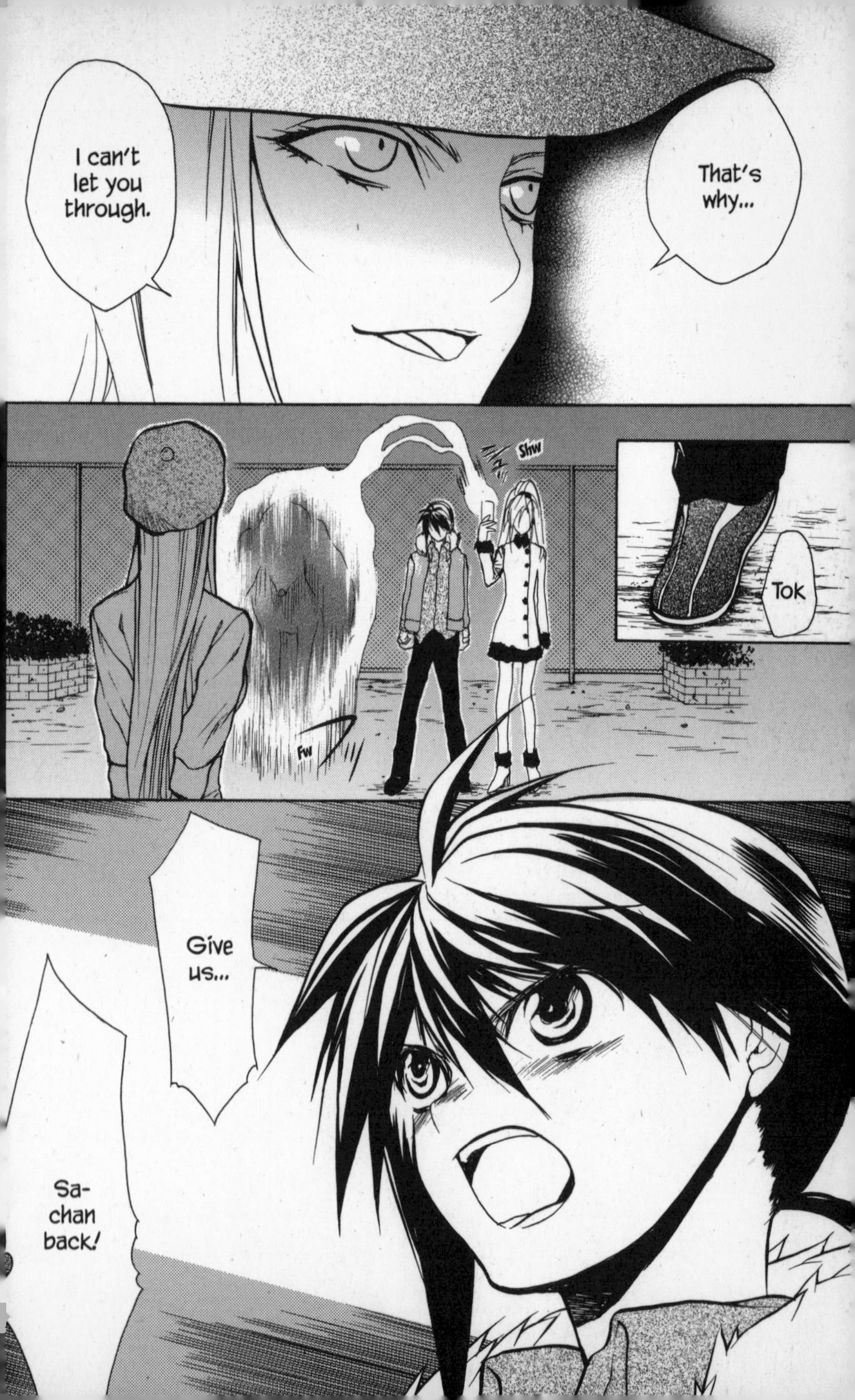
That's why...
I can't let you through.
Tok
Shw
Fw
Give us...
Sa-chan back!

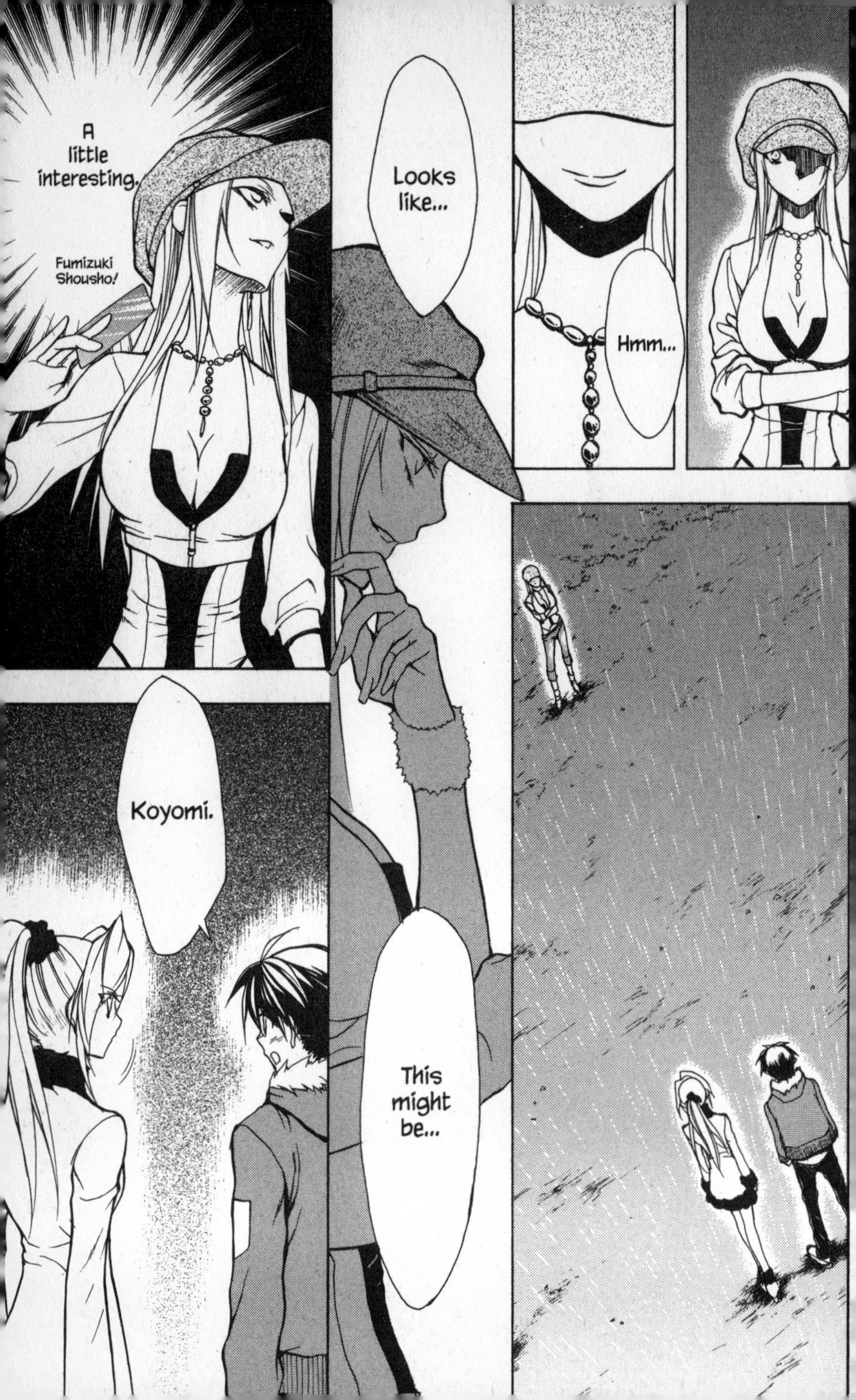
Hmm...
Looks like...
This might be...
A little interesting.
Fumizuki Shousho!
Koyomi.

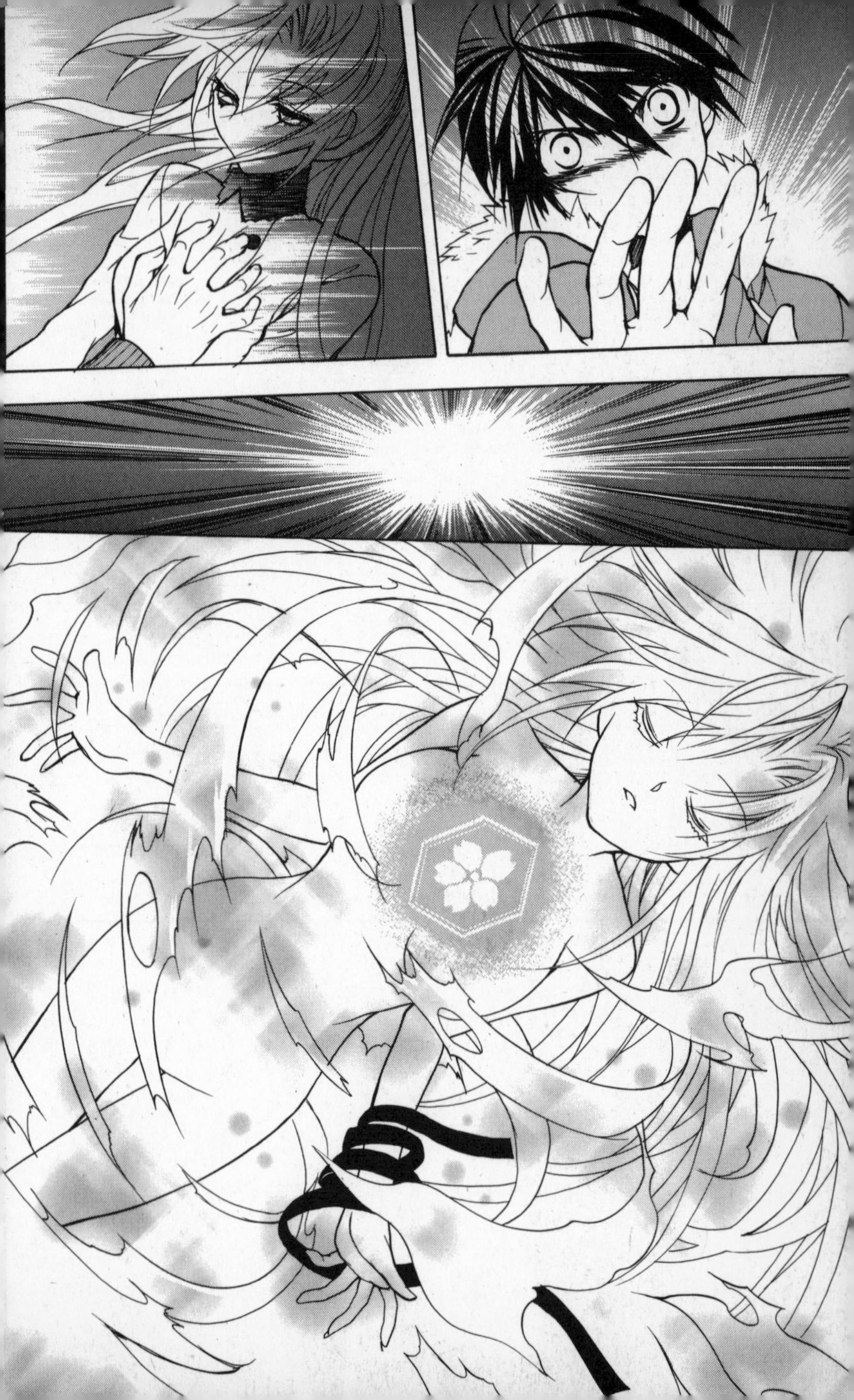

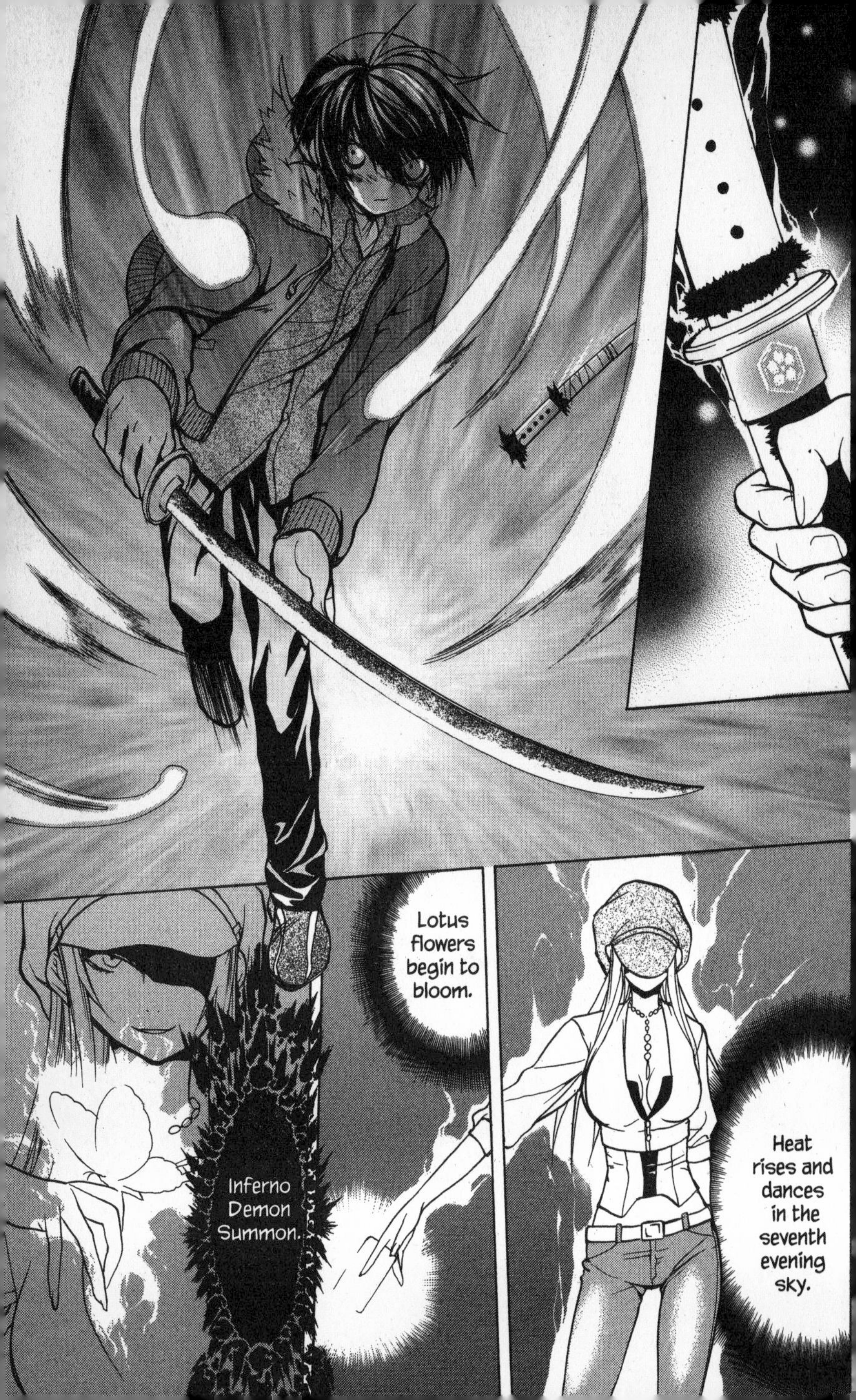
Lotus flowers begin to bloom.
Heat rises and dances in the seventh evening sky.
Inferno Demon Summon.

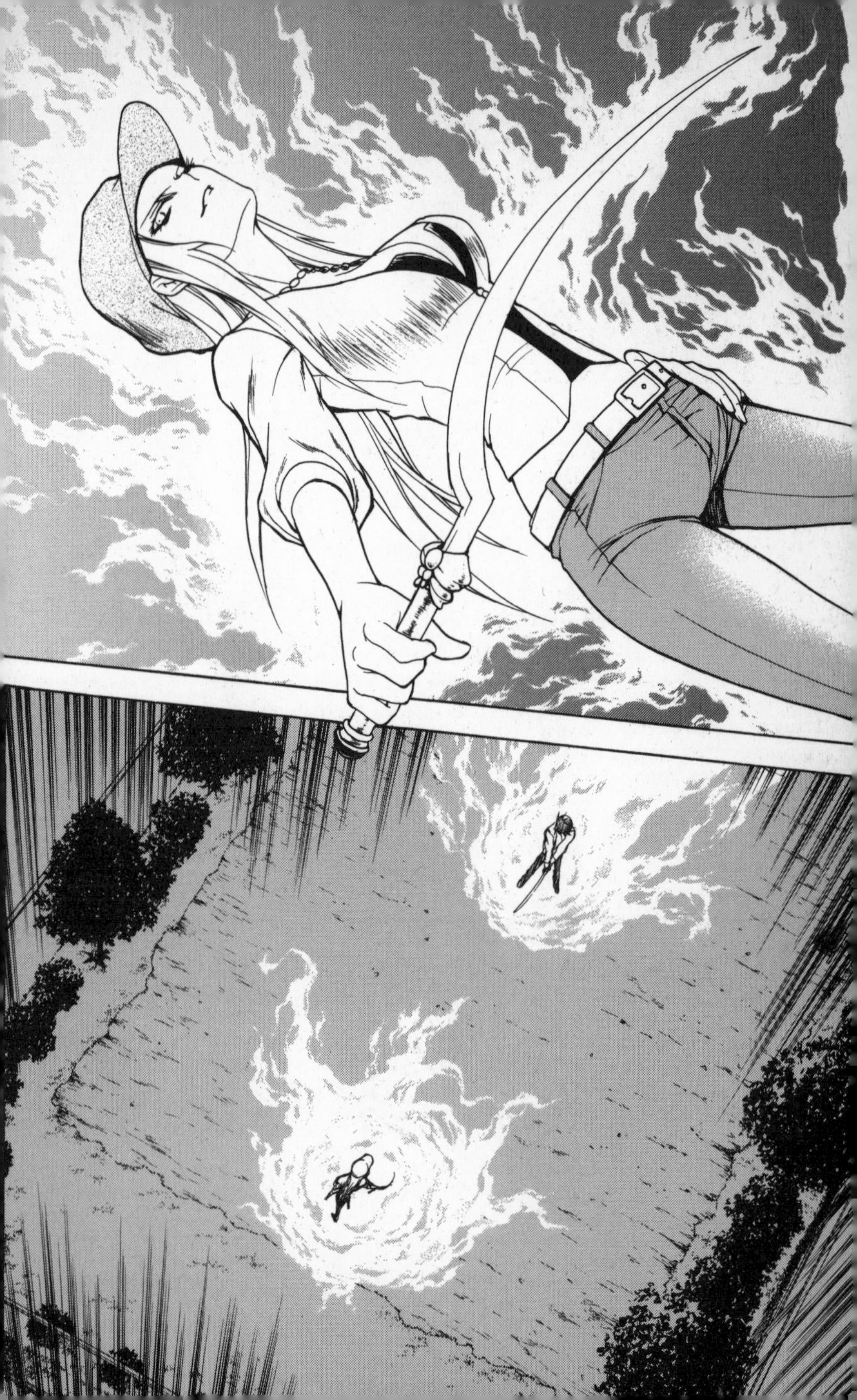

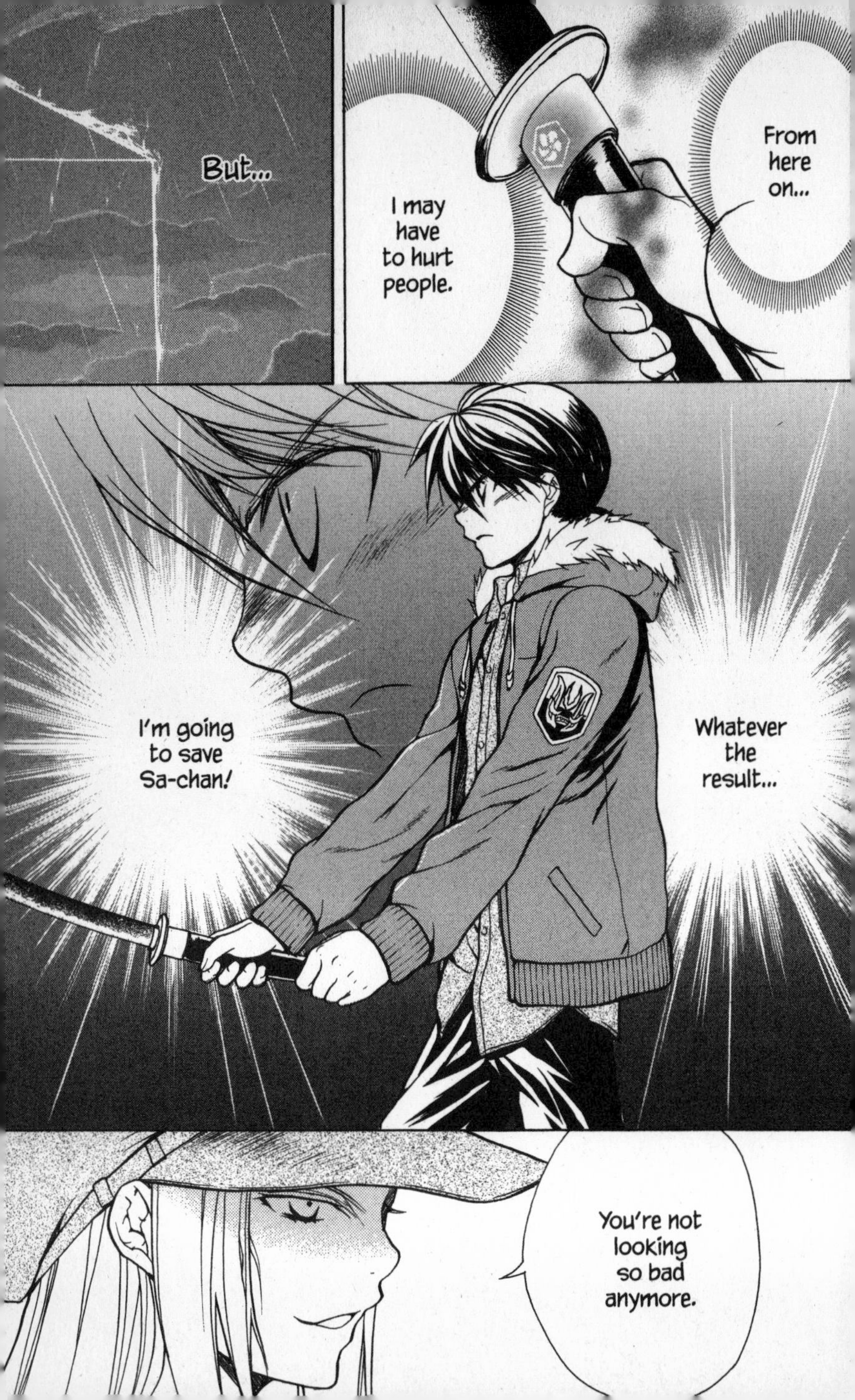
From here on...
I may have to hurt people.
But...
Whatever the result...
I'm going to save Sa-chan!
You're not looking so bad anymore.

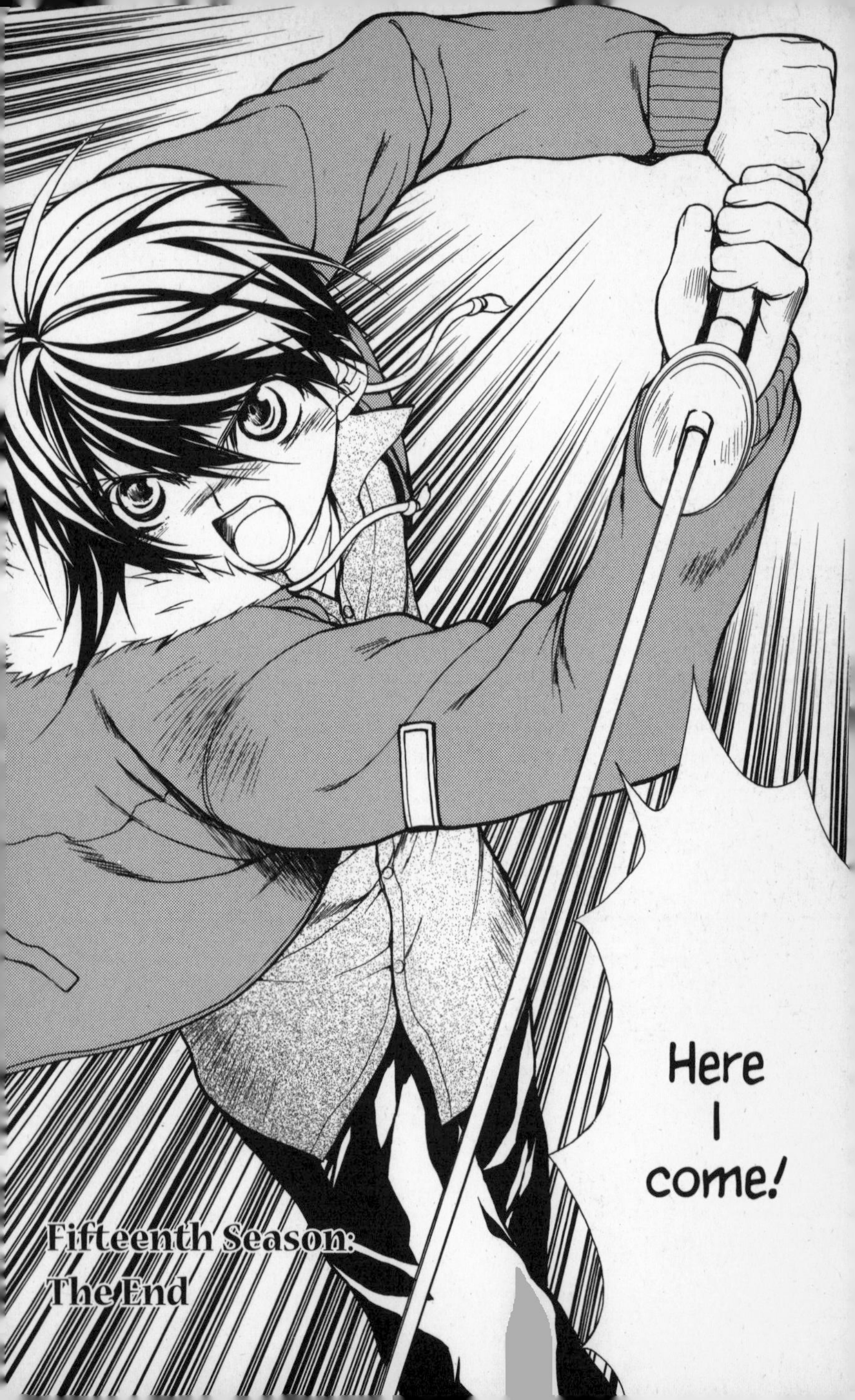
Here I come!
Fifteenth Season: The End

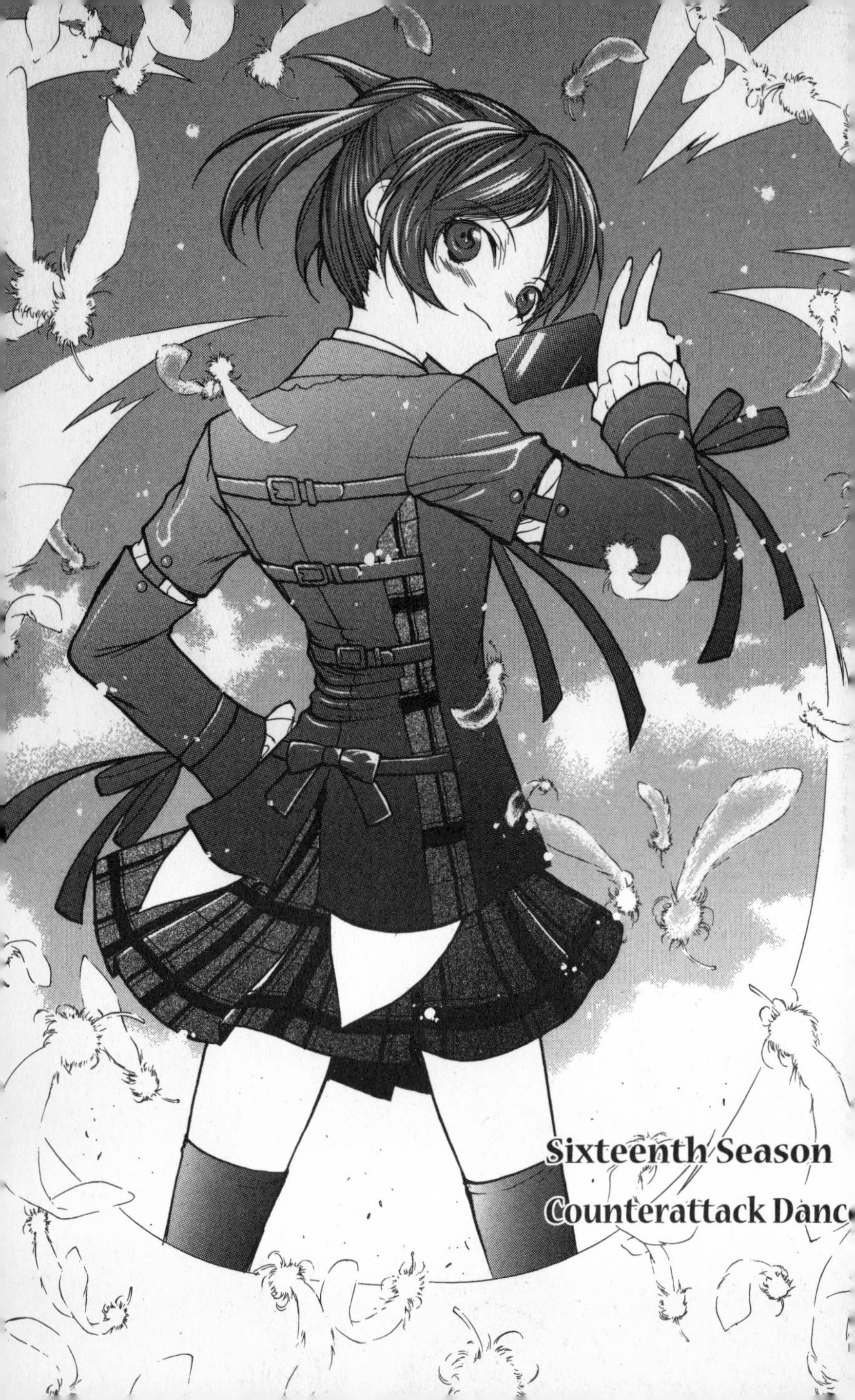
Sixteenth Season
Counterattack Danc

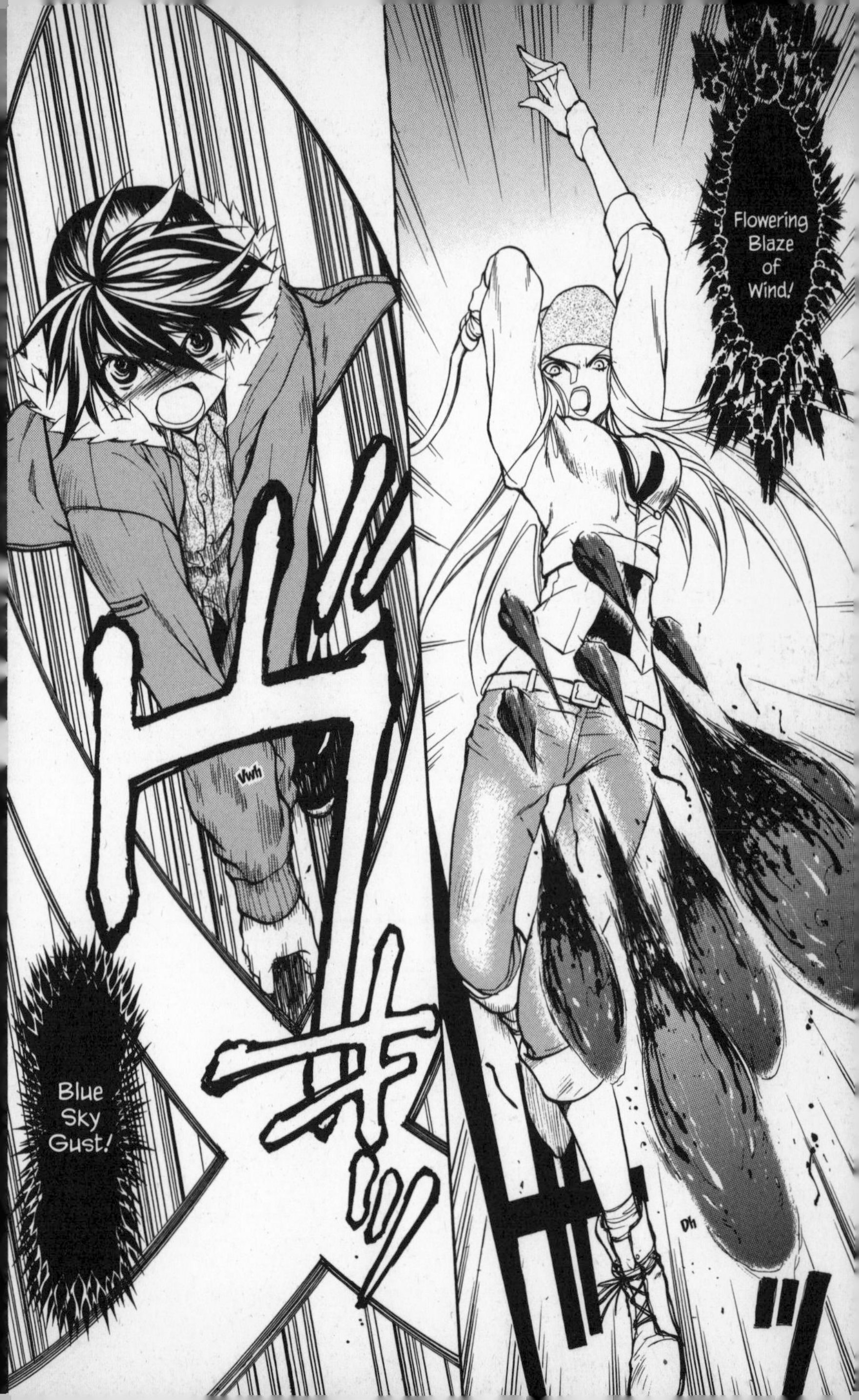
Flowering Blaze of Wind!
Dh
Vwh
Blue Sky Gust!

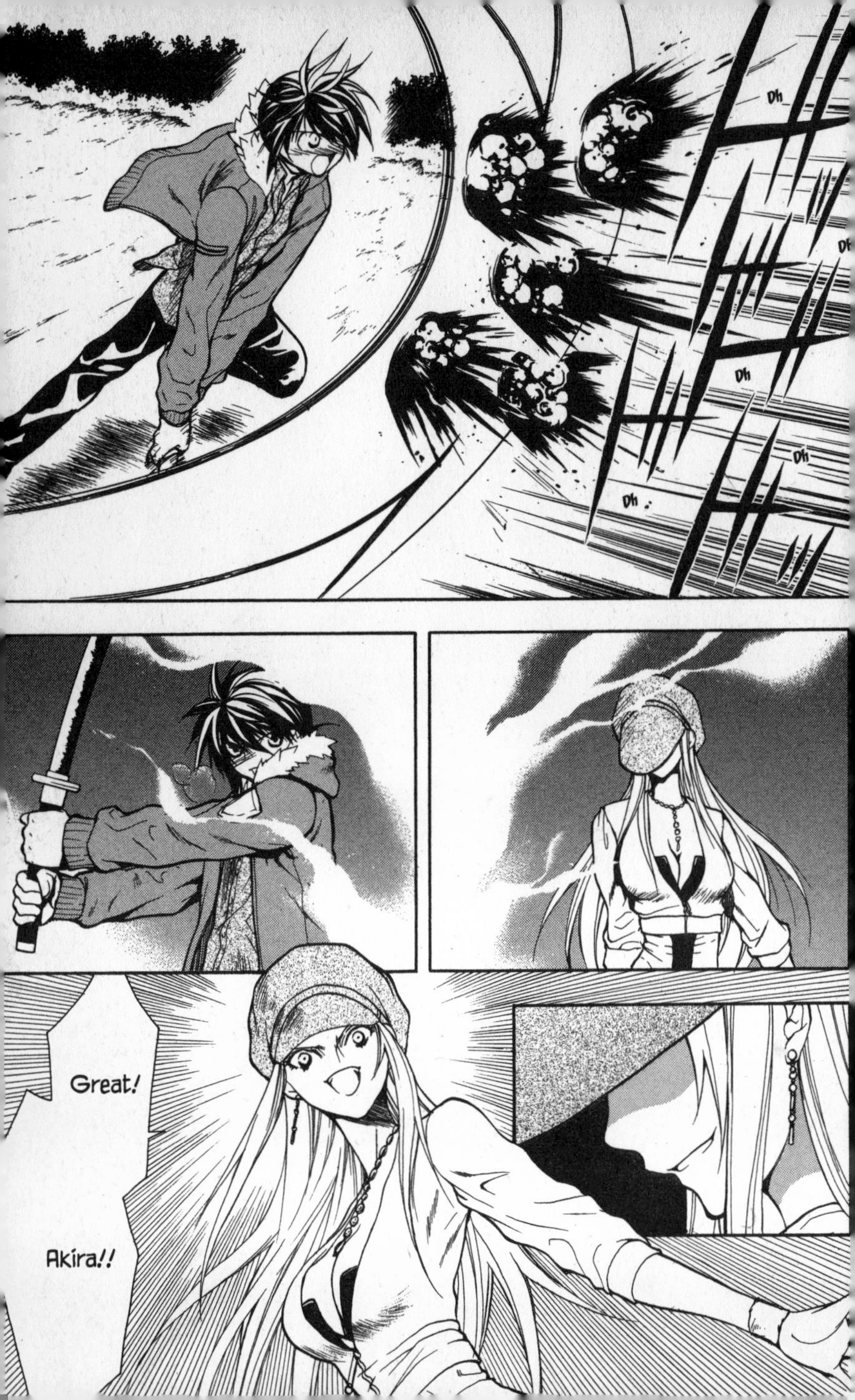
Dh
Dh
Dh
Dh
Great!
Akira!!

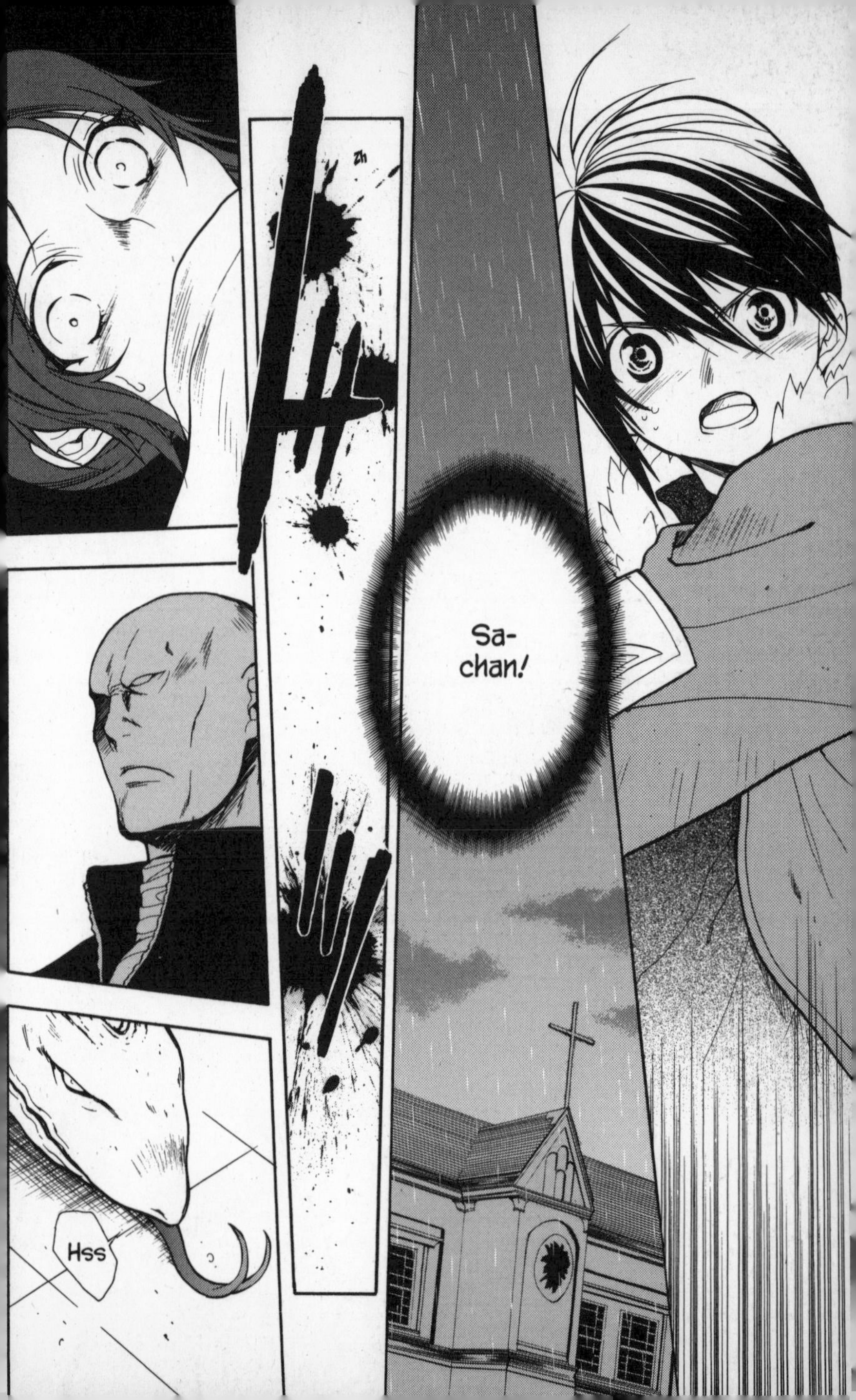
Sa-
chan!
Zh
Hss

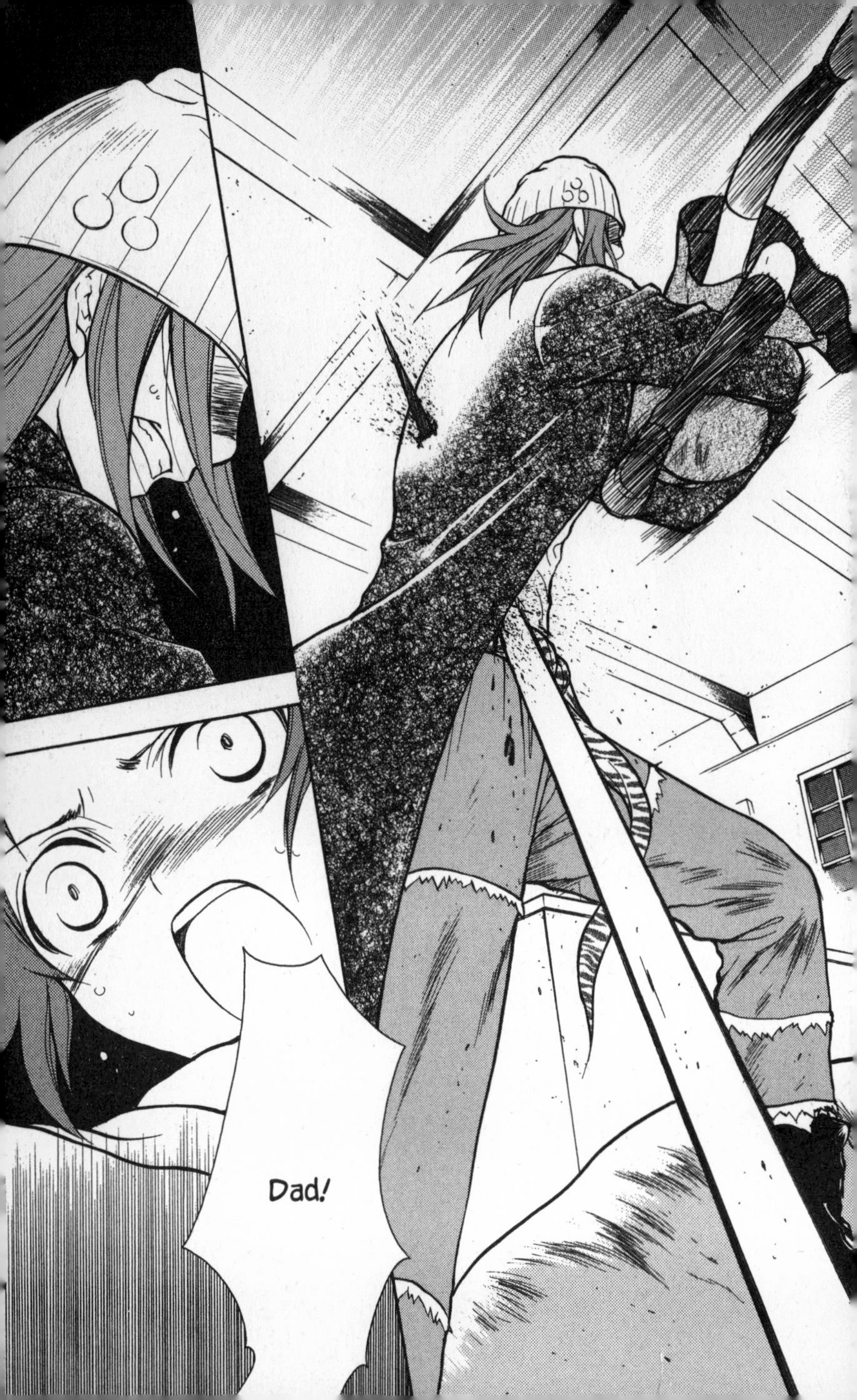
Dad!

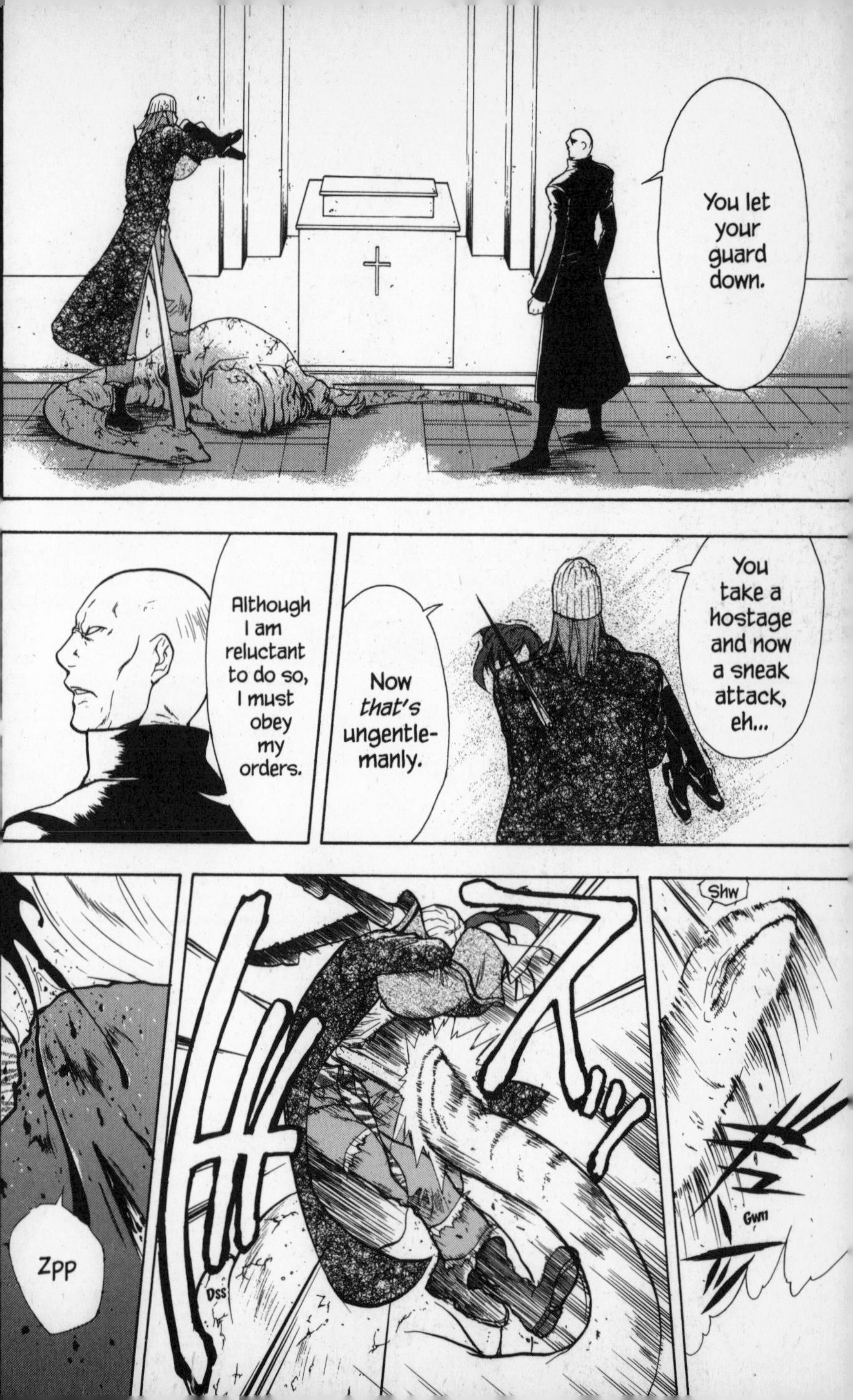
You let your guard down.
You take a hostage and now a sneak attack, eh...
Now *that*'s ungentlemanly.
Although I am reluctant to do so, I must obey my orders.
Shw
Gwn
Dss
Zpp

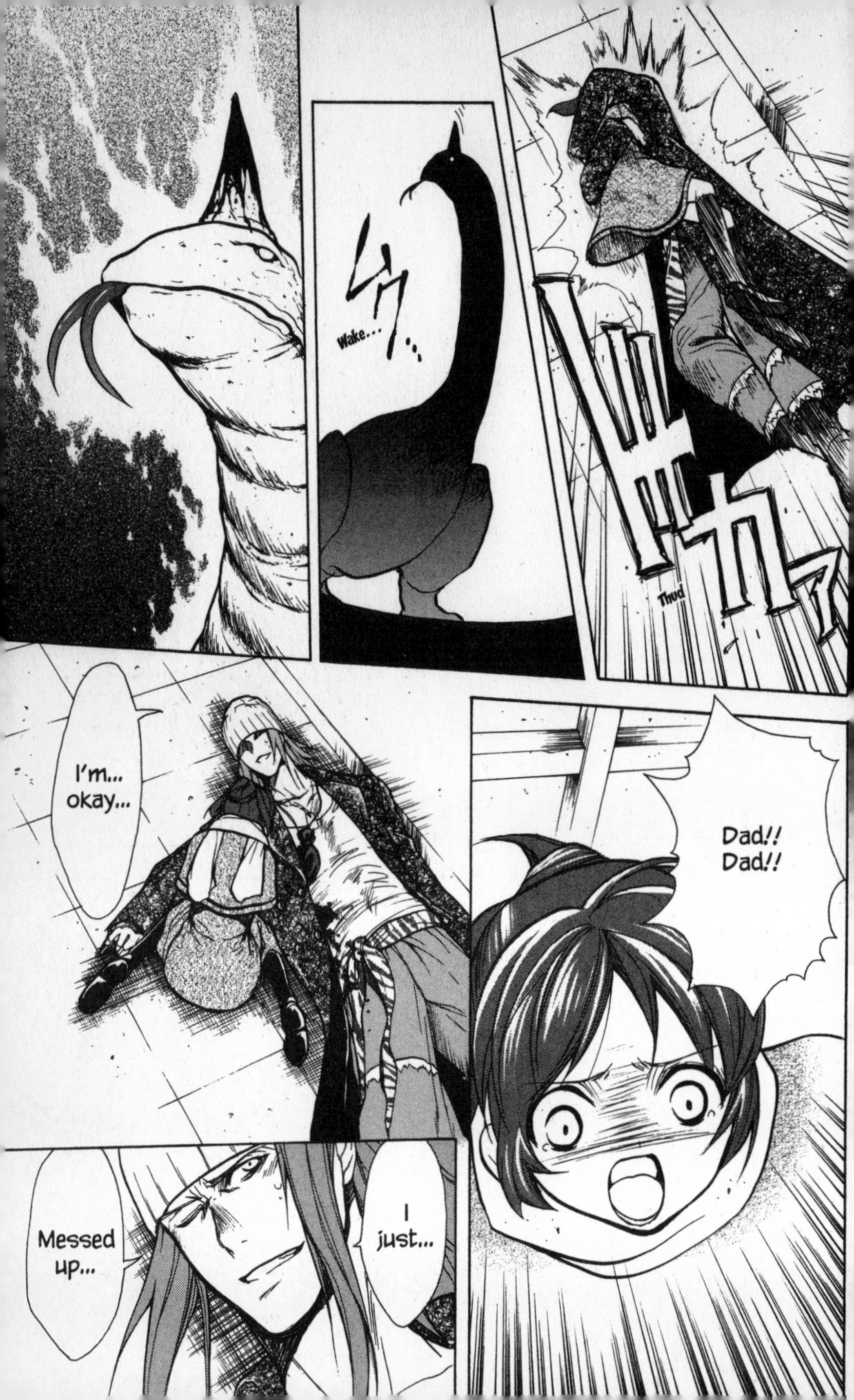
Thud
Wake...
Dad!! Dad!!
I'm... okay...
I just...
Messed up...

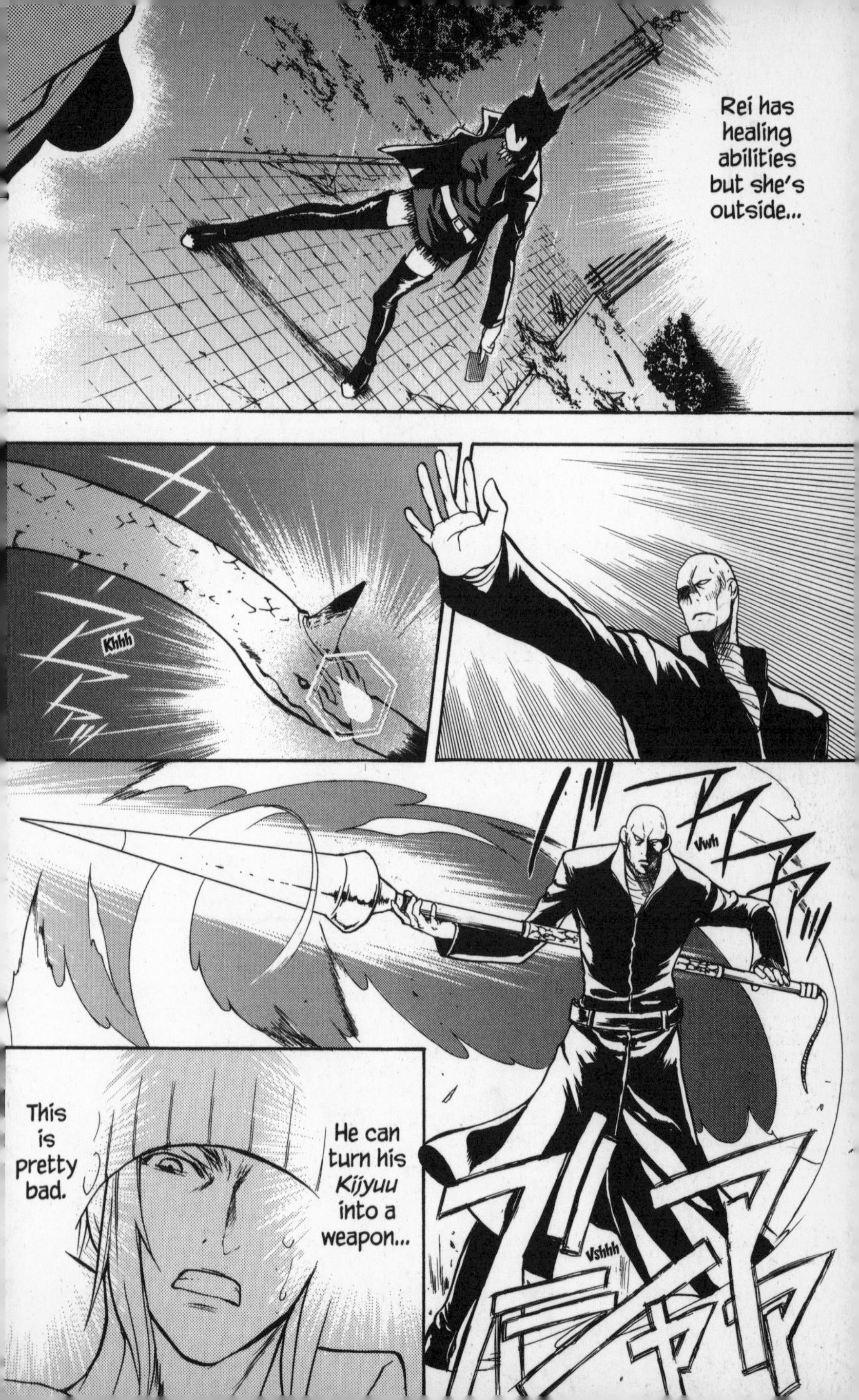
Rei has healing abilities but she's outside...
Khhh
Vwh
Vshhh
He can turn his *Kijyuu* into a weapon...
This is pretty bad.

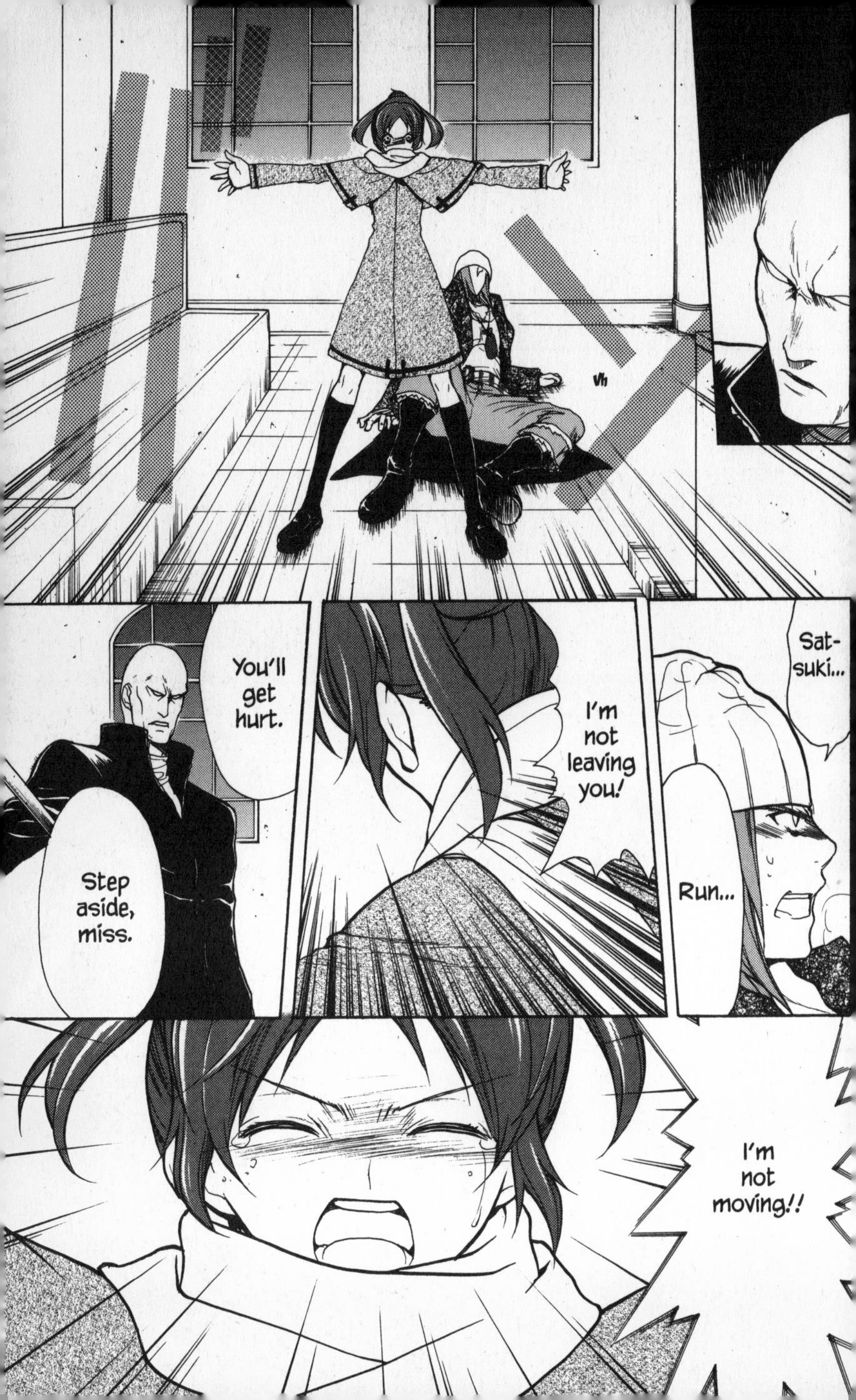
Sat-suki...
Run...
I'm not leaving you!
You'll get hurt.
Step aside, miss.
I'm not moving!!

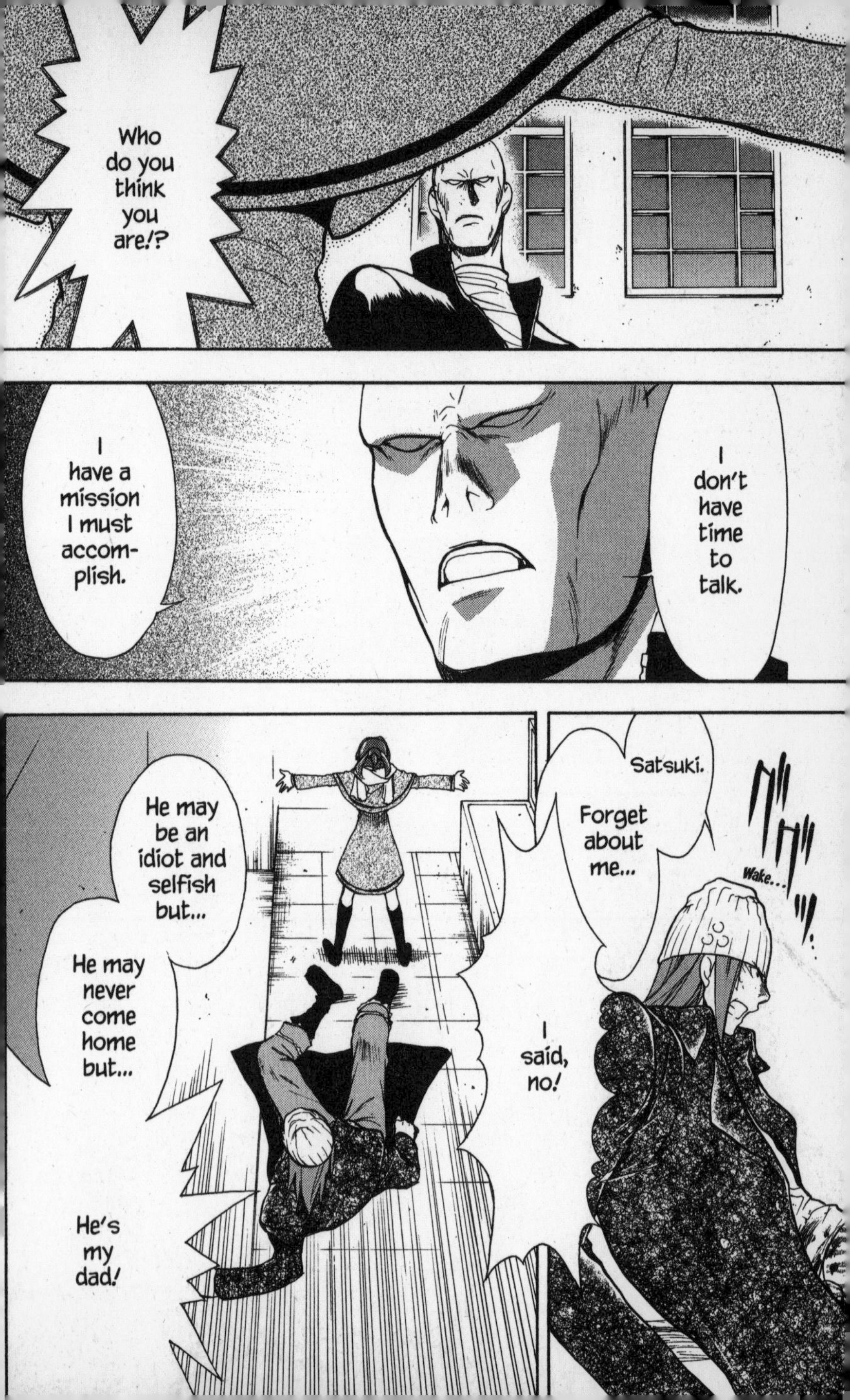
Who do you think you are!?
I don't have time to talk.
I have a mission I must accomplish.
Satsuki.
Forget about me...
Wake...
I said, no!
He may be an idiot and selfish but...
He may never come home but...
He's my dad!

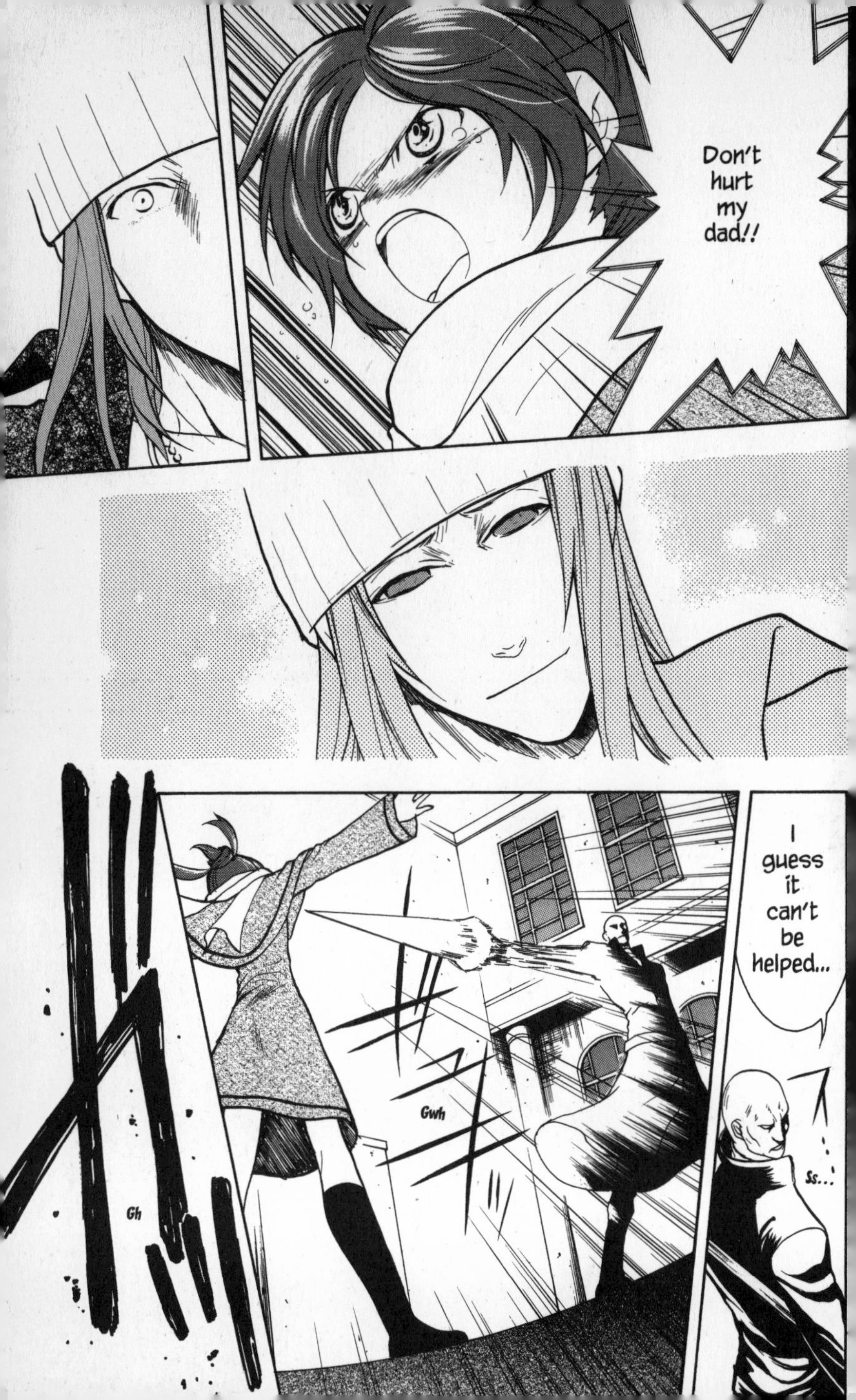
Don't hurt my dad!!
I guess it can't be helped...
Ss...
Gwh
Gh

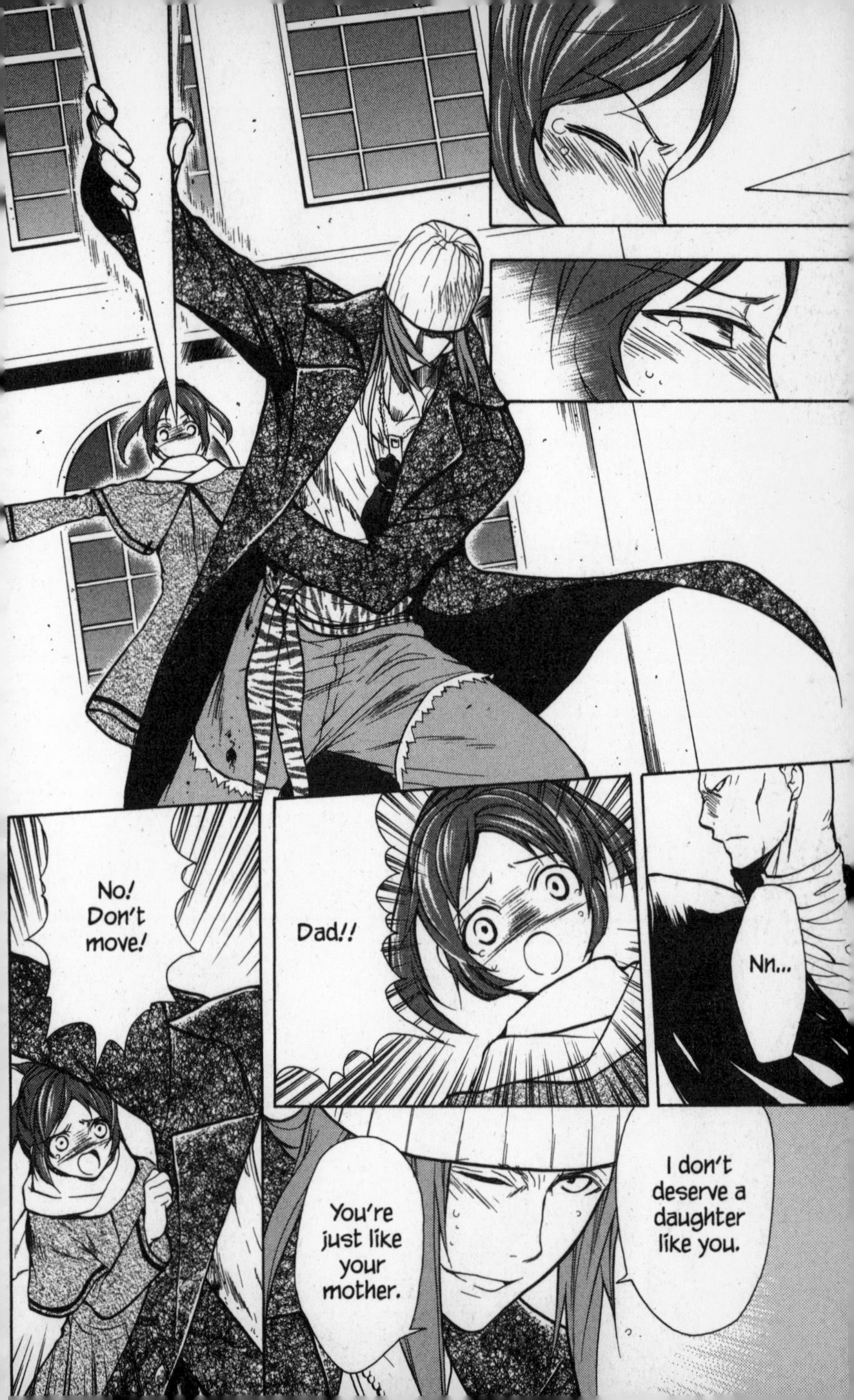
Nn...
Dad!!
No! Don't move!
I don't deserve a daughter like you.
You're just like your mother.

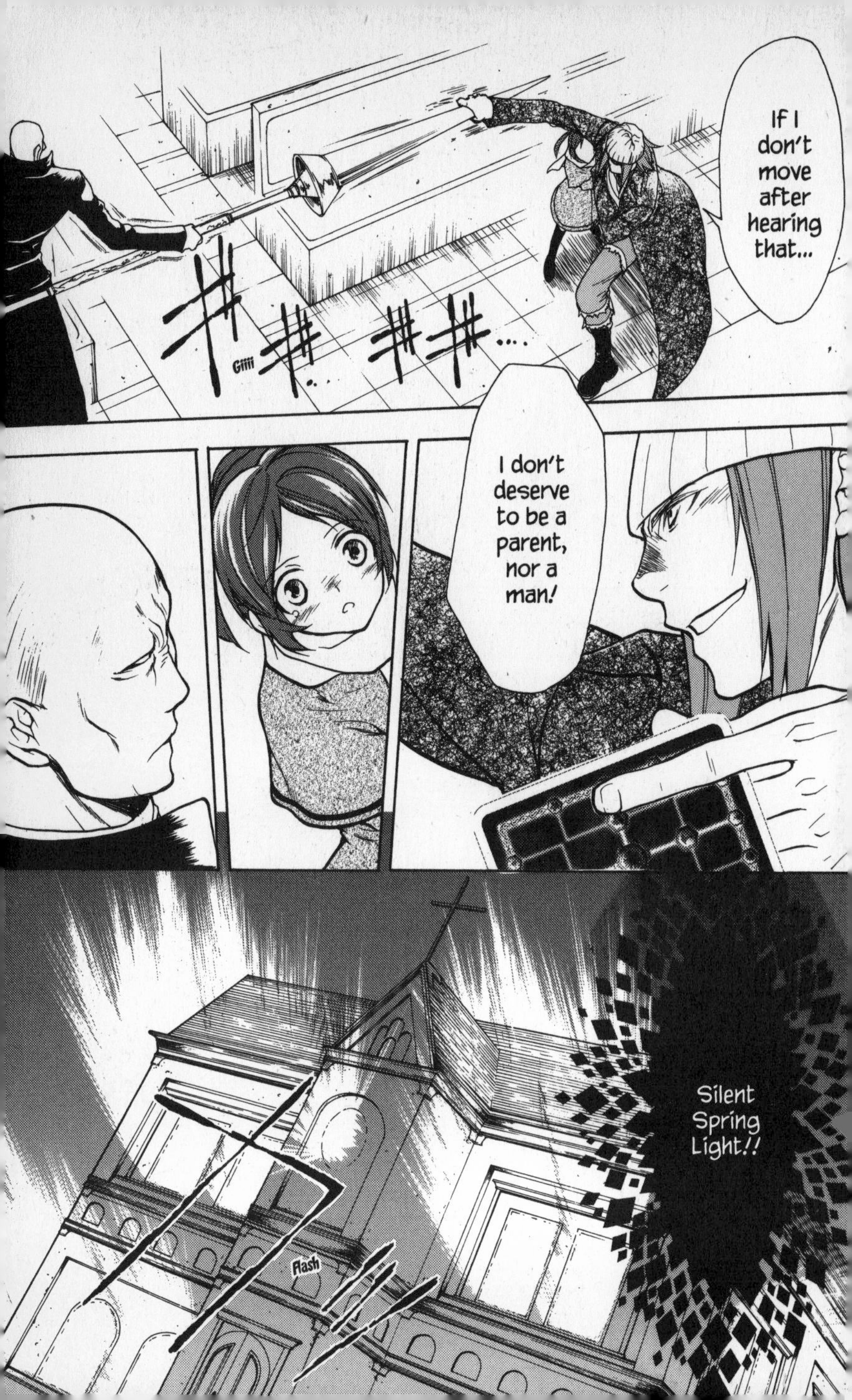
If I don't move after hearing that...
Giiii
I don't deserve to be a parent, nor a man!
Silent Spring Light!!
Flash

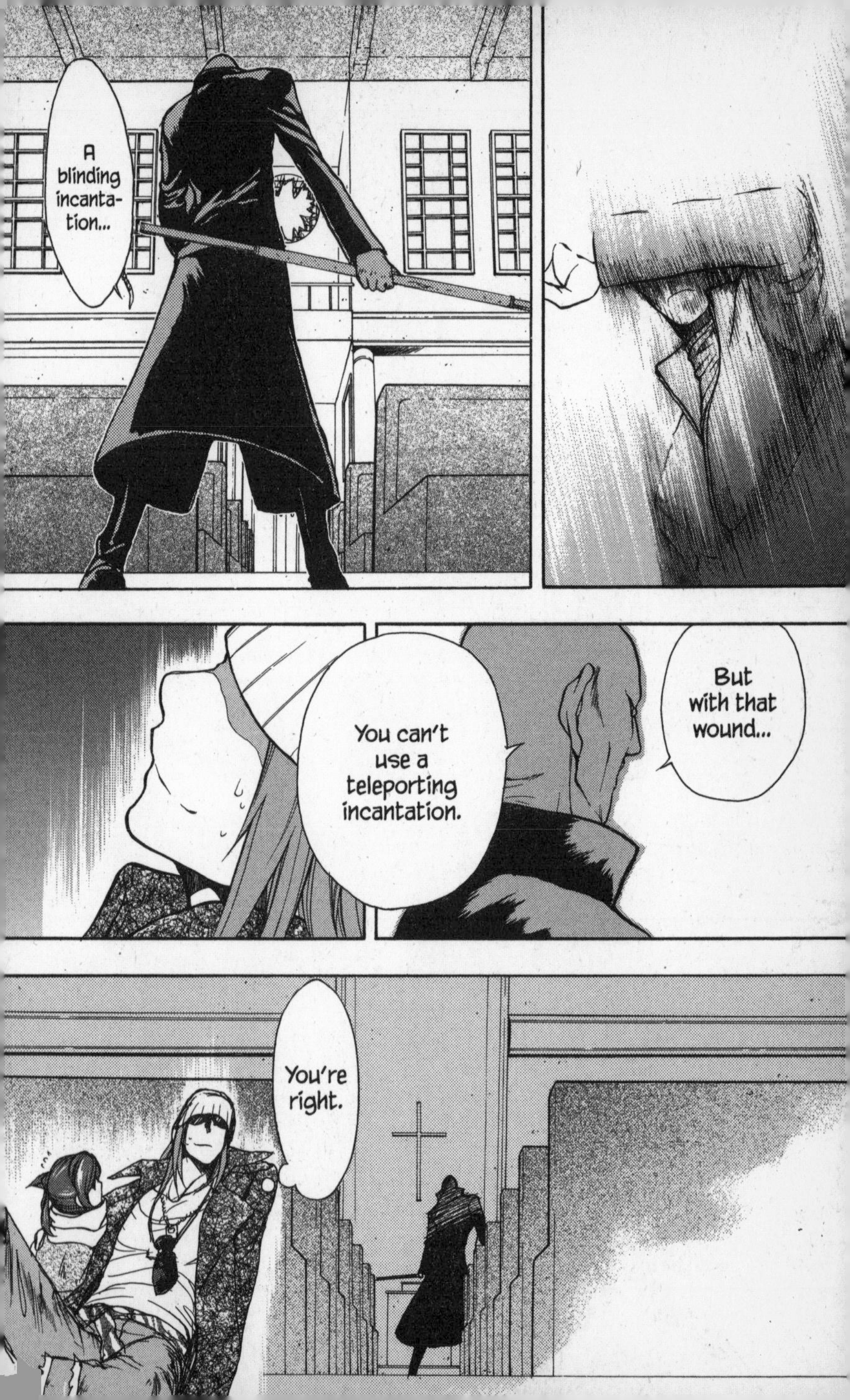
A blinding incantation...
But with that wound...
You can't use a teleporting incantation.
You're right.

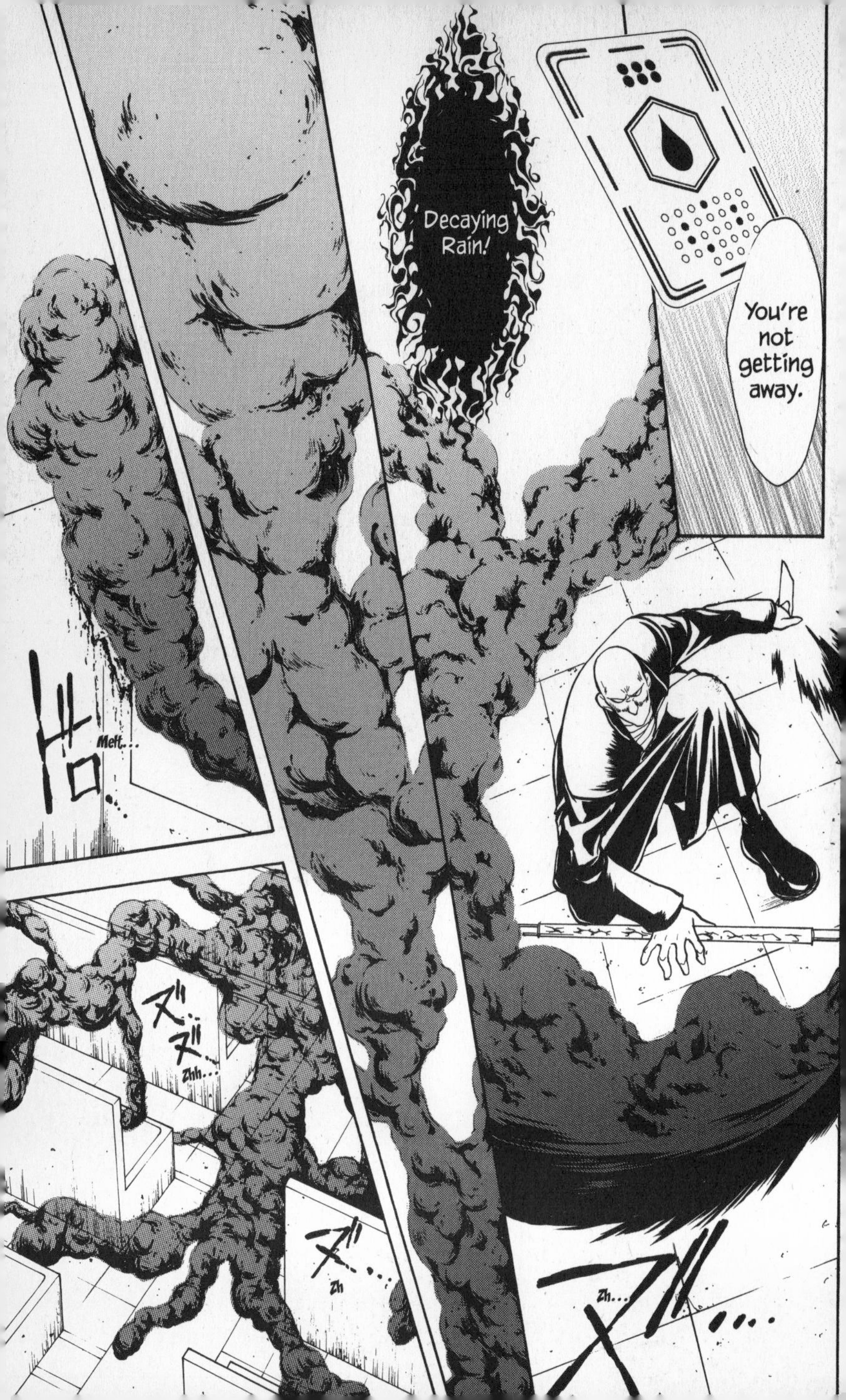
You're not getting away.
Decaying Rain!
Zh...
Melt...
Zhh...
Zh...

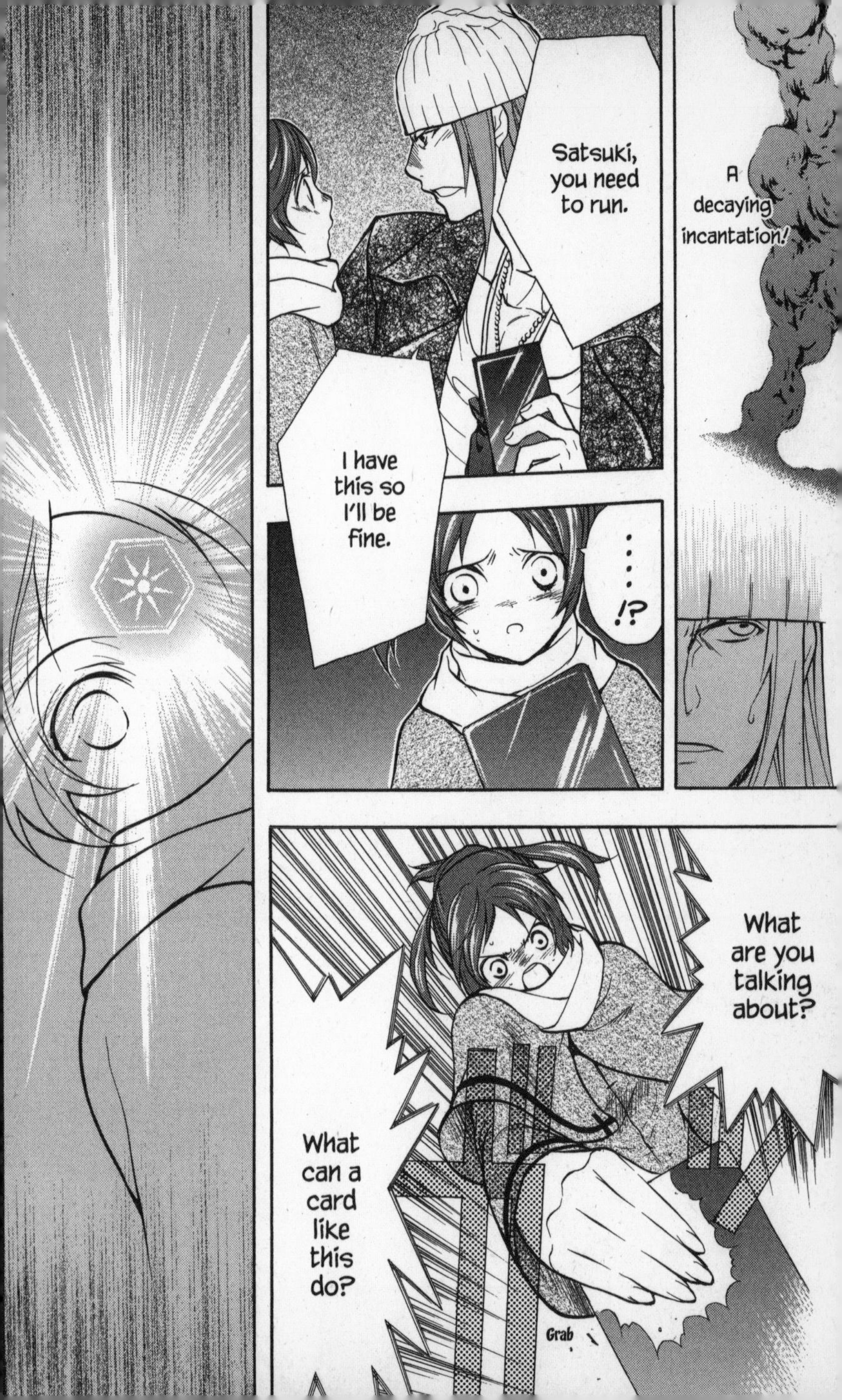
A decaying incantation!
Satsuki, you need to run.
I have this so I'll be fine.
…!?
What are you talking about?
What can a card like this do?
Grab

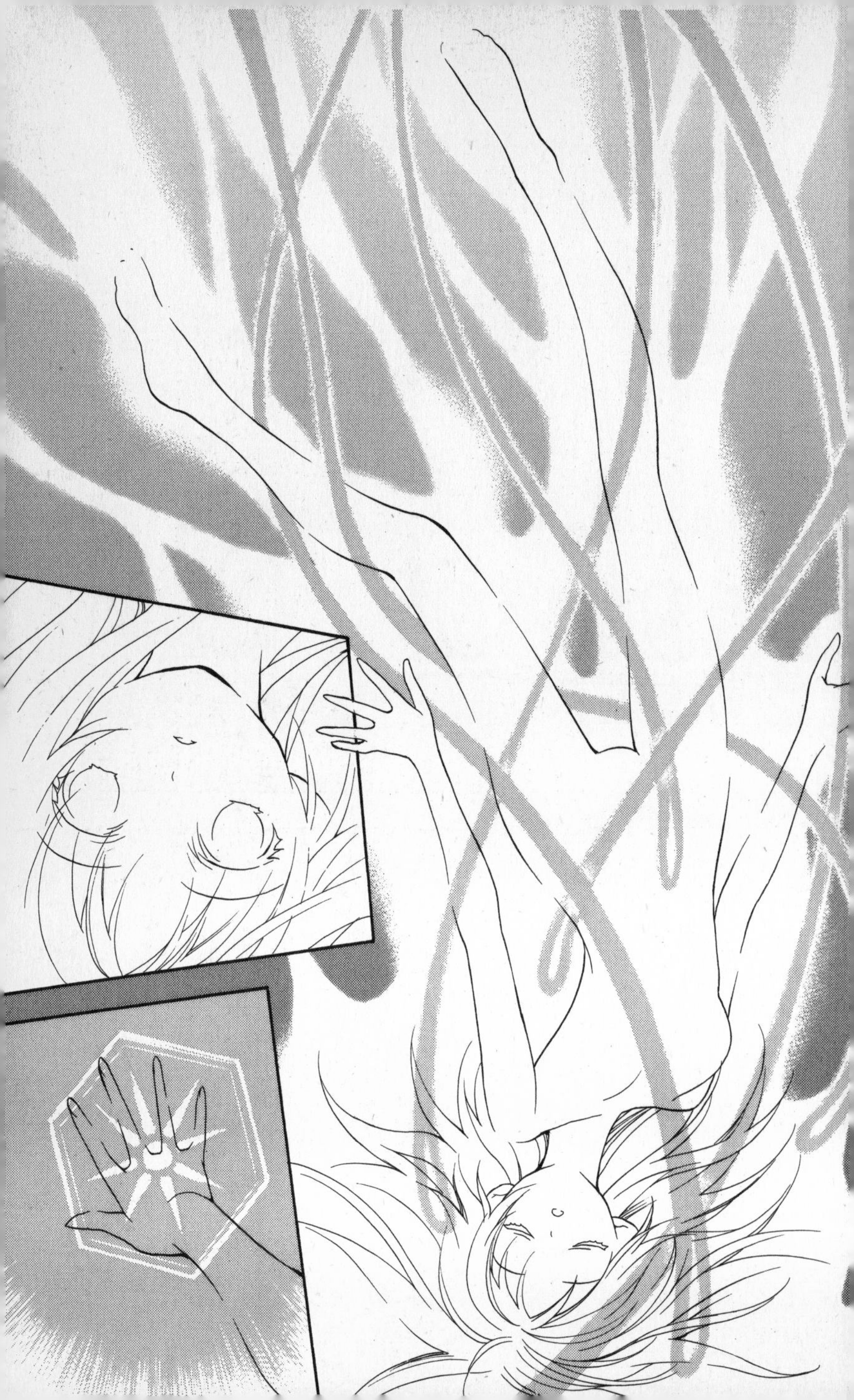

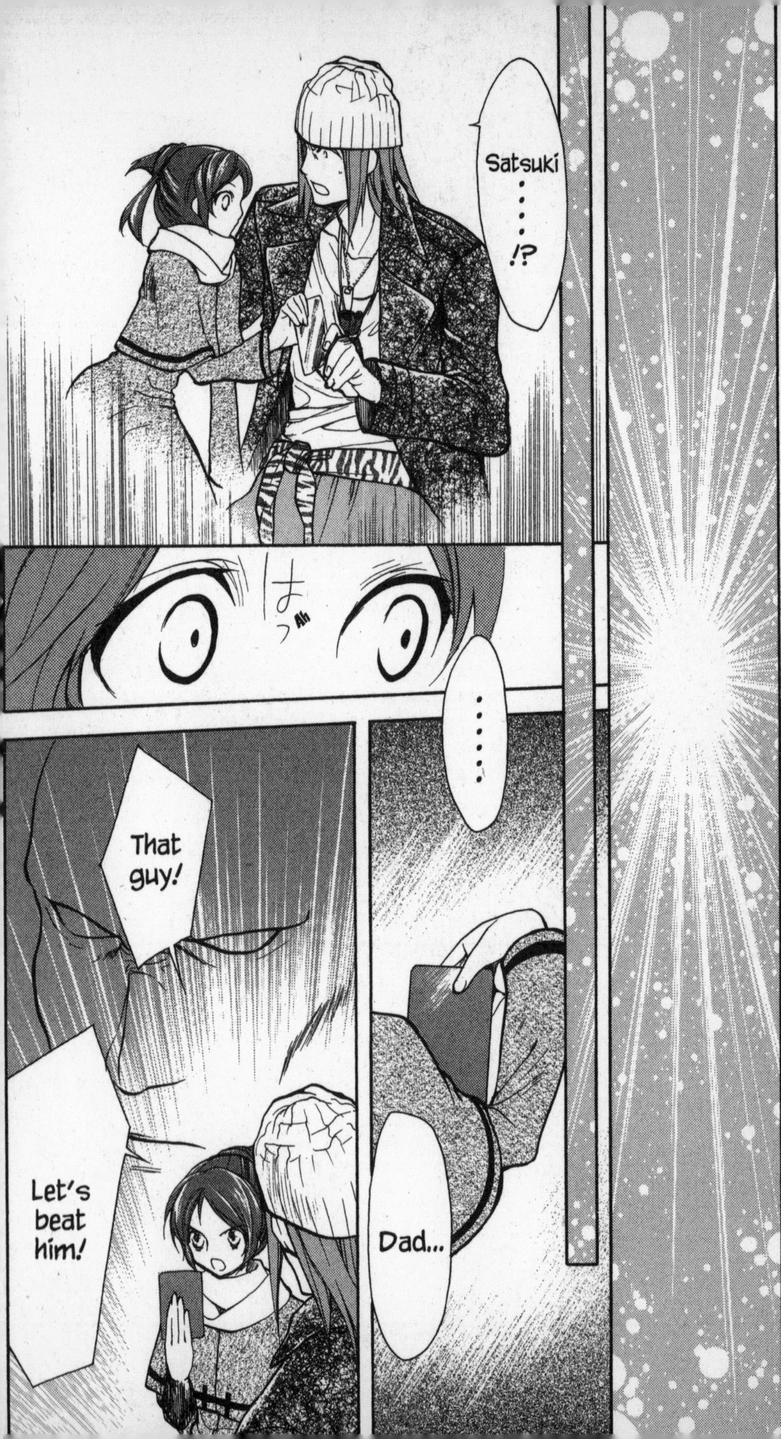
Satsuki......!?
はっ
Ah
......
Dad...
That guy!
Let's beat him!

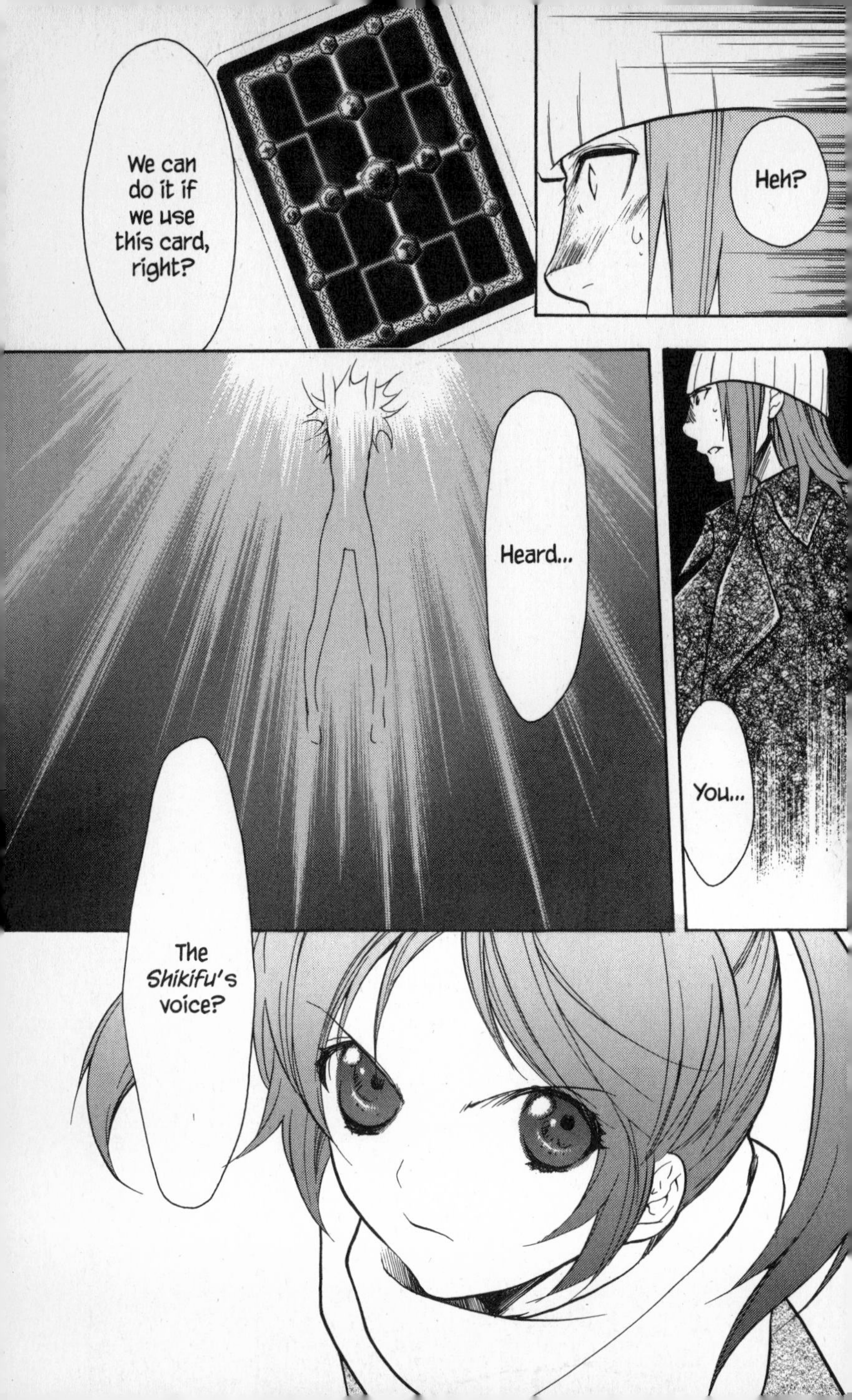
Heh?
We can do it if we use this card, right?
You...
Heard...
The Shikifu's voice?

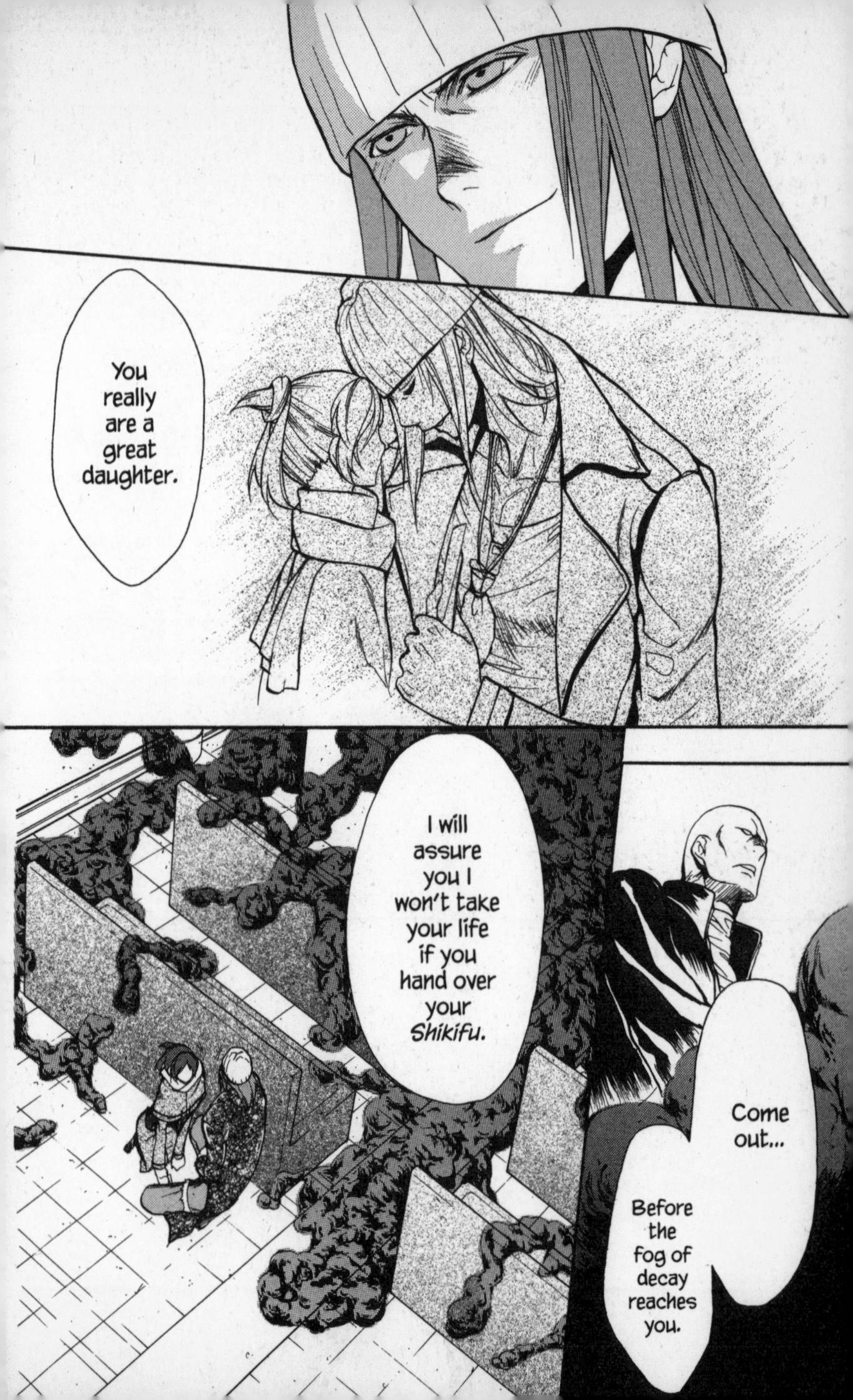
You really are a great daughter.
Come out...
Before the fog of decay reaches you.
I will assure you I won't take your life if you hand over your *Shikifu*.

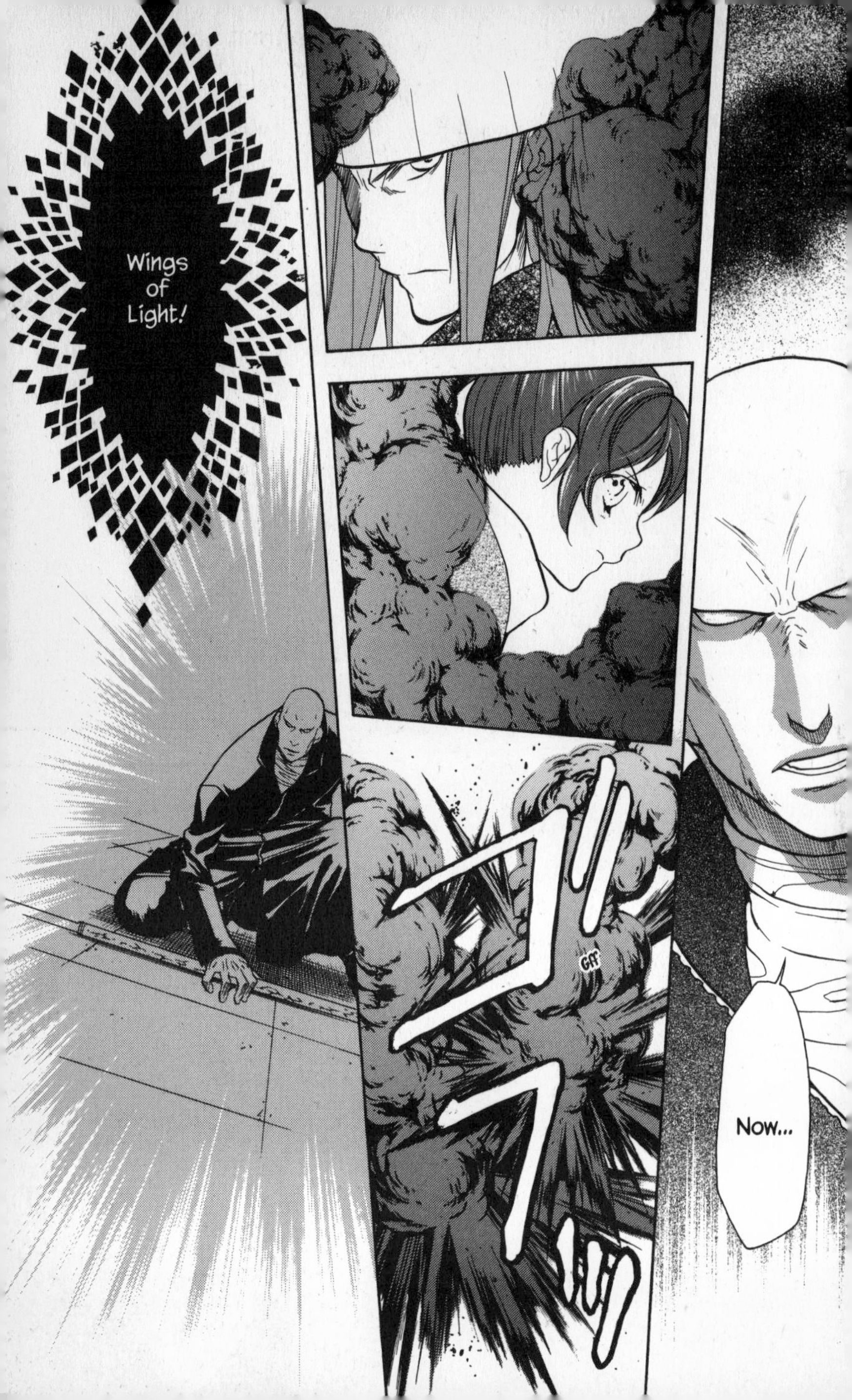
Now...
Gff
Wings of Light!

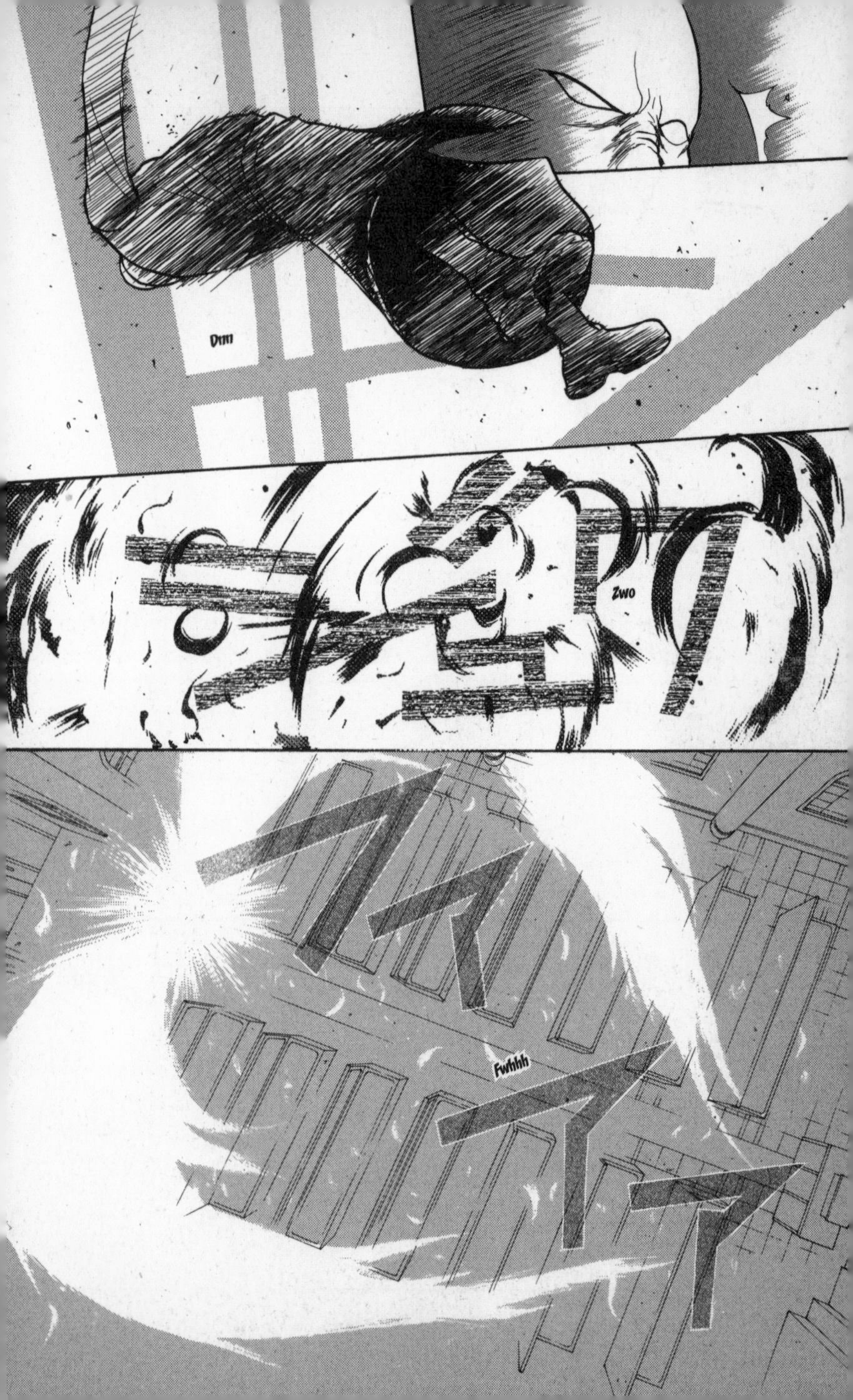
Dm
Zwo
Fwhhh

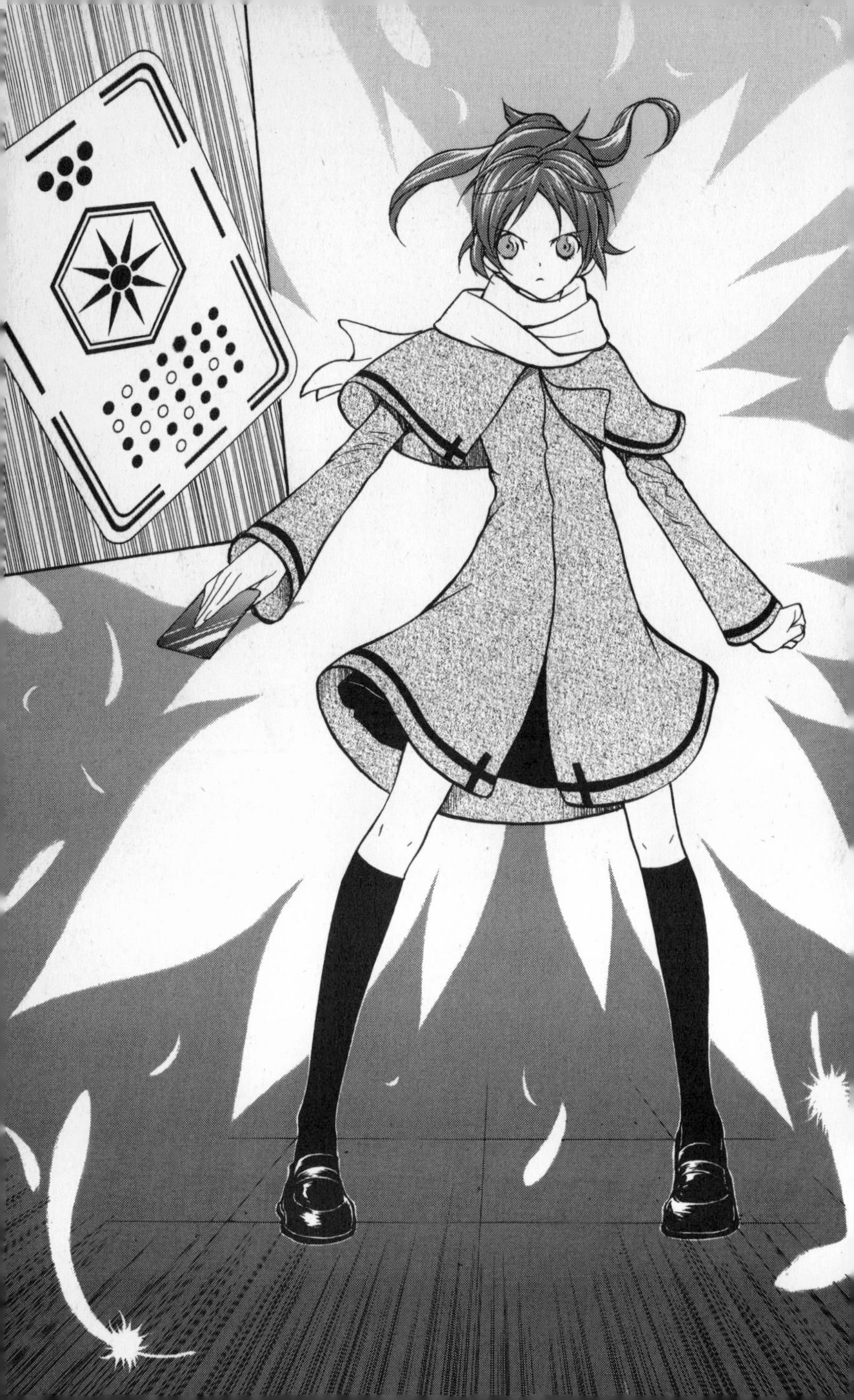

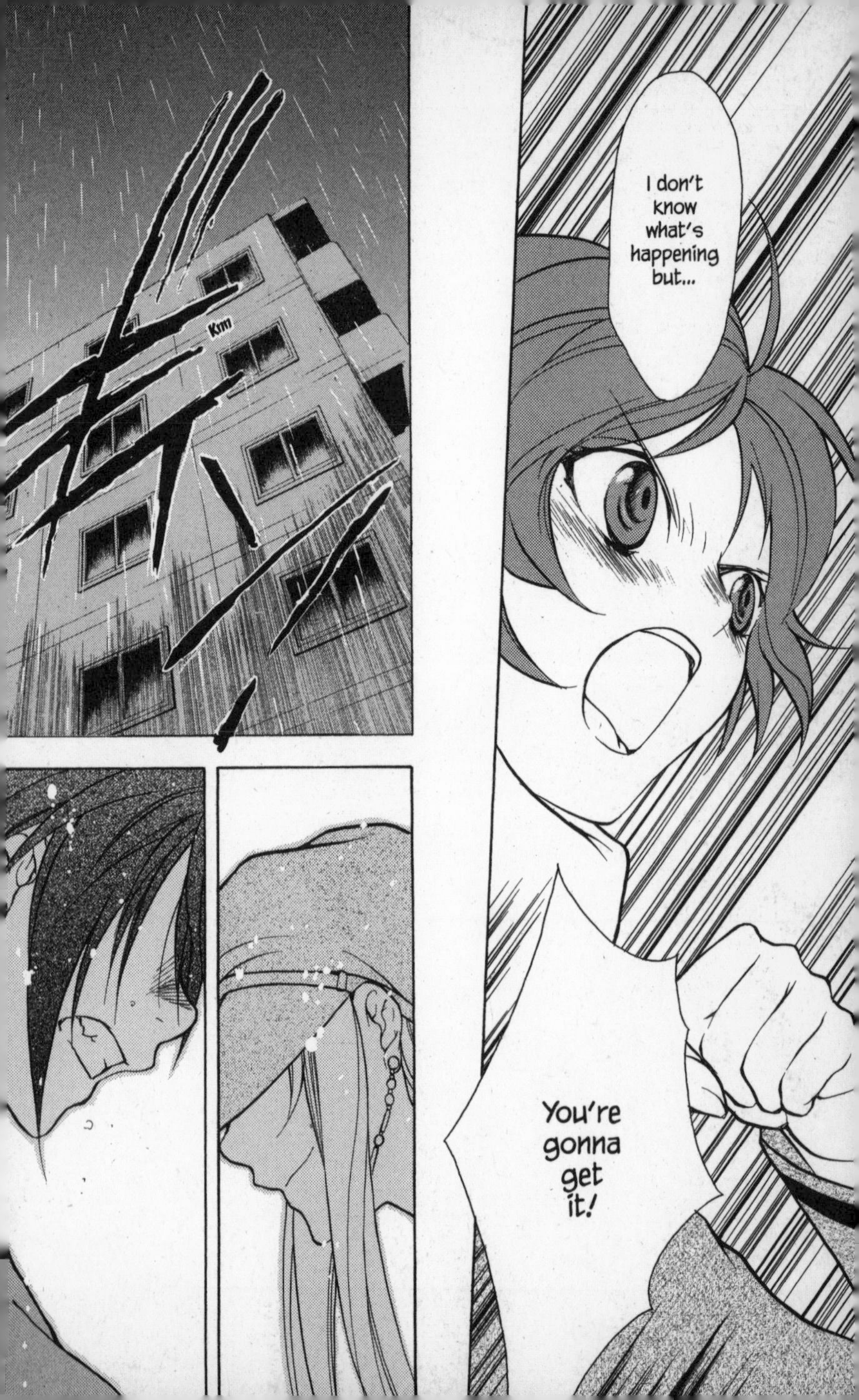
I don't know what's happening but...
You're gonna get it!
Krrn

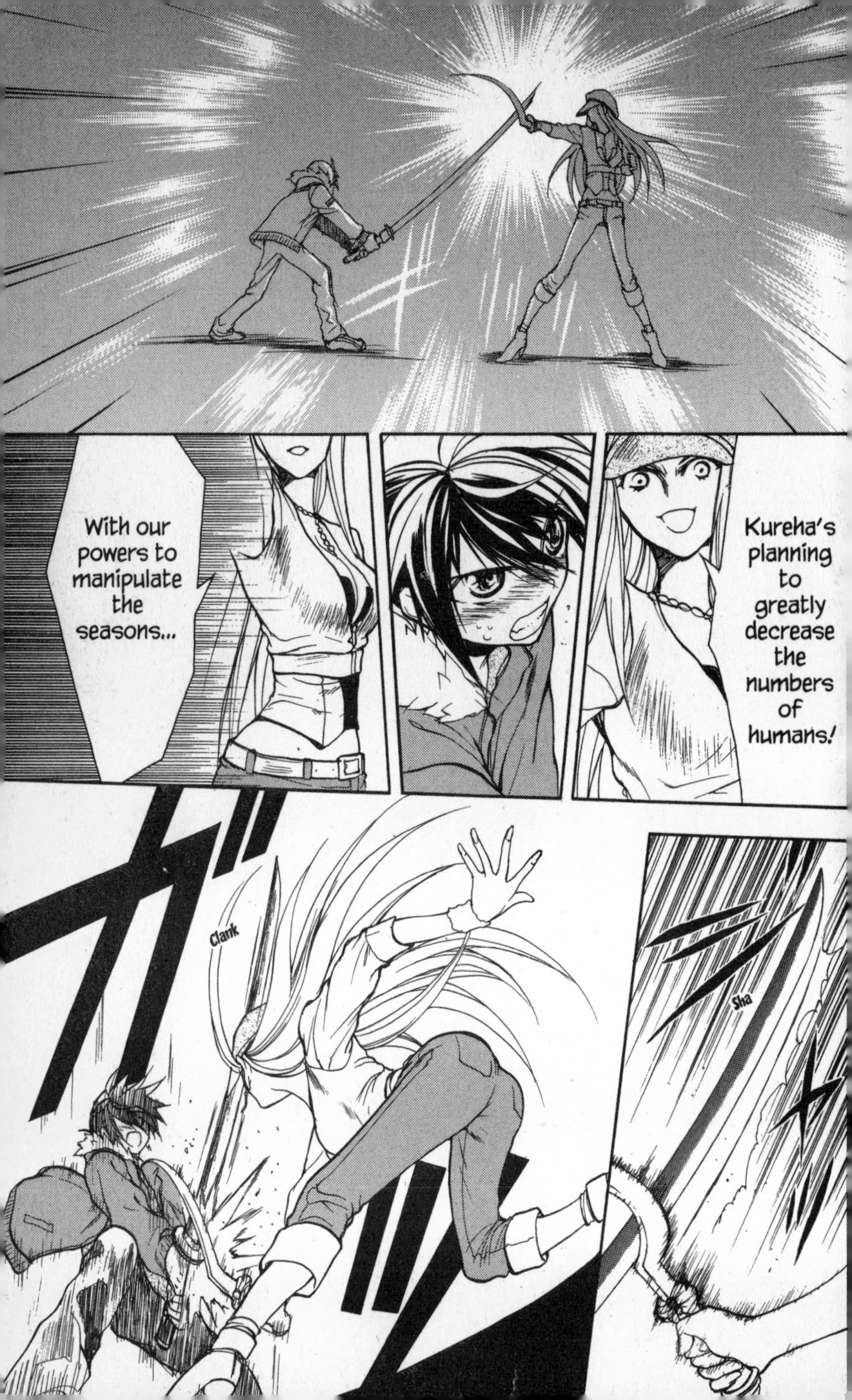
Kureha's planning to greatly decrease the numbers of humans!
With our powers to manipulate the seasons...
Sha
Clank

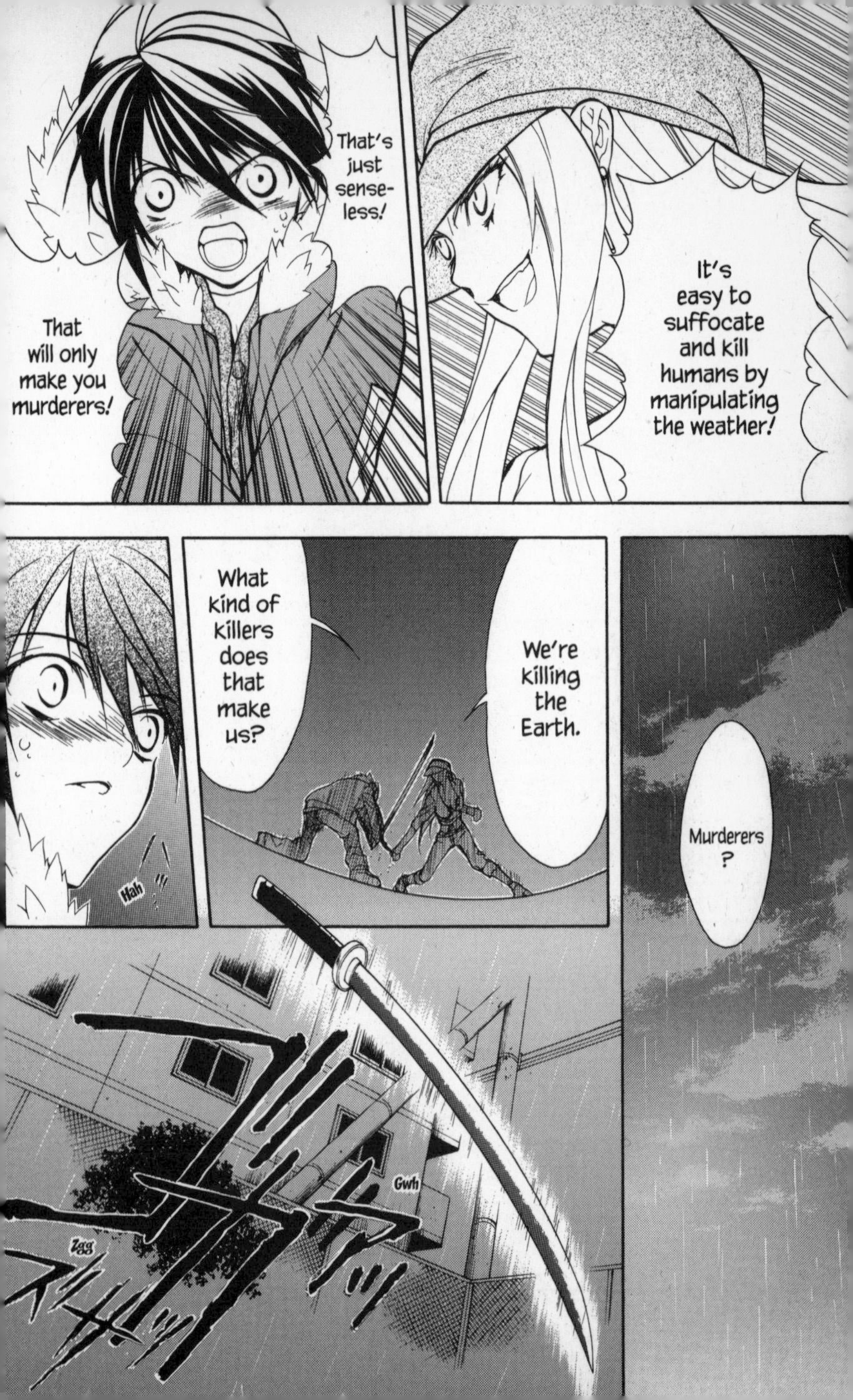
It's easy to suffocate and kill humans by manipulating the weather!
That's just sense-less!
That will only make you murderers!
Murderers?
We're killing the Earth.
What kind of killers does that make us?
Hah
Gwh
Zgg

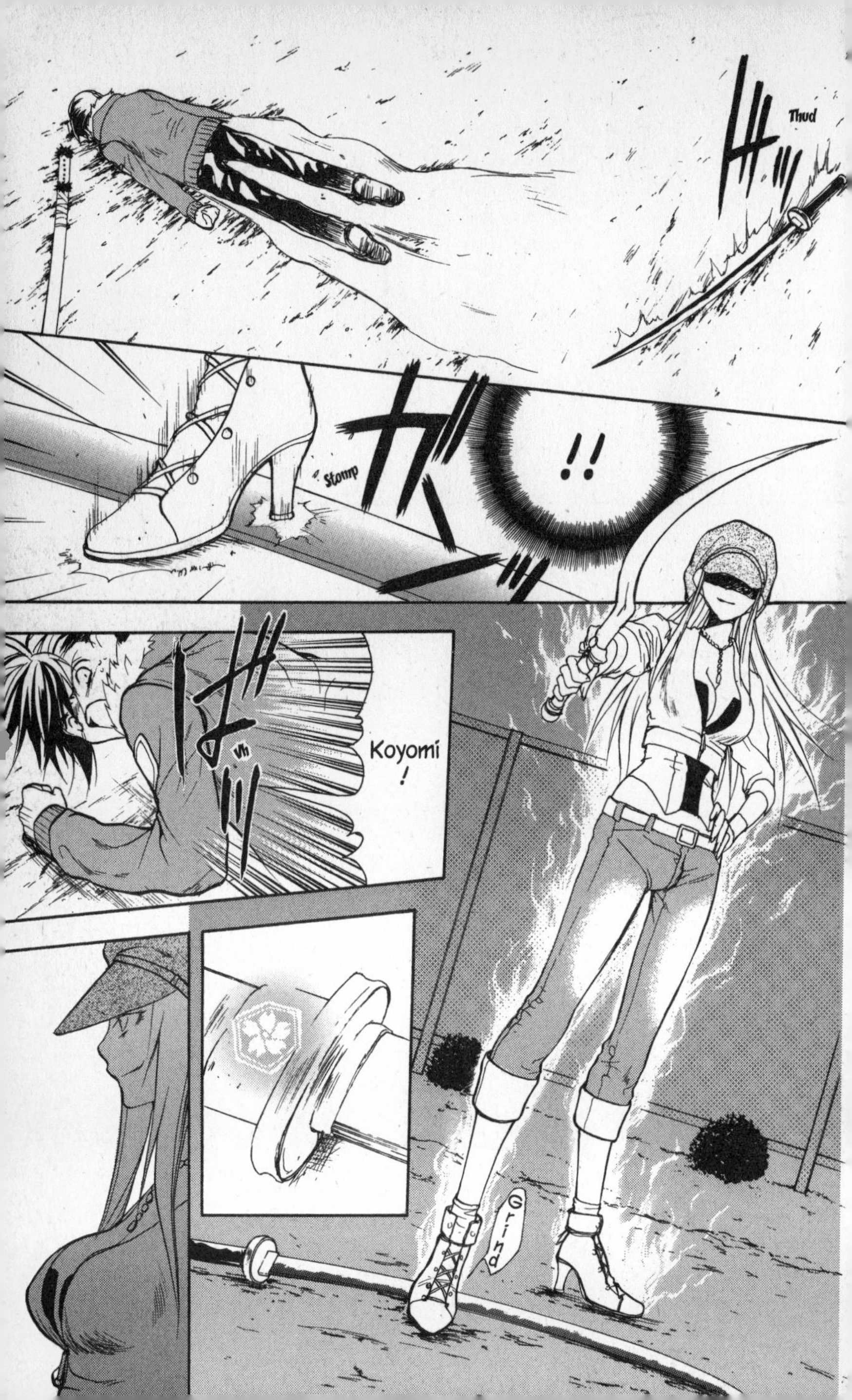

Thud
!!
Stomp
Grind
Koyomi!

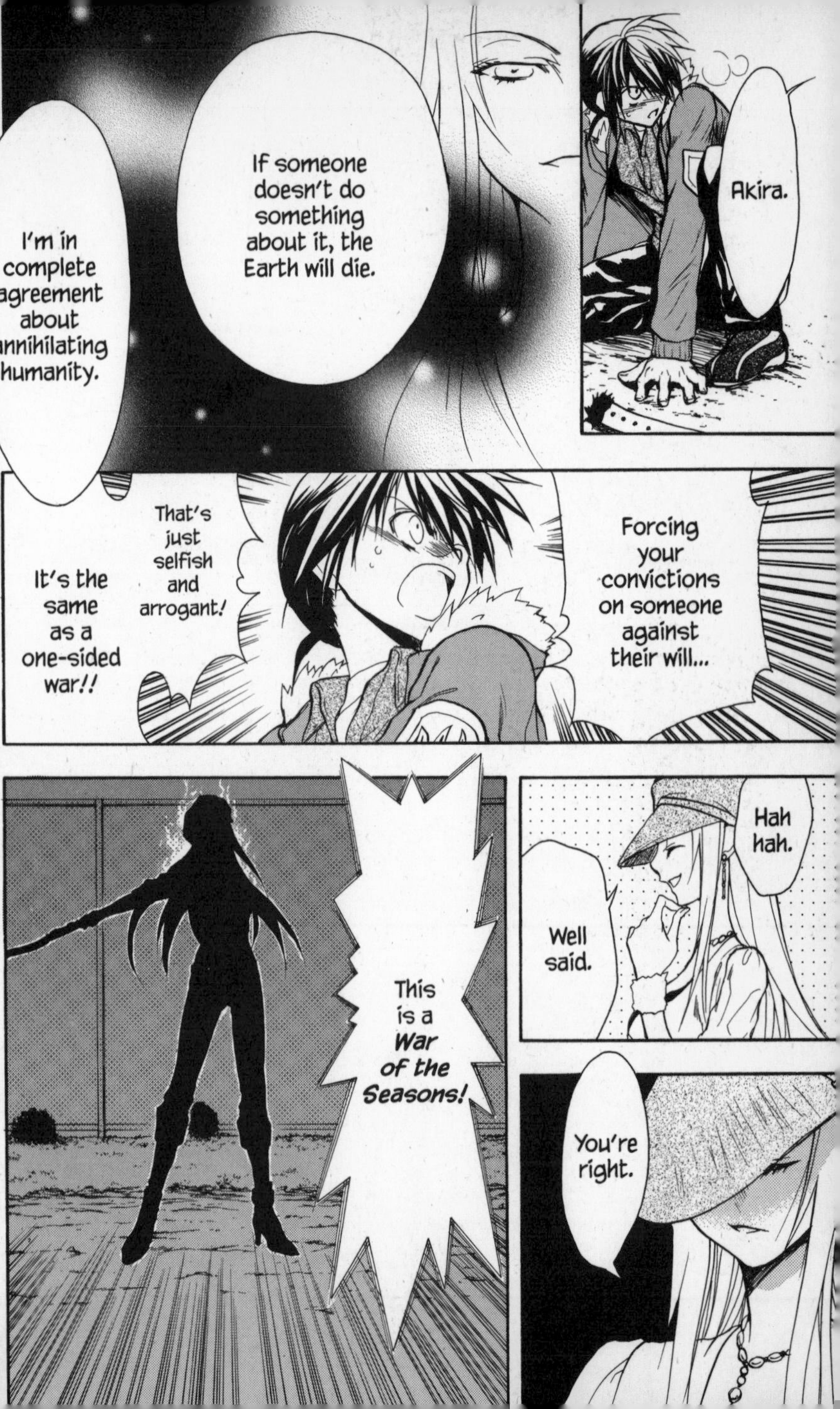
Akira.
If someone doesn't do something about it, the Earth will die.
I'm in complete agreement about annihilating humanity.
Forcing your convictions on someone against their will...
That's just selfish and arrogant!
It's the same as a one-sided war!!
Hah hah.
Well said.
You're right.
This is a *War of the Seasons!*

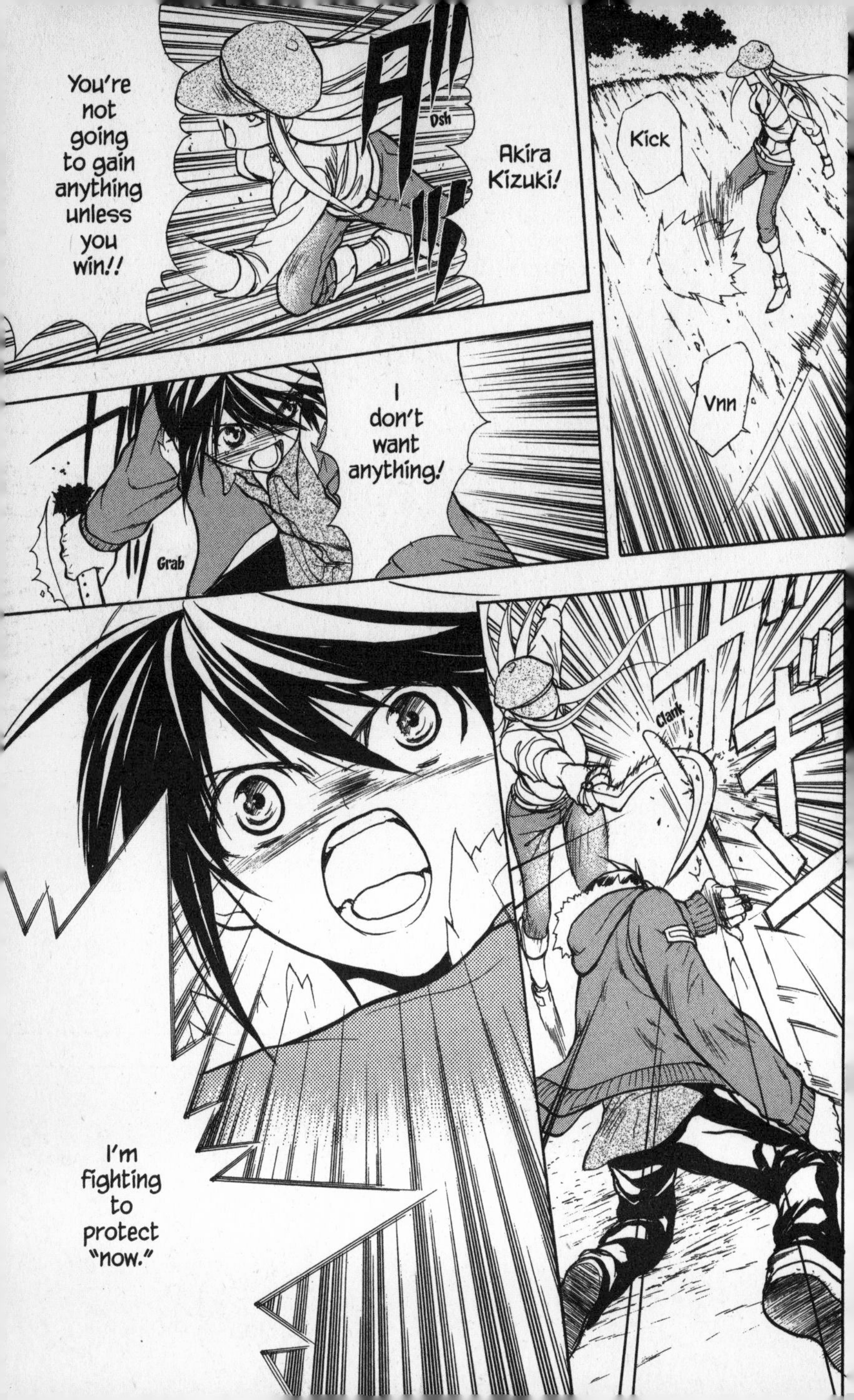
Kick
Vnn
Akira Kizuki!
Dsh
You're not going to gain anything unless you win!!
I don't want anything!
Grab
Clank
I'm fighting to protect "now."

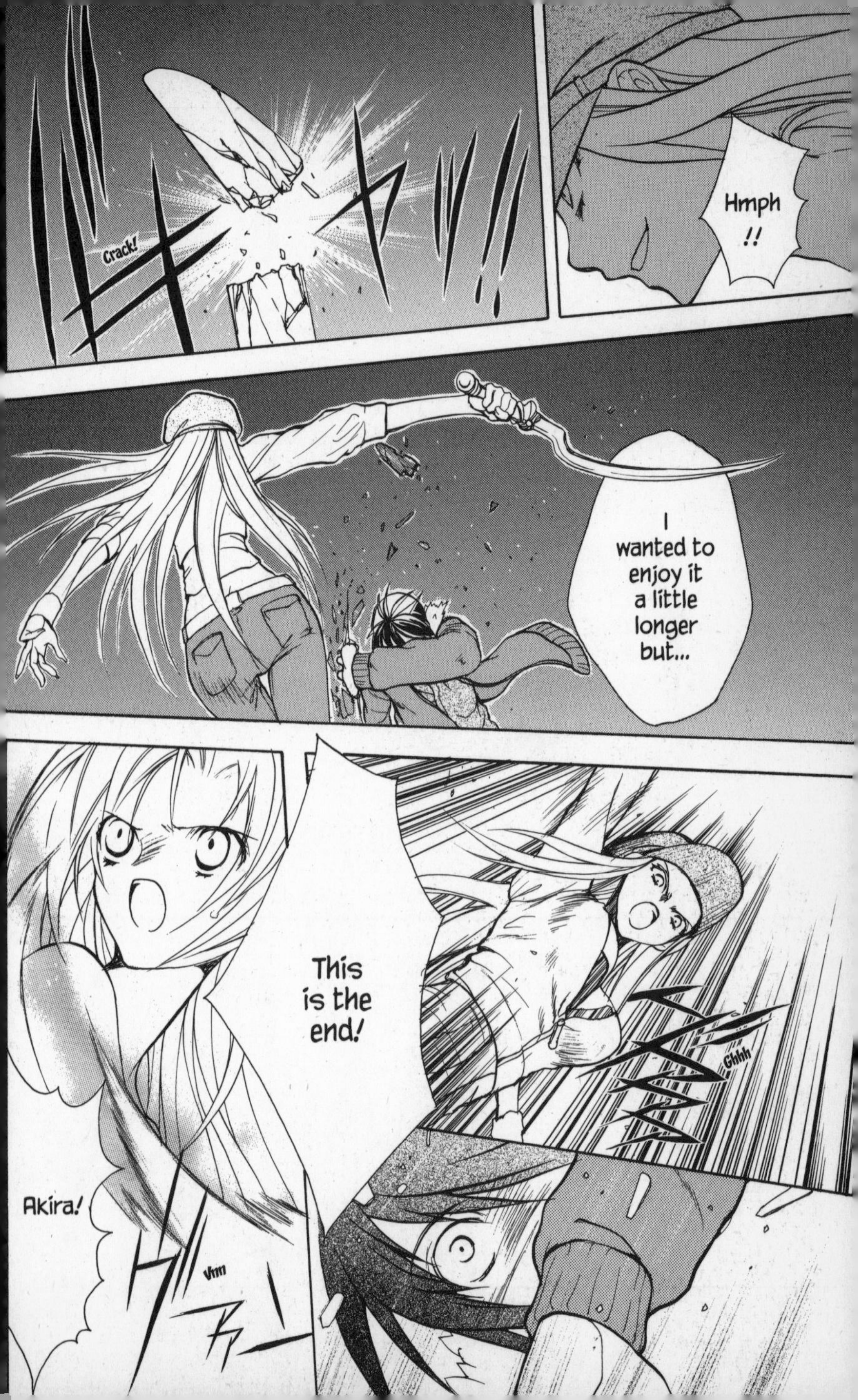
Hmph !!
Crack!
I wanted to enjoy it a little longer but...
This is the end!
Ghhh
Akira!
Vnn

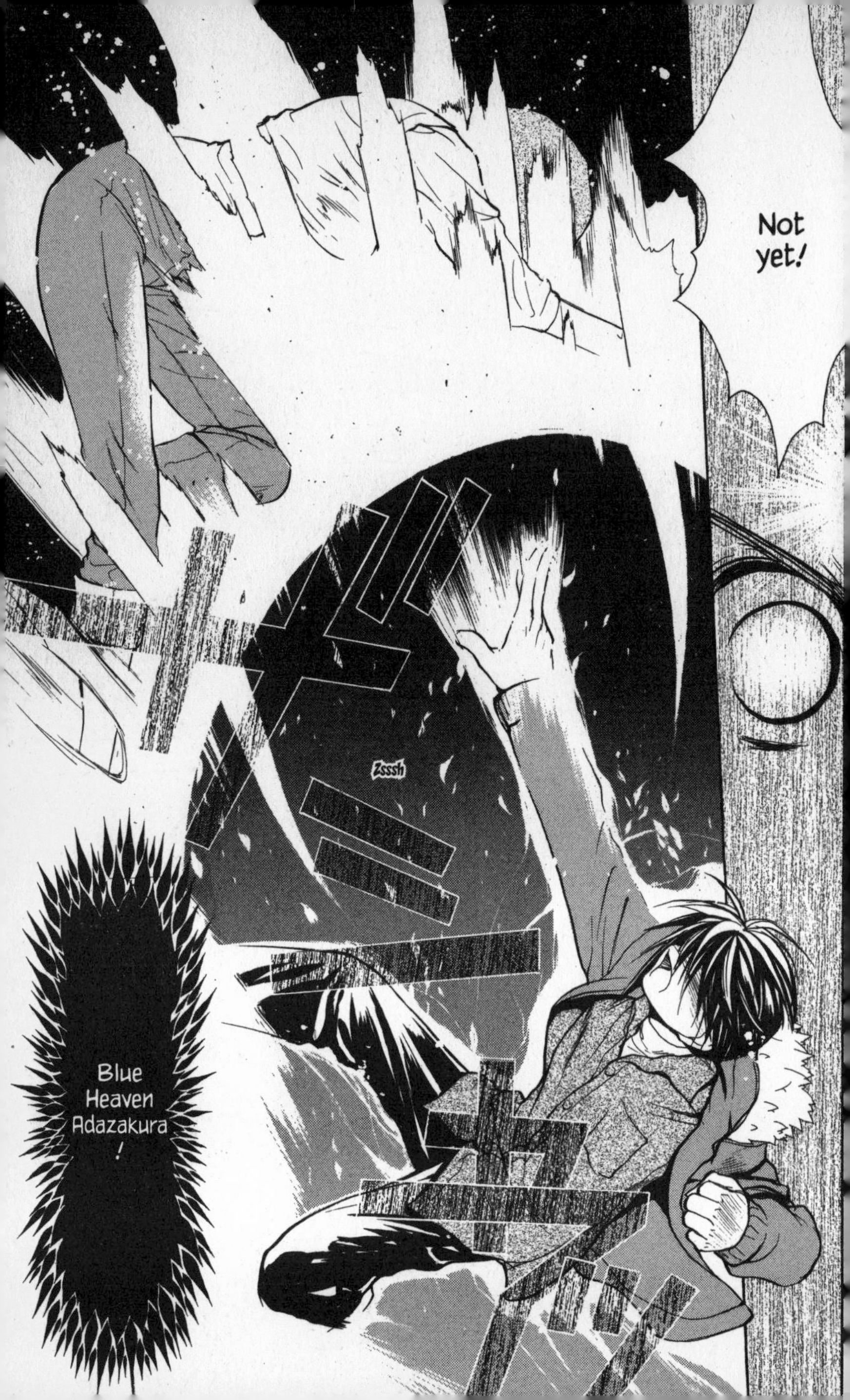
Not yet!
Zsssh
Blue Heaven Adazakura!

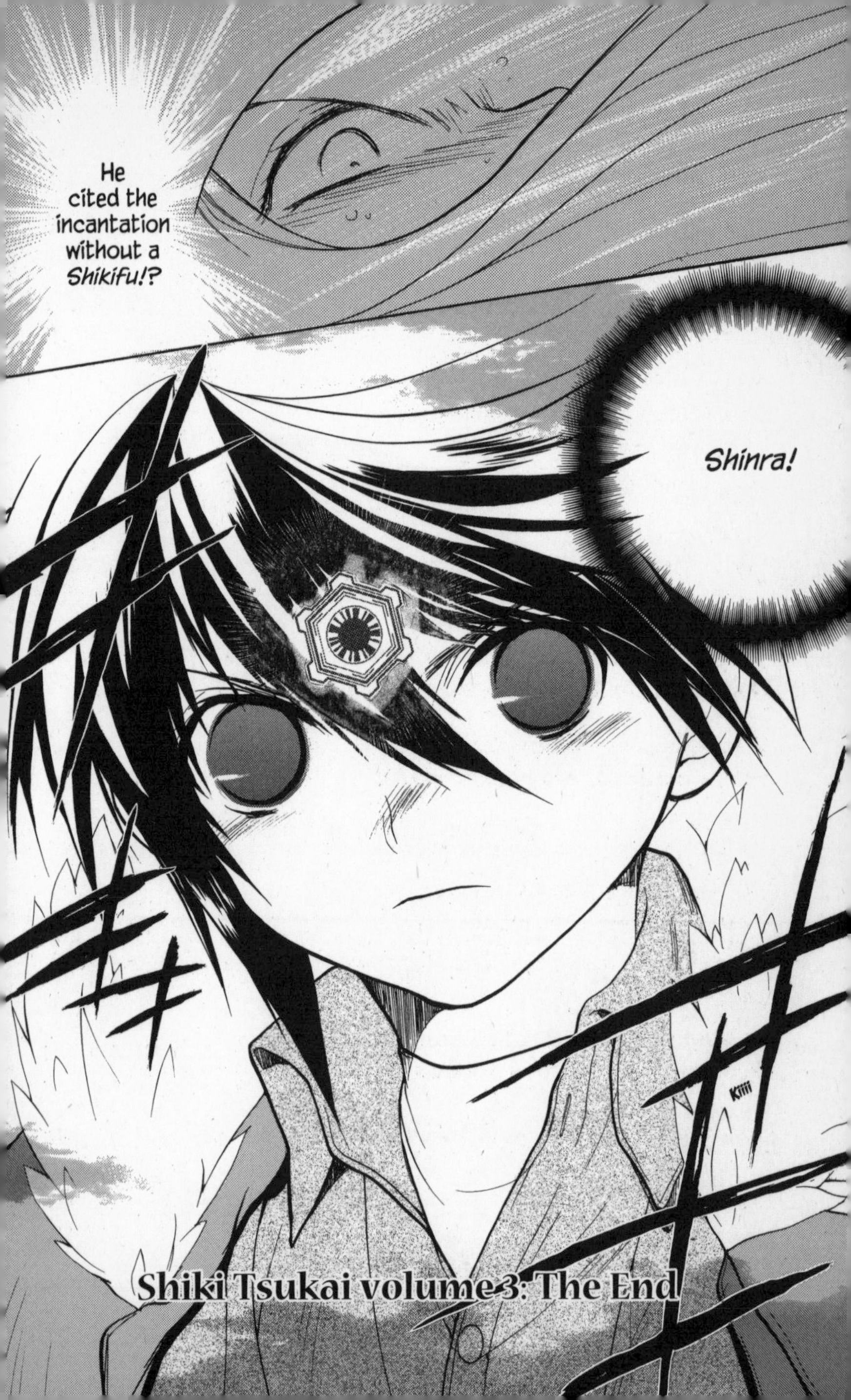
He cited the incantation without a Shikifu!?
Shinra!
Kiiii
Shiki Tsukai volume 3: The End

Staff List (Birthday: Birthstone: Meaning)

Written by: To-ru Zekuu
(September 8: Akoya Pearl: Dignity)

Manga by: Yuna Takanagi
(November 24: Cobaltian Calcite:
Anxiety Relief)

STAFF

Kira Ryuhi
(July 1: Bloodshot Iolite: To Be Directed Toward a Path)

Yu Hikawa
(August 28: Pink Coral: Cherishing Love)

Kouta Amatsuki
(November 20: Hessonite: Ability to Convince Oneself)

Character Design Assistance

Ouji
(January 5: Golden Zircon: Sorrow and Removal of Suspicion)

Takehiko Harada (Rei Seichouji)
(February 19: Water Drop Quartz: Life)

Okama
(May 25: Blue Amber: Quietly Burning Heart)

Hiroyuki Utatane (Mina Suzukure)
(June 15: Yellow Jasper: Safe Travel)

Yun Kouga (Nanayo Rangetsu)
(July 9: Brown Diamond: Unyielding Belief)

Kenichi Muraeda (Kureha Kazamatsuri)
(September 5: Golden Pearl: Mature)

Season Symbol & Shikifu Design Assistance

t-Design Lab

Naoki
(November 24: Cobaltian Calcite: Anxiety Relief)

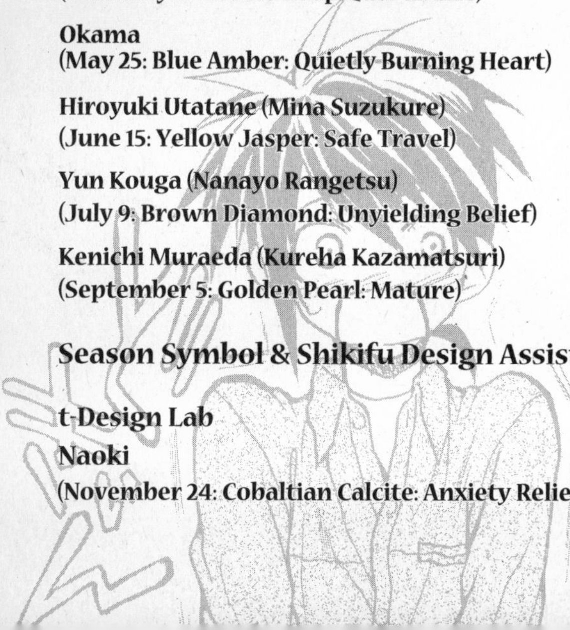

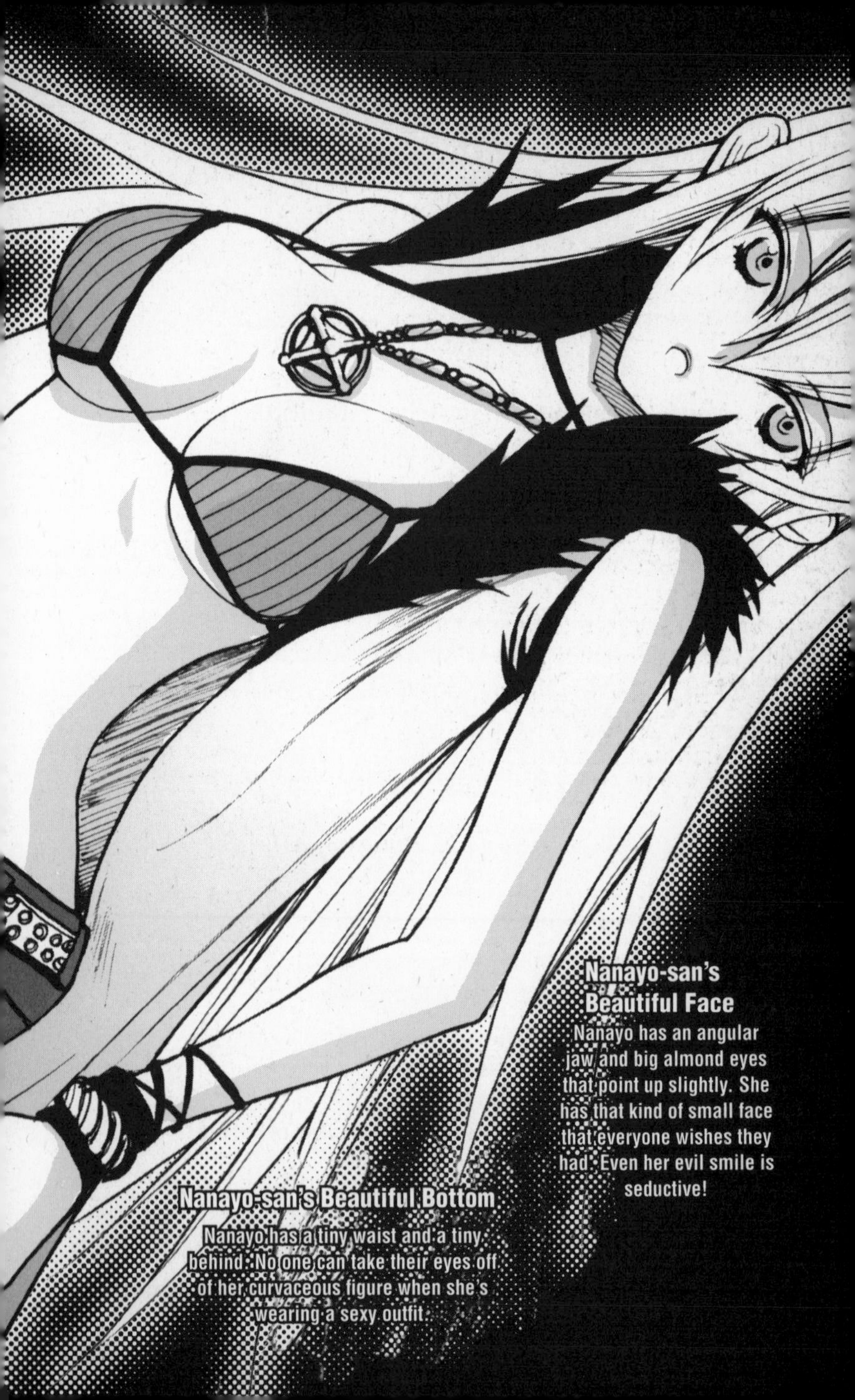
Nanayo-san's Beautiful Face
Nanayo has an angular jaw and big almond eyes that point up slightly. She has that kind of small face that everyone wishes they had. Even her evil smile is seductive!
Nanayo-san's Beautiful Bottom
Nanayo has a tiny waist and a tiny behind. No one can take their eyes off of her curvaceous figure when she's wearing a sexy outfit.

It's volume three! It's the volume with L-O-T-S of Nanayo-san action scenes…!? I like drawing her *a lot*. Being able to draw a perfect body is so wonderful. She also has a lot of different outfits, which is good. I'm always wondering what to write at the end, and I was thinking about drawing a male character, like Junichiro but… My hand has a mind of its own and ended up like this. (What the heck? LOL)

There's a stereotype that girls from the Kansai region wear revealing outfits but… I once saw a TV show where they were doing research on just how low low-rider jeans can actually go. They were doing this in a famous shop in Kansai. The majority of the jeans they carried only went as high as four inches above the crotch seam. Okay… so that had nothing to do with the manga but it would make me really happy if you read the next volume, too.

Yuna Takanagi

Nanayo-san! Body Research!

Nanayo-san's Beautiful Legs

A beautiful body line, from her thighs to the tips of her toes. Her high-speed kicks are formidable during battle! You can stare at her legs…but make sure you remember to dodge them!

Nanayo-san's Beautiful Breasts

Nanayo's breasts are the perfect shape, size and firmness. Even though she's toned, it doesn't mean her breasts aren't soft—plus they're really bouncy!

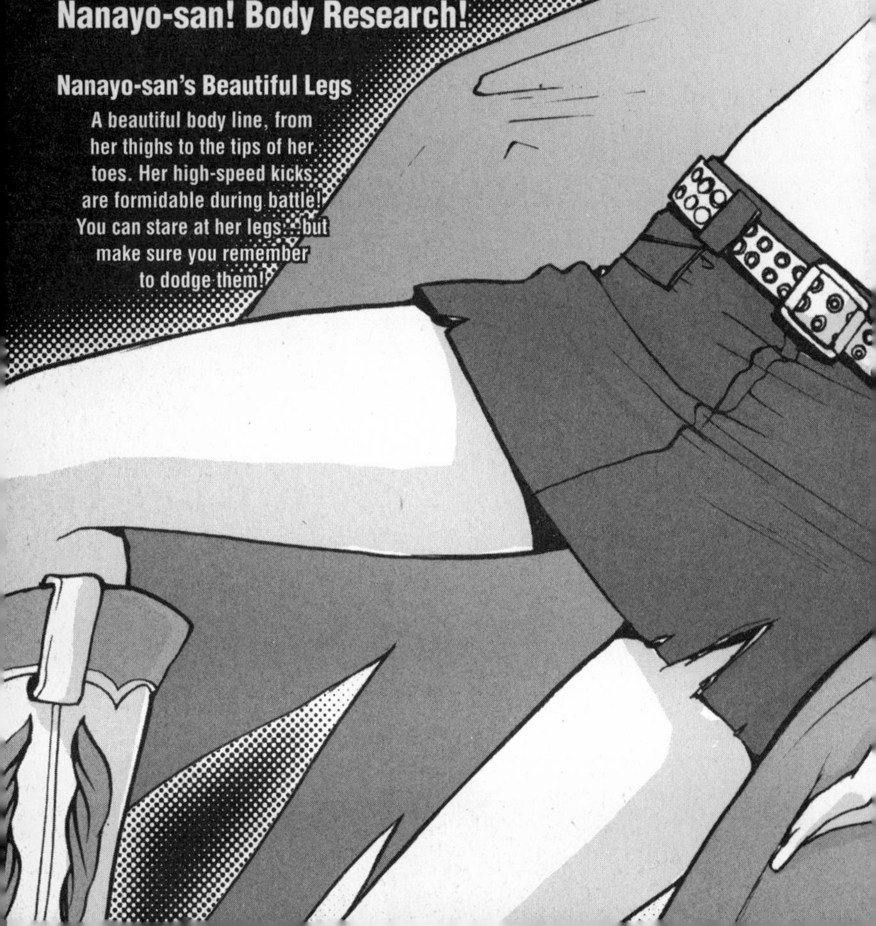

Kureha Kazamatsuri

■ Hello, it's To-ru Zekuu. What did you think of volume three, in which Summer and Winter finally clash? It's like a dream come true to have both Hiroyuki Utatane Sensei's design (Mina Suzukure) and Kenichi Muraeda Sensei's design (Kureha Kazamatsuri) in my book! They're both my Senpai, and I couldn't be happier! Yuna Takanagi and I were so overjoyed we danced like loonies in front of our fans. I can't thank them enough.

■ Now, back to reality: The manga takes place in 2013. I wonder what humanity and the environment will be like in the future? According to statistical research, the sea level will rise, and climate patterns will change because of the effect of meteorological phenomena, such as El Niño. Epidemics—especially those spread by mosquitoes—will become more common, caused by ecosystem shifts. Energy sources, such as oil, will be depleted. Other things that might change are the legal and jury system, the school system (schooling may last just a couple of semesters), etc. Even though it's only six years away, a lot of things will be different. Fumiya says something that can be applied to our changing world: "Unless we alter our relationships, I don't think anything will change."

■ The relationship between humans and the Earth, the relationship between people… There are many types of relationships, and if we can figure out which relationships should stay the same and which should change, I think it will make Earth a better place.

■ I haven't written anything that is completely pessimistic about the environment, but sometimes I get scared when I'm researching the issue. I didn't mean to talk so much about such serious issues, but I think you'll enjoy reading *Shiki Tsukai* more if you spend some time imagining what the future of the Earth will be. Thank you for reading *Shiki Tsukai* volume 3! It would make me very happy if you enjoyed it.

■ Finally: My apologies, as this is just a personal matter, but someone dear to me had a child in January 2007. Congratulations! I wish you the greatest happiness. I guess life always finds a way.

Written by: To-ru Zekuu

366-day Calendar

As long as time flows and the seasons change, everyone has the potential to become a *Shiki Tsukai*. What's your birthstone? Check it out!

1 JANUARY

Garnet – Chastity / Friendship / Loyalty / Perseverance

January 1	Imperial Jade	Immortality
January 2	Landscape Agate	Ability to avoid misfortune
January 3	Topazolite	Good news is on its way
January 4	Crisocola	Mentally sound
January 5	Golden Zircon	Sorrow and removal of suspicion
January 6	Star Garnet	Divine ability to make things happen
January 7	Ammolite	Memories of the past
January 8	Chrome Tourmaline	Strengthen one's inner self
January 9	Hydrogrossularite	Love becomes true
January 10	Gold	Helpful advice and strength
January 11	Specularite	Ability to recognize oneself
January 12	Obsidian	Eliminate distraction
January 13	Fowlerie	Binding love
January 14	Fresh Water Pearl	A harmonious love
January 15	Pigeon Blood	Eternalize
January 16	Blue Moonstone	Love between adults
January 17	Antimony	Defense against evil
January 18	Roselite	Symbol of hope
January 19	Amblygonite	Power that last an eternity
January 20	Snow Flake Obsidian	Sustained love
January 21	Peacock Color Opal	A feeling of a proposal
January 22	Star Beryl	Grace
January 23	Alexandrite-type Garnet	Change of night and day
January 24	Milky Quartz	Motherly love
January 25	Sardonyx	A happy marriage
January 26	Pyrope	Flames of love
January 27	Almandine	Being proactive leads to victory
January 28	Pink Topaz	Recovering strength and intelligence
January 29	Phantom Crystal	Ice fossil
January 30	Parti-Colored Fluorite	Past and future
January 31	Alexandrite Cat's Eye	Doubt, choice, and transformation

2 FEBRUARY

Amethyst – Ideal / Authority / Sincerity / Truth

February 1	Ulexite	Heart to see through all
February 2	Conch Pearl	Beloved
February 3	Melanite	War and victory
February 4	Bicolor Amethyst	Awakening
February 5	Prumusmume Stone	Overcome hardship
February 6	Grey Star Sapphire	Good news brought with dawn
February 7	Cairngorm	Rules and guardianship
February 8	Rutilated Quartz	Happy family
February 9	Red Jasper	Right decision
February 10	Red Tiger Eye	Fate of destruction and creation
February 11	Water Worn	Flow of time
February 12	Yellow Spinel	Self love, puberty
February 13	Bicolor Fluorite	Appeal of having two sides
February 14	Pink Opal	Encounter of love
February 15	Pink Zircon	Ease of pain
February 16	Dravite	Events in life
February 17	Tiger Iron	Courage, strong conviction
February 18	Orange Topaz	Knowledge and logic
February 19	Water Drop Quartz	Life
February 20	Brown Onyx	Chastity
February 21	Horn	Yearning of love
February 22	Cat's Eye Quartz	Prediction of the future
February 23	Cherry Pink Ruby	Love's distrust
February 24	White Pearl	Sincerity
February 25	Phantom Amethyst	Illusion
February 26	Gold Quartz	Eye to see the world
February 27	Cuprite	Multiple faces
February 28	Parasite Holed Coral	Perseverance
February 29	Pallasite	All things taking flight

3 MARCH

Aquamarine – Luminosity / Knowledge
Bloodstone – Devotion / Gallant

March 1	Fluorite	Secret Love
March 2	Shell Opal	Unite
March 3	Pink Beryl	Appeal of a sweet disposition
March 4	Silver	Symbol of youth
March 5	Royal Blue Sapphire	Happiness and Lifespan
March 6	Copal	Silence and movement
March 7	Shell Opal	Clarity
March 8	Smithsonite	Guardianship
March 9	Silver Pearl	Reverence of religion
March 10	Howlite	Symbol of something sublime
March 11	Inesite	Passion
March 12	Kyanite	Obedient and pure
March 13	Yellow Diamond	Changing peace
March 14	Colorless Spinel	Innocence
March 15	Orange Moonstone	Love moving fast
March 16	Rose Quartz	To convey love
March 17	Dioptase	Live free
March 18	Kaolinite	Caring heart
March 19	Bicolor Quartz	Arrival of spring
March 20	Euclase	Well-considered plan
March 21	Iron	Amazing power
March 22	Sogdianite	Resurrection
March 23	Picture Jasper	Fantasize
March 24	Green Quartz	Calming the emotions
March 25	Peach Zircon	Relief from pain
March 26	Platinum	Susceptible heart
March 27	Purple Zircon	Too many conversations
March 28	Pink Diamond	Coming of love
March 29	Green Diamond	Graceful
March 30	Angel Skin Coral	Unchanging heart
March 31	Orthoclase	Attain one's goal

4 APRIL

Diamond – Innocence / Eternal Bond / Unyielding

April 1	Herkimer Diamond	Dream
April 2	Celestite	Cleansing of the Soul
April 3	Zeolite	Regeneration and harvest from the Earth
April 4	Gem Silica	Happiness and prosperity
April 5	Colorless Sapphire	Holy power and wisdom
April 6	Blue Diamond	Safety
April 7	Brazilianite	Intelligence
April 8	Padparadsha Sapphire	Flower of light
April 9	Cerasite	Mental beauty and purity
April 10	White Zircon	A heart with everything on the line
April 11	Bournite	Sense of aggression
April 12	Pink Fluorite	Mystical
April 13	Violet Pearl	Sense of pride
April 14	Colorless Topaz	Genius
April 15	Peacock Green Pearl	Love for nature
April 16	Hiddenite	Pure and modest
April 17	Green Spinel	Hope, faith, and happiness
April 18	Axinite	Continuation of effort
April 19	Violet Zircon	Earthliness and spirituality
April 20	Chloromelanite	Deceit and truth
April 21	Andalusite	Feeling of love
April 22	Astrophyllite	Trusting love
April 23	Desert Rose	Love and wisdom
April 24	Kunzite	Premonition of a future lover
April 25	Plasma	Binary decision
April 26	Sugilite	Eternal and unchanging love
April 27	Carnelian	Lucid love
April 28	Kimberlite	Guardian of love
April 29	Magnetite	Consistency
April 30	Sillimanite	Warning

7 JULY

Ruby – Passion / Freedom / Courage

1	Bloodshot Iolite	To be directed toward a path
2	Parisite	Law of nature
3	Rock Crystal	Heart that seeks pleasure
4	Diopside	Direction toward happiness
5	Anatase	Happiness toward the future
6	Apache Tears	Mystery
7	Star Rose Quartz	Rendezvous
8	Milky Opal	Excitement of love
9	Brown Diamond	Unyielding belief
10	Spodumene	Unlimited love
11	Cream Opal	New encounter
12	Red Beryl	Higher consciousness
13	Chrysoberyl	Brilliance
14	Three Color Fluorite	Multi-faced
15	Goethite	Spiritual power
16	Azurite	Ability to contemplate
17	Aventurine	Bright future
18	Labradorite Feldspar	Secret meeting
19	Hydro Rhodochrosite	Justice
20	Aquamarine Cat's Eye	Ray of light
21	Blue Jasper	Fine tuned emotions
22	Flower Obsidian	A new journey
23	Watermelon Tourmaline	Mounting happiness
24	Witherite	Poison and antidote
25	Shell	A beautiful vow
26	Fossil Coral	Conquer
27	Grey Diamond	To being from a minor role
28	Almandine Spinel	Strength and caring
29	Black Opal	Menace
30	Epidote	To be released from the past
31	Red Zircon	Time of peace

8 AUGUST

Peridot – Friendship / Harmony between husband and wife

1	Citrine	Sweet memory
2	Blue Quartz	Birth of life
3	Chrysoberyl Cat's Eye	Golden Eye
4	Marcasite	Memory and supposition
5	Cat's Eye Moonstone	Opportunity of love
6	Dark Green Zircon	Mental healing
7	Yellow Apatite	Suspicion
8	Rutile	Arrow of love
9	Chalcopyrite	Removal of oblivion
10	Iolite	To heighten one's spiritual power
11	Yellow Sapphire	Concentration
12	Concha Agate	Rules of nature
13	Yellow Zircon	Sorrows from birth
14	Fire Opal	Someone in love
15	Blue Lace Agate	To move one's soul
16	Labradorite	Longing
17	Pyrite	Ability to shelter
18	Orange Pearl	Recovery
19	Calcite	Splendor and prosperity
20	Star Ruby	Core
21	Jet	Oblivion
22	White Coral	Purify
23	Eosphorite	Offer one's unchanging love
24	Lava	Lover
25	Fire Agate	Belief
26	Turquoise Blue	Divine love
27	Apatite	Confuse
28	Pink Coral	Cherishing Love
29	Cactus Amethyst	Change
30	Rainbow Obsidian	Various sorts
31	Moss Agate	Nourishment for the soul

5 MAY

Emerald – Happiness / Integrity / Spousal Love / Noble / Health / Wisdom

May 1	Amazonite	Time has come
May 2	Yellow Beryl	Enduring love
May 3	Green Zircon	Wish for peace
May 4	Forsterite	Power of greatness
May 5	Red Coral	Child's heart
May 6	Idoclase	Promise
May 7	Creedite	Maturing of the heart
May 8	Emerald Cat's Eye	Imagination
May 9	Black Pearl	Silent strength
May 10	Robin's Egg Blue	Heart yearning for release
May 11	Lace Agate	Silent courage
May 12	Cacoxenite	Beginning of consciousness
May 13	Ivory	Pure, strength from reason
May 14	Blue Green Zircon	Disappearing strength
May 15	Red Jadeite	Ability to make decisions
May 16	Tektites	Freedom
May 17	Purple Sapphire	Memory of first love
May 18	Goshenite	Elegance
May 19	Noselite	Overcome a crisis
May 20	Zaratite	Inner strength
May 21	Opalized wood	Union and harmony
May 22	Dendritic Quartz	A satisfying growth
May 23	Andradite	Loyalty
May 24	Adularia	Plan
May 25	Blue Amber	Quietly burning heart
May 26	Copper	Prisoner of love
May 27	Verdelite	Perseverance
May 28	White Chalcedony	Gracefulness
May 29	Xalostocite	Victory of joy
May 30	Tsavolite	Influential
May 31	Smokey Quartz	Comforting peace

6 JUNE

Pearl – Wealth / Health
Moonstone – Anticipation of Love / A Fulfilling Love

June 1	Color Change Sapphire	Two-faced
June 2	Clear Amber	Fulfillment of a dream
June 3	Phenacite	Complete change in mood
June 4	Odontolite	Offence and defense
June 5	Alexandrite	Two-faced
June 6	Silicified Wood	Union and change
June 7	Pink Pearl	Persevering love
June 8	Sanidine	Fusion of supernatural powers
June 9	Ulexite	Brilliant mind
June 10	Quartz	Harmony, fusion and to strengthen
June 11	White Labradorite	Good rumor
June 12	Mabe Pearl	Allure
June 13	Uvarovite	Shy with a talent to steal hearts
June 14	Cyprine	Insight
June 15	Yellow Jasper	Safe travel
June 16	Blue Opal	A refreshing show of affection
June 17	Neptunite	Continuation of life
June 18	Argentite	Defense from evil
June 19	Black Star Sapphire	Soul of the dead
June 20	Green Fluorite	Secret virtue
June 21	Serpentine	Shelter
June 22	Sun Stone	Shine
June 23	Anyolite	Modest love
June 24	Water Opal	A maiden's love
June 25	Malachite	Perceptiveness and imagination
June 26	Spessartine	Loyalty and the will to obey
June 27	Liddicoatite	Various appeal
June 28	Blue Zircon	Illusion and dreaming heart
June 29	Jasper	Self-control
June 30	Ulexite	Insight

9 SEPTEMBE

Sapphire – Sincerity / Earnest

September 1	Tanzanite	Prideful
September 2	High Quartz	Victorious love
September 3	Red Diamond	Secret to creation
September 4	Sphene	Will of the universe
September 5	Golden Pearl	Mature
September 6	Zoisite	Symbol of spiritual powe
September 7	Jacinth	Relieved
September 8	Akoyo Pearl	Dignity
September 9	Aragonite	Show one's ability
September 10	Danburite	Vast knowledge
September 11	Rainbow Fluorite	Wish come true
September 12	Fayalite	Fated bond
September 13	Golden Beryl	Bright good day
September 14	Iron Rose	Courage, power to save oth
September 15	Paraiba Tourmaline	Return to the starting po
September 16	Prehnite	Natural beauty
September 17	Dioptase	Reunion
September 18	Mandarin Garnet	Wealth
September 19	Lazurite	Meditation
September 20	Blue Spinel	Spice of love
September 21	Selenite	Self consciousness
September 22	Zircon	Innocence
September 23	Ametrine	Light and shadow
September 24	Demantoid	To run
September 25	Bicolor Tourmaline	Symmetry and harmony
September 26	Orange Diamond	Promised love
September 27	Trapiche Sapphire	Living freely
September 28	Amethyst Quartz	Sound thinking
September 29	Imperial Topaz	Remarkable strength
September 30	Blue Star Sapphire	A guide to knowledge

10 OCTOBE

Tourmaline – Wealth / Health
Opal – Anticipation of Love / A Fulfilling Lov

October 1	Elbaite	To re-create
October 2	High Quartz	To attain
October 3	Violet Diamond	Appealing relationship
October 4	Opal Jasper	Precise intervals
October 5	Larimar	Silent observer
October 6	Chrysoprase	Fertility and happiness
October 7	Rhodonite	Heighten one's self
October 8	Blue Chalcedony	Reminiscence
October 9	Blue Onyx	Good news
October 10	Tourmaline Cat's Eye	Eye opener
October 11	Rhodolite	Proactive love
October 12	Party Colored Sapphire	Calming the hatred
October 13	Hematite	Guide to victory
October 14	Trapiche Emerald	Rotation
October 15	Aventurine Quartz	Opportunity for love
October 16	White Onyx	A guide to success
October 17	Magnetite	To overcome fear
October 18	Blue Agate	Artistic
October 19	Scarab	Regeneration and eternal lif
October 20	Chalcosiderite	Wish
October 21	Schorl	Recover one's strength
October 22	Lepidolite	Reform
October 23	Thulite	Mystical recovery
October 24	Indigolite	Artistic sense
October 25	Red Spinel	Curiosity
October 26	Tiger's Eye Quartz	Ability to see through things
October 27	Hauyne	Divine occupation
October 28	Cornflower Blue Sapphire	A straight line
October 29	Matrix Turquoise	Insight and imagination
October 30	Pin-Fire Opal	Correct direction
October 31	Hawk's Eye	Decision and to move forwa

11 NOVEMBER

Topaz – Friendship / Loyalty / Prosperity

November 1	Cinnamon Stone	A chance for success
November 2	Black Onyx	Thinking based on religion
November 3	Golden Sapphire	Shining appeal and brilliance
November 4	Scepter Quartz	Joy of birth
November 5	Nephrite	Charming eyes
November 6	Sphalerite	Balance and moderation
November 7	Pit Amber	Embrace, a grand love
November 8	Red Topaz	Life and prosperity
November 9	Tortoise Shell	Long life and depth
November 10	Fossil	Ancestor's guardianship
November 11	Black Diamond	Beginning of happiness
November 12	Violet Sapphire	Graceful transformation
November 13	Crystal Opal	Strengthen of the inner self
November 14	Lavender Jade	A little rumor
November 15	Crimson Coral	A generous and silent love
November 16	Ammonite	Variations of thought
November 17	Green Rutile Quartz	Grab an opportunity
November 18	Anthophyllite	Generosity and plentiful love
November 19	Blue Topaz	Culture and learning
November 20	Hessonite	Ability to convince one's self
November 21	White Jadeite	Purified soul
November 22	Yellow Opal	Hidden instinct
November 23	Keshi Pearl	Momentary rest
November 24	Cobaltian Calcite	To be relieved from feeling anxious
November 25	Red Amber	Appeal of a little demon
November 26	Scapolite	Thinking towards the future
November 27	Petrified Wood	Fusion
November 28	Orangeish Brown Topaz	Guardianship and infinite patience
November 29	Alexandrite Tourmaline	Love and saga
November 30	Star Enstatite	Deep trust

12 DECEMBER

Lapis Lazuli – Health / Love and Harmony
Turquoise – Valor / Prosperity / Success / Life

December 1	Iron Opal	A caring gesture
December 2	Black Coral	A cool wit
December 3	Meteorite	A regeneration of the soul
December 4	Sodalite	Subconscious and manifestation
December 5	Angelite	Shining truth
December 6	Enstatite	Innocent justice
December 7	Gypsum	Furtile earth
December 8	Rubellite	Proactive action
December 9	Alabaster	To bring victory
December 10	Blue John Fluorite	A balanced heart
December 11	Cassiterite	A well planned strategy
December 12	Soft Pink Zircon	Aphrodisiac
December 13	Apophyllite	Clairvoyance
December 14	Pink Sapphire	Lovely
December 15	Trapiche Ruby	Transformation and challenge
December 16	Azuromalachite	Cooperativeness
December 17	Labradorite	Passionate and dangerous love
December 18	Tourmalinated Quartz	Oppositions unite
December 19	White Opal	Divine guardianship
December 20	Hemimorphite	Strange opposite
December 21	Black Moonstone	A new journey for two
December 22	Uvite	Creative thinking
December 23	Orange Jade	A heartwarming confession of love
December 24	Staurolite	Strong ability to shelter
December 25	Cross Stone	Holy pact
December 26	Purple Diamond	Hidden secret
December 27	Moldavite	Symbol of love
December 28	Rhodochrosite	Welcome a new love
December 29	Faustite	Regeneration and the power of life
December 30	Kosmochlor	Nature's knowledge
December 31	Ajoite	Purification of all

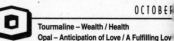

Every season incantation that the *Shiki Tsukai* use is predetermined. It is thought the *Shiki Tsukai* learn the season incantations with guidance from their *Shikifu*.

The phrases needed to use the incantations.

Shows the incantation type.

72 Kou	Incantation Variety	Incantation Known name	Incantation Type
Grains begin to sprout under the snow Water celery plants shall grow remarkably fast	Silent Chill	Frost Pillar	Special: Snow
Water beneath the surface shall begin to flow Male pheasants shall begin to twitter	Ice Sin		Manipulate: Cold
	Ice Demon	Ice Demon Summon	Summon: *Kijyuu*
	Ice King	Silver Ice Flower	Weapon/Armor: Snow
Japanese butterbur plants begin to bud Thick ice shall cover the mountain streams Hens begin laying their eggs	White Flower		Shoot: Snow
	White Cry		Special: Snow
	White Night		Special: Illusion
Hens begin laying their eggs Eastern winds shall melt the ice	White Night	Midnight Sun of Snow	Special: Illusion
Japanese nightingales begin to chirp in the mountain villages Fish shall jump through the cracks in the ice	Chi Bullets	Ice Storm Bullets / Rime Snow Bullets	Shoot: *Chi*
	Chi Beast		Summon: *Kijyuu*
	Chi Weapon/Armor	Frost Wind Bullets	Weapon/Armor: *Chi*
Rain shall fall and the Earth will soak up the water The mist shall begin to flow	Sacred Ground	Ice Crane	Manipulate: Chi
	Holy Heal	Divine Healing	Special: Healing
The grass and the trees shall lay their roots Hibernating insects shall appear from their burrows	Holy Eye		Special: Plant
Peach tree flowers begin to blossom Caterpillars become small white butterflies	Tree Shadow		Shoot: *Chi*
	Tree Banish	Tree Summon, Peach Wall	Manipulate: Bugs
	Tree God	Tree God Summon	Weapon/Armor: Plants
Sparrows shall begin to build their nests Cherry trees shall begin to blossom Thunder can be heard from the distance	Blue Sky	Spring Storm	Summon: *Kijyuu*
	Blue Heaven	Blue Heaven Adazakura	Shoot: Wind
	Clear Blue Sky		
Thunder can be heard from the distance Swallows arrive from the south	Clear Blue Sky		Special: Cherry Blossom
The geese shall migrate north Rainbows appear after the rain Reed plants begin to flower	Stiffness		Special: Lightning
	Great Strength		Shoot: Minerals
	Strong Mind		Weapon/Armor: Minerals
The frost shall cease and the grains shall grow Peony flowers begin to bloom	Earthquake		Manipulate: Earth
	Earth Dust		Special: Magnetic
	Earth Flower		Special: Plant

SHI	KI
TSU	KAI

Season Incantation Chart

The four *Shiki Tsukai* groups: shows which months belong to which season.

The *Shiki Tsukai* can use only the incantations corresponding to the Sigil dates on their *Shikifu*.

SHIKI TSUKAI

Season	Month	Sigil Dates	Month Name & 24 Sekki: Month Name	Month Name & 24 Sekki: 24 Sekki	Meaning of 24 Sekki
Winter	January	1/1–1/4	Mutsuki	Touji	The Dark Emperor takes the throne and the sun shall not rise
		1/5–1/9			
		1/10–1/14		Shoukan	Cold air shall encase all as we enter the dead of winter
		1/15–1/19			
		1/20–1/24		Daikan	A feast to the arctic cold begins and the cold shall find its light
		1/25–1/29			
		1/30–1/31			
Winter	February	2/1–2/3	Kisaragi	Daikan	A feast to the arctic cold begins and the cold shall find its light
		2/4–2/8			
		2/9–2/13		Risshun	Spring arrives from the North in search of its *Zassetsu*
		2/14–2/18			
		2/19–2/23		Usui	Snow shall cease, thus turning into rain and the Blue Emperor shall weave his water
		2/24–2/28			
Spring	March	3/1–3/5	Yayoi	Usui	Snow shall cease, thus turning into rain and the Blue Emperor shall weave his water
		3/6–3/10			
		3/11–3/15		Keichitsu	Those who hide in the earth shall rise with the light
		3/16–3/20			
		3/21–3/25		Shunbun	Days and nights have split and celebrate the coming of spring
		3/26–3/30			
		3/31			
Spring	April	4/1–4/4	Uzuki	Shunbun	Days and nights have split and celebrate the coming of spring
		4/5–4/9			
		4/10–4/14		Seimei	A time when all is full of life and the flowers begin to bloom
		4/15–4/19			
		4/20–4/24		Kokuu	The tears of Heaven shall wet the crop lands
		4/25–4/29			
		4/30			

72 Kou	Incantation Variety	Incantation Known name	Incantation Type
Peony flowers begin to bloom Frogs begin to croak	Earth Flower		Special: Plant
Worms come out of the ground Bamboo shoots will begin to appear	Light Waves	Mirage of Light	Shoot: Light
	Light Wings	Wings of Light	Manipulate: Light
	Light Fangs	Light Fang Summon	Summon: *Kijyuu*
Tree worms will begin to eat the mulberry leaves Safflowers are all in full bloom	Sudden Sun		Weapon/Armor: Light
	Silent Sun	Silent Spring Light	Special: Sun
	Sun Cease		Special: Defense
Grains shall grow ripe for the autumn harvest Mantis birth	Sun Cease	Shadow Cicada Shell	Special: Defense
Fireflies shall appear from the marshes Plums shall ripen and turn yellow	Water Ogre	Water Ogre Summon	Summon: *Kijyuu*
	Water Fowl	Waterfowl Flying Rain/Waterfowl Fog Rain	Manipulate: Liquid
	Water Dragon	Water Dragon's Rain	Weapon/Armor: Water
The *Spica prunellae* shall wither Iris flowers begin to bloom	Striking Beast	Claws of Rain/Beasts of Rain	Shoot: Water
	Burial	Decaying Rain	Special: Decay
Crowdipper plants begin to grow Warm winds shall blow	Silent Attack		Special: Flame
Lotus flowers begin to bloom Falcons shall take flight	Fiery Sin		Manipulate: Heat
	Fiery Cry	Inferno Demon Summon	Summon: *Kijyuu*
	Enou (Fire King)	Enou Blaze	Weapon/Armor: Flame
The tung tree shall bear fruit The ground shall sweat and the air shall become humid	Fire Flower	Flowering Blaze of Wind Fire Flower Ring	Shoot: Flames
	Fire Cry	Fire Lighting of Screams	Special: Lightning
The ground shall sweat and the air shall become humid Heavy rain shall fall at times	Fire Cry		Special: Lightning
	Fire Night		Special: Illusion
A cool breeze sets in Cicadas begin to sing their songs Thick mists shall settle in	Bullets of darkness		Shoot: Spirit
	Beast of darkness		Summon: *Kijyuu*
	Dark Cloak		Weapon/Armor: Spirit
The boll covering the cotton fiber shall open The summer heat finally eases	Divine land		Manipulate: Spirit
	Divine restoration		Special: Heal
The summer heat finally eases Crops are ready for harvest	Divine restoration		Special: Heal
	Divine Eyes		Special: Air
The frost on the grass shines white The gray wagtail bird begins to chirp	Wind shadow	Winds of Darkness	Manipulate: Gravity
	Banished Wind		Weapon/Armor: Air
	Wind God		Summon: *Kijyuu*
Swallows begin their journey home south The roars of thunder ceases Insects seal the entrance of their burrows	Fierce Blast	Fierce Blasting Winds	Shoot: Wind
	Fierce Heaven	Fierce Heavenly Winds Heavenly Winds of Fire	Special: Storm
Insects seal the entrance of their burrows It is the time to dry out the fields	Fierce Heaven		Special: Storm
	Fierce Sky		Special: Lightning
The geese arrive from their migratory journey Chrysanthemum flowers begin to bloom	Mineral Character		Shoot: Metal
	Mineral Strength		Weapon/Armor: Metal
	Mineral Beast		Summon: *Kijyuu*
Crickets chirp by the entranceway Frost begins to fall Light rain falls quietly	Lightening Tremor		Manipulate: Lightning
	Lightening Dust		Special: Defense
Light rain falls quietly Japanese maple trees and vines begin to turn yellow	Lightening Dust		Special: Defense
	Lightening Flower		Special: Color
Sasanqua flowers begin to bloom The Earth shall begin to freeze Daffodils begin to bloom	Sound waves		Shoot: Sound
	Wings of Sound		Manipulate: Sound
	Fangs of Sound		Summon: *Kijyuu*
Rainbows can no longer be seen The northern winds shall carry away the leaves	Bright Moment		Weapon/Armor: Sound
	Bright Silence		Special: Freeze
The northern winds shall carry away the leaves The mandarin tree leaves begin to turn yellow	Bright Silence		Special: Freeze
	Bright Closure		Special: Defense
The Heavens close its gates and winter settles in Bears burrow themselves for hibernation Salmons begin to group and rise upstream	Mind Ogre		Summon: *Kijyuu*
	Mind Fowl		Manipulate: Animals
	Mind Dragon		Weapon/Armor: Life
The *Prunella vulgaris* plant shall reveal itself Deer shall lose their horns	Silent Beast		Shoot: *Kijyuu*
	Silent Burial		Special: Thought

Season	Month	Sigil Dates	Month Name	24 Sekki	Meaning of 24 Sekki
Spring	May	5/1–5/4	Satsuki	Kokuu	The tears of Heaven shall wet the crop lands
		5/5–5/9			
		5/10–5/14		Rikka	The Blue Emperor shall bring summer and all plants shall rejoice
		5/15–5/20			
		5/21–5/25			
		5/26–5/30		Shouman	A time when all life shall reach maturity
		5/31			
Summer	June	6/1–6/5	Minazuki	Shouman	A time when all life shall reach maturity
		6/6–6/10			
		6/11–6/15		Boushu	A time when all life shall reach maturity Bearded grains shall flow with the summer stream
		6/16–6/20			
		6/21–6/25		Geshi	The Fire Emperor shall take his throne and the sun shall remain in the heavens
		6/26–6/30			
Summer	July	7/1–7/6	Fumizuki	Taisho	The Fire Emperor shall take his throne and the sun shall remain in the heavens
		7/7–7/11			
		7/12–7/16		Rishuu	Heat rises and dances in the seventh evening sky
		7/17–7/22			
		7/23–7/27		Shosho	A feast to the sweltering heat begins and thus it shall reach the temperature of the sun
		7/28–7/31			
Summer	August	8/1	Hazuki	Taisho	A feast to the sweltering heat begins and thus it shall reach the temperature of the sun
		8/2–8/6			
		8/7–8/11		Rishuu	The Fire Emperor will take his leave but his fiery will shall linger
		8/12–8/16			
		8/17–8/22			
		8/23–8/27		Shosho	The heat subsides and the winds shall carry it away
		8/28–8/31			
Fall	September	9/1	Nagazuki	Shosho	The heat subsides and the winds shall carry it away
		9/2–9/7			
		9/8–9/12		Hakuro	The White Emperor descends and creates a trail of frost
		9/13–9/17			
		9/18–9/22			
		9/23–9/27		Shuubun	Days and nights have split and celebrate the coming of fall
		9/28–9/30			
Fall	October	10/1–10/2	Kannazuki	Shuubun	Days and nights have split and celebrate the coming of fall
		10/3–10/7			
		10/8–10/12		Kanro	The dew shall embrace the cold and solidify
		10/13–10/17			
		10/18–10/22			
		10/23–10/27		Soukou	Starry frost shall fall and begin to silence all
		10/28–10/31			
Fall	November	11/1	Shimotsuki	Soukou	Starry frost shall fall and begin to silence all
		11/2–11/6			
		11/7–11/11		Rittou	The White Emperor shall bring winter and thus bring rain
		11/12–11/16			
		11/17–11/21			
		11/22–11/26		Shousetsu	Rain turns into snow and all will be blanketed in white
		11/27–11/30			
Winter	December	12/1	Shiwasu	Shousetsu	Rain turns into snow and all will be blanketed in white
		12/2–12/6			
		12/7–12/11		Taisetsu	Snow continues to fall and all life shall fall into slumber
		12/12–12/16			
		12/17–12/21			
		12/22–12/26		Touji	The Dark Emperor takes the throne and the sun shall not rise
		12/27–12/31			

Kureha Kazamatsuri

Character Design by:
Kenichi Muraeda

- Birthday: September 9, 1982
- Age: 31
- Blood Type: O
- Height: 5'8"
- Weight: 138 lb.
- Measurements: Bust 37" / Waist 22" / Hip 37"

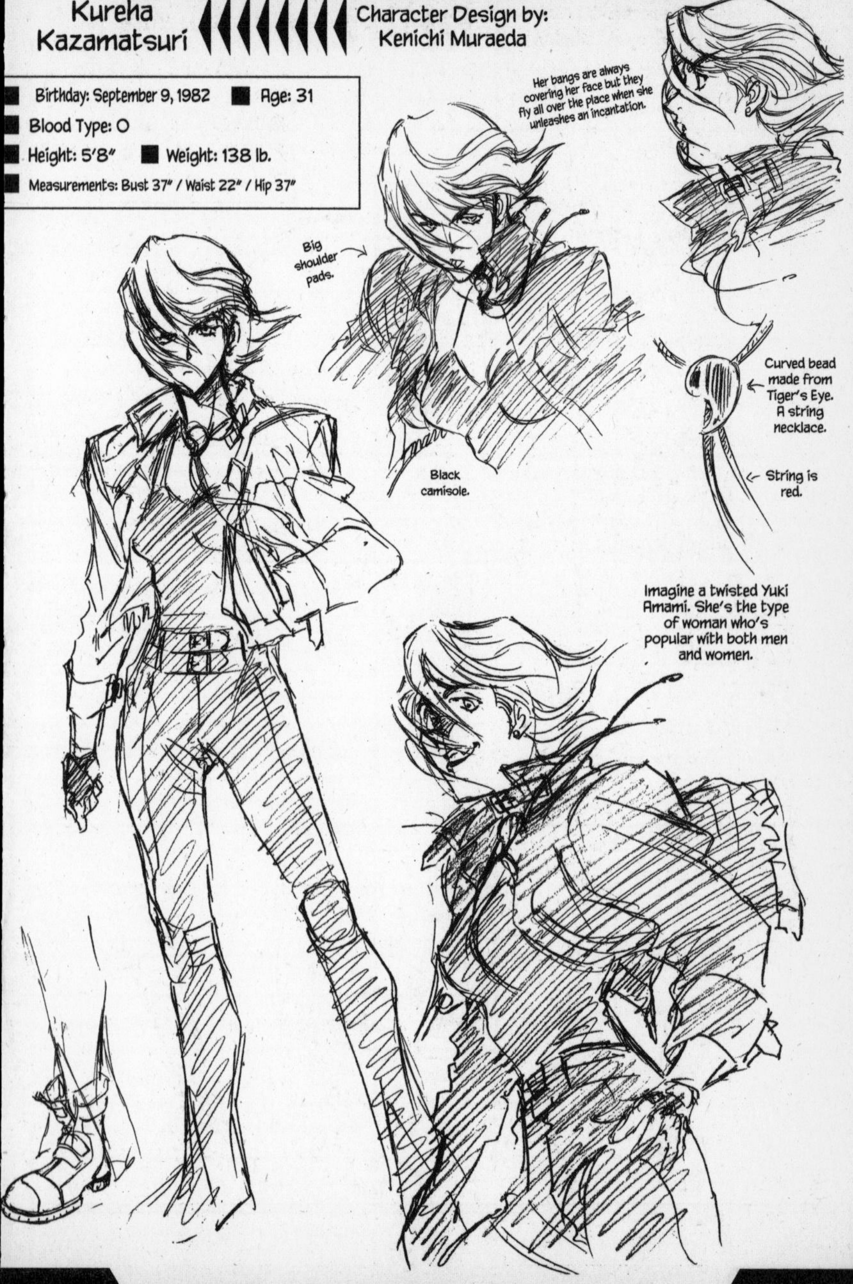
Her bangs are always covering her face but they fly all over the place when she unleashes an incantation.
Big shoulder pads.
Black camisole.
Curved bead made from Tiger's Eye. A string necklace.
String is red.
Imagine a twisted Yuki Amami. She's the type of woman who's popular with both men and women.

Character Design by:
Hiroyuki Utatane

Mina Suzukure

- Birthday: June 6, 1997
- Age: 16 — Blood Type: Unknown
- Height: 4'9" — Weight: 84 lbs
- Measurements: Bust 30" / Waist 20" / Hip 3

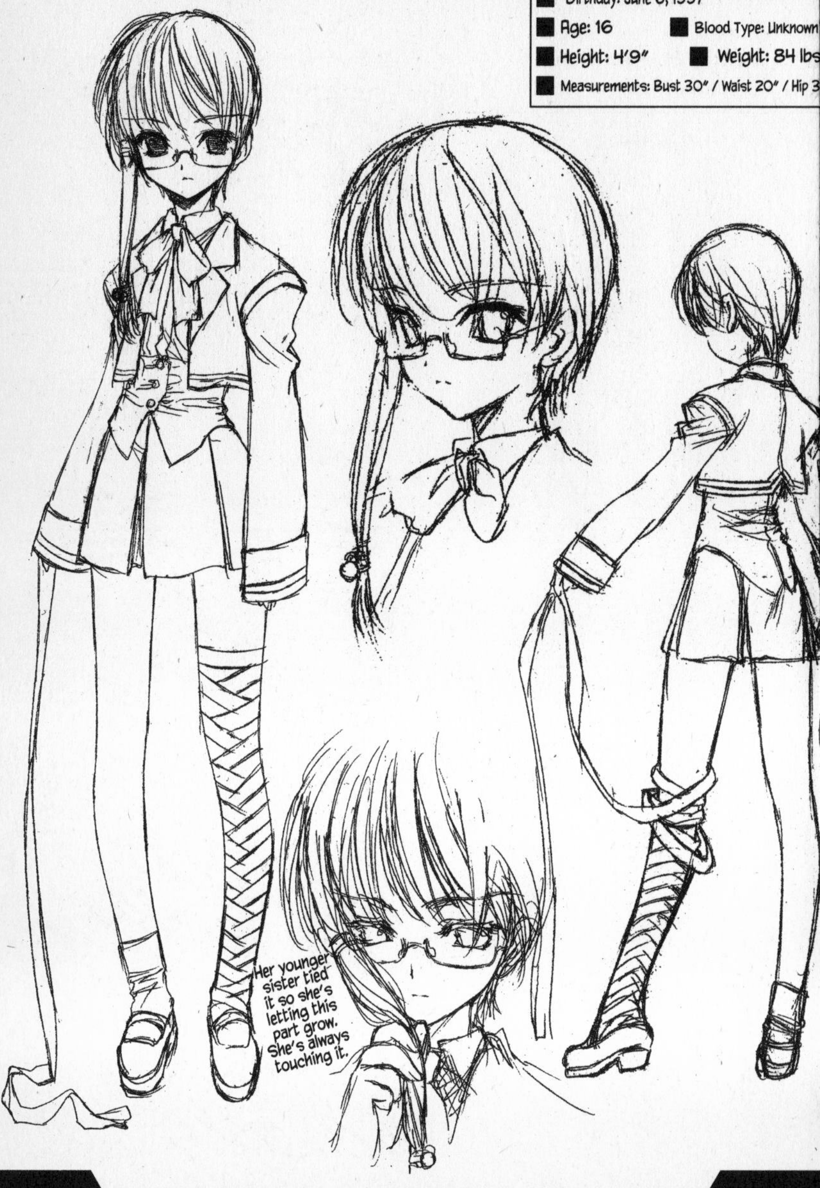
Her younger sister tied it so she's letting this part grow. She's always touching it.

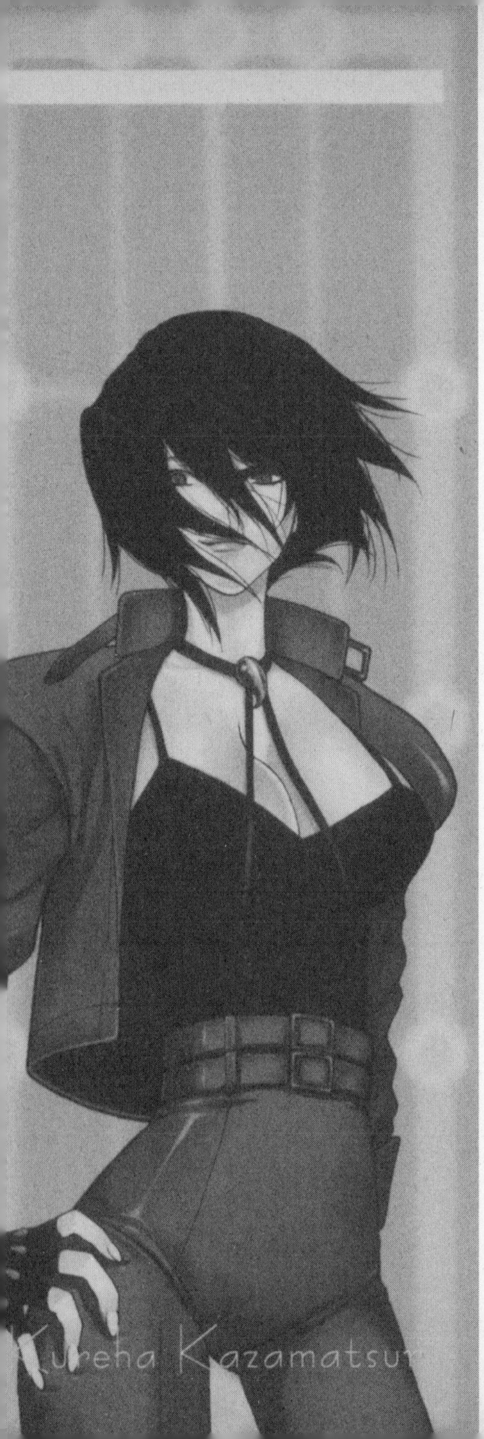
Kureha Kazamatsuri

Kureha Kazamatsuri

Shikifu: Aragonite

***Shiki Tsukai* of September**

Birthday: September 9, 1982
Age: 31 years old
Blood Type: O
Height: 5'8"
Weight: 138 lb.
Measurements: Bust 37" / Waist 22" / Hips 37"

- The boss figure of the battles in the battle.
- Around the same age as Rei Seichouji. Previously married.
- Kureha is from an ancient family of *Shiki Tsukai*. A perfectionist.
- She's a bit crazy.
- Plotting the annihilation of mankind to protect the Earth.
- Note: Data is current as of the present date—December 2013.

Mina Suzukure *Shikifu:* Silicified Wood

Shiki Tsukai of June

Birthday: June 6, 1997
Age: 16 years old
Blood Type: Unknown
Height: 4'9"
Weight: 84 lb.
Measurements: Bust 30" / Waist 20" / Hips 30"

- The daughter of the prestigious Suzukure family.
- Loves Japanese sweets
- Ever since a certain incident, she doesn't show much emotion.
- In general, she is hostile to others.
- She cherishes her hair tie more than her life.
- Note: Data is current as of the present date—December 2013.

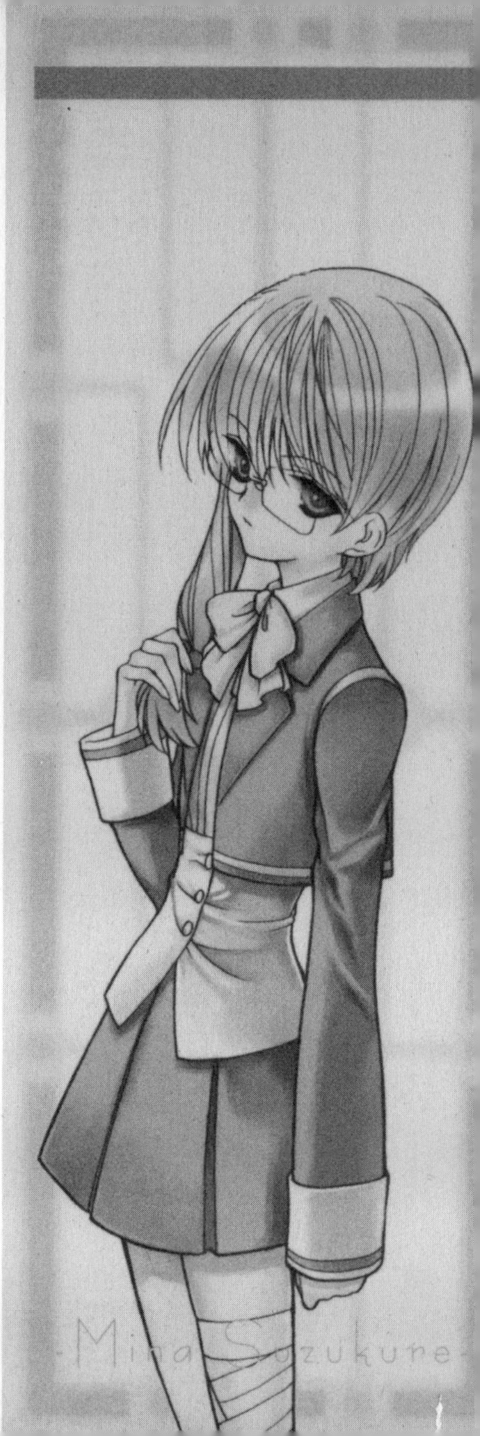
Mina Suzukure

Translation Notes

Japanese is a tricky language for most Westerners, and translation is often more art than science. For your edification and reading pleasure, here are notes on some of the places where we could have gone in a different direction with our translation of the work, or where a Japanese cultural reference is used.

Shiki Tsukai, page 3

One who possesses the power of the seasons. *Shiki* means the "four seasons" and *Tsukai* literally means "one who uses" (in this case, the seasons).

Shikifu, page 3

The *Shikifu* is a magic card from which *Shiki Tsukai* derive their power. We'll learn even more about *Shikifu* as the series progresses!

Kijyuu, page 5

Kijyuu is an elemental beast that's born from the seasons. *Ki* means "seasons" and *jyuu* is the character for "beast."

The White Emperor, page 10

"The White Emperor" refers to Winter.

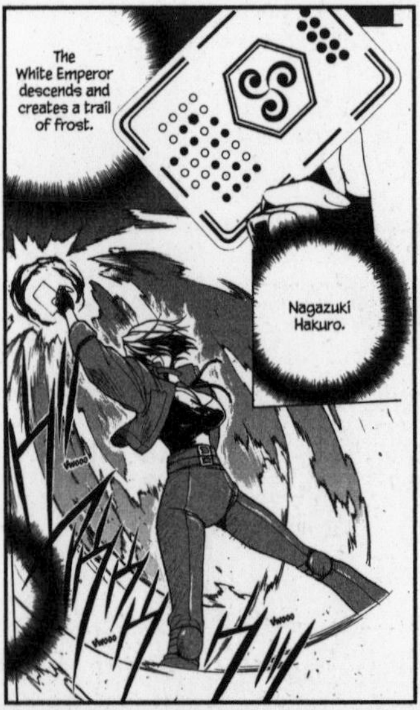
The White Emperor descends and creates a trail of frost.
Nagazuki Hakuro.

New Calendar, page 24

"The new calendar" refers to the Gregorian calendar—the modern Western calendar now widely adopted throughout the world.

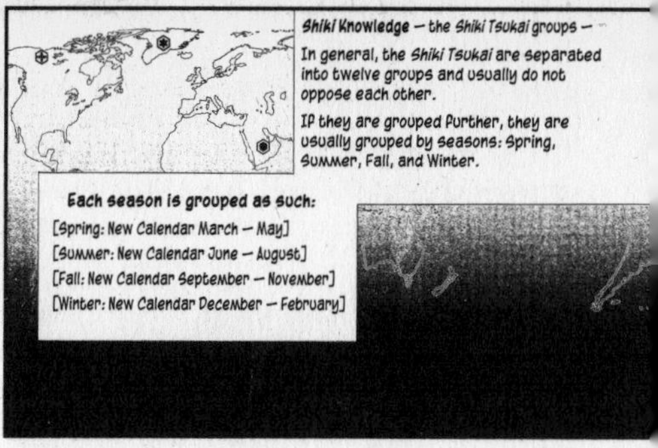
Shiki Knowledge — the Shiki Tsukai groups —
In general, the Shiki Tsukai are separated into twelve groups and usually do not oppose each other.
If they are grouped further, they are usually grouped by seasons: Spring, Summer, Fall, and Winter.
Each season is grouped as such:
[Spring: New Calendar March — May]
[Summer: New Calendar June — August]
[Fall: New Calendar September — November]
[Winter: New Calendar December — February]

Inclusion, page 39

The creators of *Shiki Tsukai* borrow many terms from biology, ecology, geology, meteorology, and other natural sciences in inventing this series' unique world. A great example is the term "Inclusion." This term is on loan from geology, where it describes any material that gets trapped inside a mineral during its formation. But in the world of *Shiki Tsukai,* "Inclusion" is the mysterious, magical process of a *Shikifu* absorbing another *Shikifu.*

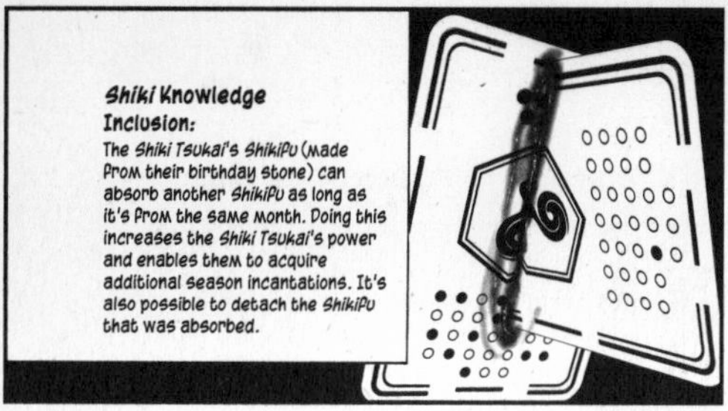
Shiki Knowledge
Inclusion:
The Shiki Tsukai's Shikifu (made from their birthday stone) can absorb another Shikifu as long as it's from the same month. Doing this increases the Shiki Tsukai's power and enables them to acquire additional season incantations. It's also possible to detach the Shikifu that was absorbed.

Formation, page 72

The special "sealed dimension" that only a *Shiki Tsukai*'s magic powers can create.

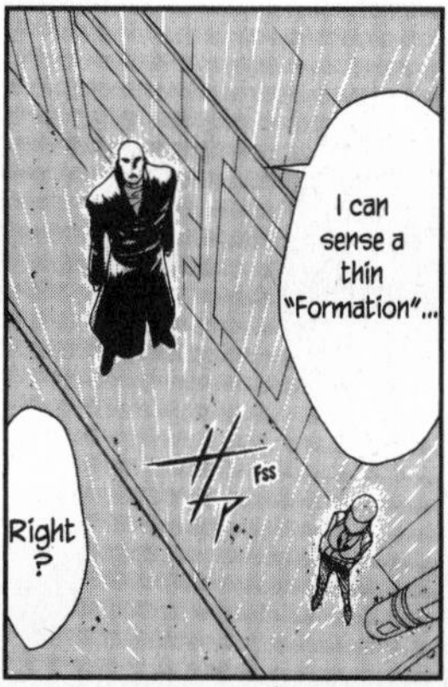
I can sense a thin "Formation"...
Fss
Right?

Fugu, page 82

Fugu is the Japanese word for "pufferfish"—and is also one of Japanese cuisine's most notorious dishes. As is well known, when fugu is not prepared exactly right, it's lethally poisonous. This doesn't stop it from being one of the most sought-after and expensive dishes in Japan—it's coveted for its extraordinary flavor as well as the thrill of the risk!

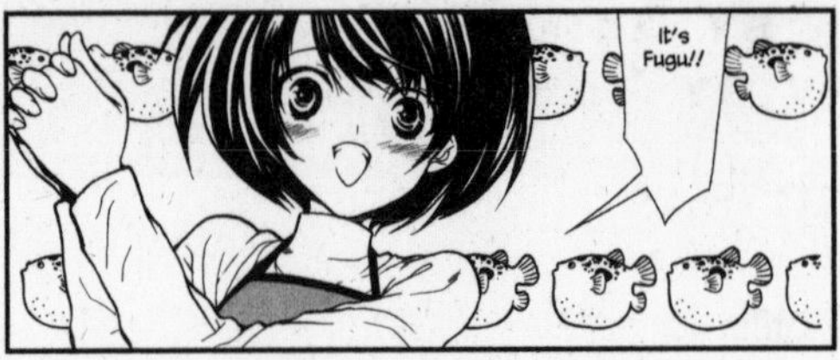
It's Fugu!!

Sashimi, page 82

A Japanese delicacy primarily consisting of fresh raw seafood, sliced into thin pieces. Try ordering some sashimi the next time you go to a Japanese restaurant!

Nabe, page 82

Nabe, or a hot pot dish, is a seasonal dish most often enjoyed in winter.

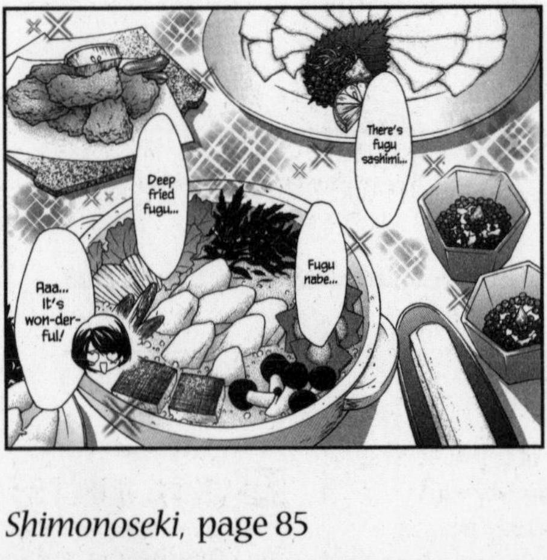
There's fugu sashimi...
Deep fried fugu...
Fugu nabe...
Aaa... It's won-der-ful!

Shimonoseki, page 85

A city located in Yamaguchi Prefecture, Japan, known for its superb fugu.

Psycho Busters

MANGA BY AKINARI NAO
STORY BY YUYA AOKI

PSYCHIC TEENS ON THE RUN!

Out of the blue, a beautiful girl asks Kakeru to run away with her. This could be any boy's dream come true, but there's something strange afoot.

It turns out that this girl is on the run from a shadowy government organization intent on using her psychic abilities for its own nefarious ends. But why does she need Kakeru's help? Could it be that he has secret powers, too?

Manga by
Akinari Nao
Story by
Yuya Aoki,
the creator of
Get Backers

• Story by Yuya Aoki,
  creator of *Get Backers*

Special extras in each volume! Read them all!

BY YASUNORI MITSUNAGA

HAVE A NICE AFTERLIFE!

Werewolves, demons, vampires, and monsters all thrive on fear, but now there's one new warrior who has them quaking in their supernatural boots: the beautiful Princess Hime, who fights the forces of evil with a chainsaw and a smile.

Not only does she look great in a tiara, she has magical powers that allow her to raise the dead. She's a girl on a mission, and with the help of her undead servant and a supercute robot, there's no creature of darkness she can't take down!

Special extras in each volume! Read them all!

RATING AGES OT 16+

VISIT WWW.DELREYMANGA.COM TO:
• Read sample pages
• View release date calendars for upcoming volumes
• Sign up for Del Rey's free manga e-newsletter
• Find out the latest about new Del Rey Manga series

DEL REY MANGA デルレイ

The Otaku's Choice.™

TOMARE!

止まれ

[STOP!]

YOUNG ADULT
GRAPHIC NOVEL

You're going the wrong way!

Manga is a completely
different type of reading
experience.

To start at the *beginning*,
go to the *end*!

That's right! Authentic manga is read the traditional Japanese way—
from right to left. Exactly the opposite of how American books are
read. It's easy to follow: Just go to the other end of the book, and read
each page—and each panel—from right side to left side, starting at
the top right. Now you're experiencing Manga as it was meant to be!